A PROFESSOR IN PARLIAMENT

Experiencing a Turbulent Parliament and Reform Party Caucus, 1993-97

Herbert G. Grubel

Professor of Economics,
Simon Fraser University
David Somerville Fellow of Taxation and Finance,
The Fraser Institute

VANCOUVER, CANADA
2000

Copyright © 2000
by Herbert G. Grubel

Canadian Cataloguing in Publication Data

Grubel, Herbert G.

A Professor in Parliament:
Experiencing a Turbulent Parliament and Reform Party Caucus,
1993-97

ISBN number 0-9686783-0-0

1. Reform Party - Canada
2. Economic Policies - Canada, US

Table of Contents

PART I
Growing Up and Becoming an Economist

Chapter 1: Growing up in Germany 9
Chapter 2: Student Years in America 19
Chapter 3: Apprenticeship Years at Stanford and Chicago 36

PART II
Professional Life and Ideas in Economics

Chapter 4: Productive Years in Pennsylvania,
            Canberra and with the U.S. Treasury 53
Chapter 5: Vancouver and Simon Fraser University 67
Chapter 6: The Fraser Institute and International Adventures 87

PART III
The Political Experience

Chapter 7: Getting Nominated for the Reform Party 109
Chapter 8: The Election Campaign 121
Chapter 9: Caucus Life and Question Period 138
Chapter 10: The Racist Label 153
Chapter 11: Employment Equity, Homosexual Rights
            and Internal Dissent 167
Chapter 12: Preston Manning, the Leader 184
Chapter 13: Designing Policies 218
Chapter 14: Committee Work and Relationships with
            other Parties 243
Chapter 15: An Assessment and Look Forward 271

            Index of Names: 293

Preface

I WAS 63 years old when I started writing this autobiography in the summer of 1997. I did not then know whether such a project was premature or whether anyone would be interested in my account of four years in Parliament within the context of my life as an academic.

However, I decided to proceed with the project because of the phenomenal electoral success of the Reform Party in October 1993. That success caused the party's representation in Parliament to rise from one seat to 52 and was accompanied by a dramatic drop in the representation of the Progressive Conservative Party from 180 seats to only two. In the June 1, 1997 election the Reform Party increased its representation in the House to 60 and became Her Majesty's Loyal Opposition. The Reform Party has scored unprecedented success in Canadian politics, changing the distribution of political power.

Many Canadians, especially those living east of Manitoba, are curious about the Reform Party, its leader, the members of its elected caucus, influential insiders and, above all, its policies. What they know about these matters will help to shape not only the future of the Reform Party but also of Canadian politics and the economic and social future of Canada. What voters can learn from my account may influence their choices in upcoming elections.

One of the biggest problems faced by any new party is the absence of a history and policy platform which can be used to predict its likely future policies. In place of such information, the media, in recent years, has engaged in much speculation about the Reform Party's policies, leadership and supporters. This speculation has created some very inaccurate myths, while some of it has been right on the mark.

My book is a personal account of my experience as a member of the Reform Caucus serving, for about two years, as the party's Finance Critic. I hope this account will help to dispel some of the myths and draw a more accurate picture. I will tell the story as objectively as I can. However, such accounts are invariably shaped by limited personal experiences and contacts. Naturally, it is also influenced by my ego, personal interests and prejudices.

The lengthy introductory chapters provide readers with information about the events and forces which shaped my personal characteristics and perspectives. I hope this information will help readers understand 'where I come from' when they read my account of events and people.

But I also had two other reasons for writing an account of my life and career. First, I think it provides an historic record of the times and the societies in which I grew up and lived. I was born during the Depression and turmoil that brought Hitler to power in Germany. I lived through the horrors of the Second World War and its aftermath. I had many lucky

Preface

breaks in life, which led me from life in near-poverty to positions at some world-renowned universities, to association and friendship with some of the most distinguished economists of the postwar years, to prolonged stays in some of the most exotic and interesting places of the world, to a satisfying professorship at Simon Fraser University, to work with the Fraser Institute in Vancouver and ultimately to the position of Finance Critic for an opposition party in the Parliament of Canada.

Finally, I have written this book to present some ideas in economics that have, for better or worse, influenced public opinion and policies. I have had the privilege of being around economists while they did their work, and have made some contributions of my own. I hope to convey not only the main contents of these ideas but also the excitement and intellectual battles surrounding their formulation.

My life and professional experiences stand in evidence of the economic and social mobility offered by the free societies of North America. I am determined to fight for the preservation of these free societies for the benefit of my children and future generations in the face of the continued threats from statism and socialism. I joined the Reform Party, stood for election and gave up the good life of the professor so I could fight in a different arena. In an important sense, this continued fight is also the genesis of this book.

I received helpful comments on the manuscript from Ken Boessenkool, Jack Clark, Tom Flanagan, Art Hanger, Lynda MacKay, Allison and Owen Owens, Filip Palda, Scott Reid, Bob Ringma, Ray Speaker, Randy White and Ted White. Scott Reid, an academic and author, went through the manuscript with a skilled editor's pencil and considerably improved the exposition and consistency of spelling, capitalization and so on. My wife, Hélène Bertrand, discussed many sections of the book with me and made many useful suggestions for improvement. I thank her for her patience during the long period when I worked on this book.

HGG
Vancouver, Fall of 1998

Postscript

SUBMISSION of the manuscript to a number of potential publishers has caused this book to be published nearly 18 months after I had finished writing it.

Typical of the problems leading to this delay was the experience with an unnamed Vancouver publisher. It took nearly six months between submission and a letter from the Editorial Director, which said: "Your work was the focus of a lively and spirited debate within [the publishing house]. This, to me, was an indication that it could be the basis of a successful book. Alas, mine is only one voice. I do hope you persevere in trying to get it published. It can only become more timely as the next federal elec-

Preface

tion approaches. I return your manuscript with great apologies for the delay in doing so."

But I could not afford to repeat the experience with other publishers because further delays would have made obsolete much of the information contained in my work. So, I decided finally — and reluctantly — to self-publish the book at the end of 1999. But this process in turn has taken an unexpectedly long time, given the nature of the job. The preparation of the camera-ready copy, some further editing for readability and consistency and the preparation of front material were done by Ted Staunton. I thank him for his excellent work.

I have decided not to write an Epilogue on the events surrounding the United Alternative and Canadian Conservative Reform Alliance. The basic points I made in Chapter 15 about the future of the conservative movement in Canada need no change. Also, I have no particular insights into the process of creating a new conservative party for Canada. Even though I agree with the need to bring under one party umbrella the majority of Canadians who are basically conservative, I did not attend any of the meetings designed to create a new party and refused to be drawn into internal party debates about the issues. Politics of this sort frustrate me — however important they may be — because I feel that I have nothing to contribute to this kind of political process.

However, I am encouraged that the platform of the CA offers conservatives a genuine alternative to the Liberals, who have had their turn in Ottawa for longer than has been good for the country. The CA platform and Preston Manning as the Prime Minister will bring a highly desirable change of direction to politics and economic policy in Canada. I hope that Canadians at the next election will share this view and elect a new government.

Staying out of politics allowed me to devote all of my time to research, publications at the Fraser Institute and a return to networking and learning at conferences. Unburdened by the need to consider political implications I have relished the publication of opinion pieces in major newspapers and Fraser Institute books with titles revealing their contents: "How to Use the Fiscal Surplus," "The Case for the Amero" and "Unlocking Canadian Capital: The Case for Capital Gains Tax Reform." Under way are several other projects like a publication on the brain drain and "Moral Hazard: The Bane of the Welfare State." I have no illusions about the likelihood that my ideas on these subjects will have any immediate influence. My experiences in caucus and Ottawa have made me quite cynical about the short run influence of academics. But, if these subjects have merit, as I think they do, they will stimulate some public interest and the best will ultimately make it into policy. Such is the hope of academic scribblers.

– HGG
Vancouver, February 2000

Part I

Growing Up
and
Becoming an Economist

Chapter 1

Growing Up in Germany

THE GREY granite walls held many carved figures and tablets with mysterious symbolic meaning. A sergeant-at-arms, in a black robe with a broad white collar and a sword, secured the main entrance door. The green carpet made a pleasing contrast with the many dark and elaborately-carved wood surfaces of the members' benches and wall-panels. To my right at the end of the aisle was the Speaker's chair, made of carved figures and spires, towering over the chamber. The tall stained-glass windows were sparkles of color in the bright mid-day sun. Overhead was a high, vaulted and brightly decorated ceiling. I was reminded of the Gothic churches of Europe, of history and how it was being shaped in this place.

I was still relishing memories of the preceding evening's ball at Rideau Hall, to celebrate the 35th opening of the Parliament of Canada. History and tradition permeated the whole affair. As befitting Ottawa in January, the temperature was minus 20 degrees and cold winds swirled the snow beneath a star-filled sky. Rideau Hall is the Governor General's residence, with all the splendor and elegance befitting the many heads of state who had been official guests of the government, and had slept and were entertained there. The portraits of past Governors General and rulers of Great Britain looked down on the men in black ties and dress uniforms and the women in their festive long gowns, who would be running Canada's affairs for the next four years.

I participated actively in the celebration, dancing to the sounds of music being made by military men in full dress uniforms. With my spirits lifted by a glass of wine, I was introduced to Art Eggleton, who mentioned that he was from Toronto. I asked him where Toronto was, a question I have had a lot of fun with in the past. Canadians are proud of their courtesy to strangers, even if they seem ignorant of Toronto's location at the 'centre of the universe.' Most begin to answer my question seriously until my smile tells them that they have been 'had.' This time the joke was on me. Before the election, Eggleton had been Toronto's mayor!

That first day in the House I inspected my chair and desk and wondered who before me had used them. Perhaps John Diefenbaker, Pierre Trudeau, Brian Mulroney, Kim Campbell, or Jean Chretien? How had the previous occupants voted on the elimination of the death penalty, the deficits that threatened to bankrupt the country, the rate of immigration, that so many of my constituents thought excessive? What important issues might I be asked to vote on? Would my presence make any difference to anyone or anything?

Chapter 1

My hopes on this matter were raised two days before. The elected Members had assembled to elect the Speaker for the 35th Parliament. Several ballots had not yet produced a winner and I had just cast another ballot. Thereafter, with permission from the Reform Party's Whip, Diane Ablonczy, I left the House for a scheduled 2:30 meeting with John Crow, Governor of the Bank of Canada. As a professional economist I had met him before on several occasions. This was to be a courtesy call and a chance to ask for his views on Canada's economic and financial conditions.

Governor Crow terminated the meeting after exactly 25 minutes and I walked back to the House just a couple of blocks away. On the way I encountered many Members who were returning to their offices in the expectation that the election was over since they had just cast their vote for one of the two remaining candidates. As I entered the Chamber I heard the announcement that only one more minute remained for voting. I quickly dropped my overcoat and raced to cast my ballot. When the results were announced, the two candidates had received an equal number of votes. The members were recalled and in a final ballot, Gib Parent was elected. Since I voted for him in the ballot that produced the tie vote, I know with certainty that without it Gib Parent would not have been elected Speaker. Of course, in this as in so many other important events in my life, fate had a big hand. If Crow had kept me one more minute, or had I gone for a coffee with my colleagues, things would have turned out differently. As I looked back on my life that first day in the House, I wondered about the many fateful decisions which ultimately brought me this place and the prized privilege of serving my constituents as a member of Parliament. There were many cross-roads in a long journey.

Living through the war

My first memories of childhood are from Frankfurt during the War. I remember my parents, brother and I standing in the basement of the five-storey building in which we had a one-bedroom apartment. The room was dimly lit by the glow of a small bulb attached to a bulky emergency battery. Bombs were falling all around, and suddenly a particularly loud explosion shook the earth and walls. There were creaking noises and fine dust began to swirl around the room. A door to the outside had been blown away and I could see a bright red night sky; heavy smoke was reflecting the flames from hundreds of burning buildings.

It was 1942. I was eight years old and had just experienced the first major raid by Allied bombers. A bomb, causing a 20-foot crater in the street had missed our cellar by about 25 metres. After the sirens indicated the end of the raid, my parents took me and my five-year old brother to our grocery store, a couple of blocks away. The single-storey, flat roofed building was intact. A volunteer stood on the roof and, with a pail and wet mop, extinguished embers that the wind had brought from a number of burning apartment buildings across the street. As I watched, two floors crashed and made the sparks shoot high into the night sky.

A few days later, my brother and I were taken in by different relatives in small villages in Thuringia, safely distant from bombing attacks. My parents remained in Frankfurt to tend to the store. I do not have good memories of the next two years I spent in the home of my father's parents. The Frankfurt apartment had a modern flush toilet, but my grandparents' home had only a pit toilet. The house was three storeys high and to use the toilet I had to go to an unheated annex and sit on a cold, drafty and smelly seat connected to the ground with a large diameter pipe. I had nightmares about falling into that dark hole.

In school I was 'the foreigner,' speaking a strange dialect. Food was scarce and finances were tight. Family life was not warm. One morning my aunt came into my room and screamed at me to put my hands on top of the duvet and stop doing what little boys liked to do. It took me years to know what she meant. She had a big bosom. Later in life, I never was attracted to women with that type of a figure.

My grandfather on my father's side earned a living in a large porcelain factory in Kahla, Thuringia, painting flowers and gold rims on plates. In spite of a low income, he had five children. My father was the third child. He was tall, muscular and handsome. He could be very charming and the women loved him. He loved them too. This caused my entire family much grief later in life when he insisted on maintaining a permanent mistress. This experience shaped my life-long revulsion against extra-marital affairs. My mother's father was a brick-layer and often worked on three jobs to feed his four children.

My mother was very bright. In her youth she was selected to attend schools for gifted children. When she met my father, she was chief accountant for Adler-Neumann, a shoe factory located in Frankfurt owned by a Jewish family. At the time, my father worked as a clerk in a small grocery store.

My parents were married in 1928 at age 24. As children they had lived through the hunger and hardships of the First World War. In 1930 they used my mother's savings to buy a grocery store while she continued to work at Adler-Neumann. Four years later, shortly before I was born, her employers offered to establish a nursery next to her office so that she could continue with her work while she took care of me. Her intelligence, reliability and determination were highly valued. However, she decided to leave her paid position to raise me and work in the store. It prospered and brought my parents a middle-class life-style that included the ownership of motorcycles and later a car, to be used for business as well as pleasure.

My mother's determination and hard work probably saved my father's life. A few months after the war had started, he was drafted into the army. My mother was determined to keep the grocery store open. Throughout the neighborhood other family stores had closed after the male owners

Chapter 1

were drafted. As a result, the business in our store increased enormously. Using ration coupons to document the number of customers she was serving, my mother was able to persuade the authorities that the work-load was too much for a woman and that her husband was needed for the war effort at home. My father returned to civilian life. Ninety percent of his army unit died in the steppes of Russia.

After the end of the war, the U.S. occupation forces engaged in a process known as 'deNazification.' My father never belonged to the Party and was cleared. He told me later that at one time during the war he was summoned to the Gestapo headquarters. There he was accused of having sold groceries to Jews through the back door of his store. He denied the allegation and a couple of days later was informed that he was lucky because a witness to his law-breaking had disappeared.

I have two very personal memories of this terrible time in German history. I remember vividly seeing people with a large, yellow star of David on their clothing. I received no answer to my question about them. The second event occurred in a train to small village near the infamous concentration camp, Buchenwald. As the train slowed down we passed a long column of workers dressed in black-and-white striped clothes, working on the tracks. I asked my aunt who they were. A hush came over the train compartment and my aunt's finger went to her lips. There was no answer and there were to be no more questions.

In 1943 my parents built a simple wooden structure at the edge of Reifenberg, the highest village in the mountains north of Frankfurt and not a likely target for bombing. Today it can be reached in a 30 minute drive from the city. As I look at pictures of the structure today, I would describe it as a shack. It had running water and a flush toilet but everything else was rather primitive. My mother cooked on a wood-fired kitchen stove. Heat was provided by a tiled oven in the living room.

When it was cold, we went to sleep in unheated rooms. Beds were pre-warmed by heated bricks wrapped in towels. Thick down covers kept us warm, even if in the morning the walls and windows were decorated with ice-flowers. We bathed fully once a week, using face-cloths while standing in a large tin pan filled with hot water heated on the kitchen stove. Until I was 17 I had never taken a shower! A telephone was something found in a restaurant nearby. When the war was winding down my parents brought my brother Alfred and me to this place where I would live for the next eleven years. My father would stay in Frankfurt to operate the store and live in a small apartment. My mother would join him for the busy Fridays and Saturdays at the store. They both came to Reifenberg Saturday evening and my father stayed all Sunday.

My parents' life during the postwar years was spent working. After having seen the effort they put out, I have the greatest respect for people who own small businesses. By example my parents instilled in me a strong work ethic and taught me how to perform tasks efficiently. But my parents and some close relatives employed in the store also knew how to enjoy themselves. I have very fond memories of the feasts we would have on the weekends, the walks we would take and, the encouragement we received to participate in sports.

Because there is always food in a grocery store, my brother and I never went hungry even when shortages during our youth haunted many Germans. Food and ration coupons were also good for bartering in the underground economy. After currency reform in 1948 and the end of food rationing, Germans went through what was called the 'Fresswelle', a time when they spent all their money 'eating like animals.' The grocery store prospered, but not enough to make us rich.

The prosperity led to the acquisition of an electric stove in Reifenberg. It eased greatly mother's cooking chores (and my duties of fetching wood). We owned a Fiat, which when equipped with a trailer, was used to transport vegetables from the wholesale market to the store, but was also used for pleasure and weekend trips. In 1950, when I was 16, my father entrusted me with a most beautiful, big motorcycle. We always had skis and acquired a love for the sport. Weather permitting, I often hiked up the local mountain for an hour after school and schussed down its slopes from 880 to 650 metres. We raced and jumped on skis and won trophies. We honed our skills in training in the Alps during several Christmas holidays. We played on the village's soccer team and my brother became a star sought by major league teams.

Measured by living standards in Canada 50 years later, I grew up in poverty. However, I always considered myself to be a member of the middle class and never felt poor.

Living in Reifenberg as a 'refugee' from the city, I encountered what today would be called bigotry. I spoke a different dialect and was known to be a Protestant, while the population in Reifenberg was almost totally Catholic. Indelible in my mind are incidents where local bullies waylaid me on my way to the village bakery. They would send two girls to spit at me and remind me of my refugee status. The larger boys in turn called me a coward and dared me to hit the girls. The resultant humiliation and fear drove me to use back paths and gardens to get to the shops. The final solution to my problem was simple. As soon as I could, I left the place where I was not accepted.

The high school years

In my youth I never saw anyone in my family read anything other than magazines and business ledgers. I do not remember any discussions involving ideas or the arts. It was not an environment to prepare me for my later career as a university professor, intellectual and author.

To this day it remains a puzzle to me how it was decided that I should attend a Gymnasium, the equivalent of a North American high school

Chapter 1

plus two years. At the time, only about 10 percent of my age-group attended this type of school, graduation from which was a precondition for university attendance. I remember very little about my elementary school years. I have no memory of having taken tests or any evidence that I did particularly well. Yet I remember that during the war I was told that soon I would attend an élite Hitler School. In fact, I never did. In 1946 I was enrolled in the Realgymnasium Königstein. There were no entrance or aptitude tests. My parents had no 'connections.'

The Gymnasium in Königstein is about eight kilometers away from Reifenberg on a winding road through a densely forested nature preserve. Today, Königstein prospers as a bedroom community for professionals and business people working in Frankfurt. After the war it was a sleepy resort town known for its large mediaeval castle ruins and its benign climate, due to its location at the southern slopes of the Taunus mountains.

Entering the Gymnasium at age 12 did little to alleviate the social isolation that I had experienced as the Protestant refugee kid in a Catholic village. The eight kilometers were too far to walk and the mountains and weather made it unsuitable for travel by bicycle. In 1946, the aftermath of the war left Reifenberg without any public transportation and to get to school I had to hitch rides on local trucks. A year or so later regular bus service resumed. At first we were served by a tiny, smoke-belching, bright yellow bus that had somehow survived the war and on occasion forced me to travel by hanging onto the roof-ladder in the back. Later, new and roomier buses plied the route. While the public transportation system was satisfactory in getting me to and from school, its use meant that I could not participate in any social activities with my classmates in Königstein.

There was very little other than homework and sports for me to do after school in Reifenberg. This fact probably contributed to my good grades in a rather competitive school. At age 12, the class had 60 members. Of those no more than six were left in the graduating class of 15, ten years later. The education was broad and demanding. It included many years of study of Latin, English and French as well as the standard mathematics, chemistry, physics, religion and history. All courses were mandatory and there were many tests.

One of my class-mates was Jürgen Schneider. At school he was rather reclusive and all we really knew about him was that he wanted to follow in his father's footsteps and become an architect and developer. He did so with mixed results. In 1992 he was celebrated as Germany's largest real estate tycoon, giving extravagant parties that were reported in national magazines. I was told that upon my next visit to Germany he would have a party for me and some other former class-mates in his spectacular estate in Königstein. Alas, the party never took place. He had built an empire on speculation and alleged fraud. The collapse of his business left unpaid debts of several billion dollars. In 1997 he was convicted of fraud and sentenced to several years in jail. His experience is not typical of my class.

Most of us became comfortable members of the professional middle class.

While in the Gymnasium I felt the effects of the German class system. This system was important until the 1950s and 1960s when the economic miracle began to break it down. I simply did not fit into the social circle of class-mates whose parents were so-called *Akademiker,* who had attended university and were doctors, lawyers, teachers and journalists. The parent of one of my class-mates, Renate Kaus, was one of the richest men in Germany. I attended some parties at her house, only to find myself totally out of place in the presence of people who had all the social graces that came with good breeding. Some of them later would make the society pages as 'jet-setters' having breakfast in Nice and dinner in New York. As the son of a corner-grocer, I felt lost.

At age 16 my social life began to improve, since I was freed from the constraints of public transportation by the use of a motor-cycle. I could drive to Königstein to socialize and make friends with youngsters from my own socio-economic background. I fell in love, and joined a tennis club. I was settling into the more normal life of a teenager when an extraordinary event changed the entire course of my life.

Going to America

I still have the tiny one-paragraph story from the local newspaper which one of my class-mates brought to school in March 1951. In the name of the U.S. occupation forces, it invited Germans between the ages of 16 and 17 to apply for scholarships that would allow them to spend a year attending a U.S. high school as the guest of a family in the United States, all expenses paid. The program was administered by the American Field Service, an organization originally operating voluntary ambulance services during the two World Wars. In 1945 its leaders decided that the likelihood of future wars could be reduced if people from different nations had more personal contacts and understood each other better. They started an international exchange student program for high school students. They were supported financially by the U.S. government and volunteers who took students into their homes without compensation. The program is still active and now brings not only foreigners to the U.S., but also places young Americans abroad.

I was the only student in my class who survived the four rounds of interviews and landed in New York in August of 1951. The change in my life could not have been more radical in terms of living standard and social relations. My 'parents for the year,' as they liked to call themselves, were the Walter Morgans of Glen Ridge, New Jersey. Mrs. Morgan was one of the heiresses to the fortune left by Walter Kidde, one of the world's leading manufacturer of fire-extinguishers.

I spent August of that year in the family's summer home in West Hampton Beach, the Long Island playground for the very rich. We had a private

Chapter 1

tennis court and used a small private swim-club at the beach. I was introduced to sailing, and given a small boat for my own use. The house in Glen Ridge, a wealthy bedroom community serving New York, was large and in a very upscale neighborhood. I was assigned one of the family's three current-model cars, though I had to ask permission each time to use it. I had my own room with a shower. Food and drink were the best. I appreciated it all, even if sometimes I had to pinch myself to accept that it was real!

My American mother and father treated me wonderfully and I admire the courage they had in taking into their home a 17-year old stranger for an entire year. They set strict but reasonable rules that left me lots of freedom to develop and enjoy life. I have no memories of emotional or other problems, probably because my parents were such sensitive and sensible people and had already raised two teenaged daughters. I remember but one very serious talk with father, when he warned me not to fall in love with his 19-year old daughter. I can understand what he meant. She was beautiful but fortunately she was away at college. Chip, my 16-year old brother, I got along with alright but we never became close.

That year my life revolved around the high school. English immersion worked wonders on my language skills. The teachers probably were generous with the grades they gave me. I was a member of the varsity football team, where my skill for kicking a soccer ball came in very handy. I also was a member of the track team and was chosen to represent the school in the annual Penn relay races for high schools in Philadelphia.

I fell in love with my class-mate Helen and fully agree with those who say that one's first, teenage love is one of the most exciting experiences of life. My memories of the many social affairs we attended together totally relate to being there with her. In the end, the class year-book named us the most popular couple in the class.

Helen and I corresponded intensely for four years after our graduation and the idea of marriage was between the lines. But when Helen had finished her university degree in 1956 and visited me on the then obligatory group tour of Europe, I was not ready. That fall I was slated to start college in the U.S. and could not accept the responsibility of having a wife. I still sometimes wonder how my life would have turned out if I had married that beautiful, very bright and sensitive woman.

The year in the U.S. ended with an unforgettable adventure after highschool graduation. A Greyhound bus took 37 exchange students from 30 different countries on a six-week trip through the United States. We traveled from New York to New Orleans, north through the Prairies back to New York. Every night we were hosted by different families in small towns and big cities and experienced a real cross-section of American society. One night I stayed in the home of a man who was off delivering milk door-to-door when we had breakfast the next morning. Another night saw the entire bus load of students stay on the Indiana farm of Louis Bromfield, the author of the then famous book and movie about India, *The Rains Came*. The trip ended in Greenwich, Connecticut, where three of us were hosted by Frank Altschul, a famous Wall Street investment banker. We roamed a mansion that easily could have been the setting for one of Hollywood's glitzy films about the rich and famous.

Wherever we went on our bus-trip, we saw the local tourist attractions and mingled with high-school students and community leaders. We had some serious and frank discussions. One concerned race relations in the South. After my return to Germany I wrote a long essay about it. Our excitement about the discovery of America was matched only by the enthusiasm of Middle America which had been shaken out of its isolationist complacency by the war and was reaching out to the world. I am sure I was the first real German many of them had met and that our contacts helped offset some of the effects of the stereotyping of Germans they had experienced during the war.

The year around my 18th birthday spent in the U.S. influenced my life profoundly, not only because I was an impressionable teenager magically transported from a very modest living standard in Germany into a life of affluence. It also made me a friend and supporter of the American economic and social system. I had seen first-hand the riches it produced. I had experienced the openness, generosity and friendliness of Americans. I appreciated the economic and social mobility of the society. Later I would benefit from it, though at the time I only noted that no one asked me who my father was. They were only interested in me and what I had to offer.

Returning home

We had been warned about the problems we would encounter upon returning to our homes and schools after the exciting year abroad. The culture shock was indeed severe. Envy made some school-mates and friends quite hostile. It was difficult to get used again to the discipline of a German Gymnasium after the relative freedom of an American high school. Everything at home and in school appeared to have shrunk!

In the end it all turned out alright. I rejoined the class I had left a year earlier, was able to keep up with the work and get very good report cards. I had resolved that I would return to America in the future, but only after time had brought proper perspectives to my teenage year abroad. I also was determined to finish my education and learn a trade so that I would always have a base for work in Germany. The final two years of school flew by and in 1954 I received the Abitur, the graduation certificate for the Gymnasium. It entitled me to attend university.

However, my goal was to become a successful businessman with a large company. This could be done by joining a company's apprenticeship program. I was lucky and was hired by LURGI, an engineering firm that built refineries and chemical plants throughout the world. It is the subsidiary

Chapter 1

of Metallgesellschaft, a large trading company and producer of non-ferrous metals, which in the early 1990s shocked the world by billions of dollars in losses which had arisen out of speculation in oil futures.

During my apprenticeship I rotated among different departments of these two firms. Stays of about two months brought familiarity with a wide variety of tasks ranging from the preparation of payrolls of factory workers to sales, to pricing and taking inventory. I was most fascinated by my work in the foreign exchange division of the banking department. This experience probably had much to do with my choice five years later of a doctoral dissertation on forward exchange markets, which I wrote at Yale University. The dissertation in turn determined my teaching and research interest in international finance.

During my apprenticeship I was paid $50 a month, which even at that time was a paltry sum. We did not deserve more because we actually cost the company money. We did very little productive work. One day a week was spent in a state-operated school to teach us some business skills and theories. We were taught shorthand and took regular trips to inspect factories. Rudi Ebel and I became close friends at and after work. Rudi had lost his father during the war and had made it to the apprenticeship program through his own smarts. He now is a partner in a very successful law firm in Bonn, specializing in anti-combines litigation.

When the two year program came to an end, Rudi and I did some careful research about career options. We could stay on with LURGI. But during our training period we had met many very bright employees who had chosen to do so after their apprenticeships. Almost all of them were very unhappy. They saw themselves stuck without hope for advancement in a large, hierarchical and political bureaucracy. We sought advice from a director of the company. He had a university degree and told us: 'Get out of here. Go to university. We are just abusing you.' I asked him about the merit of attending university in the U.S. He thought that this was a great idea.

My generation had a strong inclination to emigrate. Just how strong this inclination was is evident from the fact that during the summer of 1953 my brother and a class-mate and his brother piled into a Volkswagen Beetle and toured Europe for three weeks. We went on the cheap, camping and on occasion foraging potatoes for our meals from the fields we passed. Of the four of us, only my brother Alfred made his life in Germany. My classmate Rainer Pappon emigrated to Brazil, where he headed the subsidiary of BASF, one of the giant German chemical firms. His brother Eberhard settled in Melbourne, Australia. I ended up in North America.

Perhaps we all would have done better staying in Germany. We will never know. After we left, the economic miracle took off and class barriers broke down. At the peak of my academic career I was invited many times to take up permanent university teaching positions in Germany. But by that time it was too late. I had become a Canadian.

CHAPTER 2

Student Years in America

NO ONE welcomed me when I arrived on a passenger ship in New York that hot August day in 1956. I had a small suitcase full of clothing, a couple of hundred dollars in traveller's checks, the promise of support of 50 dollars a month from my parents and youthful determination and optimism. I was determined to obtain an undergraduate degree and a Master of Business Administration at Harvard. My ultimate, only vaguely perceived objective was to become a business executive somewhere in the world.

Rutgers University in New Brunswick, New Jersey, had accepted me as a student for the bachelor's degree. I was given a tuition scholarship.

Working my way through college

At age 22 I did not want to remain dependent on income from my parents. So the first problem upon arriving at Rutgers was finding a job. My student visa formally prohibited me from working, so I entered the underground economy and became a live-in housekeeper in a suburban home. I cleaned house, kept the garden and looked after the children, in return for a room and some meals. Soon I found out that at that time no one asked about visa status in the formal sector and I started to work for the university in a variety of jobs. I cleaned the cafeteria floor, served hamburgers, helped the baker, operated the cash register, catered receptions and evaluated assignments for a professor of accounting.

My lifelong devotion to soccer gave me the opportunity to play for the Rutgers varsity team. One season we went undefeated, but we lost in the first round of the national championship series. I was never a star but scored enough goals to become elected to the second all conference team. The Dean rewarded me with a small cash scholarship in the second year.

The work for pay took up 20 hours a week. The pay of $1.25 an hour was sufficient to make me financially independent and even allowed me to buy an old car. The work taught me a lot about operating a food service department at a university, but my most memorable experience occurred at the graduation in the spring of 1958. My class filed into the stadium for the handing out of the diplomas. I was working in a tent selling coffee and box lunches. All the cash went into a box. When it was my turn to receive my diploma, I took off my white jacket, put on an academic gown, went through the ceremony and quickly returned to my job. At this point the supervisor handed me the cash and told me to go to his car and count it. I will never forget the strength of the temptation to put a few bills into my pocket. Rationalizations were easy. Surely the supervisor is giving me a graduation present, rewarding me for the last two years' loyalty and hard work for unreasonably low pay? The older I get, the prouder I am for resisting the temptation and easy rationalizations. The university did not lose a penny.

The academic experience and choice of graduate school

When classes started I was required to meet the Registrar to determine whether I should be given enough credit from my German education to be a sophomore or a junior. He listened to me for five minutes and concluded, "I will arrange it so you can be a junior." As a result, I never took introductory courses and obtained my BA in two years. Later, in graduate school I often wondered whether it would not have been better in the longer run to have been required to take more courses. As it turned out I found myself in relatively small, advanced courses in business and economics and took a smattering of courses in fields like psychology and philosophy. I wish that today all students had to take a large number of courses outside of their field of concentration; I found my experience broadening and useful.

The only B I received was in French, the rest of my grades were As, resulting in a bachelor's degree *summa cum laude*. In a paper written for a course in economic history, Professor A. Meadows gave me an A+ with the comment "You have an unusual ability to grasp essentials." When the time came to apply for graduate school, Professor Kenneth K. Kurihara, who taught Keynesian economics, gave me the copy of the letter of recommendation he sent on my behalf. In it he recommended me as "one of the best students we have ever had in economics at Rutgers." My mother would have been proud.

Consultations with some of my professors produced the advice that I should not waste my time getting an MBA and instead seek a PhD in economics. Following their advice, I applied for admission to both the Harvard Business School and a number of the best U.S. graduate programs in economics. The results were gratifying but also required me to make a tough decision.

On a beautiful spring day in 1958, two years after arriving in America, a deadline set by the universities forced me to decide whether to seek an MBA at Harvard or a PhD at Yale, Princeton or UCLA. That fateful morning I posted a letter of acceptance to Harvard, planning to send letters declining the offer to the other universities the next day. During lunch I went for a long walk with Toni, who was soon to be my wife. She listened to me very patiently and asked important questions, as I sorted out the arguments for and against the choices facing me. She did not try to influence me one way or the other, but our conversation had a very profound effect on me. It moved me to go to the local post office and ask for a return of the letter I had mailed to Boston that morning. Unbelievable as it may sound today, the postal clerk gave me back my letter! The next day I committed myself to attend Yale and become an economist.

The choice of graduate schools was based on two considerations. Harvard would lend me all the money I needed to pay tuition and living expenses, but I had a moral obligation to repay it. Yale had the most generous scholarship of all the graduate schools, paying for both tuition and some living expenses.

But as I would do at other crossroads in my career, I also ended up choosing the PhD over the MBA program because the former would open more alternatives. It would permit me to become an academic as well as work for industry and government.

Finding Toni

In spite of the many hours spent working, playing soccer and studying, I had some time for socializing. I was guest at Gamma Sigma, a fraternity which had been founded in the immediate postwar years by mature veterans. It was full of talented but 'different' Americans and several foreign students. Traditional fraternities referred to it as "the zoo." One of the fraternity brothers was a student from Greece, Lucas Samarras, who during the 1960s he became a famous artist in the New York scene. Another student from Greece, Costa Tsipsis, became a physicist and now holds a professorship at MIT. I have lost track of the others in the fraternity, but I would not be surprised if many became outstanding professionals. I was tolerated socially and made no lasting friends. I did not have the time or skills to cultivate personal relationships beyond those formed from eating meals together.

At one of the infrequent parties at the fraternity I met Toni. She was an intelligent, vivacious, attractive and athletic sophomore from New York and I fell in love with her. She had had an unusual childhood, growing up in a hotel room just north of Times Square in the care of a childless aunt and uncle. The aunt had been a famous, beautiful actress in the silent movies and lived on the modest income of a trust which a rich admirer had established for her. Her uncle was a retired impresario who once had arranged an American tour for Leoncavallo, the composer of the opera *Pagliacci*.

The theatre background of her adoptive parents brought Toni to play the role of a child in the Broadway musical *Finnian's Rainbow*. For several years she toured the U.S. with the performing company. As a result she attended the School for Professional Children in Manhattan, where she had many brushes with the famous and an active circle of friends. Toni never had what most people would consider to be a normal family and social life. Her playground was Broadway and Central Park in mid-Manhattan. She never came close to her mother until she was well into her twenties, and never knew her father.

Chapter 2

When we met and fell in love, she had plans to quit college that summer and work in New York. Instead, we were married in June, in a very small ceremony in Fifth Avenue Presbyterian Church. The day after the wedding we returned to our summer employment in Manhattan. I worked for the American Bankers' Association. They liked my work so much they offered me a salary in excess of what I was to earn at my first academic appointment four years later at Stanford University. However, I was committed to go to graduate school and declined the offer.

While I was a student in New Haven, Toni showed the intelligence, drive and communications skills I admired. She started as a receptionist for a group of insurance salesmen, graduated to secretary to the investment officer at Yale and during our last two years worked as a research assistant to Tony Carpenter, a professor of psychology at the Center for Research in Alcohol at the university. I am sure she could not have been more successful with a bachelor's degree than with the two years of college she actually had.

Always looking for opportunities to earn extra income, I participated in a study involving the paid consumption of alcohol, which Toni administered in her capacity as a research assistant. The hypothesis was that individuals' ability to perform certain intellectual tasks was enhanced through the consumption of alcohol up to a certain dosage. Toni and her boss laughed for a long time about my behaviour, which they observed from behind a one-way mirror.

I had been required to consume, in five minutes, a water glass of pure Scotch on an empty stomach. My memory of the following hour is nearly blank, but allegedly I sang nursery rhymes in German and failed all tests. It is interesting to note that the study's hypothesis was actually confirmed. The consumption of small to moderate amounts of alcohol facilitated the performance of analytical tasks. But the experiment was designed to use only tasks that did not require interaction with memory. The report on the results of the research stressed that taking exams slightly drunk does *not* bring better grades!

Getting through graduate school examinations

I was fortunate in my choice of economics as a field of study. In the postwar years economics blossomed. It was caught up in the optimism of the times, which expected that technology and science would result in a continuous improvement of the human condition. Science and technology were conquering the atom and space. Economics, adopting the scientific method, would provide the tools for stabilizing the economy, producing rapid growth and an equitable distribution of income.

Mathematics and rigorous modeling of economic processes proceeded rapidly. The availability of computers at increasingly more reasonable

Student Years in America

costs resulted in an explosion of empirical work, testing hypothesis and measuring phenomena. Econometrics, the application of statistics to time series developed into a major field. Soon, economists' status would be raised by the annual award of a Nobel prize. I was privileged to have been studying economics when the excitement and optimism were largely unchallenged. At the time, Friedrich von Hayek and Ludwig von Mieses with their doubts about the new approach to economics were cries in the wilderness and did not penetrate the graduate curriculum.

I was also lucky to have chosen Yale University to study economics. Yale had a long tradition of excellence in the field. Its most distinguished faculty member had been Irving Fisher, whose monetary theories live to this day. But he had suffered a great personal tragedy and set back economics at Yale for some time. In the initial phases of the Great Crash of 1929 he had recommended to his colleagues to hold on to their stocks. They believed him, lost their investments and ostracized the greatest U.S. economist of the period.

In the late 1950s Yale's economics department was beginning to return to greatness. The process coincided with the arrival of Professor James Tobin. He is an intellectual giant. His scientific works are landmarks in monetary theory and econometrics; in 1981 he won a Nobel prize.

Tobin's presence and vision had been instrumental in persuading the Ford Foundation to provide a substantial number of scholarships to attract to Yale the best students from around the world. I had come to Yale partly in response to the generous offer of financial help: so had over 20 others. They were the brightest and the best. Some came from the top U.S. colleges like Swarthmore and Williams, known for the high proportion of graduates that end up in careers as academics. Others came from Australia and Europe, where they had been extremely well prepared, often as teachers.

Many years after my graduation I asked Tobin whether my generation of students was outstanding or whether I was myopic in noticing that so many of them had made significant contributions to economics and held positions at the world's leading universities. He replied that indeed my generation was extra ordinarily successful and, he added, for reasons that he did not know.

Whatever the reasons, I found myself in a tough competitive environment. For what was demanded of me, my knowledge of English and my preparation in economics at Rutgers were inadequate. I read enormous amounts of material but could not see the forest for the trees. For the first time in my life I was not at the top of my class — I was near the bottom. The worst came when I failed the comprehensive examinations given to my class at the end of the second year. I was so discouraged that I arranged an interview with McKenzie, the management consulting firm. The man who interviewed me said that he would be willing to offer me a job but that he would much rather see me finish my degree. Several professors told me that my failure was only a message from the faculty that I needed more training, that Tobin was upset about my plans to quit. For the first time six, or 25 percent of students taking their comprehensive examination did not pass. I was told that Tobin was determined to raise the standards of the Yale graduate program. Four of my failed colleagues were denied further opportunities to take the comprehensive examination. I had just made it under the wire and was allowed to return for another try at passing the examination.

In the end Tobin offered me some individual coaching that would help me get over the last examination hurdle. This was most encouraging and to this day I appreciate the gesture he made, even if I never asked him for extra help. I took another year of courses, served as a teaching assistant and passed the examination on the second try, nearly getting distinction, as one professor privately told me.

In spite of the uncertainty surrounding my status that year, I began to work on my dissertation while still taking courses. By finishing it in August of 1962 I had caught up with my classmates who had passed their comprehensive examinations on their first try. I had also published two papers in top professional journals, which further distinguished me from my colleagues.

The four years of graduate work were one of the toughest parts of my life, but it was worth it. I learned much and, as Professor Ray Powell, the graduate chair used to say to people when he congratulated them upon meeting all the requirements for the PhD, I received my "license to get started" on a professional career. Perhaps more important, the experience launched me on a lifelong search for understanding of how the economy works and how people respond to economic stimuli.

The 'Keynesian Revolution' at Yale

During my term at Yale, the intellectual life of the department was very exciting. The Keynesian revolution was in full swing. As a result, it was no longer considered proper for governments to balance their books and for central banks to give assurance that prices were stable. Instead, it became an obligation of governments to run spending deficits during recessions and for central banks to create inflation, in the expectation that it would lower unemployment.

Tobin and Professor Arthur Okun contributed theoretical arguments justifying these Keynesian policies. Tobin applied 'portfolio theory' to illuminate the role of money in the economy. This task involved the argument that money was not just used to finance cash transactions; money holdings were also seen as a method for diversifying asset holdings. Such diversification results in more stable portfolio values than are associated with holdings of only one type of asset. For example, a portfolio consisting only of bonds will fall 10 percent in value if bond prices are reduced by that percentage. On the other hand, a portfolio made up half of bonds

Student Years in America

and half of cash would be reduced in value by only five percent if bond prices dropped 10 percent. This analysis was designed to open the 'black box' of monetarists like Milton Friedman, who, according to Tobin and other Keynesians, did not have a good explanation of money's role in the economy.

'Okun's Law' about the relationship between economic growth and unemployment is in the toolkit of every economist today. It suggests that for every one percentage increase in the unemployment rate, the nation's total income is decreased by three percent. The same percentage decrease in the unemployment rate raises national income by 2.5 percent. The implication of Okun's Law was that policies which lowered unemployment benefited not just the unemployed but others in the economy as well. Both Tobin and Okun advocated the concept of the 'Phillips Curve,' which suggested that if the government increases inflation, the unemployment rate is reduced, potentially to as low a rate as one or two percent. They helped integrate the Phillips Curve concept into the main body of Keynesian economics and helped provide the rationale for the inflationary policies of the 1970s, which swept the entire world and caused much hardship.

The Keynesian ideas promoted by Tobin and Okun faced challenges at Yale from two more traditional economists. Professor William Fellner was a Berlin-trained Hungarian Count; Professor Henry Wallich was a German-born economist who had earned a Harvard PhD during the war. Both had fled Nazi Germany. Neither used mathematics or econometrics in their research, but drew on the core of economics found in Adam Smith and refined by generations of economists thereafter. This core made them question the validity of the Phillips Curve. How could deficits and the printing of money add to a nation's real income wealth, which other parts of economic theory postulated were determined by capital, labour and technology? They also were concerned about providing politicians with a rationale for running spending deficits to lower unemployment due to recessions. Fellner and Wallich predicted (correctly, as it turned out), that politicians would be tempted to make these deficits permanent.

I have unforgettable memories of a small graduate seminar at which these committed Keynesians and sceptics of Keynesianism fought it out. Fellner and Wallich lost the argument by the standards of the time at Yale. The committed Keynesians had too much 'science' behind their arguments. Rigorous mathematical models of the economy had been built. Innumerable economists had examined these models. Keynesianism carried the day, and the Yale-Harvard-MIT axis ruled.

At MIT especially, the postwar economics wunderkind Paul Samuelson did much to popularize this vision through his bestselling textbook and weekly columns in *Newsweek*. Robert Solow trained many outstanding economists who taught at leading U.S. universities for the next 30 years; both Samuelson and Solow won Nobel prizes for their work. Many graduates from these establishment universities returned to their native countries in both the industrial and third world, where they in turn became influential teachers and government advisers.

It is interesting to note that all four of my Yale professors left their 'ivory towers,' at least temporarily, to work at the highest level of policy formulation in Washington. Tobin became a member of President Kennedy's first Council of Economic Advisers and the famous 'Camelot' he had assembled. Ted Sorensen, the historian whose book *A Thousand Days* chronicled the Kennedy administration, called Tobin "the economic conscience of President Kennedy." Returning to Yale for a seminar, Tobin said that while he was in Washington he saw President Kennedy almost every day and called him "one of the best graduate students I have ever had." Okun became the chief of President Johnson's Council of Economic Advisers during the Vietnam war. Fellner became the chief of President Nixon's Council of Economic Advisers.

Wallich became an influential adviser to the Secretary of the Treasury John Connally. He received much public exposure as a regular columnist in *Newsweek*, alternating with Paul Samuelson and Milton Friedman. Later he was a member of the Board of Governors of the Federal Reserve, where one of his roles was to liaise with European Central Bankers. They appreciated his sophisticated love of good wine, food and cigars (to which I can give personal testimony).

Keynesian economics won not only the intellectual battles but also the hearts of the policymakers during the 1960s and 1970s, who acted on the Phillips Curve and Okun's Law. Inflation was seen as a reasonable cost worth accepting, as it reduced unemployment and brought higher incomes to others. The politicians also accepted the idea that deficit spending during both recessions and prosperity involved little cost since resultant government debt was owed almost totally to the people who incurred it. Taxes needed to pay for the interest on the debt was returned to the same citizenry which collectively held the debt. At a meeting of U.S. Treasury consultants as late as 1970 in Washington I heard Okun make these points central to Keynesianism with such eloquence that I was sure Secretary John Connally was persuaded by them. If I had not been exposed to Milton Friedman's ideas a few years earlier in Chicago, I too might easily have been persuaded by Okun.

The monetarist challenge

Economists now know through analytical and empirical work that the Phillips Curve tradeoff works only if workers can be induced to accept lower wages through unexpected inflation. For example, workers might accept a pay of $5 per hour but unexpected inflation lowers the real value of the wage, or what the workers can buy with it, to $4.50. Under such conditions, the real cost of labour for employers is only $4.50 and they hire more workers than they would have at a cost of $5 an hour. Through this mechanism inflation was expected to lower unemployment and give rise to the Phillips Curve tradeoff.

But, as Friedman, Edmund Phelps and Robert Lucas have argued, this mechanism does not operate for any length of time because it is based on a false perception of reality by workers. Eventually workers learn from their experiences and are unwilling to settle for $5 if inflation is expected to be 10 percent over the year's contract. They will insist on wages that compensate for the expected inflation. In the above example, they will accept only a wage of $5.50. But at this wage employers real labour costs are $5 and they do not hire the extra workers they would have if they pay had been $4.50. Therefore, unemployment does not fall. The only way the Phillips Curve tradeoff works if in every successive period the actual inflation is greater than the workers expected it to be, and that they do not learn to anticipate the pattern of accelerating inflation.

The unfortunate consequences of Keynes

During the late 1960s and well into the 1970s Washington politicians were advised by Okun and other economists who believed in the existence of the Phillips Curve tradeoff. Critics of the concept were voices in the wilderness. Therefore, the world went through a period of high and accelerating inflation which brought some serious upheavals.

One of these upheavals involved the international monetary system, which had been based on the dollar gold exchange standard. The U.S. Treasury was willing to exchange U.S. dollars held by foreign governments for gold at a guaranteed fixed price of $35 an ounce. Therefore, governments held many dollar-denominated U.S. treasury bills. They were as good as gold and yielded interest. However, the inflation of the late 1960s and early 1970s made this price of gold increasingly unrealistic. While the official price of the metal remained at $35, the free market price rose dramatically. Countries who had been happy to hold U.S. dollars in the past now demanded gold at the official price from the U.S. Treasury, which in turn did not want to surrender it. The resultant political and economic tensions in 1970-71 produced a collapse of the postwar international monetary system. Exchange rates among the major countries of the world were no longer fixed and were free to adjust to each nation's competitiveness.

The move to a floating exchange rates system was hailed as a great advance by the Keynesians, who believed in the Phillips Curve tradeoff. Under the new system countries could use inflation to lower their unemployment rates without the foreign constraints which had plagued them under the fixed rate system. If inflation made a country's prices too high and imports were higher than exports, a lower exchange rate would correct the imbalance.

Chapter 2

In response to the establishment of this new international monetary system, many countries formerly reluctant to have inflation to lower unemployment embraced inflation with a vengeance. There was an unprecedented economic boom because initially workers could be fooled into believing that there would be no inflation; they accepted lower real wages and unemployment dropped. But workers soon learned about the effects of inflation on their income and changed their wage demands. Governments had to increase inflation ever more to keep unemployment low and soon the second major consequence of the inflationary policies manifested itself.

Shortages of natural resources developed. Throughout history the known recoverable supply of reserves of oil, copper, coal and so on were sufficient to meet world demand, for about 15 years ahead. When reserves were depleted, new ones were discovered and brought onstream. Such conditions are good for the world, because it is costly to discover and develop reserves which are not needed in the near future.

The delicate balance of reserves and expected demand disappeared as a result of the worldwide inflation. The supply of reserves of many natural resources suddenly became so small that it was projected that severe shortages would occur within a very few years. The Club of Rome, a collection of business leaders and natural scientists, used what at the time were impressive computer simulations to project future trends, predicting that the world had entered a new phase of scarcity and would soon run out of a wide range of resources. Stanford Professor Paul Ehrlich added into the debate his neo-Malthusian spectre of overpopulation.

We now know that these ideas of the Club of Rome had no economic content. It is true that all resources are finite, but this is not the same as being exhaustible. Increased scarcities and the resultant high prices will lead to the development of substitutes and reductions in demand such that the world will never completely exhaust any resources. Moreover, in the context of the 1970s, the apparent development of shortages was only temporary. It was attributable to the unexpected world wide economic boom accompanying the victory of the Keynesian economic theories. It disappeared with the elimination of inflation. In fact, oversupplies have resulted in falling price indices for these products.

There was another tragic consequence of the Keynesian economic policies. President Johnson had been led to believe that the inflation would decrease unemployment and increase revenues enough so that the Vietnam war could be fought without tax increases and sacrifices to his 'War on Poverty.' He was convinced that it was possible to have both guns and butter. It is doubtful that he would have committed his country to the Vietnam war as strongly as he did had his advice been based on traditional economics.

Keynesians involved in Washington policymaking at the time have a different story today. They claim that they had warned Johnson of the dangers of inflation, asking him to raise taxes. According to them, the refusal of Johnson and Congress to follow this advice are responsible for the economic upheavals brought on by OPEC, inflation, the Vietnam war and student unrest of the late 1960s and 1970s. The definitive economic history of this time has yet to be written, but there is no doubt in my mind that the Keynesian economics brought to the highest levels in Washington by Tobin and Okun had a decisive influence on the political process.

But of course, at the time when the Keynesian Revolution was refined and I was a graduate student at Yale, these adverse consequences were not foreseen. There was great enthusiasm for the ideas and optimism about the benefits they would bring. If Tobin and Okun had any doubts, they never showed them. I was caught up in this spirit. It was irresistible. I was drawn into it powerfully by an experience that was heady stuff for the son of a Reifenberg grocer.

It was a bright Sunday morning in January 1960. New Haven was enveloped in a blanket of fresh snow. Tobin telephoned and invited me to go skiing with him and his family if Toni could babysit for his smaller children at home. Toni agreed and we were off in the Volkswagen bus for a ride to the northeastern part of Connecticut. On the way, Tobin's son, who was in his early teens, asked me whether I had heard that President Kennedy had called his father? I then got the story.

The preceding evening the President had asked Tobin to be a member of his Council of Economic Advisers. Tobin had answered that he did not think that he was a suitable candidate since he was an "ivory tower economist." Kennedy replied that this was fine since he was an "ivory tower president." The media reported this event widely during the next week. It added to the 'Camelot' image of the Kennedy administration that Tobin accepted the invitation.

Understanding free enterprise

The most fundamental ideas of economics are simple, but it takes much effort and time to understand them fully and integrate them into one's thinking about the world. Sometimes the final insights come from unexpected sources and thought-processes. My full understanding of how the 'invisible hand' works came under ironic circumstances and so dramatically that I remember the incident to this day.

I had read the basic textbooks. I even had read much of Adam Smith's *Wealth of Nations* in the original. While in class one day, I could not understand an argument about economic planning, which Professor Michael Montias had presented, on comparative economic systems. In the library in the evening I discussed my problem with Parvez Hasan, a classmate from Pakistan. He referred me to a book by Oscar Lange on the use of economic planning. As I read this book, I felt the proverbial penny drop. By understanding how Lange envisioned the imitation of market processes

Chapter 2

through computers at a central planning agency, I finally understood fully the way the invisible hand of competition allocates resources efficiently. I had finally become an economist!

Ever since then I have been trying to pass on this understanding to my students. I will never forget the great success I once had in 1989 with a group of Chinese students. Having been sponsored by the Canadian International Development Agency, these junior level executives were likely to become business leaders in the future, and were required to attend some special lectures on business and economics at Simon Fraser University.

During one of these lectures I asked them whether they had ever thought about the way in which the capitalist system created the high quality, good service and low prices they found in Canadian bakery shops. I had seen the shortages and poor services and products in Chinese stores myself, and their initial reaction showed that they were really impressed by the good services and products they encountered in Canada. I pointed out to them that importantly, no one told the bakers what to do; they were selfish human beings and were free to charge any price they wanted. Having been trained to understand that planning and commands were essential to the functioning of an economy, they had no idea what made the capitalist system function as well as it did.

It took me some time to explain the essence of Adam Smith's story of the baker's motives and constraints. Under free enterprise, individuals like the baker are always in the selfish pursuit of gain by buying inputs and labour as cheaply as possible and selling their products at the highest price they can get from consumers. However, their freedom is severely constrained. If they pay too little, they cannot obtain the inputs and labour they need. If they charge too much for the bread, consumers refuse to buy it from them and purchase it from another baker. So eventually they have to pay the going price for what they buy and sell at the going price for their products. Competition from other bakers ultimately results in the condition where all of them earn just enough profits to stay in the business. There are no large fortunes to be made baking and selling bread.

The baking industry is in constant flux. A baker who does not offer good bread and service will lose consumers and go out of business. Incentives to improve the quality of bread exist all the time. A baker producing superior bread can charge a higher price and expand his business. If he can keep his trade secret hidden from others, he even has a chance to get rich. However chances are that competitors soon imitate his innovation and profits go back to normal. Nevertheless, the desire to get rich through the invention of better bread results in every higher quality goods and services for consumers.

When I was finished with my explanation several students said: "You must visit China and tell this story everywhere." After my term in the Canadian Parliament I think that it should be told there as well. There are many who do not know how free enterprise works, that it is not possible to have improved goods and services without changes in industries which impose hardships on some, and that it is not possible to improve on the functioning of the market by selective intervention by government. The bureaucrats engaged in such intervention cannot possibly have the knowledge to do better. If the knowledge were available anywhere to anyone, entrepreneurs would already have exploited it. As Nobel Laureate Friedrich Hayek pointed out in an article of fundamental importance, the knowledge required by the bureaucrats can only be produced by the trial and error of entrepreneurs testing their ideas on consumers. Free markets, in essence, are the only practical method available to society for finding out what new products, services and technologies are worth adopting.

Developing an interest in the international monetary system

My early research as a full-fledged economist was in the field of international finance. It started through a course taught by Professor Robert Triffin, a Belgian-born, Harvard-trained economist. During the immediate postwar years he had headed missions to developing countries, helping with the creation of their national central banks. He also worked at the OECD in Paris, where he developed a system of accounts for measuring the effects of monetary policy. In a study of currency upheavals in Western Europe in the postwar years he suggested as a remedy the establishment of the European Monetary Union for cooperation among Europe's central banks. This Union was the initial step in a process which is expected soon to result in a common currency for Europe.

In 1960 Triffin published the book *Gold and the Dollar Crisis* (Yale University Press). It made him famous as a visionary, following in the footsteps of Keynes by proposing a common currency for the world to be issued by a reformed International Monetary Fund. The book also increased his fame since it was published just when the dollar was under speculative attack for the first time in 30 years. His analysis had predicted this attack, explained its causes and proposed policies to prevent recurrences.

I was strongly attracted to Triffin's ideas on international monetary affairs. As a result, in 1963 I edited a volume published by Stanford University Press entitled *World Monetary Reform: Plans and Issues*. It consisted of reprints of alternative reform proposals made by a number of economists, many in response to Triffin's latest book. It gave me a great thrill as a young economist to see a 10-page review of this book published in Russian in a Russian academic journal. The Soviet Union obviously was interested in the development of the international monetary system and what it implied for the future price of gold. This publication in turn led to the invitation from Penguin Books to write a textbook in the field. I entitled it *The International Monetary System*. It was published in 1969 and sold 200,000 copies through four editions worldwide.

I also worked for Triffin as a paid research assistant. Following up on his ideas I used his OECD monetary accounts and model for an econometric study of the international transmission of monetary policy. Computers were just becoming accessible and I had to write a regression program to do the estimates. The results of the study were inconsistent with what Keynesian theories would have predicted. When a European country expanded its money supply more rapidly than its neighboring countries, Keynesian theory predicted that it would experience inflation. Our calculations showed that instead prices remained stable or moved in unison with those of neighboring countries. The newly created, excess supply of money resulted in higher imports and reduced exports. The resultant trade deficit was financed by the extra money until, in effect, it had moved abroad. This finding was important for the policy discussions of the time. It implied that countries with fixed exchange rates and much trade with other countries could not use inflation to lower the unemployment rate as the Phillips Curve suggested.

Triffin suggested I show the study to Tobin, who reacted by saying that our results were very interesting and should be published for consideration by a wider, critical audience. We followed Tobin's advice and submitted it for publication in the prestigious *Review of Economics and Statistics* published at Harvard. It was accepted and appeared promptly. Triffin had been most generous in making me a co-author of this paper, even though I worked for him as a paid research assistant when it was written. The paper did not receive much attention in the U.S., since it did not fit into the dominant Keynesian paradigm. However, in the 1970s Rainer Masera, an Italian academic involved also with the Bank of Italy, referred to it as the first published International Monetarist model. Just at that time monetarism, under the intellectual leadership of Milton Friedman, had begun to gain respectability as a systematic criticism of Keynesian economics.

The doctoral dissertation

Until the postwar years, doctoral dissertations were expected to produce major contributions to knowledge. Since then, criteria for dissertations have become much less ambitious (or, as some would say, realistic). The results of the research are expected to result in the publication of a refereed journal article. Like most such articles, it was expected to make only a relatively minor contribution to knowledge. The main purpose of the publication was to show that the student is able to design and carry out a scholarly research project. I chose my research project keeping in mind this new concept of a dissertation, even though in the end it was published as a book by Stanford University Press.

My research involved the development of a theory of forward exchange rates and its empirical testing. The topic came up in lectures by Egon Sohmen, a German who had obtained his PhD at MIT and was a visiting assistant professor at Yale. Forward exchange rates are the prices at which one can purchase foreign exchange today for delivery at some point in the future. Most of these forward contracts are for 90 days in the future, though they also exist for other time periods, including a year or more. The forward exchange market is used by importers and exporters to assure that they will be paid a known sum for the goods they produce today but ship later. For example, on February 1 a Canadian company sells lumber to an American company at a certain U.S. dollar price. However, the lumber will be in the hands of the purchaser only three months later, at which point the bill is also paid. When the sales contract is signed the Canadian exporter does not know how many Canadian dollars the sale will bring in March. This uncertainty creates difficulties for financial planning. The forward sale of the U.S. dollars eliminates this uncertainty.

Forward exchange is also used by investors. For example, a Canadian finds that a British government bill due in 90 days carries a higher interest rate than a Canadian government bill with the same maturity; however, purchase of the British bill carries an exchange risk. It is quite possible that by the time it matures the exchange rate has moved and results in a loss. This loss can reduce, eliminate or even exceed the extra earning from the purchase of the British bill at the higher interest rate. The forward sale of the British currency undertaken at the same time the investment is made eliminates this exchange risk and the investor knows exactly the return from the foreign investment. Forward exchange markets offer also an opportunity to speculate. Someone who believes that the spot rate in three months will be higher than the three month forward rate today may want to sell the currency forward. If the guess is correct, the transaction is profitable. One reason why people find speculation in this market attractive is that only a small margin down payment is required when a forward exchange contract is entered into. As a result, large speculative positions can be taken with very little owned money. Of course, opportunities for large gains are accompanied by the risk of large losses. But this is what some speculators want.

For all participants in the forward exchange markets it is of considerable interest to understand the determinants of forward rates so that they can act rationally in their buy and sell decisions. My dissertation involved essentially a systematic analysis of the determinants of forward rates, what causes people to buy and sell and how their decisions are influenced by existing spot rates, interest rates and expectations about the future. Such an analysis is challenging and interesting in its own right, even if it makes dull reading for students and others not involved in the market. However, my interest in forward exchange theory stemmed less from the desire to do such theoretical work but from the fact that governments at the time regularly intervened in forward markets to set rates different from those free markets would have produced.

Such intervention by central banks was seen as a method for maintaining a high effective interest rate for foreign investors and a low rate for domestic investors. It was thus believed to permit countries to pursue expansionary monetary policies without having to worry about the outflow of capital to countries with higher interest rates. This possibility had important implications for the practicality of using inflation to reduce unemployment. Countries could exploit the Phillips Curve tradeoff between inflation and unemployment without fear of capital outflows, the loss of international reserves and currency devaluations.

The selection of my dissertation topic was based on the same criteria used in the many research projects I would undertake later. There was an actual or potential government policy which was expected to result in substantial benefits. What were the chances that these benefits would be realized? What were unexpected results of the policy? The theory would be used to deal with these questions and direct the empirical work. I was not interested in advancing theory for its own sake.

For the theory of forward exchange rate determination I used the graphic exposition of a model already in the literature and modified it to incorporate Tobin's portfolio theory. There were few published data on exchange rates and I obtained a large data set from the Dresdener Bank in Frankfurt with the help of my good friend Rudi Ebel. Coding and keypunching the data was a boring and time-consuming job, but with my wife's help we got it done quickly and I could return to the real work of analysis and writing.

The calculations made with these data were simple but large in number. The new electronic computer at Yale, an IBM 650, was ideal for such a task. In today's world of highly efficient personal computers the job would be trivial. With the slow-working IBM 650 and expensive and limited access, the calculations were quite difficult and time-consuming. Word processors were unheard of at the time. I wrote the first draft of the dissertation by hand. Toni typed it on stencils which were relatively easy to correct and permitted running off a number of copies.

After about nine months of work, I had a first draft ready for Triffin and two other professors in June 1962. Over the summer, they read it and made some suggestions for changes. I made these promptly and the dissertation was formally accepted in September 1962. The official award of the degree was at the 1963 convocation in New Haven. I was unable to attend the ceremony because at that time I was teaching at Stanford University in California and could not afford the cost of flying across the continent.

As Professor Gustav Ranis said in his evaluation of the document, it was "a solid piece of workmanship." It was not an important contribution to knowledge, but it was good enough so that in 1966 after some revisions it was published as a book by Stanford University Press. Professor Harry Johnson recommended it in his graduate classes at the University of Chicago for a number of years. Professor Michael Levi at the University of British Columbia, who was a student of Johnson's in Chicago, in turn used my

Student Years in America

work in his lectures and own textbook. In the summer of 1998 I met an economist working for the OECD on a visit to the Fraser Institute. He told me how he had used my book in his studies at the University of Paris in the 1970s. Such feedback about the use of one's research by others is important in keeping up one's morale. Research and writing is a very lonely and tedious affair. Once a paper or book is published, it goes out of one's life much like children do. There is a void and a longing to know how the offspring is doing, but it has a life of its own and information about its performance is rare.

My formal schooling had been completed in September 1962, six years after I had arrived from Germany. Ahead of me lay a turbulent decade full of professional and personal challenges. It saw the birth of two children, academic positions at four different universities in California, Illinois, Pennsylvania and British Columbia, a year as a researcher at the U.S. Treasury Department, and visiting research and teaching positions at institutions of higher learning in Europe, Asia and Africa.

CHAPTER 3

Apprenticeship Years at Stanford and Chicago

ONE OF the hallmarks of the North American labour market is that most people change jobs and move their residences a number of times. After a decade or so of such wanderings most settle down and stay for a long period with the same employer. New PhD economists seeking an academic position are no exception.

The period of mobility is like an apprenticeship. Learning by doing improves teaching and research skills. Teaching evaluations and publications produce a resume useful in finding new jobs. Expectations about career paths are made increasingly realistic through contacts with competitors and familiarity with market opportunities. My apprenticeship period was perhaps a bit longer and far ranging than average. It certainly started with a bang.

Early in April 1962, while I still held the position of an Assistant Instructor at Yale, I was contacted by telephone by Professor Lorie Tarshis, the chair of the Department of Economics at Stanford University near San Francisco in northern California. His department needed someone with my qualifications and background for a one year appointment to replace a number of faculty members who had unexpectedly gone on leave. The pay would be $8,600 for the year plus the option of having first refusal if the department were to hire for the following years. Was I still available?

The inquiry came as a complete surprise. I had not been seeking a job, expecting instead to remain at Yale for one more year while I finished my thesis and worked as an Instructor for $3,000. I consulted some of the Yale faculty about the wisdom of accepting this position. Everyone encouraged me to take it. They considered it to be a great opportunity for getting started on an academic career.

So, in the middle of June Toni and I left New Haven after a tough but productive four years. The first draft of the thesis was with the advisers. As we set out to drive across the continent Toni was six months pregnant. A new Volkswagen bus was loaded with personal belongings. The mattress on top was so close to the roof that Toni had some trouble turning around when we slept in the car during our camping trip across the continent.

The travel was a wonderfully refreshing experience. There was the thrill of seeing the mountains of Colorado rise out of the flat, hot and seemingly endless prairies. The cool, flowering mountain meadows and the sparkle of stars in the clear night sky high in the mountains were like a reward after a big job had been completed. Great excitement overcame us as we drove through the grass-covered hills that led us to a first view of the fabled San Francisco Bay with the Golden Gate Bridge and skyline shimmering through the haze. I would not just visit but actually live and work in this beautiful part of the world.

Teaching at Stanford

The work came quickly and in large amounts. It did not take me long to revise my thesis and return it to Yale for final approval. Then came the preparation of lecture notes for courses I had to teach in September. The job was difficult, as any teacher knows. One course was on international trade and finance, a subject I would teach for the next 30 years and for which I wrote a large textbook in the 1970s.

The second course involved teaching a rather unusual and difficult subject to economics majors in their last year. The course was traditionally taught by Professor Paul Baran, who was on leave that year. Baran's writings were full of Marxist analysis of capitalist exploitation and the coming revolution of the working class. In its wisdom, the Stanford faculty had decided that every economics major at Stanford in the last year should be exposed to such a course. It was expected to help them gain better understanding of capitalism. I used Baran's book but focused on a more standard approach to the study of alternative economic systems.

I had the normal anxieties coming with a new occupation. They were increased by the fact that Stanford students were known for their brilliance and high expectations. Was I ready for them? The Stanford faculty in economics had an outstanding reputation. It was led by Professor Ken Arrow, whose work in mathematical economics later would bring him the Nobel Prize. Jack Gurley and Edward Shaw were famous for their work in monetary theory. Gurley held the prestigious position of editor of the *American Economic Review*. Professor Emile Despres was a brilliant economist who published little but inspired many. How would I fit into this environment?

On September 20, at seven o'clock in the morning, Toni gave birth to our son Eric in the Palo Alto hospital after a long labour. I was awake and waited all night for the event outside the delivery room. When the wait was finally over I went straight to my office where I was committed to my first official office hours for students. My mind did not function well that day.

As if teaching two new courses, having a new baby and doing research was not enough, I had unexpectedly been given another burdensome responsibility. Despres was the manager of a large Ford Foundation grant that went to financing the Pakistan Development Institute in Karachi. Without any consultation I was simply told that I would oversee the affairs of this grant during Despres' absence that fall. An able secretary helped me greatly and somehow I managed. But sometimes it was not easy.

Chapter 3

One evening I returned home from the university to a just-arriving telephone call from Karachi. Professor Mark Leiserson, the Institute's director, was in panic. Several Pakistani students were ready to leave and attend universities in the U.S. They could not get visas because I had failed to send letters acknowledging financial support from the Ford Foundation Program. Just when he began to explain what I had to do so urgently, a voice cut in over the crackling telephone: "The circuits are now closing." Transcontinental telephone calls in 1962 were dependent upon the angle of the sun. There were no faxes or e-mail to take the place of the telephone or slow mail. After a long wait the next day, Leiserson and I resumed our conversation. Upon his suggestion I sent Telex messages to all of the students, certifying that they had been granted financial support and they all were promptly granted their visas.

Then there was the pressure to do research. I knew that my entire academic career depended upon the publications I produced and that they would ultimately help me overcome my mediocre graduate school record. So I went to work. By November, leading journals accepted two papers on forward exchange. Stanford University Press awarded me contracts for the publication of two books. For the first I edited a number of papers proposing international monetary reform. The second was for the publication of my doctoral dissertation. With the two articles published already as a graduate student, my resume looked very good and I was quite optimistic about the future.

But at the end of November devastating news arrived from Arrow, the temporary chair of the department. The faculty had just voted not to extend my contract. I would have to find another job. The decision was reached before there was time to evaluate my teaching and research performance. At the same time, the department had begun to interview new candidates for employment in the next academic year.

This unfair reneging on a promise made to me by the chair during the negotiations for employment six months earlier turned out to be one of the best things that ever happened to me. It brought me one of the very best jobs in economics at that time, a position at the University of Chicago. Later I learned that the treatment I had received from the Stanford faculty at the time was not at all unusual. Unfair amounts of work and disregard of promises were all part of the game.

However, Stanford was kind enough to pay my expenses for a trip to the meetings of the American Economics Association in December of 1963 in Pittsburgh. Economists at these meetings present papers, socialize and operate what graduate students call the 'slave market.'

Three years at Chicago

I went through the official interviewing process in Pittsburgh with several universities that were looking for young academics. There was also

Apprenticeship Years at Stanford and Chicago

an interesting informal market. One evening I was invited by Herbert Giersch to join him for a meal in a restaurant. Giersch, a famous German economist and head of the economics department at the University of the Saar, later became President of the Institute for World Economics at Kiel (and, much later, I would be in the running as his successor there). Another person at the table was Herbert Stein, head of the American Enterprise Institute in Washington, Chair of the President's Council of Economic Adviser 1972-72 and a very popular writer for *Fortune* magazine. Here the two eminent Herberts were persuading the lowly assistant professor that he should take a job in Germany! It was a tempting thought, but too much spoke against it. My wife was an American. It would have been very difficult for her to learn German and fit into the socially much more rigid German society. Most important, I would have wondered forever whether by returning to Germany at that time I would have missed the opportunity to 'make it' in the big American pond. With my year at Stanford, I had already seen what it took to make it at an American establishment university.

Through the more formal market I had obtained an attractive offer for a teaching position at Dartmouth College in New Hampshire. However, the position I finally accepted came to me through another initiative in the informal market. During the first day of the Pittsburgh conference I ran into Tobin and told him that I was looking for a job. A day later, as he was leaving, he asked me whether I had seen Harry Johnson. I had not and quickly searched out Johnson. The next morning I had breakfast with him in his room.

Harry, as everyone called him, was a big man with a big reputation. He would soon have the longest list of publications of any living economist. He was a specialist in international and monetary economics at the University of Chicago. The Rockefeller Foundation had awarded him a large fellowship grant under a program designed to give free time and financial resources to a small number of especially promising young U.S. academics. In a one page proposal, Johnson had promised that during the next two years he would rewrite international trade theory.

His financial arrangement provided for the hiring of a research associate. He had arranged with the Department of Economics at the University of Chicago that his associate would have a joint academic appointment. A couple of weeks later I was in Chicago to give a seminar and meet the faculty. Soon I had an offer to be Harry's research associate and an assistant professor teaching half the normal load. I accepted it happily. The University of Chicago is famous for its outstanding graduate schools in many disciplines. The Department of Economics is among the best. The 1960s saw the Department's 'Golden Age.'

Nothing in my memory describes my Chicago experience better than the following episode. One Wednesday I walked to the regular weekly luncheon meetings of the faculty with Professor Milton Friedman and

Chapter 3

Donald Baer, a fellow Assistant Professor. As Baer described it later, I was 'feeling my oats' and started a conversation with the opening gambit: "Milton, do you really believe that the U.S. should not have any national parks?" According to Baer I put myself into the meat grinder and then kept pushing.

At the luncheon I got some help from the faculty present and in fact Friedman's views were shared by only one or two others. The discussion was most exciting and enlightening as might be expected since of the 10 faculty members there, six would end up with Nobel prizes. There was George Stigler, a great wit and father of a new approach to the economics of regulation, who received his prize in 1982.

Theodore Schultz was the 'grey eminence' and very influential in departmental hiring policies. He won his prize in 1979 for work in agricultural economics and human capital theory. Bob Fogel was the Secretary of the Communist Party of New York when Krushchev's revelations about Stalin's crimes changed his political values. He wrote *The New Economic History*, for which he received his prize in 1994.

Ronald Coase brought to economics the Coase Theorem, in a widely cited article on economics. Merton Miller, teaching at the Business School, was given the prize for his work in financial theory. And then there was Milton Friedman, one of the best known economists of this century, who was honored with the prize in 1976.

Other faculty members were or would become famous. Robert Mundell's writings are still on the reading lists of most graduate students in economics. Later he was known as the intellectual father of supply side economics. George Shultz, dean of the Business School, later became the U.S. Secretary of Labour and would leave his mark as Secretary of the Treasury (and, ultimately, Secretary of State). Arnold Harberger, who was married to a Chilean, ran a successful graduate program for students from Latin America. Today his former students are serving in numerous Latin American countries as Presidents, Ministers and Central Bank Governors.

Albert Reese would become Provost of Princeton University and President of the Sloan Foundation; Zvi Griliches moved on to become a distinguished professor at Harvard; Lloyd Metzler, Greg Lewis, Lester Telser, Hirofumi Uzawa, Bert Hoselitz and Larry Sjaastad are the authors of influential research familiar to most economists.

The intellectual life of the department was most exciting, partly because the faculty was small and tightly knit. Senior faculty numbered only about 15 and taught only graduate courses. The University of Chicago College had its own faculty responsible for teaching undergraduates. Three other assistant professors, like myself, also taught some undergraduate courses.

In addition, there were always bright visiting faculty like UBC's Tony Scott and Albert Breton from the University of Toronto. Seminars and workshops were frequent and well-attended. Anyone who was anybody in economics came through Chicago for short visits. Almost every week day evening saw a party at someone's home for a visitor. There was almost a problem of intellectual over stimulation. It was necessary to engage in rationing if one wanted any time and energy for one's own research.

The secrets of success of the University of Chicago

The outstanding success of the Chicago faculty was due to the example set by its most famous and widely published members like Friedman, Stigler, Johnson and Harberger. But it was also due to what I can best describe as cooperative competition. There was a daily lunch at the Quadrangle Club, well attended by faculty and visitors. The discussion focussed on ideas and the latest research being done anywhere in the world. I usually came away from these meetings anxious to get back to work. I sensed that my colleagues always were worried about their own output and reputations that seemed endangered by all the talk about scientific achievements elsewhere. The anxiety affected everyone. At no other university have I ever seen such a process at work.

Another secret of the university's success is its independence from public funds and the absence of a faculty association, which operate like a labour union in most universities. There was no need to hire according to a union scale. The dean, D. Gale Johnson, himself a well known agricultural economist, tended to authorize hiring for senior faculty by setting no limits on the salary that could be offered to an economist the faculty wanted to hire. At one faculty meeting it was decided that a person was needed to teach monetary economics whenever Friedman was on one of his frequent leaves. The search procedure started with the preparation of a list of the best monetary economists in the world. The chair was then asked to contact persons on this list, starting at the top. He had complete freedom in the salary he was able to offer in each case.

Another Chicago practice cannot be used in universities with strong faculty associations. Any tenured faculty who did not perform according to expectations would be given extra work responsibilities and no pay increases. It never took long before such persons left for greener pastures elsewhere. This practice allowed Friedman to say that "tenure means nothing at Chicago." The graduate program also contributes much to the success of the Department. It is rightly known for its competitiveness and the great opportunities it opens for those who survive it. I learned first hand about the operation of the admissions process. One year I was asked to study the background papers of about 150 candidates for admission. I was astounded to find that practically all of them were in the top one percent of their under graduate classes and of the annual global Graduate Record Examination scores. Students with less than such top credentials did not even bother to apply!

A ranking of the graduate students was circulated among the senior

Chapter 3

faculty like Friedman, Schultz and Harberger, who had financial resources provided by foundations. They offered generous fellowship to the candidates they liked best, but the fellowships were renewed only if the students received the grades that were expected of them. After the first and second year of course work, a substantial proportion of students lost their financial support. Some were asked to leave.

Like Friedman, who used some interesting criteria when he selected students, the senior faculty took great personal interest in the admissions procedure. One year, one of the top students had an undergraduate record of straight As. He was at the top of the list I had helped prepare. Friedman put him near the bottom, on the grounds that from personal experience he knew the quality of the faculty at that university. He also vetoed the admission of a mature student with outstanding qualifications. His grounds were that by the time this person joined the profession he would have so few years of productive life left that the social rate of return of investment in him was much below that of investment in a younger person. I wonder what would happen to this policy in today's spirit of group rights and non-discrimination! Would a university with such criteria face civil suits on the grounds of age discrimination?

One of the most intellectually interesting activities took place in a rather unique Chicago institution, the so-called 'workshops.' They were much like seminars — but with a twist. Presenters had 10 minutes to introduce their paper, which had been distributed at least one day before. The discussion then turned immediately to the critical evaluation of theory and empirical evidence. Friedman in particular was incisive in his comments and students competed fiercely in their attempts to imitate him. Often the workshops brought out fatal flaws in papers. One distinguished visiting professor had tears in his eyes at the end of a workshop in which serious flaws in his paper had been exposed. He wondered whether it was too late to withdraw the paper already in print with a leading journal.

But the workshop also raised the productivity of graduate students and faculty. Constructive suggestions for improvement often were invaluable. The entire process was not for the timid, but those with the mental toughness to withstand the pressure walked away well prepared for future academic battles.

There were many subtle rivalries at Chicago. Upon leaving a party Johnson once noted slyly: "Have you noticed how Friedman always says, 'Why don't we all sit down?'" (Friedman is 'vertically challenged,' being only about five feet tall). Friedman in turn once described Johnson as "the writing machine that feeds on alcohol." Johnson indeed liked alcohol, dying in 1979 at age 56 from the complications of alcoholism. A small group of faculty used to retire to the Quadrangle Club several evenings a week. When Johnson had offered me employment I accepted under the condition that I was not expected to join that group. He agreed. I wonder what opportunities for learning economics I had foregone.

Apprenticeship Years at Stanford and Chicago

Research done

I thrived as an economist in Chicago. One year I published seven papers. Someone who studied publication records placed me with this rate near the top of all U.S. economists that year. Johnson had given me many useful tips on research and writing style through his comments on the first few papers I sent him. This coaching was invaluable.

However, Johnson and I did not work on joint projects in the field which he had promised to rewrite in his application to the Rockefeller fellowship. Johnson was always traveling and his main role in the world was to integrate, synthesize and publicize the different strands of research he found. As such, he played a valuable role for the profession. Economists might say that he made more perfect the market for economic knowledge. But this role left him virtually no time for basic, innovative research. I had neither the skill nor the interest in pursuing the topic he had identified in his Rockefeller Foundation research proposal. This topic involved the important task of integrating traditional international trade theory with the theory of imperfect competition. The closest we came to joint work on this topic was when he asked me to do a literature search. The results of this search produced no insights that allowed us to push the theoretical frontier.

However, while in Chicago I had begun work on the same topic of international trade in very similar products which pointed out its importance empirically. Traditional international trade theory considers trade in goods which require very different inputs. The best example is one first used by David Ricardo in the 18th century: Britain exports cloth manufactured with the abundant textile machinery in that country. Britain in turn imports wine from Portugal, which uses the country's good soil and climate.

Tariffs against cloth import into Portugal and against wine imports into Britain protect local industries. Ricardo's theory demonstrates that tariff reductions in the two countries leads to expanded trade and an increase in the total income in both countries. However, the tariff reduction comes at a cost. In Britain the producers of wine (or a substitute product like beer or whisky) go out of business. Workers in the industry lose their jobs. The same adjustment takes place in the Portuguese cloth industry. Because of these costly adjustments countries tend to resist free trade initiatives.

Ricardo's theory was useful in demonstrating how countries gain through free trade, but it is also misleading in its choice of industries to illustrate the process. Most of international trade consists not of products requiring much different input, like cloth and wine, but products which have very similar production requirements and meet very similar needs of consumers. Examples of these industries are steel, automobiles, electronic equipment, clothing, food and machinery. The different varieties of goods are recorded in domestic statistics as belonging to the same industry. The problem I attacked with my research was the measurement of the relative impor-

Chapter 3

tance of what is called 'intra-industry trade,' relative to the trade in goods from different industries, the so-called 'inter-industry trade.'

I considered it important to document the importance of intra-industry trade because of the implications it has for the cost of lowering tariffs. Reduced protection does not mean that Canadians, for example, would be condemned to be the "hewers of wood and drawers of water." Free trade instead is likely to result in increases in both Canada's imports and exports of automobiles and a wide range of other manufactured products. Experience has shown that adjustments to the increased level and new pattern of trade was relatively easy. Machines did not become obsolete. Workers did not lose their jobs. The main changes involved the expansion of some product lines and the contraction of some others in the same company.

These changes in the industries with expanding imports and exports resulted in substantial productivity gains. Canadian firms which under protection might have produced 20 types of refrigerators — of different capacity, style and colour — under free trade produced only six. Consumers' choices increased because of varieties imported from the U.S. At the same time, the six remaining varieties produced in Canada would be exported all over the U.S. The shrinking of the number of varieties produced in Canada and the U.S. made production more efficient in both countries. Inventories of inputs and finished products could be smaller. Assembly lines had to be shut down less often to change from the production of one variety to another.

I had observed the growth of intra-industry trade in Europe during the postwar years: at one point my father carried in his store in Frankfurt only German cheeses. After free trade among the countries of Western Europe, he carried French, Italian and Dutch cheeses alongside the German products. And the German products had labels in several languages, suggesting that they were sold all over Europe. It was for those reasons that previous work by the American economist Bela Balassa and the European Paul Verdoorn on the nature of intra-industry trade had caught my attention.

I built on the work of these pioneers in my first article, which was published in 1967. It had not interested Johnson. Yet, in the 1970s others developed a 'new trade' theory which is based on the recognition that most of world trade is in goods produced under conditions of imperfect competition and serving very similar consumer demands. At the beginning of this new theoretical research reference was often made to the measurement of intra-industry trade done by myself and some others. Trade in such products also underlies the theories of economic development by Professor Michael Porter from Harvard Business School. During the 1980s he had published a number of well-known books extolling the merit of industrial strategies based on the development of national market niches in such products. He once told me personally that his work had been influenced strongly by my work on intra-industry trade.

Apprenticeship Years at Stanford and Chicago

The cost of being the 'world's banker'

As result of Johnson's own interests, I was basically left free to work on subjects that interested me. First I had a series of articles discussing the role the U.S. played in the international monetary system of immediate postwar years, the so-called 'dollar gold exchange standard.' The U.S. government held very large amounts of gold, which it promised to exchange against U.S. dollars held by foreign central banks at a fixed price of $35 an ounce. Under these conditions, initially central banks were very happy to hold U.S. dollars as reserves which they used to defend their currencies. These dollars yielded interest and were as good as gold since they could be exchanged for the metal any time. But when inflation became substantial the price of gold in the private London market began to rise. Some central banks began to ask for their gold from the U.S. Treasury. It was rumoured that some used it to make quick profits by reselling it at higher prices in the private market. The U.S. Treasury, with the help of the Defence and State Departments, began to apply pressures on foreign governments not to cash in their dollars. Clearly, the system could not be sustained.

The big policy question at the time was about the merit of the system for the U.S. Foreigners took dollars in return for goods they sold to the U.S. In a sense that was a good deal, since the Americans seemingly could print dollars at no cost. This process irritated Charles de Gaulle very much and he insisted that the Bank of France hold no dollars and cash them all in for gold. But the idea of no cost dollars was somewhat misleading since foreigners did not hold dollar bills but U.S. government securities. Interest had to be paid on them. This was one cost of the system for the U.S. Still, having the world on a quasi dollar standard was a source of pride to many Americans and worth the interest cost.

The biggest problem for the U.S. stemmed from the need to maintain stable prices to assure the world that their dollar holdings were safe and would not be paid off with currency worth less. At the time the Phillips Curve tradeoff was considered to be relevant. Not being able to foster inflation was seen to involve large losses in terms of unemployment and lower national income. In one paper I analysed the costs and benefits brought to the U.S. in its key role as the 'world's banker.' I thought that the costs far outweighed the benefits. Fred Hirsch in *The Economist* discussed my analysis. It was the first time a popular media outlet had taken note of my scholarly work. It was a great thrill to me.

Forward Exchange speculation

I also published a paper which simulated how much money a speculator could have earned in the forward exchange markets following simple rules. Using the computer and a large data base of spot and forward exchange rates I simulated what profits could have been earned by following different strategies. One of them was that the spot rate 90 days later would always be the same as it is today. If the 90 day forward rate today is above that spot rate, sell, if it was lower, buy. A profit was earned if forward exchange was sold and indeed in 90 days the spot rate was lower than the forward rate. The speculator would buy spot exchange at, say $3 per pound and deliver it to the person who had bought his forward contract at $3.01. I also tried more complicated assumptions about behaviour, like positing for example that the spot rate would continue on a trend that had occurred during the preceding month.

The results of my simulations suggested that speculators could earn very high rates of return. This did not sit well with Friedman. According to basic economic theory in free markets such opportunities for earning extraordinary returns cannot persist. Other will find out about them and quickly eliminate them. Friedman suggested that I had not taken sufficient account of occasional, catastrophic outcomes like large official devaluations when speculators are heavily committed. During the time period used in my study, there had been no such events. His comments helped me put a valuable perspective on my results. The paper was published in the *Quarterly Journal of Economics* at Harvard. The methodology I had used was employed later by many economists who tested the profitability of using mechanical rules in the purchase and sale of common stocks until that methodology was replaced by the theory efficient markets and simpler tests were developed.

The theory of the 'Brain Drain'

In 1963 Johnson had written a very provocative analysis of the 'Brain Drain,' the economics of the international migration of highly skilled people. I wrote a number of papers, several in co authorship with Professor Anthony Scott, who was spending a year at Chicago on leave from the University of British Columbia. We elaborated on Johnson's theory and produced some original research to quantify it. The argument was essentially that such voluntary emigration raised world welfare. This was inconsistent with the conventional wisdom that it retarded economic development in the Third World and lowered the average income of its people while at the same time it raised the average income of people in the already developed and high income countries. The issues remain controversial in Canada to this day.

Here is the essence of what would become known as the 'Internationalist' view of the Brain Drain. When emigrants leave a country, they reduce the nation's output but they also take along what they would have contributed to it. According to fundamental economic theory, a person's pay is equal to his or her contribution to the output of the firm and country. Under these assumptions, emigrants leave unchanged the incomes of those they leave behind. In the country of immigration, similarly the migrants' income allows them to make an equal sized claim on incomes, leaving unchanged the welfare of the people in their new country of residence.

The migrants also stop paying taxes in the country they leave and start paying them in the country of immigration. However, in the two countries the migrants also respectively withdraw or add to their consumption of the services governments offer with the tax money. On average, citizens' taxes pay for the average government services consumed. By this reasoning, the migration of the average person improves the well-being of the migrants and has virtually no effect on the welfare of those in the countries of emigration or immigration.

However, it is argued that many migrants with high skills do research and produce knowledge which brings benefits to others for which they are not paid. As it turns out, most knowledge is patented and therefore the benefits accrue to its producers. Some knowledge is pure and cannot be patented. But such knowledge is a free good for the entire world, including the emigrants' home country. A cancer cure found by an Indian scientist working in the U.S. accrues to all humanity, including the people in his home country of India.

Many see a problem arising from the Brain Drain because migrants were educated at the expense of their home country. Taxpayers there do not get a return on the investment they made in the emigrant's education. But again this argument involves only one side of the equation. When migrants leave, they take away not only the taxes they would have paid but also their children on whose education these taxes would have been spent. By analogy, in their new country of residence they pay taxes but their children also make claims on educational and other government services. On average, the effects are a 'wash' in both countries. There are no gains or losses to the people left behind or in their country of new residence. As private individuals, the migrants gain from their move. Therefore, there is an increase in world welfare.

There is one possible way in which brainy migrants affect the welfare of people in their home country. If they have high incomes and the income tax system is progressive, less money is available for transfers to the poor. Perhaps this is the most important reason for believing that a brain drain is bad for a country. The question is one of empirical magnitude. Even large numbers of such migrants tend to be only a tiny fraction of the population of most countries.

It is clear that this analysis would cause much controversy and interest. It brought me invitations to international conferences and published papers in *Science* and *The Bulletin of Atomic Scientists*. One of these papers brought an amusing result. I received requests for reprints from a number of neurological institutes around the world. The title referring to the brain drain had led many to believe that my article dealt with a medical procedure.

Chapter 3

I have described my work on the Brain Drain at length because, ironically, during the election campaign in 1993 I would be accused of racist views on immigration. Such views are not compatible with my analysis in support of the free movement of highly skilled migrants and the beneficial effect it has on their welfare and that of the countries receiving them.

The theory of effective tariff protection

Towards the end of my stay in Chicago, Johnson wanted me to produce some joint work, presumably to show that we had collaborated successfully while he received the grant money from the Rockefeller Foundation. At the time, the theory of effective protection created much intellectual excitement because it offered new insights into the failure of many development plans in Third World countries.

Consider the producer of a widget costing $100 to produce in a developing country. It requires $80 of imported inputs and $20 of labour for local assembly. Now assume that this developing country puts a tariff of 20 percent on the imported inputs in order to encourage their local production. The assembler of the widget now has a cost of $100 for his inputs after payment of the tariff. If the world price for the assembled widget is $110 and it can be imported without a tariff, the local assembler cannot compete. The assembly of widgets is killed by a protective tariff on other products.

A recent example in U.S. tariff policy illustrates this relationship. The U. S. imposed a high tariff on flat computer screens needed for portable computers on the grounds that these screens were widely used in military applications and that a domestic production capability was in the national interest. No tariff was imposed on the importation of portable computers. As a result of these policies, U.S. manufacturers of portable computers moved their production abroad and imported them. We have here one of these unintended consequences of well-intentioned policies which as an economist I delight in pointing out.

In the real world, of course, there might also be a tariff on the widgets which might wipe out the cost increasing effects of the tariff on inputs. The theory of effective protection has formulas which allow estimation of the precise net effect of tariffs at various stages of production on the industries producing these products.

Johnson and I co-authored several papers on this subject. They extended the theory and estimates by the inclusion of domestic excise taxes on inputs in the calculation since such taxes also raise domestic costs of production and give a competitive advantage to foreigners. This fact is one of the justification used for the replacement in Canada in the early 1990s of the manufacturers' sales tax with the GST, a so-called value-added tax which avoids raising the cost of inputs into further manufacturing. Harry and I also organized a conference on the subject in Geneva. I edited the proceedings, wrote an introduction and GATT published a volume of papers. My introduction was reprinted several times in a widely used collection of readings for undergraduate students.

Other life in Chicago

Family life in Chicago also prospered. Toni was pregnant and the birth was imminent when we attended a public lecture by John Kenneth Galbraith in 1965. The room was crowded and overheated. Galbraith is not known for his scintillating talks. The start of Toni's labour gave us a good excuse for leaving the lecture. Ten hours later we were the proud parents of Heidi, born on December 4, 1965 at Michael Reese Hospital in Chicago.

I pursued sports with much vigor and have some amusing memories of tennis matches with distinguished economists. One day a fellow assistant professor, William DeWald and I had challenged Milton Friedman and George Stigler to a match at the Quadrangle Club. As we walked onto the tennis court Stigler, renowned for his wit, said "Remember now, boys, who has got tenure around here." A short time into the match, DeWald hit Friedman on the forehead with a ball. It was all downhill from there. We lost more or less graciously.

On another occasion Robert Mundell and I played a match against Paul Samuelson, the brightest star on the horizon of economists at the time, and George Shultz, Dean of the University of Chicago Graduate School of Business and later Secretary of Labor and Secretary of State during the Reagan administration. After I had made a good shot Samuelson said to me, "Show me a good tennis player and I show you a poor scholar." Mundell and I had won the first set and were close to winning the second for the match when Mundell's play suddenly deteriorated seriously. We did not win another game and the match went to Samuelson and Shultz. To this day Mundell has refused to say whether or not he lost his playing edge deliberately. Winning in tennis is supposed to be largely a mental affair and psyching out opponents is all part of the game. The world's top economists appeared to be particularly adept at it.

Only one thing was wrong in my professional life in Chicago. I felt that I was under the shadow of all the great senior faculty members. I had no graduate students to inspire and work with. I received only few invitations to conferences and other academic involvements signalling professional acceptance and status. Given my publication record, I thought I deserved better.

I was therefore very receptive when out of the blue came an offer from the Finance Department of the Wharton School at the University of Pennsylvania in 1965. It offered promotion to the associate professor and a significant increase in pay. Harberger was the chair of the Chicago Economics Department at that time. His response to the offer from Pennsylvania was to raise my pay for the rest of the year. He also told me that if I asked, the faculty would probably extend my contract as an assistant professor

Chapter 3

for three more years but that it was too early in my career to request promotion and tenure. I decided to move on.

It was a fateful decision. If I had stayed I would have been present during the most outstanding phase of the department's 'golden age.' It produced important research which influenced both academic work world-wide and public policy in the U.S. and elsewhere. Friedman and his students laid the foundations for Monetarism. Johnson pushed it into the international sphere. Some of the graduates from the PhD program during this period would have outstanding careers. Rudi Dornbusch is a star at the Massachusetts Institute of Technology; Michael Mussa is the director of research at the International Monetary Fund; Jacob Frenkel is the Governor of the Bank of Israel after an illustrious career at Chicago and the IMF. Could I have made it in such a competitive environment? Where would I be today, if I had taken up Harberger's offer and stayed at the University of Chicago for three more years? I will never know.

Part II

Professional Life
and
Ideas in Economics

CHAPTER 4

Productive Years in Pennsylvania, Canberra and with the U.S. Treasury

IN THE fall of 1966 I started to teach in the Department of Finance at the Wharton School of the University of Pennsylvania. Wharton is the oldest business school in the world, with an excellent reputation for both undergraduate and graduate education. Its MBA program consistently ranks among the best in the world, according to employers and graduates.

The academic atmosphere was different from that at Chicago, partly because my academic home was in finance and partly because Wharton was a Business School. The average quality of the faculty's research was not as good as that done in Chicago. There were seminars but no workshops, and much less social and professional interaction with colleagues and visitors. The research interests of my colleague were very specialized and typically had less significant policy implications than I was used to in Chicago.

Professor Irwin Friend was the senior faculty member by age and reputation. His policy work was known mostly in a small circle of specialists. Professor Doug Vickers was working on (and ultimately published) a book which showed theoretically that all financial functions of firms are interdependent and simultaneously determined. His craftsmanship was impeccable but the idea is fairly obvious, once stated. He did not draw out any management policy implications.

Professor Marshall Blume was a recent graduate of the University of Chicago Business School; his massive data bases were producing more evidence on the efficient market hypothesis but to me were not very interesting. Professor Hans Stoll, also a recent graduate from the Chicago Business School, did more interesting work on forward exchange markets, but we never collaborated on any research. Blume and Stoll went on to excellent careers in Finance.

I had the best personal relationship with Professor Jack Guttentag. His main interest was in the market for housing and mortgages, in which he was well known. I remember the remaining Finance faculty more for their talk about what research they were about to do than what they produced.

The research agenda and faculty in the Department of Economics were much more suitable for my background and I probably would have felt much more comfortable as a member of this department. However, there was an institutional rivalry between Finance and Economics, which limited formal contacts and made informal contacts more difficult.

Teaching bright and motivated MBA students was a real pleasure. I was assigned to teach a course in international finance. When I first started to teach the course, there was only enough interest in the subject to fill one class with 25 students in one semester. When I left Wharton three years later in 1969, the subject attracted many more students.

The growth of interest in International Finance was due partly to the increasing internationalization of U.S. trade and finance. My own approach to the subject may also have something to do with it. I discussed the determination of exchange rates and methods by which firms could protect themselves from exchange risk. I also covered the operation of international capital markets and the economics and politics of direct foreign investment. My past research was put to good use in the analysis of the international monetary system and its likely future evolution.

While the growth in enrollment in my course was gratifying, it also had a serious disadvantage, which played heavily in my decision to seek employment elsewhere. Teaching one and the same subject all the time is wearing. Diversity of teaching subjects keeps one intellectually keen. My pleas for help from another professor in the field fell on deaf ears. Perhaps I was too impatient. International Finance was a relatively new subject at the time and I am sure that eventually Wharton would have hired others in the field, as indeed was done within a few years after I had left.

While in Philadelphia I wrote a book, *The International Monetary System.* It was published by Penguin Books and sold 200,000 copies world wide through four editions, one of them also in Spanish. Unfortunately, the royalties were very small, given the low price of the book and the fact that it sold mostly outside of North America. Much later I would meet economists at international conferences abroad who expressed their amazement at my age. They had read my book as students and told me that they had expected me to be an old man!

The international diversification of portfolios

In the 1960s the most exciting fields of financial research involved the theory and empirical study of the benefits of diversified wealth portfolios. In simplest terms this theory suggests what is true for the transportation of eggs. If they are all transported in one basket, an accident means the loss of all. The use of two baskets assures that if one encounters an accident, at least half of the eggs get to the destination. The same is true for holding wealth: it is better to hold a number of different shares than just one. Whenever people ask me for investment advice, I always point to this strategy as the only one I can give with any confidence. If I knew how well certain specific stocks will perform in the future, I would be very rich.

Over lunch one day a colleague, Doug Vickers, suggested to me the application of the concept of diversification to international assets. The theory was that the stock markets of individual countries were subject to some strictly national economic developments and changes in their

Productive Years in Pennsylvania, Canberra and with the U.S. Treasury

exchange rates. Inclusion of foreign stocks in U.S. portfolios would therefore permit investors to earn higher rates of return with unchanged risks. For example, if there is a recession in the United States and the stock market are down, sometimes European markets are up. A portfolio which includes both American and European stocks under these conditions would hold its value better than a portfolio which includes stocks from only one of the two markets.

I wrote a paper extending the theory of diversification into the international sphere and, as the most important contribution, demonstrated the empirical magnitude of this benefit from international diversification. I had obtained information on the stock market indices, dividend yields and exchange rate changes from eleven different countries over about ten years. The monthly return from holding the stock market average of each country in terms of U.S. dollars was estimated. A sophisticated computer program used this information to select foreign and U.S. assets in different percentages until for every possible rate of return for the entire portfolio it discovered that set of holdings which minimized the fluctuations of value through time.

The paper was published in the most prestigious journal in economics, *The American Economic Review*. Its methodology was copied by several dozen papers published later, using different data and time periods. It was reprinted many times in textbooks for investment analysts. I received phone calls from mutual fund managers who told me how well they had done using the ideas in my paper, asking me whether I had any other good ideas. I was so much into academic work that I did not recognize that such calls might have led to some lucrative consulting, had I played my cards right. Oh well, I guess I was never meant to be rich!

The paper was not appreciated by everyone. Once a semester advisers to the Finance Department of the Wharton School visited campus for a day, to talk about curriculum, research and current economic issues. The advisers were drawn from the U.S. business elite. The Treasurers of major corporations like Ford and AT&T flew to Philadelphia for this meeting in their company jets.

Donald Regan, president of Merrill Lynch, the largest U.S. brokerage house, attended regularly before he became Chief of Staff for President Reagan. In 1968, when it was my turn to talk about my research, I proudly began to report how my estimates had shown the large benefits wealth holders could gain from the diversification of their stock portfolios. I had only been speaking for a few minutes when Regan told me in no uncertain terms that I should shut up and sit down. My research was totally irrelevant, he asserted, because Americans would never be interested in foreign stock markets and foreigners would never play a significant role in the U.S. market. Naturally, I was crushed. I had no difficulties believing that his personal arrogance had later caused him to lose his job as the personal adviser to President Reagan.

Chapter 4
Moral hazard

Wharton has one of the few Departments of Insurance in any university of the world, its courses preparing students for careers in the insurance industry. Graduates with PhDs in the subject often become university teachers. One day I was asked by the dean to attend a PhD examination as his representative and report my views of the quality of the thesis and examination to him. I have forgotten the theme of the examination, but my questions revealed that the student had not been exposed to the idea of moral hazard. I had just encountered this fascinating concept in an article I had read in an economics journal. My questions evoked a lively debate among the examiners. The student passed, but later several of my colleagues from the department of insurance said this examination had been one of the most interesting seminars they had ever attended.

Moral hazard arises when groups of people insured against a risk change their behaviour and end up afflicted by the hazard more often than when they were not insured. One could say that buying insurance puts peoples' morals at risk. The phenomenon explains why restaurants which are insured have fires more often than uninsured ones, and homes insured against burglary are broken into more often than those without such insurance.

I do not like to attribute these phenomena to changes in morality induced by the insurance; they are simply rational responses to altered incentives. Some insured restaurants might be torched, but most of the increased incidence of fire is due to carelessness and lack of prevention. It is costly and time-consuming to be careful and take fire prevention measures. Since insurance lowers the cost of having a fire, the returns to care and prevention are lower. It is rational to undertake less of both. In the case of home insurance it is equally rational to take fewer burglary prevention measures. They are worth less, and fewer are bought for houses with than for houses without insurance.

The reaction of my colleagues in the Department of Insurance led me later to write a paper in which I worked out the economics of moral hazard. The paper was published in *The Journal of Risk and Insurance* and for many years was cited widely in articles by other economists. Most important, after I had moved to Simon Fraser University, it stimulated me to co-author a paper with a colleague, Professor Dennis Maki, and a graduate student, Shelley Sax. It brought us much notoriety in Canada.

Our paper was based on the notion that moral hazard also operated with social insurance provided by government. We showed that the increased generosity of the unemployment insurance program initiated in 1971 two years later had raised Canada's unemployment rate by about 1 to 1.5 percentage points. At the time this finding was considered radical and 'politically incorrect.' How dare we suggest that some workers become and remain unemployed of their own volition? I will discuss this and related studies some more in the next chapter.

Productive Years in Pennsylvania, Canberra and with the U.S. Treasury

The Australian National University in Canberra

By 1968 I felt secure enough in my position at the University of Pennsylvania that Toni and I agreed we would take advantage of an offer to attend the Australian National University as a Research Fellow for a year. The pay was miserable, but there was some 'sabbatical' money from the University of Pennsylvania, and I would have no teaching responsibilities for the entire year. In addition, we would make the trip to Australia an excuse for a trip around the world. The entire package was exciting, even if it was full of uncertainties.

The trip was a wonderful experience. The children, Eric at six and Heidi at three, were good travellers. Professional contacts had brought invitations to give papers at universities and institutes in Athens, Karachi, Bangkok, Kuala Lumpur and Singapore before we reached Canberra. Only in New Delhi were we pure tourists. Eric had quickly become used to traveling in style and wondered at the Delhi airport where our car and driver was — we had been picked up at every other stop. It was very sweet to learn that at least some of my publications had been read, or at least noticed, by economists in the places we visited. Exposure to conditions in developing countries and to local academic thinking considerably broadened my horizons and increased my appreciation of Western free societies.

The stay in Australia exposed Toni and me to a world that we had not known. After the pressure-cooker of academic life in New Haven and Chicago and the heated atmosphere of Philadelphia, Canberra was like an oasis. Everything moved at a slower pace. The Institute of Advanced Studies offered superb research facilities and superior, modern housing for visiting faculty. Fellow visitors in the housing facilities were doing fascinating work. David Lewis, a Londoner who was a physician by profession and a sailor by avocation had come to Australia in a small sailboat. He wrote about his experiences and the complications and joys of having a wife and two small children on board in a best-selling book titled *Daughters of the Wind*. He was collaborating with Ben Finney, an anthropologist from the University of Hawaii. A traditional war canoe constructed by Finney is on view in Hawaii. They worked together on a paper explaining how ancient South Sea natives found remote islands without the help of a compass. Later they tested their theories in an expedition which was reported on in *National Geographic* magazine.

The Fellows at the Institute of Advanced Studies were very bright and worked on important subjects. However, the Australian work ethic was not the same as that in the leading U.S. universities I knew. After my arrival I worked my standard day of eight to five, Monday through Friday. But eventually I became acclimatized. I arrived for work at ten, had tea at 10:30, enjoyed long lunches and was home before five. Every Friday afternoon my colleagues and I played squash and joined other throngs of Australians in overcrowded and noisy bars.

Chapter 4

Australia's flora and fauna were fascinatingly different from what I had known. Eric and Heidi still remember the drill they had been taught in their school on how to protect themselves against the dive-bombing attacks of magpies which were raising their young in the trees on the way to their school. Using their hands to protect their faces, they bowed their heads and ran to the next building as fast as they could.

I had eerie, atavistic emotional reactions to the total absence of insects and birds in certain forests around Canberra, which consisted entirely of imported species of European pine trees. The different smells, sights and noises of the Australian bush were similarly unsettling. Nevertheless, we greatly enjoyed the Australian outdoors, which is easy to reach from Canberra. We even went skiing a few times under the leaves of eucalyptus trees at Thredbo in the Snowy Mountains.

A book on intra-industry trade and meeting Phillips

Peter Lloyd was a Fellow in the same department of the Institute of Advanced Studies. He was a New Zealander who only a few years earlier had obtained a PhD from Duke University. During the year, Peter and I wrote a book entitled *Intra Industry Trade: The Theory and Measurement of International Trade in Differentiated Products* (London: MacMillan, 1975). In the preceding chapter I have described the nature of Intra-Industry trade and why it is important for understanding the real world in terms of economic policy design.

While expanding on the theories I had published in earlier papers, our main contribution consisted of a more detailed empirical analysis than anyone had ever before attempted. We were able to obtain data on Australian trade to measure the extent of the phenomenon at different levels of aggregation. Our data forced many economists to reconsider the ability of the traditional international trade theories to explain the very significant phenomenon of trade in goods which are very similar in design, function and cost of production.

The book's very technical chapter on the statistical properties of our measurement index was written mainly by Lloyd, and contains such a clear definition and analysis that it has become the standard for studies in this area.

There are many references in economics literature to the 'Grubel-Lloyd Index of Intra-Industry Trade.' It has made our book join the small rank of books in economics that are widely cited but very rarely read. Statistics Canada offers to calculate and make available the Grubel-Lloyd Index for the country's trade pattern to anyone interested enough to pay a fee.

Shortly after I had arrived in Canberra I met Professor Bill Phillips. While teaching at the London School of Economics during the 1950s, he had discovered that, in England, periods of low inflation were associated with higher unemployment rates than periods with high inflation. This relationship became known as the 'Phillips Curve.' Phillips' finding was interpreted by many as evidence that unemployment could be lowered by the simple expediency of accepting some inflation. This was a revolutionary idea when the conventional wisdom was that inflation was bad for the economy. I discussed above the nature of the trade-off, how it influenced policies and what damage it to the smooth functioning of Western economies.

During one brief encounter (in a corridor!), I talked to Phillips about attacks on his ideas which had been made in the preceding few years by my colleagues at Universities of Chicago and Pennsylvania. He said, "Friedman and Phelps are probably correct. Let's talk about it over lunch on Monday." That weekend Phillips had a stroke: I never saw him again.

The false idea of the existence of a Phillips Curve useable for the permanent lowering of the unemployment rate still is not completely dead. In the 1990s when I was serving as a member of the House of Commons Finance Committee, we were lobbied for 'a little' inflation rather than the near price stability targeted by the Bank of Canada. Pierre Fortin, a professor of economics at the University of Quebec, had made a scholarly argument in favour of such a change. I will discuss the nature of his findings in a later chapter. As a result of my involvement in the development and criticism of the Phillips Curve, including a conversation with Phillips himself, made me a strong opponent of witnesses to the Finance Committee still adhering to this idea.

The legacy of the visit to Australia

At the end of a most enjoyable and productive year in Canberra we returned to Philadelphia via the Philippines and Japan, again making contacts with local universities and institutes. The year's experience had deeply changed my attitude towards life in general and life at major universities in particular. I had seen that there was a beautiful and interesting world beyond the advancement of scientific economics that had so dominated my life in the preceding decade.

The year 1969 was spent teaching again at Wharton. But where before we had seen opportunities in the difficulties of living in that large city and teaching in a finance department, we now saw almost only disadvantages. Toni and I were ready to leave Philadelphia and move to Canberra, to one of the best sinecures in the profession. Senior Fellows at the Institute of Advanced Studies were tenured. They had a salary about 10 percent above that of professors at regular Australian universities. There were no teaching obligations. Computer, secretarial and research assistance were provided in generous amounts.

The Canberra environment suited our love for the outdoors. Sabbatical leaves permitted frequent stays in foreign centres of learning. I was look-

Chapter 4

ing forward to extensive collaboration with Peter Lloyd; we were going to rewrite the theory of international trade by incorporating the phenomenon of intra-industry trade.

However, the promised offer for such a position was slow in coming. It had been caught in some internal politics of the Institute. Professor Heinz Arndt was a brilliant, mostly self-taught economist with strong interests in applied development economics. He was the head of the department which I had visited and hoped to join. He had vetoed my appointment on the grounds that my work was "too theoretical."

In 1971 the offer for a position in another department at the Institute arrived, but by then it was too late; I had been attracted to Simon Fraser University in Vancouver. However, before moving there, we were to spend the calendar year of 1971 in Washington, D.C.

The U.S. Treasury

I had always wanted the experience of working inside government; in 1970 an opportunity arose to do so. The U.S. Treasury Department was like all government departments around the world that controlled the purse strings. It wielded great power and its bureaucrats were the most powerful and influential of all. However, during the late 1960s the Department had begun to lose some of its influence. In interdepartmental negotiations its position often lost. Other departments had hired professional economists and presented better reasoned and documented policy alternatives. After some soul-searching, top Treasury officials decided to establish their own research department, to be staffed by graduate economists.

Through the good services of Henry Wallich, a former teacher at Yale and adviser to the Secretary of the Treasury, I was offered an appointment in the research department of the Office of the Assistant Secretary for International Affairs, known as OASIA. I shared responsibilities with three other professional economists.

There were many filters between us researchers and Secretary John Connally, who was famous for his role as the hosting Governor of Texas when John Kennedy was assassinated; he was sitting near the President and was injured. We reported to Wilson Schmitt, a professional economist with the title of Deputy Assistant Secretary, who in turn reported to Richard Petty, Assistant Secretary for International Affairs. All of these mandarins were under the direction of Under-Secretary Paul Volker, who in the late 1970s was to gain great notoriety as Chairman of the Federal Reserve when it raised interest rates into the high teens.

It took some time for the FBI to provide me with the required top secret clearance papers before I could start work in January 1971. This security designation was necessary since my work often involved classified documents, though to this day I am not sure why so many of them were stamped 'Top Secret.' For the FBI to do its work, I had to fill out long forms and account for what seemed every day of my life. Neighbours in Philadelphia confided in me how agents had approached them with questions about me and my family. I still wonder how they dealt with my life in Germany.

The pay at the Treasury was 50 percent higher than in academia. We had sold our house in Philadelphia and could afford to rent a fine house in Annandale, Virginia. This part of Washington was known as 'Colonel Country' because of the many officers who lived there within easy commuting distance to the Pentagon. It was pleasant enough, with a sports club nearby and quiet, treed streets; typical suburbia, but it was not a friendly place. Contacts with neighbours were few.

I commuted to Washington daily by bus, reading a professional paper every morning and adventure novels on the way home. The routine allowed me to feel free from the burden of thinking about economics. It was a surprising relief from the life of the professorial economist which seemed never to allow a break from thoughts about teaching and research.

As a family we took full advantage of all of the wonderful tourist attractions of the American capital. In the spring we experienced the glory of the cherry blossoms around the tidal pool of the Jefferson Memorial. We saw the greatest firework display of our lives during the July 4 Independence Day celebrations on the mall between the Capitol and the Lincoln Memorial. The Smithsonian Museum and National Gallery of Art provided us with many hours of educational entertainment when the weather did not allow for outdoor activities.

My office was on the fifth floor of the historic Treasury building at the top of Pennsylvania Avenue adjoining the White House, and from my window I could overlook its famous Rose Garden. On occasion Treasury employees and their spouses were invited to attend official events there. President Nixon needed a friendly, FBI certified safe crowd as a backdrop to his official greetings of visiting heads of state. We were rewarded with a few hours off work.

Research for policy

The creation of the new research department was not welcomed by George Willis, the Deputy Under Secretary for Monetary Affairs. He held one of the top two civil service positions in the Treasury. Rumour had it that after the second world war, Willis worked overtime all days of the week and many weekends. Family life suffered and at one point his wife gave him an ultimatum: It's me or the Treasury. He chose the Treasury.

Willis was a one-man research department with an encyclopedic knowledge of history and issues. Every new Secretary, recruited from the private sector, relied on him for information and guidance. People like him are indispensable to the efficient operation of government departments. They provide continuity and introduce realism into the often starry-eyed agendas of new political appointees.

Chapter 4

Soon after arriving in Washington I approached him with a request for a meeting. I suggested that we academic economists in the research department needed to learn from his knowledge and experience and to get his guidance in our research agenda. He grudgingly agreed to the proposal, with the stipulation that the meeting would be at 4:30 on Friday. Presumably he had hoped we would not show up at such a time, but we disappointed him.

As it turned out, the session was very productive. We listened, asked the right questions and made just enough substantive comments to persuade him that we could help him do a better job advising the Secretary. It also became obvious that we could never take his place or perform his function. Soon we had regular weekly meetings at more civilized times of the week. I learned a lot from Willis about both international monetary affairs and the way government works.

At one meeting Willis told us that the main source of power in the bureaucracy was held by people who controlled the flow of information to 'decision-makers.' He confided in us that he personally decided what letters, memos and reports the Secretary would see. Through this process he had enormous influence over the Secretary's agenda and the positions taken in policy debates. Shortly before I left the Treasury for Simon Fraser University Michael Keran, one of my professional colleagues, gave a farewell party for me. Willis was there and made my day. In a manner full of symbolism he took hold of my arm and, carefully steering me into an alcove away from the other guests, said: "Do you have any other papers that the Secretary should see? Send them to me, I'll make sure he does."

The research work was rather frustrating. In spite of George's briefings we were outsiders, a threat to the established bureaucratic hierarchy that had to be tolerated. I never met either Volker or Connally while I was there. Many years later, at a reception following an International Monetary Fund conference, Henry Wallich introduced me to Paul Volker. When I told him about my year in his research department, he said: "Oh yes, I remember reading your memos." This was the first time I knew that anyone other than my colleagues had noted them. Indicative of the strange ways of the bureaucracy was Wilson Schmitt's telling me that he had seen a copy of my book *The International Monetary System* on the desk of one of the 'Principals.' Though insisting he could not tell me who that Principal was, I suspect it to have been Volker.

Volker needed good perspectives on the history, economics and politics of the international monetary system because during his regime the old order collapsed. In 1945 the Bretton Woods Agreements created a world of fixed exchange rates, with the United States serving as the world's banker. In a preceding chapter I have already described my research on the merit of this role for the U.S., and the forces which put the system under strain.

It was an exciting experience to be in the middle of the institution

Productive Years in Pennsylvania, Canberra and with the U.S. Treasury

which was at the heart of the system and to participate in the discussions of how to change it. Some analysts proposed a change in the official price of gold at which the U.S. would exchange dollars. This was vetoed because it rewarded countries like France that refused to play the rules of the game and punished the 'good guys' like Germany and Japan. My own view was that the U.S. should adopt a law which would stop all conversions of dollars into gold for all times. Some gold in U.S. vaults could be sold on the private market; countries that no longer wanted to hold dollars could sell them and buy gold at market prices. Eventually interest and exchange rates would adjust and governments would be satisfied with the mix of gold and dollars in the reserves of their central banks. The problem of gold, dollars and international reserves would be solved by impersonal market-forces.

My preferred solution, based on the official demonetization of gold, was considered unfair to those countries holding dollars and providing correspondingly unfair gains to those who had obtained gold for their dollar holdings. The solution was also decried as 'dollar imperialism' because it would free the U.S. government from all responsibilities over its international payments imbalances. Private investors and traders would determine the value of the exchange rate. As a result, governments in the rest of the world would lose all influence over American monetary and fiscal policies they had had when exchange rates were determined through collective action. Under these conditions the U.S. government could behave like an imperial power, constrained only by its self-interests.

Importantly, the solution was also opposed by leaders in the financial sector, who lamented the loss of prestige and benefits which the U.S. was alleged to obtain through the foreign holdings of U.S. dollars bearing low interest. These dollars were used to finance high-paying direct investment abroad. I vigorously questioned the aggregate value of these benefits, especially when seen in the light of the costs they brought in the form of restraints on domestic U.S. policies.

Throughout 1970 the price of gold in the free London market was extremely sensitive to rumours about pending U.S. action. My superior, Wilson Schmitt, had nightmares that a reporter would walk into one of the offices of the research department and find a memo recommending the revaluation or demonetization of gold. The leak of such a document could cause massive speculation and force the hands of the government. In his nightmares he would see himself standing in front of Richard Nixon trying to explain what had happened. He calmed his nightmares by sending us a memo threatening to immediately fire anyone who did not lock up all papers after hours in designated safes.

A few weeks later another somewhat bizarre memo followed. My colleagues and I interpreted it as saying that we were not allowed even to *think* about the price of gold, much less talk or write about it!

Eventually, the world adopted essentially the system that I had recom-

Chapter 4

mended at the time. However, it would take some time to get there. In 1971 Volker travelled over 400,000 miles in a few months to hammer out the Smithsonian Agreement, named after the Washington museum where it was signed. On that occasion, early in 1972, Nixon called it "the most important international monetary agreement of the century." I do not know who wrote that speech for him, but it did not show good judgement.

The agreement was a typical compromise, that satisfied no one while only postponing the inevitable. Gold would officially be revalued to $37.50 an ounce; countries with payments surpluses would appreciate their currencies against the dollar in order to reduce U.S. deficits, while others would devalue their exchange rates.

Some of my colleagues, experts in econometrics and what was then the infant use of computers, helped in these negotiations. They developed a formula allowing for estimates of the effects of currency revaluations on U.S. and other countries' balance of payments to be made. During the negotiations we had telephone lines to meeting rooms in places like London and Frankfurt. When the finance ministers at the meetings proposed sets of new exchange rates, we were informed. A few minutes later Volker announced the estimated implications of the proposed exchange rates. Everyone was impressed by the modern technology and eventually, through a process of iteration, an acceptable set of exchange rate realignments was agreed upon.

Of course, the seeming precision in the calculations was a sham, even if some of my colleagues thought otherwise. The econometric models did not take account of inflation, the expansion of the Vietnam war, OPEC and vast flows of speculative capital that were on the horizon. These events were much more important than exchange rates in the determination of the balance of payments of the U.S. and other countries. But the telephone link to the computer, albeit through some intermediary human brains, brought some respect to the U.S. government and Paul Volker when they were in great need of it.

Learning about power in the government

Once a year Henry Wallich organized a conference of America's leading economists at the U.S. Treasury. The Secretary sat through the papers and discussions all day. He often asked penetrating questions and obviously enjoyed the sparring between the coterie of Keynesians and the new breed of monetarists opposing them. I am not sure how he could sort out the widely diverging recommendations, but the meetings were considered a great success by many.

One of the highlights of the 1970 meeting of Treasury Consultants was a presentation by my former Yale teacher, Arthur Okun. He had been the chairman of the Council of Economic Advisers under Lyndon Johnson.

Productive Years in Pennsylvania, Canberra and with the U.S. Treasury

While Nixon was in the White House, he and other top economists from the Johnson years were 'in waiting' (some would say 'exile'), at the Brookings Institution, a think-tank financed mostly by private foundations.

Okun argued very eloquently about the merit of letting inflation rise even more so that unemployment could fall and output and tax revenues would increase. It was an impressive rhetorical performance, much better than what I had been exposed to during my graduate school days by him. I could only shake my head in disbelief that in 1971 he would still propound the merit of the Phillips Curve tradeoff. Had he not heard of the devastating criticism of the concept by Friedman and Phelps and of Phillips' own doubts about it?

The episode taught me much about the difficulties faced by policy makers who get advice from eloquent economists with outstanding reputations as scientists. I concluded then that, as Finance Minister, I would surround myself with a number of advisers certain to have differing points of view, listen to all and then use my own best judgement.

An important insight I gained from my work in Washington was the role of political power, which is the ability of an institution or people to force others into doing something against their own will. The Treasury was universally considered to be the most powerful ministry in Washington. Inside the Treasury, the strength of that power was always considered to be very small. Here, those concerned with the financial soundness of the country knew exactly what the best policies were. Yet, in trying to get their way, there always were obstructions. The President, the Council of Economic Advisers, the Secretary of State, Congress and many others often opposed and blocked Treasury's policy initiatives.

When I talked to people in other institutions, they typically voiced similar views about the lack of power to get adopted the policies they had designed for the outstanding benefit of all Americans. Yet, in the minds of outsiders, such institutions as the International Monetary Fund and even the President and Congress have very great power. Upon reflection, of course, the diffusion of power among institutions and individuals is very beneficial to society. It means that policies in the end reflect the broadest possible spectrum of interests and that change is slow and deliberate. This fact should be remembered by all those who are frustrated by existing institutions in Canada and other democracies. No one person or institution has the key to solving the complex problems of modern economies and societies.

Lunching at the IMF and social limits to growth

My stay in Washington allowed me to establish some interesting professional relationships at the International Monetary Fund. For a period I had lunch in the executive dining room at least once a week.

My host was Fred Hirsch, an economic adviser to the executive direc-

Chapter 4

tor. I gained many insights into the operation of the international monetary system and the political constraints under which the IMF was working. Hirsch was in the process of writing *Limits to Social Growth*, a book which rode the coat-tails of the widely discussed and very influential book *Limits to Growth*, published by the Club of Rome, the central themes of which I have discussed in a preceding chapter.

Hirsch had built on the idea that growth in population was not accompanied by a corresponding increase in the top positions in society attainable by individuals. There could be only one President of the United States and one chief executive officer for General Motors. This limit interacted with the physical limits of the world. There was only a finite amount of shoreline along which those in top social positions could reside and thus give expression to their status. He argued that these facts limited the attainment of peoples' social ambitions. These limits were as detrimental to their well being as were the limits on economic ambitions caused by the scarcity of real resources.

I disagreed with Hirsch on the basic facts, noting that free societies have always created new institutions which permitted people to achieve their social ambitions. The number and variety of clubs, civic organizations and governmental institutions increases with income and population. As a result, there are now probably per capita more clubs for such activities as tennis, hiking, bowls, cooking, singing, stamp-collecting, travelling and politics than ever before. All these clubs need presidents and other officers, and provide them with corresponding social status.

Hirsch obviously enjoyed our conversations because he kept inviting me back for lunch. However, his published and widely reviewed book in the end noted only very cursorily the arguments I made. I suppose that if he had accepted them, his analysis and conclusions would have lost much of their punch.

The Washington experience was valuable in my development as an economist in ways which I could not have achieved had I remained in academia. The experience provided me with insights about the operation of government, the role of the bureaucracy, the problems of international monetary organization, the politics of exchange rate alignments and other problems which greatly influenced my future teaching and research. It certainly provided me with valuable insights when, 23 years later, I arrived in Ottawa as a Member of Parliament to serve as my party's shadow Finance Minister.

CHAPTER 5

Vancouver and Simon Fraser University

AFTER a long drive from Washington D.C, Toni, Eric, Heidi and I arrived in Vancouver on Boxing Day 1971. The next day the city was bathed in bright sunlight shining on two feet of freshly fallen snow. We could see the shimmering ocean, the distant mountains of Vancouver Island and the city skyline through the large windows of our new house in West Vancouver.

It was as if nature had given us a special welcome. Little did we know that for the next 20 years, Christmas weather would be grey and rainy! To add to our welcome, neighbours presented us with a freshly baked ham. We felt that we had arrived in Paradise. We would settle down and make this our permanent home after a little more than a decade of what seemed like endless journeyings, which had seen me leave Germany and live for at least a year each in New Jersey, Connecticut, California, Illinois, Pennsylvania, Australia and Washington, D.C.

Many motives had brought us to this wonderful place. The city was beautiful, new and clean. The environment and climate suited our love for skiing, hiking, the mountains, ocean and tennis. Canada was a friendly place for immigrants.

The population and economy were growing. This growth brought a positive spirit of adventure and optimism to the people. The cost of airline travel and electronic communication had fallen and promised to become lower still. These developments would end the region's relative isolation at the edge of the continent. The school system was great for the children. Crime and violence were known only to our neighbours through American television.

The University and its left-wing image

Simon Fraser University is a spectacular place and popular with tourists. One drives up a steep hill through a dense forest when suddenly, after a turn in the road, a large structure appears, covering the top of a hill for about a kilometre. The views include downtown Vancouver, the Straits of Georgia with the snow-capped mountains of Vancouver Island in the distance, the menacing shape of the 4,000 metre Mount Baker and the Indian Arm fjord surrounded by pine forests clinging tenaciously to steep slopes carved by the Ice Age, 10,000 years ago. In the distance, the remainders of these glaciers glare in the sun.

Chapter 5
History of Simon Fraser University

The university had been founded just four years before I arrived. It had been built in record time from an award-winning design by the famous architect Arthur Erickson and his colleague, Jeff Massey.

Even today, the atmosphere of the place is one of excitement, modernity and community, brought on by the unconventional use of space, concrete and buildings. The sterility which hangs over modern architecture using much concrete has been avoided through the widespread use of lawns, bushes and trees.

The university owes its existence to the rapidly growing population of the area and the limited capacity of the existing University of British Columbia, which had reached its planned maximum size. Important for me was also the decision of the Government of Canada to encourage the creation of academic programs for advanced degrees.

These PhDs were required to meet the needs of the 'baby-boomers' who were soon expected to swell the ranks of undergraduates. The federal government supported these programs because of growing nationalism and a desire to be different from its neighbour to the south. Nationalists wanted Canadians taught Canadian subjects by Canadians trained in Canadian universities.

Simon Fraser University was designed to teach undergraduates, the number of which (in 1997) has reached about 15,000. It also has graduate programs in the arts and social and natural sciences. It has no professional schools like medicine, dentistry or law. It has a system of tutorials for undergraduates designed so as to allow the discussion of learning material in small groups. This has turned out to be an important asset for the graduate programs because the staffing of the tutorials by graduate assistants was built into the university budget from the beginning. It brought many good graduate students to economics.

During the 1960s all North American universities expanded in order to accommodate the 'baby-boomers.' This fact resulted in a shortage of PhDs available for employment, creating serious problems for SFU in its quest for faculty.

To become competitive two important steps were taken. The first was to hire European academics, who were receptive to offers for employment with high salaries and the challenge of creating a new university, whose founders had promised them the opportunity to experiment with innovative teaching and research techniques.

The second step involved a financial inducement made possible by a federal government initiative: faculty from abroad would not have to pay Canadian income taxes for two years.

The first of these inducements created serious difficulties. A German political science professor was hired to head the new department. He was a Marxist scholar with an outstanding reputation. His first task was to hire a full complement of teachers. He decided to hire a number of graduate students and new PhDs from Berkeley on the recommendation of their teachers whom he knew from international gatherings. These graduates had been activists in the Berkeley student protest movement. Their lives were dominated by the desire to use universities as the base from which to launch a Peoples' Revolution, which would create a democratic, egalitarian, Marxist society. This faculty thought that SFU and Canada were the perfect places for such a revolution.

In their efforts they found allies in other departments and among students, some of whom were Americans avoiding the military draft. These people issued demands for egalitarian grading standards and salaries, using demonstrations and sit-ins to press their demands.

The resultant upheavals played havoc with an organization which had only just started to function. Sit-ins in the office of the president and confrontations with the police were Berkeley tactics new to Canada. The media loved the events and SFU gained its reputation as a hotbed for left-wing ideology and politics, which still lingers in the 1990s. Under the able leadership of President Ken Strand, a labour economist skilled in negotiations, calm eventually returned and the university flourished. In the 1990s it has been ranked by *McLean's* magazine as the best Canadian university in its class. This ranking is based mainly on the superb facilities for students and the high quality of instruction offered.

As a result of internal upheavals, the department of economics lost Professor William Scammell, who had come to SFU from Britain with a distinguished list of publications in international finance. He became discouraged about the poor atmosphere for learning and took up a position at McMaster University in Ontario. His departure left an opening for me. The university offered me a professorship with an attractive salary and fringe benefits; the federal government helped by allowing me tax-free status for two years.

The Department of Economics and Commerce

One of the experiments of the new university was to combine in one department the teaching of both Economics and Commerce. The synergies created by this arrangement were not large. Conflicts over teaching, research and academic standards reduced productivity. One of these conflicts involved proper credit for promotion and pay based on performance. The economists had strong publication records, which the Dean of Arts was alleged to have valued more highly than the good records of the Commerce Faculty in consulting, case studies and similar activities. Because of this alleged discrimination, Commerce faculty believed that only a separate Dean of Business would remedy this situation. After many drawn-out battles, about 15 years after the experiment was launched, it ended with the creation of a separate Faculty of Business.

Chapter 5
The cost of the B.C. Milk Marketing Board

The synergism of having colleagues with a commerce background was quite strong for me. It resulted in two joint research projects and publications. At a casual lunch one day, Professor Richard Schwindt told me about a dairy farmer in the Fraser Valley who had just sold his property. This farmer had received more money for his milk marketing quotas than he had for the land, improvements and cows combined. Schwindt was able to obtain prices for these quotas and we quickly agreed to study the determinants of their value.

The resultant short book, *The Real Cost of the B.C. Milk Board*, was one of the first publications of the Fraser Institute, a privately financed economic think-tank about which I will have more to say.

The study caused an uproar. In B.C., only the owners of quotas are able to sell milk to a marketing authority. The price of the milk paid to the farmers is set by a formula designed (allegedly) to reflect the cost of production and leave only normal profits for the farmers. In fact, the formula is seriously defective, mainly because it totally neglects the increased quality of cows. Every year, on average, cows produce about one percent more milk for the same amount of feed. This increase in productivity continuously results in a widening gap between the price of milk and its cost of production. The larger the gap, the higher the value of the quotas. In effect, quotas give their owners the right to sell a litre of milk for a sum which is higher than the cost of producing it by continuously larger margin.

Of necessity, marketing boards with the power to limit supply require protection from foreign imports. When the marketing board system was introduced in Canada, imports of dairy products were frozen at existing levels. Importers were given quotas, which entitled them to bring in these quantities in the future. Eventually, these quotas became worth a fortune, because they allowed the import of products bought at world prices to be sold in Canada at domestic prices, which were greatly inflated by the actions of the marketing boards.

When the basic quotas for domestic production were first introduced, farmers received them free of cost. Most of them are now millionaires — or will be, once they sell their quotas. They have become millionaires at the expense of B.C. consumers, who pay excessively high prices for their dairy products. The irony of the system is that it has failed to encourage the creation or even maintenance of family farms. A young ambitious person who wants to become a dairy farmer has to borrow a large amount of money to buy a quota. The cost of interest is equal to the difference between the price of milk and the cost of its production. Initially, the new farmer has to struggle just to make ends meet and pay the interest. Things tend to get better with time, as the gap between the price of milk and the cost of its production continues to increase, but even this outcome is uncertain. The value of the quota and the size of the loan needed to buy it may well reflect the expectation that this gap will continue to increase.

The new farmer has great difficulty entering the business because of the larger need for capital than was the case before the quota system was put into operation. As a result, large agricultural firms with easy access to capital often outbid for quotas farmers who would otherwise have carried on as traditional family farmers.

It is easy to understand that dairy farmers did not and still do not like the analysis Schwindt and I had done. They disputed our estimate that the system cost the average B.C. family $48 per year in 1975. Some argued that quotas did not have a specific value. Others admitted that quotas were valuable but that market prices meant nothing, since they would drop sharply if everyone tried to sell theirs at the same time. John Van Esch, a farmer and officer in the Association of B.C. Dairy Farmers, sent vitriolic letters demanding our resignation for incompetence to the President of the University, the Premier of British Columbia, the Prime Minister of Canada and the Secretary General of the United Nations. On the other hand, our study was used as supplementary reading in some economics courses at other Canadian universities, and we were consulted by numerous organizations.

A bank in the Fraser Valley, which had made large loans for the purchase of quotas, once organized a meeting of people for and against quotas. The bank was worried that if the government would introduce a policy to end the quota system, their loans would be in default. NDP politician Dave Stupich, who had introduced the system when he was Minister of Agriculture for British Columbia, attended this meeting.

He defended quotas very vigorously with arguments which did not deal with the economics I have just outlined. He justified it essentially on the grounds that the system was fair to farmers who otherwise were treated badly by a free market. He used effective political rhetoric in suggesting that Canadians were willing to pay more for their dairy products to assure the existence of a healthy, family-operated farm sector which produced high quality products. (As an aside, it is interesting to note that in 1998 Stupich was convicted of defrauding charities in connection with bingo games, accounting for which was done by a special association he had formed.)

Schwindt and I like to joke that we should have bought quotas rather than publish the study — we would have been financially secure a long time ago! As a footnote I should note that free trade agreements signed by Canada in the 1990s are likely to result in an end to marketing boards with supply management powers like the B.C. Milk Board. In order to facilitate the transition to a free market, by international agreement the dairy market in Canada is protected by a tariff so high that imports remain at their present level. The tariff needed for this purpose has been set at over 300 percent for butter by a politically neutral international organization. The level of this tariff is a clear measure of the extent to which Canadian dairy products have gotten out of line with world prices and the true cost of production. By agreement, this tariff is slated to be reduced five percent per year over the next six years. Thereafter, a new treaty will have to be negotiated. I am not confident that the quota system will be dismantled in my life-time. There are too many millionaires and banks fighting to keep it, and B.C. consumers do not care enough to call for changes.

The National Energy Policy

Professor Sam Sidneysmith and I collaborated on a study of the effects of the National Energy Policy on government revenue. The NEP had imposed special taxes on producers of energy on the grounds that the world-wide increases in energy prices caused by OPEC in the early 1970s resulted in a large windfall gain to them. The argument was that the oil and gas in the ground, mainly in Alberta, belonged to *all* Canadians, not just the firms which previously had bought the right to extract them. The federal government also considered it unfair that the people of Alberta should enjoy large increases in royalties from natural resources while the rest of the country reeled from the effects of dramatic increases in the cost of energy.

The NEP was a very ill-conceived policy. It fuelled Western resentment and stimulated the creation of the Reform Party. The research by Sidneysmith and myself addressed a subtle but important economic consequence. The taxes imposed on producers raised the revenues of the federal government immediately. But in the longer run, they would lower the price governments would be able to obtain from the auction of new drilling and exploitation quotas. We hypothesized that in the longer run, revenue losses would be larger than the short run gains from new taxes. This conclusion was based on the idea that bidding on the right to drill for these resources would depend on expected future energy prices. Such estimates are never precise and include the possibility of both large increases and decreases. In the middle 1970s, prices rose dramatically.

The NEP eliminated producers' gains from these price increases. The government had set an important precedent. When the gamble taken by producers turned out favourable, they could expect to lose their extra profits. On the other hand, if future prices were lower than they had expected, the government would not give them a rebate on the money they had paid for the drilling rights. As a result of this new, asymmetric treatment of future gains and losses, investors could be expected in the future to bid less for these rights than they would have before the NEP precedent had been set. It is impossible to test empirically this kind of theoretical reasoning, since it deals with future developments in the longer run. However, our analysis attracted the attention of some specialists. A leading textbook on the economics of natural resources contains a chapter entitled 'The Grubel-Sidneysmith Hypothesis.'

Vancouver and Simon Fraser University

Unemployment insurance and the rate of unemployment

The most important research I did at SFU involved an analysis showing that Canada's unemployment rate was *raised* as a result of the increased generosity of the benefit system initiated in 1971. The paper was based on the insights I had gained from my study of the phenomenon of moral hazard discussed above. The important empirical findings are due to the work of my co-author and colleague, Professor Dennis Maki, an accomplished econometrician, and a graduate student, Shelley Sax. Like most of my research on the follies of government policy, this study disputed conventional wisdom and affected many who stood to gain from the policy. It was highly controversial.

We presented our findings at a seminar at SFU after I had published articles in the *Financial Post* and *The Vancouver Sun,* and a wide public debate had begun. The seminar had been arranged by faculty in other social science departments and the audience included a large number of graduate students. The hostility in the overcrowded room was palpable. As I entered the seminar room the atmosphere was so charged that literally the hair on my forearms stood up. The audience was not interested in the paper's analysis or empirical evidence; they had come prepared to question our motives and character. One comment remains burned into my memory: "We know how much you love your work and that it would be difficult to induce you to work less. So why do you infer that less educated and poor people behave differently?"

To my surprise I was invited to appear on a popular CBC radio program, *Cross Country Checkup*. The response of callers reflected a strong dichotomy between the views of the chattering classes and the general population. The former mainly attacked my motives and character. Average Canadians agreed with our findings and wondered what all the fuss was about.

I had wondered about the origin of my invitation to *Cross Country Checkup,* but many years later it became clear. Simon Reisman, Trudeau's powerful and colourful Deputy Minister of Finance, had arranged it. He had an interesting motive: in the preceding couple of years Canada's unemployment rate had risen, and the Cabinet was considering combatting it through increased deficits and lower interest rates. Reisman opposed these policy initiatives because he agreed with the findings of our study. The higher unemployment rates were due to the increased generosity of the insurance system initiated a few years before. He needed my paper and the opinions voiced on the radio program to persuade the Cabinet. As he told me later, they reluctantly went along with his views but insisted that the Economic Council of Canada be asked to do a study to confirm the 'findings of that right wing economist in Vancouver.' The Council took two years to produce its paper. It found that we had *underestimated* the effects of the increased generosity of the system on unemployment!

Chapter 5

I had not been asked to work with the McDonald Commission of Enquiry into the Future Prospects of the Canadian Economy, which conducted its research during the period 1983 - 1985. However, in a private conversation some years later, the Hon. Donald McDonald told me that our paper's findings "hung like a shadow" over the commission's deliberations. Professor Mark Blaug, a student of the history of economic doctrine, once told me that if I ever were to win a Nobel Prize, it would be for this work.

My work, which applied the concept of moral hazard to social insurance programs, had been an important innovation. I believe that moral hazard will ultimately offer the most profound understanding of the crisis of the welfare state in all Western democracies. Without it, there are only feeble explanations of a very strange fact. Since the 1960s the growth in spending on social programs has by far outstripped inflation, population growth and the aging of the population. Yet poverty and unemployment rates have not improved. Indeed, social activists claim, and some statistics show, that they have become worse. I am convinced that these developments are due to moral hazard and the needs created by the generous supply of government assistance itself.

I plan to write a book-length study of this subject after my retirement from active teaching in 1999. In my position as a researcher with the Fraser Institute, I expect to use many examples from recent history, including the failure of Canadian programs of support for natives and the Atlantic provinces, where changes in behaviour induced by the 'insurance' programs have worsened the problem they were designed to ameliorate. The study will also show how some other jurisdictions in the world have begun to deal with the problems of moral hazard. Such important reforms of social insurance programs have succeeded in the State of Wisconsin, the United Kingdom, New Zealand and the province of Alberta. My study will also deal with proposals for the privatization of social insurance programs, and interpret them as efforts to limit moral hazard induced by the actions of bureaucrats administering these programs.

Measuring the productivity of academics

During my work on the Brain Drain (see page 85), an entrepreneur in Philadelphia approached me with a proposal for its reduction. This man had started a novel service made possible by the falling cost of computers. He had hired a large number of individuals who paged through almost all professional journals in the physical and social sciences, and whenever they encountered a reference to some previously published work, would enter it into a database. Computers were then used to arrange this information by various criteria, one of them being the name of the cited author. He thought that ready access to this database would allow scientists in developing countries keep current with scientific developments and make them less likely to move to industrial countries.

Vancouver and Simon Fraser University

However, of great interest to me was the ability to use the author listing to measure the extent to which the work of individual economists had been noted by others. Such information would reflect the productivity of economists much more accurately than the traditional measure, which simply counted the number of publications. The measure is not perfect. There may be citation cartels among top economists, and self-citations are a small problem. In spite of these limitations, citation counts are now considered in decisions about academic tenure and promotion, along with other measures of productivity.

I obtained a list of all professional staff teaching economics at Canadian universities, looked up the numbers of citations in their name and compiled the mean and median number of citations per faculty member of Canadian universities. The President of the University of Toronto at a meeting of the Finance Committee in Ottawa remarked, approvingly, that I once had the audacity of measuring the productivity of academics. He had obviously appreciated my effort, even if his economic faculty probably did not, for obvious reasons.

In an article published in the *Canadian Journal of Higher Education* (1981) I showed that the highest average number of citations was to the publication of economists at the University of British Columbia. Simon Fraser University was second. Toronto and the other establishment universities in Canada lagged far behind the upstarts from the West Coast. This study did not endear me to my academic colleagues. Some saw it as self-serving, since my own university did so well and my personal citations placed me second in Canada, behind Professor Richard Lipsey, then at Queens and later at Simon Fraser University.

My work on citations led me to a fascinating insight into the nature of competition and the sociology of science. A philosopher named Lotka had found that in all fields of human performance involving complicated tasks, the top 10 percent of all people engaged in that activity produced around 50 percent of all output, while the bottom 50 percent produced none. I found 'Lotka's Law' to hold in the case of publications in economics and citations to them. I believe it also works, with some qualifications, in hockey and other sports. It is also found in a field that comes as a surprise to many: the top 10 percent of income earners in Canada pay 50 percent of *all* income taxes!

Economics departments in many universities of the world are losing student enrollment. Graduates with PhDs in Economics are frequently shunned by both private and government sectors. The main reason for this development is that economics has become increasingly rigorous through the use of mathematics in the refinement of theory. But in the process, economics and the theory have also lost much of their relevance to the real world. I have long been conducting a personal crusade to arrest this trend, part of which involved the publication of an article titled "On the Efficient Use of Mathematics in Economics," co-authored by Professor Larry Boland, which appeared in the journal *Kyklos* (1986).

Most of my economist colleagues at Simon Fraser University agreed with my position. I think the department's popularity with students and employers of graduates has had much to do with our moderate and efficient use of mathematics. Our teaching and research remain relevant to real world problems. In addition, SFU has had a long tradition of demanding good teaching techniques from their professors. In economics student evaluations of teachers and courses always have been a substantive criterion for promotion and compensation. It did not come to me as a surprise that *MacLean's* magazine in the 1990s has ranked SFU as the best university of its type in Canada (that is, universities without professional schools for law, medicine and dentistry).

During the 1990s, economics at SFU was strengthened by the arrival of several distinguished professors, such as Richard Lipsey, Curtis Eaton and Richard Harris. These individuals had outstanding records of accomplishment in large Ontario universities. Like free agents in sports, they were persuaded to move by SFU's favourable salaries, working conditions and living environment. They have raised the international stature of SFU, and continue to attract good students to the graduate program.

Graduate students

The best and most rewarding graduate programs in the world are at such famous U.S. universities as Harvard, Yale, Princeton, Chicago, Stanford and Berkeley, with a 'second tier' of programs at the larger U.S. state universities. The quality of education and the employment opportunities for graduates of the SFU program are comparable to those in the U.S. second tier. As a result, SFU attracts of good number of talented graduate students from around the world.

I have had the privilege of teaching international trade and finance to many of these students. It has been a rewarding experience. They have forced me to keep current and rigorous in my teaching. They have stimulated and complemented my research.

Every doctoral student has to write a dissertation, a task which takes about two years. Students select faculty supervisor to help them with their work. Between 1971 and 1993 about 20, or 60 percent of the total graduating from SFU with a PhD, chose me for this job. It was time consuming, involving much personal contact and potential opportunities for conflict. None of my students ever chose another supervisor and all completed their dissertations, except for one who had to return to Korea for family reasons. About 75 percent of these students were natives of African and Asian countries. It was therefore ironic that during the 1995 election campaign I was branded a 'racist.'

Several of the students I supervised have found employment in universities. Some are working for international organizations such as the IMF and United Nations; some are working for governments and in the private sector. I follow their careers with interest and pride.

Other research and publications

One of my largest and time-consuming writing projects during the 1970s resulted in a 600-page textbook, *International Economics*. Its first edition appeared in 1977, the second in 1981 and the Japanese edition in 1980. The book was published by Irwin, which at the time was the largest and most prestigious publisher of textbooks in business and economics in the United States.

However, the market for texts in international economics is small and at best yields royalty income of a few thousand dollars a year, not the hundreds of thousands earned by a small number of successful authors of introductory texts. The reason for such small royalties for international economics texts is that the subject is taken by only a relatively small number of students.

In addition, I had a special problem. I had only a few students who were teaching the subject at other universities. This put my text at a great disadvantage relative to those written by professors at the large U.S. universities. They had many former students who routinely adopted their textbooks when they started to teach international economics. For this reason it is difficult for non-U.S. professors to take a large share of the U.S. market in any field.

My text was written using very little mathematics. Theory was used to create rigorous analysis and empirical evidence, not for its own sake. Much time was devoted to explaining institutions and putting matters into historic context. It contained several innovations which have been adopted widely by other authors. For example, I used a facsimile of a table of foreign exchange quotations from the *Wall Street Journal* to describe foreign exchange markets, using this information as a base for the theoretical analysis of the determination of exchange rates. Actual data on international trade were used as a starting point for the explanation of why countries trade, what they trade and what benefits such trade brings.

The book had a large overseas market, but sales were quite limited since pirated copies were readily available and much cheaper. While visiting a professor in a developing country, he showed me with a sheepish smile a copy which had been published in Taiwan without authorization, and which was being used in his class. The University of Cape Town library had indeed bought two copies of the book, but at the same time 10 photocopies of several chapters were on the shelves, with the suggestion that students make copies of them for their own use!

In the mid-80s the publisher of my text, Irwin, was bought out by Dow Jones, a large U.S. conglomerate known as the publisher of the *Wall Street Journal* and *Forbes*. Soon, sharp-penciled MBAs with finance degrees began to cut costs at Irwin. Many textbooks with insufficient sales were culled. Mine was one of the "last victims of rationalization," as an editor told me.

Some good memories yet remain. At an academic conference I was approached by a young woman who was a teacher at a small midwestern U.S. college. She had just been assigned the task of teaching international economics. Since she had no background in the field, she had obtained a copy of each of the leading textbooks. She found mine the most informative and interesting. However, she had assigned her students another text, telling me apologetically: "I kept your book from the students so I would know more than they could learn from theirs."

Most important, the wide use of the book abroad brought to SFU a number of students who had come expressly to study with me. These students were among the best and most successful I encountered.

In the fall of 1997 I attended a conference organized by the Fraser Institute in Berlin. Present were academics from a number of Central European countries. One of them approached me with this story. When the Communist government of Poland relaxed its tight control over universities during the mid-80s, he was the member of a committee charged with finding a Western textbook in international economics worthy of being translated into Polish for use at Warsaw University. He told me that after the committee had studied all of the major texts available, mine was chosen. It had just the right admixture of theory, history, institutions, empirical information and policy implications to suit the University's objectives. Alas, the translation and publication never took place. The providers of the traditional Communist reading material, fearing the loss of their monopoly, had been able to kill the project.

Conferences and changing research priorities

Professors who publish regularly and whose work attracts the attention of their colleagues around the world often face important changes in their professional lives and research agendas. These changes are brought about by invitations to conferences and accompanying requirements to write articles for publication in the proceedings. After my arrival at SFU I received a steady flow of such invitations.

The Institute for World Economics, located in Kiel, Germany, had me attend their annual conference about ten times. In addition, I attended conferences all over the world on exchange rates, the international monetary system, the Brain Drain, trade in services, unemployment and tariff policy. They kept me current on theory, empirical work and policy issues. I never returned from any one of these without at least one important insight that influenced my research, teaching and view of events. Such conferences represent one of the most efficient ways of ensuring that professors are kept abreast with developments in their fields and do not teach obsolete knowledge and facts.

Vancouver and Simon Fraser University

Some of these conferences were also rewarding from a personal point of view. The trips to Germany allowed me to visit my family and friends. Some conferences brought unique insights into bureaucracy, power and jealousies.

One year I attended a conferences at the IMF on the topic 'The Future of the International Monetary System.' The venue was awe-inspiring. As one of the paper presenters, of which there were 12, we sat around a huge oval table in the meeting room of the executive directors. Many of the directors sat behind us, where normally their assistants would be found.

In my paper, I argued that the IMF should raise the interest rate it paid on the Special Drawing Rights, which it issued for use by foreign governments as international reserves. My analysis showed that this would help move the world towards an optimal degree of exchange rate stability. At a reception that evening, Jacques Polak, IMF Director of Research and Chief Policy Adviser, spoke to me alone, suggesting that my paper was too theoretical and unrealistic. As tends to happen at such receptions, just at that moment a distinguished-looking gentleman had joined us and overheard the criticism. He looked Polak straight in the eyes and said: "Quite to the contrary, I found Professor Grubel's the most interesting paper at the conference."

I found out later that these words had been spoken by Sheik Yamani, executive director for Saudi Arabia and a major OPEC player. He was known to have been in a running feud with Polak over some other matters. I never found out what other directors thought about my paper, but ironically, at a follow up conference a few years later, Polak opened the proceedings by remembering the new ideas he had obtained from the first conference.

The most important of those he identified as the need for higher interest rates on Special Drawing Rights, which had been introduced by the IMF in the interim and he had thought unrealistic at the time I had introduced the idea (though he did not credit me as its originator).

The international conference circuit is personally and professionally very satisfying, but it also has a cost. Typically, invitations are based on work already done and the conference papers tend to be rewrites and minor extensions of that work. They also use up a lot of time and energy. For these reasons, the originality and depth of my research after the early '80s was less than it had been in earlier years. But I have no regrets; most scientists go through life cycles in their work.

Originality in theoretical and conceptual work comes when they are young and is followed by more applied research and more devotion to the passing on of knowledge through teaching. Economists at the second stage often get involved deeply with giving advice on economic policies to governments and international organizations.

My professional life went through these cycles. In a sense, entering Parliament was an organic part of it.

Chapter 5
Commitment to Vancouver and Canada

Since arriving at SFU in 1971 I have been approached by a number of universities for possible employment. Typically, I would receive a telephone call or a letter. "We are seeking to hire a professor and your name has come up as the ideal candidate for the position . . ." It is always flattering to receive communications of this sort, even if it is not certain that one actually could count on being hired for the position.

Some positions were interesting and promising. The University of Miami in Florida, for instance, offered a professorship in international finance. As I was told, the financial connections with South America offered great opportunities for both study and consulting work. A chair at the University of Southern California would have paid well, but on telling my wife about it she responded by saying that she hoped that I had negotiated for weekend return trips to Vancouver, because she was not willing to move to California. Vanderbilt University in Nashville Tennessee has a great reputation and superior student body, but I could not see myself happy with the climate and recreational and cultural opportunities of that part of the U.S.

Several German universities asked me to join their faculties, the most intriguing offer being the chair for economic policy at the University of Bonn. The proximity of the federal government would surely have exposed that position to much immediate involvement in current and relevant policy analysis. The University of Konstanz offered a location ideal for my recreational interests, right at Lake Konstanz and a short distance from some of the best skiing in the Swiss and Austrian Alps. A professorship at the Free University of Berlin did not appeal to me, especially after I had some not so good experiences teaching there.

The Institute for World Economics at the University of Kiel in Northern Germany is a major research organization. It operates a library for the government of Germany, specializing in the collection of publications related to international trade and finance throughout the world, and publishes a number of well known professional journals. The President of the Institute is also a professor at the university and has one of the most prestigious academic positions in Germany. All past presidents had ready access to the media. Their counsel was sought by the government, even if it urged the greater use of markets. I had visited the Institute regularly for international conferences held every June. I felt at home ideologically and had a good personal relationship with its most recent president, Herbert Giersch.

I think I would have been willing to accept the position of President of this Institute, had it been offered to me; however, it never was. When Giersch retired in 1988 I was near the top of a list of possible successors. As some friends at the Institute told me, in the end I lost out to fighting among Kiel University and the local state and federal governments, all of which helped finance the Institute and had their own agendas in the choice of a new president.

In 1995 the Institute awarded me the Bernard Harms Medal in recognition of my contributions to economics and the Institute. During my visit to accept the medal I had many conversations with some of the Institute's former leaders, now in retirement. Some left me with the impression that I was lucky *not* to have become the president! Of course, I will never know the truth. However, I do know that the move to Germany would have enormously complicated my family life and I would never have had the opportunity to become a member of the Canadian Parliament.

Looking back at the many opportunities I had to move to other universities, I occasionally wonder whether I was right in turning down the possibilities for earning a higher income and enjoying more prestige or professional growth. I have decided that such contemplation is unfruitful. After many moves made during my period of education and professional apprenticeship I had settled and put down roots at SFU and in Vancouver. I had become a Canadian citizen. My family had grown up here. Having a home and belonging were, and remain, an important part of my emotional well-being.

The family

After the family arrived in Vancouver in 1971, we had a busy and happy family life. Our house in West Vancouver was large and comfortable, in an upper middle class neighbourhood. Our immediate neighbours were doctors, salesmen and teachers. The acquisition of two dogs and two cats symbolized that we had finally settled down. They also helped to turn our house into a home.

At first, Eric and Heidi went to schools which were only a short distance away. In 1974 Eric was enrolled as a day student at St. George's, a private school in Vancouver. As soon as he was old enough to drive, I passed on to him a 17-year old Mercedes Diesel which I had bought very cheaply on one of my visits to Germany, and which had served me well for a number of years. Though the car provided him with reliable transportation, being heavy and safe, it certainly did not lend itself to the kind of racing that some teenagers are tempted to engage in! Heidi graduated from West Vancouver High School, located close to home. Both children have fond memories of their high school years and benefited from superior educational opportunities.

Hollyburn Country Club was very near our home, and we became members soon after our arrival. It has superb facilities for racquet sports, ice hockey, curling, exercise machines, swimming and social events. The entire family played tennis and squash. Eric and Heidi took up competitive swimming. For years Toni took them to the pool at 5:30 every morning and to meets all over the Lower Mainland. Both children had large

Chapter 5

collections of ribbons in evidence of their competitive successes. The tennis at Hollyburn has always been important to me for exercise, a change of pace from work and opportunities to meet non-academics.

We hiked on all the local mountains on weekends. An overnight trip to Lake Garibaldi was the biggest expedition we ever undertook as a family. In the 1980s a student with much interest in mountaineering guided Professor Zane Spindler and me to the top of Mount Baker, a little over 4,000 meters high. We used ice picks, crampons and ropes and proceeded with extreme caution over glaciers that are known to have deep crevasses covered by snow that can give way any time. Our student did not want to lose his teachers!

Everyone in the family loved skiing. We made frequent trips to Whistler during the early 1970s but stopped them for a few years when line ups were too long and did not warrant trips starting at six in the morning and expenses equal to a month's food budget. We enjoyed cross country skiing on Hollyburn Mountain instead. However, during the Labour Day weekend in 1977 we visited a new real estate development at Whistler, which offered condominiums for sale at a reasonable price and in a great location. We were very disappointed when we did not like the design of this particular development.

As we left the site we saw Jeff Massey, the tall, lanky and aristocratic looking co-architect of Simon Fraser University, working on a small condominium development near completion. His design would later win a prize for excellence. We fell in love with it but the price was more than I thought we could afford. However, eventually Toni persuaded me that the added income I would get from expected text book royalties and her own part time work would allow us to make the extra monthly payments. In the end, the condo offered the family much enjoyment and turned out to be a good investment. We were part of Whistler's growth from the visionary beginnings of a few pioneers to a destination resort rated as one of the best in the world by skiers around the world.

Early in life Eric showed great entrepreneurial spirit. At St. George's he was elected captain of the swim team. He was disappointed that the team was very small. So he proposed the unification of the swim teams of St. George's and Crofton House, a nearby private girls' school; after the merger he was suddenly the captain of a large team. After completing high school in 1980 he went to Queen's University in Kingston, where he majored in computer science and economics. He always had extra sources of income, grading examinations for a professor and operating the computer centre in the evenings and on weekends.

During one summer break he worked for a company selling vacuum cleaners door to door in Vancouver. This is how the company worked. Every morning he and his sales associates would knock on the doors of houses in lower middle income neighbourhoods. They informed inhabitants coming to the door that their company was about to open a store nearby selling vacuum cleaner bags. In order to know what bags to put into inventory they needed to know the make and age of the cleaners they owned. In return for the information their name would be entered into a draw for a prize. That afternoon the information thus obtained was used to single out people who had cleaners of an age likely to need replacement. These targeted residences would be contacted by telephone and a date for the delivery of the gift — a low-quality carving knife — was arranged. Eric loved his sales job and sold more vacuum cleaners that summer than anyone else in Western Canada!

After graduating from Queen's, Eric enrolled in the PhD program of the New York University Graduate School of Business. He had a scholarship and had earned enough money from different jobs to pay all his living expenses. He passed all his courses, specializing in international finance and had behind him all the examinations which qualified him to write his doctoral dissertation. However, at that point he decided that he did not want to be an academic. He wanted instead to be a successful businessman and a millionaire by the age of 40.

He left graduate school and joined a high-tech company developing software for computers, using the skills he had acquired as an undergraduate major in computer science and his talent and love for selling. From this job he joined a large computer company, eventually took over marketing for Canada and settled down in Toronto. He then became president of a small high-tech company that was developing a new product, being financed by a venture capital firm. In the end, this company was taken over by a company in Los Angeles, where he moved in 1996, only to join yet another company as an executive in marketing. His income is much higher than mine has ever been. He has a very good chance of reaching his goal of being a millionaire by the time he is 40. All that is needed is a high price for his company's stock when he is permitted to exercise his options.

Eric is married to Sharon. She is a lovely, lively, energetic and very intelligent modern woman. She has a BA in engineering, an MBA from Queen's and had become an account executive in a major food marketing firm and the marketing director for a medical service company. In 1995 she left her career to give birth to my grandson Andrew and to look after him during his formative years. Twin girls were born to them in October 1998.

My daughter Heidi is also a thoroughly modern woman but with more interest in non-material things in life. She had good grades at Queen's but after earning a general degree in arts and economics, she enjoyed herself for a number of years. A girl friend at the university had inherited some money and the two used it to travel all over Africa and Asia. I now shudder when she tells me about her adventures of travel through African countries engaged in civil war and the dangers of travel in primitive areas. While canoeing down the upper reaches of the Congo River in July 1988 with some other Canadians, she needed to reach land and find an airport

Chapter 5

that would allow her to fly to Toronto to attend her brother's wedding. Insisting that her friends drop her off on land rather than the shallow waters on which their canoe floated, it was later discovered that if she had stepped into the water, she would have been swallowed by quicksand.

Heidi repaid the debt owed to her friend by moving to Japan, where she earned a high income teaching English. In 1994 she left Japan with a young American she had met abroad and was deeply in love with. They moved to San Francisco, where he worked as an architect. Eventually the relationship broke up and Heidi found herself working as a receptionist at a conservative think-tank in San Francisco. On her 29th birthday she went through a wrenching personal crisis. She had realized that she was soon to be 30 and needed to decide on a career.

So in 1995 she enrolled in the program for a Master of Public Health at Columbia University in New York. In December 1997 she graduated with a superb academic record. She has a debt of $30,000 in spite of much part time work as a research assistant. In the spring of 1997 she took on her first professional, paid, full time position. She works for a company in Washington D.C. which provides evaluations of family planning projects undertaken by U.S. foreign aid granting agencies. Heidi hopes that before long she will be doing work that she loves and considers to be important: doing field work in managing family planning programs in developing countries. In September 1998 she accepted a Fellowship administered by the University of Michigan in Ann Arbor and financed by the U.S. Agency for International Development to evaluate U.S. development programs in Africa. She will be stationed in Nairobi, Kenya, where about 20 years earlier she had attended high school for a year.

After our marriage in 1958 and our arrival in Vancouver in 1971 Toni and I got along well. We shared many interests in sports and recreation. We enjoyed the challenges of living in the many different places of the world described above, finding strength in each other through the normal struggles of life, raising the children, making ends meet and my pursuit of a professional career. However, once the children had gone off to university, the struggles that had given us a common goal had disappeared. Our activities and interests increasingly diverged.

After the children had grown enough to leave Toni some discretionary time, she did much volunteer work for the SPCA and similar organizations. Once the children were away at university left volunteer work and took on part time paid employment in the Eaton's store at Park Royal, a large shopping centre near our home. It meant that often on weekends she had to work and could not come with me to Whistler, where I belonged to a group of regular and ardent skiers. Owen Owens, a geologist and senior vice president with the large mining company Cominco, and I found that we shared strong interests in skiing, books, politics, business and the economy. For many years we spent many happy and interesting hours in conversation riding on chairlifts and racing down the steepest slopes.

Vancouver and Simon Fraser University

It was on one of these weekends alone at Whistler that I met Hélène Bertrand on a chairlift. She too was alone; her husband and children in Victoria were not interested enough in skiing to come to Whistler for most weekends. Hélène and I soon found out that we had in common not just our love for skiing but many other interests. Most important, we shared the pleasures of talking and getting enthusiastic about ideas. Hélène was the youngest graduate of the McGill Medical School and constantly works on innovative methods for treating illnesses. She always wants to know and discuss with me aspects of my work, much as I ask her about the fascinating work she does. Friends and relatives often comment just on how similar we were in our interests and temperament.

In the summer of 1988 Hélène and I began living together. We were divorced from our spouses within a year. I had been married to Toni for 30 years; Hélène's marriage had lasted 26. For me the divorce was the most dramatic event of my life. I still have bouts of sadness about it.

Hélène and I were married in the snow on top of a Whistler mountain on April 18, 1992. Hélène's three children and my two attended the ceremony, along with many friends. All of our children have remained neutral during the difficult time of the divorce. Now they all have two Christmas celebrations every year. Eric and Sharon's son Andrew has two grandmothers in Vancouver. Hélène has a thriving medical practice in North Vancouver. We continue to share the interests and activities that brought us together ten years earlier.

Hélène is a francophone, being born and raised in Montreal. Her father was a Rhodes Scholar and professor of neurosurgery at the University of Montreal. Her mother was one of the pioneers in the restoration of Old Montreal and served on the boards of a number of public and private corporations. Hélène has two sisters and a brother, all of whom are married and have children. This large Bertrand clan has accepted me readily. Almost every summer I have been spending a week or two at the large family compound at Lake Nicolet in the Eastern Townships of Quebec. This membership in a large Quebecois family has enriched my personal life enormously.

An interesting fact about our five joint children is that by 1998 three had moved to work and live in the U.S., part of the large 'brain drain' from Canada; only Hélène's sons remain. One is a struggling artist with a high school degree and some university education who uses computers to do his work. The second is in a home for the mentally handicapped and is employed in a sheltered workshop.

Heidi was able to pursue her professional interests in family planning in developing countries only in Washington, D.C. For Heidi, income and taxes are not important, and she left Canada reluctantly. Eric was moved to Los Angeles by his company but tells me he is unlikely to return to Canada, where he had found job opportunities much more limited and taxes much higher. Hélène's daughter Claire and her husband Ken work

Chapter 5

as animators for Spielberg's film-producing company, Dreamworks, in Los Angeles. They were attracted to the U.S. by the professional opportunity and say they would return to Canada for a similar job even if the pay were lower and they had to pay higher taxes.

After the 1998 budget was brought down by Finance Minister Paul Martin, the *Globe and Mail* head of the Ottawa office, Ed Greenspon, called me for a comment. In my comment I deplored the absence of tax cuts for high income earners because there was a large gap between the tax burden of such people in Canada and the U.S. To underscore my point I mentioned what had happened in my own family. A few days later Greenspon called and asked for Claire's and Eric's telephone numbers. His editor had agreed to do a story about Canada's brain drain, made more interesting by a case study of the motives of these two. The article was published in the *Globe and Mail* in the spring of 1998. Eric's picture was very small, but Claire's was spread over nearly a third of a page. I think I know why: for many years before she turned to animation, she had been one of Canada's leading fashion models!

Hélène would play an important role in my short political career. Without her emotional and practical support I never would have embarked on, no less succeeded, in that great adventure of becoming a Member of Parliament.

CHAPTER 6

The Fraser Institute and International Adventures

THE TENDENCY to shift more and more of my time and resources into the analysis of economic and financial policies had started in the middle 1970s in another important forum, the Fraser Institute, which owes its existence to the 1972 election of the first avowedly socialist government in British Columbia. At that time the business leaders of Vancouver could not believe that the people of their province could have been so poorly informed about the consequences of such a government that they brought it into office. They had thought an advertising campaign extolling the merit of free enterprise would prevent the repeat of such a mistake.

At that time, Pat Boyle was the senior vice president for long range planning for MacMillan Bloedel, the largest forestry company in British Columbia. Singlehandedly, he persuaded the B.C. business community to use the money they were about to spend on advertising to support a research institute, to be modeled on the Institute for Economic Affairs in London, which would later gain fame (or notoriety, depending on one's political views) as the place where Margaret Thatcher developed the policies she put into effect as the Prime Minister of Great Britain.

With seed money from MacMillan Bloedel and other large companies, the Fraser Institute opened its doors in 1973. Michael Walker was its Director from the beginning, and they could not have found a better person. The son of a Newfoundland coal miner, he had earned a PhD in economics from the University of Western Ontario and had worked in the Bank of Canada and the Department of Finance. He was thoroughly disenchanted by the political and bureaucratic processes which he had witnessed in Ottawa and which, he believed, were ruining the prosperous, free society that he loved. He jumped at the opportunity to take on the challenge of running the non-profit Fraser Institute.

Tall and muscular, Walker works as hard as he plays at squash, tennis and windsurfing. With a ready smile and a good sense of humour, he often tells jokes, sometimes at his own expense. He is very loyal to his friends, defending them against all attacks. At the same time, he demands high quality work of everyone. As a result, he manages the affairs of the Institute very effectively, making difficult decisions, moving people to different responsibilities when necessary and occasionally asking one to leave. He is very approachable; his office door is always open. The problem is being able to catch him when he does not have a telephone at his ear!

Today, the Institute has an annual budget of around two million dollars.

Chapter 6

It still receives no money from government and is supported entirely from private sources. About 60 percent comes from donations by foundations, 30 percent from corporations and 10 percent from individuals. It distributes a monthly magazine, *Fraser Forum,* which has the widest circulation of any publication of its kind in Canada. Publishing dozens of studies in pamphlets and books, most of the longer studies are written by academics and economics practitioners who are paid small honorariums, but have the satisfaction of seeing their ideas circulated widely in print.

The Institute has become a respected (and, by some, feared) source of objective information about economic developments and of rhetorically effective ideas about the merit of a free market economy and society. Twice, attempts have been made to hire Mike Walker to head similar institutes in the U.S. Large increases in his own income and much larger budgets and organizations were not enough to draw him away from his important task in Canada. He is deeply involved in the running of a global umbrella organization for free market think-tanks that have developed in many countries.

The development of the Institute was not always smooth sailing. About a year after the Institute was formed, Prime Minister Pierre Trudeau announced wage and price controls. The Institute published papers opposing them. MacMillan Bloedel and other Canadian corporations liked the controls and gave the Institute an ultimatum: "Withdraw your opposition to the wage and price controls or lose our support." The Institute stood by its decision. The financial situation deteriorated to where Canada was very close to losing the Institute. But it survived this and other, similar crises. The rest is history.

Within two years of its founding, I became a member of the Institute's Board of Editors. I was in good company, as it included Nobel Laureates Friedrich Hayek, George Stigler and James Buchanan, as well as Sir Alan Walters, Britain's Prime Minister Margaret Thatcher's influential personal adviser, and famous Canadians Richard Lipsey and Tom Courchene. It was more or less an honorary position, though on a few occasions we were requested to adjudicate disputes between Walker and authors. Since the Institute is strictly non-partisan, I lost my position as a member of the Board of Editors immediately upon my election to Parliament in 1993.

Studies published by the Fraser Institute

My professional involvement with the Institute was extensive and resulted in the publication of a number of studies. I was instrumental in organizing a conference on the effects of unemployment insurance on the rate of unemployment. The papers presented by authors from the U.S. and Europe broadened the evidence we had for Canada. The conference proceedings are to be found in many libraries. The study of the Milk Marketing Board, co-authored with Richard Schwindt, has been discussed above. It helped the Institute early in getting a reputation for publishing studies that exposed the ways in which interest groups benefited at the general public's expense. It taught me about the strength of these interest groups and of their ability to mobilize the media to defend their causes.

My study titled *Free Market Zones: Deregulating Canadian Enterprise* (1983) had an influence that still brings me periodic calls from Canadian municipalities who want to set up such zones. At an international conference of libertarians at Whistler in 1996, Michael Van Notten, a Dutch entrepreneur, informed me that he was in the process of creating a free economic zone in Ethiopia. At his side stood his wife, dressed and with a bearing appropriate for her position as an Ethiopian princess. If the project is ever realized, I hope to have a chance to visit it.

In 1985 I published a study titled *On the Insurance Corporation of British Columbia: Public Monopolies and the Public Interest.* The study presented data on its excess costs, evidence on how they were hidden and principles on why one should expect such results and behaviour from a monopoly. This is still the only economic study of such an institution in existence. As a result, the head of the commission studying the feasibility of such a monopoly for Ontario visited me to discuss the subject. Two state senators from Hawaii took me out for lunch for the same purpose. Neither jurisdictions adopted state sponsored automobile insurance systems. I cannot be certain, but my analysis might have had some influence on this outcome. I wish I had the time to update the study, which is now over 12 years old.

Josef Bonnici was recently Minister of Finance of the Government of Malta, and holds a doctorate in economics from SFU. In 1984, while still a Professor of Economics at the University of Malta, he visited SFU on a sabbatical leave. During that year he and I collaborated on a study titled *Why is Canada's Unemployment Rate so High?* which was published in 1986. Our analysis focussed on the difference in the Canadian and U.S. unemployment rates, which was negligible until the early 1970s, when Canada's unemployment insurance system was made much more generous. Thereafter, the difference in the two countries' unemployment rates diverged to where in 1997 Canada's for a time was about twice that of the United States.

Many Canadian economists and politicians still do not accept our conclusion that these differences are due to the greater generosity of the Canadian unemployment insurance system in the past. They think that traditional determinants of unemployment like deficits, trade surpluses and monetary policy in the two countries can explain the differences in unemployment rates. In the summer of 1996 a special conference organized by the Centre for the Study of Canadian Living Standards gathered in Ottawa to consider the problem raised in our 1985 Fraser Institute publication. The conference reached the conclusion that less than a quarter of the unemployment gap, which at the time was six percentage points, is due to the unemployment insurance gap. I do not accept this conclusion, but am happy that at least and at last, after ten years, the issue was consid-

Chapter 6

ered to be worthy the close attention of my distinguished economist colleagues.

In 1987 Mike Walker was approached by the federal government to have the Fraser Institute undertake a study of the economy's service sector. After assurances that there would be no government interference in the design and publication of the research, Walker accepted the challenge. He appointed me the academic manager of the project. The following two years were hectic but also very interesting.

We developed a template of questions which about a dozen academic specialists answered in their studies of individual service industries. The industries studied covered the fields of medicine, law, education, culture, construction, insurance and so on. We organized a conference to help us set the questions and research agenda. At a final meeting researchers discussed their findings.

I edited all 12 volumes in the series, which occupies about 20 centimetres on the shelves of libraries. Walker and I contributed to this series a lengthy study of the more general developments affecting the service industries in Canada. It was published in 1989 under the title *Service Industry Growth: Causes and Effects*. The basic problem it addresses is well known. In recent years, about 70 percent of all employment has been in the service sector, the rest in goods production and agriculture. The growth of service sector employment was foreseen by many to incur a number of problems in the future. Allegedly, it would result in the creation of too many low paid jobs, like those of the proverbial hamburger flippers. It was also identified as the major cause of a marked slowdown in the economy-wide growth of labour productivity, since there are few technical opportunities to increase the productivity of the many people who work in services like retailing, teaching, medicine, restaurants and others, since personal contact plays an essential role in the delivery of the services. Some were worried how Canada would pay for its imported goods if almost all employment would be in the service sector, the output of which could not be exported. Many wondered whether the trend towards service sector jobs should not influence the strategy for granting development aid by regional development authorities. In fact, the latter concern caused the government to initiate this study.

Our study showed that most of the growth in the service sector industries was due not to the expansion of the hospitality industry that employed the hamburger flippers. Rather, it took place in services used by business: advertising, law, engineering, computing and so on. These services were increasingly supplied by small businesses, which are nimble, non-unionized and highly specialized, tending to employ highly educated and experienced workers with correspondingly high incomes. These service workers indirectly raise the productivity of workers in the goods industries. Both types of industries are highly intertwined and depend on each other.

Goods will always be needed for export, but they embody increasing amounts of services. For example, most of the total cost of computer programs on disks consists of the cost of programming, packaging, shipping, advertising, finance and so on. The cost of actual manufacture of the disks is a relatively minor factor. Small employment in the production of the disks is accompanied by large employment in the service sector. Services enter international trade *after* they have been embodied in goods. For government policy, all this means that regional development agencies should pay more attention to the development of skills used in the service sector, and less to the building of factories.

I do not know how widely the Fraser Institute studies on the service industries were read, or how much influence they have had on policies in Canada. However, our main volume detailing the above findings was published in Chinese. In 1988, at the invitation of the Chinese government, I visited some centres of learning in China, where I presented our findings. In 1996 Mike Walker made a similar tour. He noted with great satisfaction that at least in that country the insights produced by our study are well known.

Foreign adventures: Oxford

The English-speaking world is wonderfully large and diverse. It offers academics from that world many opportunities for prolonged foreign assignments. I took some advantage of these, and spent time in Oxford, Nairobi, Cape Town and Singapore.

In 1974 a sabbatical leave from SFU brought me to Nuffield College at Oxford. During that academic year my salary was only two-thirds of normal, but renting out our house in West Vancouver provided extra income and helped with the housing costs abroad. The children attended school in Oxford. They did not acquire a British accent, but gained many new friends and enjoyed their experience. I had an office and some secretarial help at Nuffield, which I used intensively to complete my textbook.

Attending High Table and having sherry with colleagues in the inner sanctums of the College were enjoyable rituals. History is evident everywhere at Oxford. At Magdalen College I noticed a sharp corner in a narrow corridor of a building where, over hundreds of years, students' hands had noticeably worn down the sandstone. In the older colleges the walls were decorated with huge paintings of past masters. The rich oils in their gold-covered frames, darkened by age, conveyed an unmistakable sense of tradition and excellence totally absent from a university like Simon Fraser.

I enjoyed the company of, and learned much from my economist colleagues at Nuffield. Max Corden, who was responsible for my coming to Oxford, is a well known economist specializing in international trade. I attended his famous weekly seminars and he allowed me to present two papers at them. Peter Oppenheimer is the Reader in international economics at Christ Church. He has good connections to the financial community in London and through him I gained many insights into the working of that sector.

Jim Mirrlees, a recent Nobel laureate, Ian Little, Maurice Scott and John Fleming had worldwide reputations. Sam Brittain, a senior editorial writer with the *Financial Times* of London was visiting Nuffield on a sabbatical. He brought many fascinating insights to the discussion of economic issues. The students were interestingly different. Some were brilliant and became successful economists, like Peter Neary, who holds a chair at Trinity College in Dublin, and John Martin, who has an influential position at the OECD.

The University of Nairobi

During the 1970s the Canadian International Development Agency, CIDA, supplied the University of Nairobi in Kenya with technical teaching support in economics and business. In 1978 I was chosen to hold one of these positions. During briefing sessions in Ottawa, a veteran of African affairs told us about political risks and dangers. He noted jokingly "Just pray every evening that during your stay nothing happens to President Jomo Kenyatta."

On the second day after our arrival in Nairobi early in the morning I went to the reception desk at the famous Norfolk Hotel when several jet fighters roared by at rooftop level. A maid with an incongruous smile said: "Have you heard? Our beloved President died last night." The scene is burned into my memory for ever. Here I was with my family in a town which many had expected to explode into racial and tribal warfare upon Kenyatta's death. What to do?

The entire city had come to a standstill. Stores were closed and the windows boarded. Business owners of East Indian descent had gone into hiding. The university had closed. Fortunately, I had bought a car. The family quickly piled in and we drove to the tourist area on the Indian Ocean. The idea was that we would be safe there and in case of serious danger could count on rescue by foreign forces. As it turns out, disturbances in Nairobi and elsewhere were minor. There was a smooth transition to a new government headed by Daniel Arap Moi.

The government of Kenya was under the obligation to supply us with accommodation and (after much prodding) came up with a nice house on a heavily fenced lot. I was told in no uncertain terms that I was expected to hire a housekeeper, gardener and night guard. The servants' quarters soon provided shelter for a large, extended family.

The gardener performed what seemed to me like miracles. He put into the ground a cutting from a rosebush, thick end in the air. A few weeks later we had a blooming rose bush. It is said that the East African soil and climate are so benign, if one sticks a finger in the soil, a bush grows out of one's ear! As we found out later, our securely fenced lot adjoined one occupied by an army general. A guard dog and powerful lights protected his property. Our night guard, armed only with a machete, had his work made easier by this neighbour's efforts.

Eric and Heidi attended the International School. They still rave about the quality of the instruction they received and the warmth with which they were received by fellow students. All the students were the children of highly mobile parents and knew how difficult it was to enter a new school, and acted accordingly.

For me, teaching was a nightmare. I faced over 300 students in lectures on topics in finance that were of little interest to them. Yet I had to follow the curriculum, which had been laid down by the authorities. The mention of examinations always brought very vocal responses from the students. They had an attitude that was totally alien, but was explained to me as follows. In North America, examinations and admission to university provide samples of students' qualifications for entry into high-level occupations. Nothing is determined or final at any stage. One can improve or worsen one's chances of success through the quality of examinations.

In the Kenyan system, which is modeled after the British, students take critical examinations at an early age. If they pass, they join an élite admitted to university and are practically guaranteed good careers in highly paid occupations. By contrast, in North America students are tested throughout the educational process, many switching from top to average and below performance. Finishing with good grades is no guarantee for economic and personal success. As a result of the Kenyan system, students I had to deal with had great difficulties understanding why they were still being subjected to the torture of periodic examinations since, after all, they had passed the all important entrance examinations to the university.

Several times I stood in front of the hundreds of students, intimidated by their shouts and threatening gestures. Once I said that if the room was not quiet in 30 seconds I would leave the room. As I was leaving the stage, the noise died down. But when I turned back, it came on stronger than before. I left and went straight to the Dean to explain my action. Thereafter things went better, but I am sure that the students do not have a good memory of me.

The reason is that I could not get myself to do what according to rumour was a common practice. At the end of a semester, several lectures were used to discuss the examination questions that had earlier been submitted to a central authority. This did not happen in my classes. Instead, I provided students with samples of the kinds of questions they could expect. I also made sure that the distribution of grades was fair and that only a standard number of students received failing grades.

I wrote and co-authored a number of studies commenting on current policy issues. One taught me a lot about economics and politics in Kenya. At the time, Kenya's balance of payments was in serious deficit and a mission from the IMF had recommended the devaluation of the local

Chapter 6

currency known as the shilling, a year earlier. I published an article in the *Nairobi Times* supporting this view and giving reasons why this would be in the national interest. The following day I went to the Canadian Embassy and was greeted by the CIDA representative with the words: "I am glad to see that you have not been deported." In his experience the government of Kenya did not take kindly to comments like mine and often reacted by deporting the offenders. I was properly scared since deportation would have meant the total loss of pay and great upheaval for the family. As it turned out, I was told by someone inside the government that the Finance Minister had actually welcomed my comments.

As a result of the publication of my newspaper article I was invited to address a class of students at the staff college, where they were being prepared for future work in the bureaucracy. They were very adamant in their opposition to the devaluation of the shilling, the reason being that devaluation would reduce the real value of Kenya's exports and therefore lower the country's standard of living. However, this is not possible in the case of a small country.

Consider coffee as the proxy for Kenya's exports and cars for the country' imports. The rate at which these goods exchange is determined in world markets: a car might trade for, say, 100 bags of coffee. In terms of dollars, this would mean that a $10,000 car could be purchased for 100 bags of coffee worth $100 each. Therefore, whatever the exchange rate of dollars for shilling, Kenya always will get a car for 100 bags of coffee.

But a Kenyan devaluation would change the prices at which coffee and cars exchange. Consider an exchange rate of five shillings per dollar. A car in Kenya costs Sh50,000 and a bag of coffee brings Sh500. When the shilling is devalued to six per dollar, the price of the cars rises to Sh60,000 and that of coffee to Sh600. The higher domestic price of cars discourages imports and helps domestic production, given unchanged prices of Kenyan inputs like labour, land and interest on capital. Most important, the higher price of coffee helps farmers, enables them to buy more fertilizers and other inputs. As a result, coffee production and exports increase; car imports fall. The balance of trade and payments is improved, which is the objective of the devaluation.

The car-for-coffee example is the standard textbook case explaining how devaluation helps eliminate a trade deficit. However, in the leading textbooks in international economics to which these Kenyan students had been exposed, only a page or two is spent on this normal case. Three or four pages are then used to discuss the theoretical possibility that a devaluation will result in the deterioration of a trade balance. This case is discussed under the heading 'The Marshall-Lerner' condition, named after two economists who discovered it. In essence it arises when a large country devalues and lowers the world price of its exports. In the light of the above example, if Kenya were a really major exporter of coffee, the devaluation could increase exports of coffee so much that the world price would

The Fraser Institute and International Adventures

fall. Instead of a car requiring 100 bags of coffee, it may require 120 bags. Under these conditions Kenya would indeed be worse off as a result of a devaluation. More domestic labour, land and capital would be required to pay for an imported car.

The problem with this case is its irrelevance for practically all countries of the world, but especially for a small country like Kenya. Even a very large increase in its domestic production of coffee would hardly make a dent in the world price set by the very much larger exports from a host of other coffee producers of the world.

My experience reinforced my unhappiness with textbook writers and many of my colleagues who teach international economics. They are so fascinated by the logical intricacy and mathematical formulation of the Marshall-Lerner condition that they spend an inordinate amount of classroom time on it. Almost every examination in the field has a question on the topic. As a result, students concentrate their studies on this question. They do not have the needed perspective to realize its near-irrelevance in the real world. The bright and future leaders of the Kenyan bureaucracy at the staff college brought home to me with force the importance of teaching economics focussed on the real world and not theoretical niceties.

While my professional experience in Kenya was stressful, the personal experiences were outstanding. The whole family played tennis regularly at the Impala Club, whose members were mainly expatriates, many of whom had lived in Kenya all their lives. They told us many interesting stories about the past, the colonial period when they were guides to Hollywood celebrities on safaris and big game hunts. They described the times when automobiles regularly ran into big animals on the road to Mombasa at night. According to them, it was more dangerous to run into the tall legs of a giraffe than it was to collide with an elephant!

I had the good fortune of getting a club member who was also temporarily working in Nairobi to play as my partner in a mens' doubles handicap tournament. This event takes place every year in conjunction with the Kenya Open for professional tennis players. My partner was an excellent amateur player and since we were not known to the tournament organizers we were given an average handicap. As it turned out, we won the draw, which had 96 entries. Our names appear in the record printed every year in the program for the Open Tournament!

Eric and Heidi were eager swimmers. They won several events and established some records at the Kenya national swimming championships. They too some day may return to that country and look up their names in the record books.

We toured a number of game reserves and saw all of the major predators except leopards, which are nearly invisible, perched in trees. Once we felt threatened by a rhinoceros, which are known to attack cars, but escaped safely. We also had a little excitement when our car was parked in a meadow chosen by a herd of elephants for passage. A young bull was on collision course with our car. It raised its trunk and trumpeted at us. Fortunately, it got bored when we did not react, lowered its trunk and just walked around the car.

The whole family went on a safari to Mount Kenya, over 5,000 metres high and sporting a glacier even though it is just a few kilometres from the equator. The climb through the thin air was very strenuous. Passage through what is known as a 'vertical bog' left us wet. In that state we spent what for me was the coldest night of my life, in a tent in a valley at about the 4,000 metre level. At dawn a guide, Eric and I climbed to the highest level at 5,000 metres that can be reached without technical rock climbing.

During that period, Toni and Heidi tried to forget their splitting altitude headaches as they marveled at the exotic vegetation. Many plants common at lower altitudes had developed into giants, capable of resisting the regular night frosts, snow falls and hot days of the great heights. We learned that identical plants evolved separately at all high altitudes on every continent, indicating the important role played by environment in the survival of mutations.

The University of Cape Town

Africa has a way of getting into the blood. So, when in 1984 I had earned another sabbatical leave from SFU, I took up a long standing invitation to visit the University of Cape Town (UCT). Professor Cedric Nathan, a native of the Cape, had written his doctoral dissertation under my supervision and organized my stay. In 1989 I had another visit of four months.

Both Eric and Heidi were attending Queen's University, so in 1984 for the first time Toni and I were able to travel on our own. We rented a house in Llandudno, a small village a few mile south of Cape Town. The roaring waves of the South Atlantic were 100 yards away and sometimes awakened us in the middle of the night. The landscape of the Cape is spectacular. The city sits between the ocean and steep mountains. Of all the cities with this setting that I have visited, Rio de Janeiro, Hong Kong, Nice and Vancouver, I like Cape Town the best.

The vegetation of the Cape is uniquely African, adapted to the Mediterranean type climate, which means guaranteed blue skies and warm temperatures for at least six months of the year. We climbed mountains, traveled the Garden Route, swam in the Atlantic and Indian Ocean on the same day, enjoyed the local wines and fresh fruits and vegetables. A trip to Namibia allowed us to see one of the most hauntingly beautiful landscapes of the world. Outside of teaching and writing some papers, the semester was like a long and beautiful holiday.

Some of my SFU colleagues have also had several visits and teaching posts at the UCT. Several regular faculty members have visited the Fraser Institute and SFU. Several graduates with a BA from UCT have obtained graduate degrees at SFU. We all believed that we could help the cause of freedom in South Africa best by a continuing dialogue and the analysis of the merit of free markets.

The dialogue was welcomed by students and faculty at the UCT and among most of the business people I met. Even before the end of the official policy of apartheid, UCT had begun to increase the number of black students; during my 1989 visit, blacks represented about 30 percent of the total. The department of economics has had a long tradition of analyzing the disadvantages of the system of apartheid. The department was the home of researchers documenting the extent of poverty, with the help of a large grant from the Ford Foundation. Under the leadership of Professor Brian Kantor, much work was done on the cost of excessive regulation and taxation, including racial separation. I felt at home ideologically.

I was free to give my views on any and all subjects at the university and in private conversations. I never had any encounters with any government agencies. I had a visit with the Canadian High Commissioner for friendly discussions about Canadian boycotts of South Africa, its effectiveness and costs. If he disapproved of my visit at a time when the Canadian government spearheaded a boycott of South African trade and investment, he never indicated it to me.

I never visited any black townships outside Cape Town: it was not safe to do so, any more than it is to visit the shanty towns of Nairobi or the streets of New York's Harlem. During my 1989 stay in Cape Town I was accompanied by Dr. Hélène Bertrand, with whom I was to be married in 1992. While I was teaching, she provided medical services for blacks. This work required her to drive regularly into the black townships. She was instructed on these occasions to wear her white coat which identified her as a doctor. Nevertheless, she did not escape having clenched fists raised at her as she drove by. She dreaded the possibility that her car might break down.

Hélène found excellent medical facilities in the townships, paid for by the government. In special obstetric facilities, patients were counseled throughout their pregnancies. Midwives, from whom Hélène learned much, oversaw the deliveries. Ambulances were available for quick transfers to hospitals of women experiencing serious difficulties with their deliveries.

During my visits to Cape Town I learned a lot about the way the media work. We made friends with a couple of doctors from the Netherlands who were engaged in postgraduate studies with a world-renowned specialist at the famous Groote Schoor hospital, where Christian Barnard had performed the first human heart transplant. One of the hospital buildings had a large lawn with a few trees where workers could regularly be seen taking a nap after lunch. These friends had received from their concerned relatives a picture which had been printed on the front page of a Dutch newspaper. The picture showed a lawn with a few trees with a number of bodies lying on it. The story accompanying the picture referred to a massacre commit-

Chapter 6

ted by South African police in Cape Town. Of course, in a police state like South Africa, it is possible that a massacre had taken place without the knowledge of our friends. However, there was no doubt whatever that the picture showed the resting workers that they saw every day at Groote Schoor hospital.

In this context I should note a haunting experience during a visit to Chile during the Pinochet regime. I had been invited to present a paper to the graduating class at the Chilean School for Diplomats. I also gave a couple of seminars at the National University of Chile. This work left me several days for sight seeing in and around Santiago. I found a peaceful, prosperous country, contrary to what I had expected to find after having seen regular TV broadcasts by the CBC in Canada. These reports inevitably featured pictures of slums, demonstrations, riots and strong police forces.

Never a shy person, I visited the Canadian embassy and arranged for a meeting with the Ambassador. I asked him bluntly where all the demonstrations and riots were that I had seen so regularly on CBC. He told me that visiting Canadian tourists and business people often came to ask him the same question. In fact, often media representatives did the same thing. He did not have an answer to our question. So where did the CBC get its footage of demonstrations and riots? He told me that they had fostered the development of a rent a demonstration business. For a few dollars people dressed for the occasion would assemble at a garage to obtain signs and banners. They would then move to a park where their small numbers were skillfully made to appear large. After the footage was taken, the 'demonstrators' would return their signs and banners to the garage and return to their normal occupations.

Of course, my report of first hand experiences with manipulations by media in South Africa and Chile does not imply that I supported the policies of apartheid, violations of human rights and the suppression of freedoms in the two countries. I only wish to offer some unusual evidence on the power of the media to influence public opinion through means that many would consider to be unworthy of Canada's proud history of democracy. Little did I know at the time of these experiences that a few years later during my election campaign and as a politician I would experience first hand the power of the media to distort facts and pursue their own agendas.

I am glad Nelson Mandela has been able to oversee a transition to a black government without the bloodshed and revenge taking that has played such havoc with the people in other African countries. I am also glad Mandela's vision was pursued at a time when the country was no longer a battleground between the Soviet Union and the United States.

Unfortunately, however, South Africa has made very little progress in its effort to free the economy from the devastating regulations and controls of the previous regimes. My colleagues at the UCT and others familiar with conditions in South Africa fear that as a result the country will never reach its potential for development and riches. Above all, I hope and pray that Mandela's successor can continue with his pragmatic policies of reconciliation, for without them it does not matter what kind of economic system the country has.

Singapore

Institutes and universities around the world find it useful to have foreign visitors to enrich their research and teaching programs. For these visits they tend to invite academics with a proven record of publications and a certain personal and scholarly maturity. During the 1980s I received a number of invitations for shorter visits at foreign institutes and universities.

Thus, in 1985 I spent six months at the Institute of Southeast Asian Studies, which is affiliated with the University of Singapore. The Institute has a number of scholars in residence and interns and students from countries of Southeast Asia.

One of my responsibilities was to interact with the staff of the Institute. For this purpose I arranged for regular luncheon meetings. We had some great discussions. One was especially memorable. It involved two academic economists from Rangoon, Burma. They described policies in that planned economy in response to pointed questions from me. A few years later I paid a short return visit to the Institute. I was told how people still talked about and missed the 'Grubel luncheons.'

During the first week of my visit I received a quick lesson in Singapore politics and economics. I attended a talk given in a large university lecture hall to the academic community by Lee Hsien Loong. He is known as 'The Brigadier' after his position in the country's army reserves, and is the son of the famous long time Prime Minister Lee Kuan Yew. He was obviously a very bright man with great self confidence. He had a joint honours major from Cambridge University in England.

At the time he was Minister of Economics and the topic of his talk was the present economic crisis. Singapore had been growing at annual rates of 10 percent since the early 1970s when suddenly, in 1984 growth stopped and unemployment appeared. What had caused this change in Singapore's economic fortunes?

During a question period after the Brigadier's presentation I offered my diagnosis: wages are too high. This condition was attributable directly to a 50 percent increase in wage rates legislated by the government in the preceding year. This policy was initiated on the theory that it would force employers into adopting more labour saving technology and rescue the economy from what was considered to be a 'low wage trap.' The next day I received an invitation to be a panelist on Singapore television for the discussion of current economic problems. I promptly informed Kernial Sandhu, the Director of the Institute about this invitation.

Chapter 6

Sandhu immediately urged me to decline the invitation on the grounds that my views would be used for domestic political purposes. As a result, my ability to work with industrial and academic leaders during the rest of my stay would be compromised seriously. After I informed the TV station that I could not accept the invitation, I was urged to tell Sandhu that the invitation was issued by the Brigadier personally. I did so and Sandhu said he would make a few phone calls. A short while later I was given permission to appear on the program.

During the program I laid out my position about the need for wage flexibility to deal with shocks to the economy. I strongly condemned Singapore's policy of centralized wage setting, which about a year earlier had abused its position to impose a 50 percent increase in labour costs on employers. I thought that I made my points well, but to make sure that the analysis was available in print, I collaborated with a local scholar in writing a paper on the same subject. It was published in the *Straits Times*, the leading local newspaper.

It is difficult to know how much influence my analysis has had on government policies, but this much is clear. The government no longer has wages determined by a central authority and set economy wide. There are now guidelines which urge wage adjustments by individual firms according to their profitability. These policies were initiated in 1986, together with a partial elimination of the wage increase mandated earlier. Under this new regime strong economic growth resumed and unemployment promptly disappeared.

Further evidence on the merit of my ideas on the role of wage flexibility came from an unexpected source. During my presence in Singapore Charles Schultze, a former chairman of President Johnson's Council of Economic Advisers, was a visitor in the Economics Department at the University of Singapore. A grey-haired man, he had the kind of confidence that comes from advising Presidents and moving in the highest policy-making circles in Washington. In a seminar at the university, which I attended, he expressed his opinion that the then present growth and unemployment crisis was due to deficient monetary and fiscal policies. Accordingly he urged the adoption of lower interest rates and government deficit policies. We had some heated discussions over the merit of such Keynesian policies relative to lower wages.

Neither of us gave in during this debate. However, a few years later I met Schultze at a conference of the American Economics Association in Chicago. He had just returned from another visit to Singapore. I asked him about economic conditions there. He answered: "They are excellent. It is amazing what lower wages can do."

Unless there be a misunderstanding, let me deal with an objection raised by opponents to lower wages as a solution to unemployment and slow growth. Wages do not have to fall by a large amount to achieve the intended objective. Small adjustments are sufficient to attract profit hungry entrepreneurs. They are always eager to hire workers whose productivity is greater than their pay. That is how they can earn higher profits and get rich. In the longer run, flexible wages and free labour markets bring the wage increases desired by everyone. History provides the evidence. Advances in science and technology and capital accumulation increase labour productivity: at the given wage rate, employers gain from hiring workers. The actions of all entrepreneurs together create labour shortages and drive up wages. But such wages are consistent with increased productivity of the workers and therefore do not result in unemployment.

In addition, higher educational and skill attainments by workers raise their productivity, making them targets for hiring and increasing their wages. Singapore had made the mistake of wanting to exploit the productivity and wage nexus by legislated wage increases, in the expectation that productivity would follow. The economy does not work that way, as Singapore found out, at high costs in the form of unemployment and lost profits.

However, Singapore has generally benefited from much wise economic management in the years before and after the mistake was made in 1984. During my first visit in 1969 wages were low. The shops were poorly stocked with goods of low quality. The infrastructure was inferior. Workers and the government did not have the income to afford anything better. Conditions were bleak because Britain had just closed down its naval base, one of the biggest employers in the state. The country has no natural resources and virtually no land for agriculture to feed its population. It even has to import its drinking water.

During my 1985 visit to Singapore I found the improvement in living standards and infrastructure impressive. They were achieved by keeping wages in line with productivity. But the wise management of labour costs is not the only secret of Singapore's success. Another is the absence of a conventional social insurance program. Singapore has no government benefits for the unemployed, ill and retired. I asked some searching questions as to why this is so. One minister who was in office during the period immediately after independence told me the following story. Representatives from agencies of the United Nations after independence was attained in 1969 visited him again and again, suggesting that Singapore could never shed the yoke of colonialism and become a modern state unless it adopted such social insurance programs. These unwanted visits and lectures from the UN representative stopped only after this minister had threatened to end the next one by tossing him out the window.

The minister had carried out the policies adopted by cabinet under the leadership of Prime Minister Lee Kuan Yew. Lee had decided against the adoption of the modern social programs. During his studies in England he had seen the damage they had done. He also saw great merit in the traditional Chinese way of life with its emphasis on self-reliance and the family as the source of social security. His concession to the new age was a policy of forced savings. The state played the role of the wise father rather than

Chapter 6

a nanny, which is the role played by the traditional welfare state. All workers and employers had to contribute a large fraction of wages tax free to individually owned accounts in the so called Provident Fund.

This Fund is administered by the government which sets conditions under which individuals can withdraw money. Initially, withdrawals from the accounts were allowed only to be used for retirement.Gradually, withdrawals were allowed also to cover expenses arising from unemployment, illness, and the purchase of a first home. For individuals unable to work and build up their accounts in the Provident Fund, the state provides welfare. Eligibility for such benefits is strictly limited to those with unambiguously severe handicaps which prevent them from finding employment. The Singapore welfare role is small.

The Provident Fund has not been managed as efficiently by the government as it would have been by private agents. It has been criticized for other reasons, some of which are due to the unexpectedly high rate of economic growth and the effect it has on pensioners whose wages and contributions were low when they were young. Others have suggested that its investments in local enterprises like taxis and grocery stores was protected by laws restricting competition. These policies caused inefficiencies and higher prices for consumers than would have existed if the economy had been free from these interventions. However, basically it has served the people of Singapore extremely well. Spending on unemployment and the other social needs have remained much smaller than they have in Canada and other countries with modern transfer programs. My discussions about moral hazard above explain this state of affairs. The 'needs' of individuals during periods of unemployment and illness translate into much less spending if it comes at their own expense rather than at the expense of the state. People have strong incentives to find new jobs quickly. Singapore's unemployment rate always has been very low.

The government of Singapore is often criticized for being paternalistic and too rigid in its management of the affairs of its citizens, for example the death penalty for the possession of drugs, stiff fines for littering and corporal punishment in the form of whipping for some offences like vandalism. In my experience, many Canadians think that such policies are appropriate. Opposition to them comes mainly from the chattering classes. Anyone visiting Singapore will agree that the policies work. One execution for drug possession has been enough to make the city virtually drug-free. Vandalism is not a favourite activity of bored youngsters facing some painful lashes if they are caught. The streets are clean and orderly.

Another criticism of Singapore has been the alleged suppression of free speech. I think that its policy to ban international publications like *The Wall Street Journal* and *Time* for the publication of allegedly false reports about corruption in the country was ill-advised. Governments in the business of deciding what is truth and publishable are on a slippery slope that can easily lead to the demise of democracy. Similarly, the government's treatment of parliamentary opposition carries many unfortunate risks. However, to the surprise of many people, these risks have not resulted in repression and a cumulative loss of economic and political freedoms. The Fraser Institute publication *Economic Freedom of the World* by Jim Gwartney and Richard Lawson (1997) ranks countries according to the freedom of its citizens to earn and keep wealth, enjoy the stability of prices, deal with foreigners and a range of other objective statistical measures. On this list of over 100 countries, Singapore ranks as the second most economically free country of the world; only Hong Kong ranks higher. Canada comes in at 14th.

In all widely reported cases in which the government has confronted the media, the issue has been the reporting of corruption by government officials. The government is extremely proud of its integrity. The importance of having and keeping corruption and cronyism out of the government has been demonstrated by the 1998 economic crisis which has afflicted Thailand, Indonesian and Malaysia. Many observers see government corruption and cronyism as the main source of the economic woes of these countries.

I have a personal experience which shows the role played by the Prime Minister in assuring the integrity of his government. The president of the largest local brewery told me that habitually he sent to the Prime Minister as a Christmas present a case of bock-beer specially brewed for the season. He always received a note of thanks — with a cheque for the beer included.

The following story is an interesting illustration of how the media have operated in creating the impression that Singapore suppresses the freedom of speech and religion. In 1987 the world's media were hard on the Singapore government for the expulsion of some people who claimed to be missionaries. The media frenzy was fed by some Singapore leaders dissatisfied with government policies. In 1988 I met with Sandhu, the director of the Institute of Southeast Asian Studies, while I was on my way from China to India. I raised the issue of the expelled missionaries with him. He told me the following story, which I have no reason to consider to be anything but factual.

At the peak of the global media frenzy the Prime Minister invited personally a dozen of his most vocal critics to a meeting in his government's cabinet room. When these critics arrived they all were given a stack of papers. The Prime Minister asked them to read the material during the next two hours, when he would return to discuss it with them. The papers contained the well-documented report of the Singapore internal security forces on the activities of the alleged missionaries. The report showed conclusively that these foreigners were not missionaries but agents of a foreign government engaged in activities designed to destabilize the country. When the Prime Minister returned at the appointed time, most of the visitors had left. They saw no need to ask questions of him. Their criticism of the government policy ended. The media never reported on this

Chapter 6

turn of affairs. The story about the expelled missionaries to this day is used to illustrate Singapore's alleged lack of freedom of religion and speech.

The Free University of Berlin

In 1990 I spent six months at the Free University (FU) of Berlin as the Distinguished Bundesbank Visiting Professor of International Finance. This Professorship was endowed by the German Central Bank on the occasion of the 750th anniversary of the founding of the City of Berlin. I had to teach two courses and lectured in German, using notes that had generated enough interest by students at SFU so that my classes were always filled to capacity. At the FU a large number of curious students showed up for the first few lectures. Their numbers shrank gradually until in the end there were no more than a handful in each course.

The German university system is much different from that in North America. Students have great freedom in their choice of courses and the timing of their examinations. They tend to show no interest in lectures by professors who are known not to have any influence on the outcome of their examinations.

The FU was founded in the 1950s with the help of money from the U.S. It was 'free' in contrast with the historic Humboldt University located in East Berlin. The FU was a hotbed of radical student movements throughout the postwar years. These movements in Germany were and to some extent still are much more aggressive than they were at SFU or even Berkeley. The German social security and education system has encouraged the development of a hard core of permanent students. In earlier times these people would have been the leaders of movements outside the university dedicated to the establishment of anarchy, socialism, communism or simply opposition to specific government policies. They have left literally indelible marks on campus buildings with their slogans and on student life with their radical rhetoric.

My professorial colleagues were interesting but interaction among faculty and with graduate students was minimal. The exception was Professor Heino Riese. His speciality was monetary and macro economics. I tried valiantly to understand the book he had published on this subject. Perhaps I did not have the proper background. The teachings of Milton Friedman and James Tobin were obviously not enough. Riese had made it a habit to challenge to a debate everyone holding the Bundesbank visiting chair. I gladly accepted under the condition that the topic be an examination of the causes of the high unemployment rates in Germany.

I was chosen to introduce the subject and discussed the role of moral hazard discussed above. A large audience of students was attracted to what they had hoped would be a fun spectacle. Some of Riese's students promptly attacked me. One claimed that the correlation between high insurance benefits and unemployment rates was equivalent to that between the number of births and storks sighted. At one point I asked Riese to offer his side of the debate. He said he wanted to do it at the end. When the scheduled time for the debate was over, he refused to do so with the words: "I have no explanation for Germany's high unemployment rate." And this came from a professor responsible for teaching this subject at Berlin's leading university. At least it was an honest answer.

In 1990 Checkpoint Charlie still existed but without passport controls on either side. I went into East Berlin a number of times to visit the museums and the opera. They were wonderful but the rest of East Berlin was depressing with its poorly maintained infrastructure and the obvious poverty. On one visit I saw a tram tilt on its rails so much that I thought it might topple over.

One day I had given a seminar at a West Berlin Institute unrelated to the Free University. In the audience was Professor Rainer Schwartz from the East German Academy of Social Sciences. He had begun to attend academic events in the West frequently after the Wall had crumbled.

We met and developed a friendship which in 1996 brought him to Vancouver for a visit on his way to seminars all over the world. Schwartz was a member of the East German intellectual elite with a PhD in solid state physics from the University of Leningrad. He had a fascinating life that included marriage during his student years to a beautiful woman from a southern region of Russia. Her father was a powerful local head of the Communist Party and had an outstanding record fighting Germany during the war. He never approved of his daughter's marriage to a German and mostly because of his disapproval the union did not last long.

Schwartz is now married to a German physician. He lived in a spacious apartment in a rather drab neighbourhood, but since both he and his wife were members of the intellectual élite, they and their two children had all the comforts of life. He arranged for me to talk to members of the Academy who were in limbo, not knowing what would happen to them after the unification of the two parts of Germany. Some, like Schwartz, had skills that were readily transferrable, others could not expect any demand for their services. I left the meeting feeling very sad for these people, even if some of them had been part of the power structure and responsible for the crimes of the East German regime.

Schwartz was a charming and lively man who used his physics training only for a short period in his life and ended up doing research in the application of mathematical techniques to management of enterprises under the auspices of the Academy of Social Sciences. One of his many duties was to organize the acquisition of computers for the organization. I thought that he was very qualified to help me find an answer to a puzzle. Why did the East German system break down around 1989 rather than earlier or later? Here is the answer he provided.

U.S. President Reagan's embargo on the export on computers was very effective. Schwartz personally saw a drying up of all his past sources of

Chapter 6

supply of computers for the Academy. At the same time, Reagan launched the so called 'Star Wars' program for the development of an anti-ballistic defense system. The Russians could not expect to match this program, especially since they could not acquire the essential computers. The planning system was unable to duplicate the boom of innovation driven by small entrepreneurs in the U.S.

Chairman Gorbachev was the head of a group of Soviet leaders who had reluctantly come to the conclusion that the only choice they had was to modify their system. The immediate problem was to get the most favourable accommodation possible with the West.

During a later meeting in Ottawa of the Canada Europe Friendship Association, this account was confirmed. The ambassador from Russia revealed to MPs and other ambassadors at the meeting that during the 1980s he had been a member of a Kremlin group engaged in the development of longer run foreign policy. Having decided that they could no longer continue with the Cold War in its historic pattern, they planned on how to manage the transition. Out of all this came what Schwartz told me was the final and most crucial event.

The people of East Germany began protest marches and economic disruptions. The East German armed forces did not interfere as before, the reason being that Gorbachev had informed Ernst Honnecker, the President of East Germany, that Russian troops would not be ordered to take the place of East German troops if they refused to fire on their own people. The rest is history.

Part III

The Political Experience

CHAPTER 7

Getting Nominated for the Reform Party

IN THE SPRING of 1992, four different constituency associations of the Reform Party in the Lower Mainland asked me to become a candidate for nomination in their riding. I was interviewed by the selection committees of the ridings of North Vancouver and Capilano Howe Sound and formally accepted the latter's nomination. Even though I lived in North Vancouver at the time, West Vancouver and Whistler, both part of Capilano Howe Sound, had been my home for nearly 20 years.

The Capilano-Howe Sound riding is dominated by West Vancouver and part of North Vancouver, a densely populated suburb of the City of Vancouver. About 20 percent of the constituency lives in Squamish and Pemberton, where the economy is based on forestry and agriculture. Average family income in the riding in 1993 was the highest in British Columbia and third-highest in Canada. The unemployment rate was the lowest in British Columbia, reflecting the fact that its population ranks second in British Columbia in terms of the percentage with a university degree and working in managerial or business service occupations. The population is dominated by individuals with a British background and those belonging to protestant religions.

I can only speculate about the reasons which led to the invitations to seek the Reform Party nominations. During my 20 years at SFU a substantial number of students had gotten to know me and my views on economic issues. Most of these students had settled in Vancouver and reached positions of responsibility in the community. I had also published a good number of editorials in *The Vancouver Sun* and other national newspapers whenever I felt strongly about national or local issues. The electronic media had frequently interviewed me on current economic issues. In other words, I had some name recognition and a reputation as a conservative. Fiscal conservatism, of course, was the most important part of the Reform platform. As a party formed just recently by the grassroots, it was seeking candidates who had not been previously involved with other parties. In short, I fit the bill.

Motives for seeking the nomination

The idea of standing for election had never before seriously entered my mind. Therefore, the invitations to do so were completely unexpected. But they fell on fertile ground for professional, personal and political reasons. Professionally I had begun to run into diminishing returns. Teaching and research had occupied me for over 30 years. Seats in my undergraduate classes were still in great demand, but I began to feel somewhat uncomfortable teaching graduate students. At that level economics had become very mathematical and I could not equip students with the rigorous skills they needed to succeed. Some graduate students told me how much they appreciated my approach to economics and how much they missed it from other courses, but I still was uncomfortable.

Research is a self-generating process and I never had any problems finding interesting projects. But there were symbolic signals that at age 58 I had reached a peak of achievements and that from now on things would go downhill. My biography had been entered into a book, *Who's Who in Economics 1700-1986* (London: Wheatsheaf Books). Professor Mark Blaug, the editor, selected 400 deceased economists for inclusion in the volume on the basis of the lasting value of their contributions. He also included 1,000 living economists of the world who had the largest number of citations to their work in the literature. Blaug estimated that those 1,000 constituted the top six percent of the world's economists.

In 1992 Edward Elgar, a British publishing house, was about to republish 54 of my professional articles in a series entitled *Twentieth Century Economists*. There was a market for such a series by new libraries in the world that could not afford to buy expensive back issues of economics journals but that wanted to offer their readers collections of some of the most important journal articles published during the postwar years. In addition, I had been informed that soon I would be awarded a medal by the Kiel Institute for World Economics 'in recognition of my contributions to economics and the Institute.'

I was flattered by this set of indicators that my work and achievements were recognized. But at the same time I also felt that I had done it all, that I had made the best out of my abilities in academia. I had wondered whether perhaps it was time to move on to new challenges. The idea of becoming a Member of Parliament appealed to me as such a new challenge. I had some hope that my skills might help me to be a productive MP and that I would have opportunities to help shape Canadian economic policies more directly than is possible through teaching and research.

I was also ready for new challenges on a personal basis. I was 58 and healthy. My new wife's enthusiasm and love had reinvigorated me and given me new self confidence. We were at a stage in our life cycles where we were free of the burden of raising children. We had moved into an apartment and no longer had to look after pets and a garden. With my 60th birthday on the near horizon, trying out for a new career was an attractive alternative.

The problems with the other parties

I was also ready politically because of the fiscal crisis that threatened

Canada's economic stability. Something drastic needed to be done to eliminate the deficit. For eight years the Progressive Conservative government, under Prime Minister Brian Mulroney, had relied on economic growth to raise enough revenue to match expenditures but had never succeeded. For a time, revenues would rise more rapidly than spending but then economic slowdowns stalled revenue increases while spending soared. The PC government simply did not have the political will to undertake the spending cuts needed to balance the budget. The deficit rose not just because of excessive spending on traditional programs, but also because annual deficits added to the debt. When interest rates rose in the early 1990s and raised the cost of servicing the huge debt, government finances went into a death-spiral. The recession of 1992 was the final straw. Canada faced a serious fiscal crisis.

As the 1993 election approached I was in despair over the likelihood that any of the three major parties had the political will to cut spending and deal adequately with the deficit crisis. The record of the PCs was dismal. They had been elected twice by Canadian voters who wanted a balanced budget. I had voted for them myself, in the hope that they would cut spending and reverse the left-wing drift of Canada's economic and social policies. Margaret Thatcher in Britain and Ronald Reagan in the United States had shown the way. The PCs missed the opportunity.

The PC governments had enacted some excellent legislation. NAFTA brought free trade between Canada, Mexico and the United States. It reduced the power of special interest groups and their ability to gain legislated benefits. Replacing the Manufacturers' Sales Tax with the GST increased economic efficiency. These gains could have been greater if the GST had been applied uniformly and at a lower rate. Special exemptions and exceptions made the tax into an administrative monster. Unfortunately, the economic benefits of NAFTA and the GST were considerably less than the economic costs of the deficits, debt and resultant fiscal crisis.

I did not expect the Liberals to deal effectively with the fiscal crisis. They were the party of ever-growing government. The social programs they had initiated were at the root of Canada's fiscal crisis. When the Liberals were in opposition they gave no indication that they had changed their views on the role of government and that they accepted the need for spending cuts. Much the same could be said about the NDP. Its policy platforms continued to urge more and bigger government. Their views had not in the least been influenced by the failure of social democracy in countries like Sweden and of socialism in the Soviet Union. They were, and remain, in a state of denial about the seriousness of the fiscal crisis.

The promise of Reform

In 1992 only the Reform Party's platform promised to cut spending, move to a smaller government and produce a balanced budget in three

Chapter 7

years. I had met Preston Manning in 1989 at a luncheon meeting at the Fraser Institute. At that time already he had impressed me with his grasp of fiscal issues and the need for smaller government. He also came across as a thoroughly decent and honest man.

However, at that time I had not been willing to join the Reform Party or support him. Like almost everyone else in the Institute, I was worried about the split of the conservative vote that would occur if both the PCs and Reform would appear on the same ballot. I also was and remain to this day uncomfortable with Manning's populist notions. I wanted to be associated with a party committed to the conservative principles of personal freedom and smaller and less intrusive government, not one which fits principles to suit the populist demands of the day.

However, a couple of years after that meeting at the Fraser Institute I joined the Reform Party. The resultant exposure to the party's literature and election platforms eventually persuaded me that Reform offered the best hope for resolving Canada's fiscal crisis and growth in government. In April 1992 I threw my hat into the ring to get the nomination as the party's candidate in the 1993 federal election in Capilano-Howe Sound.

Assembling a team

Peter Wearing had been a student in some of my classes during the early 1980s. He is a large man with a ready smile, a good sense of humor and an engaging personality. Peter had seen me a few times in my office to talk about economic problems. We also talked party politics and I learned about his great interest in practical political affairs. In fact, his interest was so strong that he quit university before he had earned a BA degree.

Wearing had been drawn into B.C. politics to help successfully manage election campaigns of Socred candidates. The Socreds were essentially the B.C. right wing party with a platform not unlike that of Reform. After the election, he worked in the bureaucracy as a legislative assistant to the Minister of Health. In the 1990 provincial election he ran for office under the Socred banner in Burnaby but lost, as did most other Socred candidates. Premier Bill Vander Zalm had been involved in personal scandals and his government had a poor record of performance. The backlash to his behavior and policies resulted in the election of an NDP government in B.C.

For me this change in B.C. politics brought a great benefit. Wearing returned to SFU to complete his studies for a BA. By that time, he was a mature student with much experience in electoral politics and inside government. He had learned of my possible interest in seeking a Reform nomination and came to my office for a talk. I gathered from him much practical knowledge about the problems and rewards of life in politics.

A few days after our talk, I decided to become a candidate for nomination in Capilano Howe Sound. Peter agreed to become my campaign manager, a position he held through the federal election. His first contribution to my effort was to involve two fellow students with a strong interest and experience in politics. One of them, Steve Vanagas, did not stay on my team for long. He needed an income I could not provide, but he stayed in the political business: in 1998 he became the head public relations officer of the Liberal Party of British Columbia which is the official opposition in the provincial legislature and which lost the 1996 election in spite of receiving a larger percentage of the total vote than the NDP.

Poor prospects for election victory

I entered the nomination race without much hope of winning, much less gaining a seat in Parliament as the Reform candidate. At the time, Prime Minister Kim Campbell headed the PC Party and was riding a wave of popularity that seemed to make her a sure winner. Expectations were that as a new leader she would overcome Mulroney's legacy, that the majority of Canadians who basically were conservatives would remain loyal to the PCs. In addition, it was thought that many women voters would support her simply because of her gender.

The Liberals at the time were running a strong second in British Columbia. In the existing Parliament they had 83 seats. As well, they had a long tradition as the country's ruling party. There was a good prospect that they would win the upcoming election. The polls gave the NDP the traditional 15 percent of the vote which had given them 43 seats in Parliament. In the previous election the Reform Party had a low standing in the polls. It had a substantial 'grass roots' support, but none of the tradition, machinery and financial resources of the other, long-established parties.

I decided to enter the nomination race in spite of the seemingly poor odds of winning the election because I wanted to experience the political process first hand. The experience would allow me to become a better teacher and analyst in my role as a professor of economics. A win, which I thought was a very remote possibility, would simply be a bonus.

SFU obviously agreed that faculty involvement in party politics on balance had positive effects. It had a policy passed when Pauline Jewett was the President of the University. She had previously been a Member of Parliament for the NDP and informally remained one of the leaders of the party. She was widely expected to run for election again. Under the policy, a professor could take unpaid leave from the university during a campaign and while serving in Parliament for one term. I took advantage of this policy. If I had been elected for a second time, my tenure would have been terminated. As it happens, this policy did not become relevant for me.

The legacy of Doug Collins

In 1987 the members of my riding association had nominated Doug

Chapter 7

Collins, a successful broadcaster and columnist in his seventies who had migrated to Canada from Britain as a decorated war veteran. Collins holds strong views about the death penalty, Quebec politics, immigration and multiculturalism, the Holocaust, feminism and several other political hot buttons. He expresses his opinions with an acid tongue and in total disregard of political correctness. The Left despises and haunts Doug Collins and the *North Shore News,* a community newspaper which published his columns until his retirement at age 78. In 1997 he was hauled before the B.C. Human Rights Commission in response to a complaint by the Jewish Congress that the views he had expressed were violating the rights of Jewish people. He was found not guilty.

After Collins had been nominated, the national media launched a campaign linking the Reform Party to the politically incorrect views attributed to him. The ultimate goal of this campaign was to make the Reform Party appear to be a party of bigots, racists and extremists. It was not possible to achieve this goal by focussing on issues and published policy statements of the Reform Party. When the media tried to do so, they found out quickly that most people in B.C. agreed with the official party platform for reduced spending, a balanced budget and more democracy in Parliament. So the media chose instead to suggest that the Reform platform favoured policies recommended by the likes of Collins. Little did I know at the time that this media strategy was going to give me a lot of trouble during the election campaign.

In 1988 Preston Manning and the Party leadership decided that they could not let Collins' candidacy give the media the lever for their smear campaign. The strategy was for Manning to give Collins an ultimatum: "Promise to tone down the rhetoric on politically incorrect issues or I will not sign your papers that allow you to run as the Reform candidate." I do not know whether Manning expected that Collins would refuse to be bound by such a document or whether he thought that he could in fact make him become less outspoken. At any rate, Collins resigned his candidacy and a short time later party members nominated Neil Thompson in his place.

It is interesting to note as a comment on the nature of the Reform Party that after the Collins affair, grass roots members changed the party constitution. This change gave the ultimate authority to sign candidates' papers to the party's Executive Council, a body elected by members at large. They were concerned that the leader had too much power to over rule the membership at the local level.

In my frequent contacts with the people of Capilano Howe Sound I found that Collins' willingness to talk about politically incorrect issues appealed to a large number of them. They believed that since the Trudeau years in the 1970s the government has been passing legislation that was changing the very nature of Canadian society. In particular, they were upset about the rapid increase in immigration from non-European countries, pandering to Quebec, the Charter of Rights favouring the interests of criminals over those of victims, abolition of the death penalty and the more extreme agendas of the feminist, Native and other 'rights' lobbies. They believed that these policies were imposed on them by Eastern political élites without consultation and certainly without their consent. They were frustrated by the media-imposed code of political correctness which prevented public discussions of the merit of these policies. They liked Collins because he said and wrote what they thought was needed to be discussed publicly.

In my view, most of the people who supported Collins are not bigots, racists or extremists. They are genuine conservatives who believe that policies and traditions developed and tested over many generations have intrinsic merit, policies which should not be abandoned lightly and without adequate debate. They are proud of their European heritage and wish to protect it. They believe in individual responsibility. They believe that the welfare state has become too generous, that it has turned a safety net into a hammock.

The Riding Association and other candidates

As the 1993 election approached, the wounds caused by Collins' resignation healed and only few Reformers told me that they could never forgive Manning for the way he gave in to the media's demands for Collins' head. The riding association, headed by Brice MacDougall, had a large membership base. A short, intense and dedicated man, MacDougall retired as a partner from a major accounting firm in Vancouver. He is in many ways the quintessential 'back room politician.' He had previously been involved in the running of the Socred and PC party bureaucracies, fundraising and election campaigns. His accounting and auditing background assures that any task he takes on is done with diligence and according to the rules.

MacDougall led a delegation of members of the riding association to interview me, according to Party regulations. I was declared acceptable and declared my candidacy in April 1992. At the time there was one other declared candidate, Neil Thompson. He is a retired, intense man with a cherubic face, who speaks with animation but, in spite of having run for Reform in 1988, did not present his arguments well enough to large audiences. The contents of his speeches concerned much the same issues treated by Collins in his columns. Knowing much about the history of Quebec and its relationship with Canada, he tended to conclude with calls for a re-balancing of the federation, with more benefits going to the West and fewer to Quebec.

I fervently wished that the constituency association would immediately meet and endorse either Thompson or me. A loss would allow me to return to academia without further involvement; a win would allow me to start planning for the election campaign. Unfortunately, we both were left in limbo until mid-November. The reason for the delay was that party policies required nominations to be contested by as many people as possible. MacDougall took this rule seriously and also believed that a good fight among a large number of candidates would generate interest in the Party and help in the federal election.

After much effort, MacDougall and the constituency association persuaded two other persons to seek the nomination. One was Eric Cant, a lawyer and accountant, who had retired following a successful career. During meetings arranged to introduce candidates to the Party members, he did not perform well. His delivery was uninspired and his speech did not connect with the mood of the audience. He left the impression that he really did not want to be the candidate.

The second person to enter the nominations race relatively late was Margo Furk. An elegant, tall, slim and intense single mother of two daughters, she had much political experience in local government, which revealed itself in her excellent stage presence. Her talks were to the point and showed an excellent grasp of the important issues of the day. She had many friends in the community who helped her campaign. However, her previous work on the School Board had also created her some enemies.

The nomination campaign

Several meetings were held to expose the nomination candidates to Reform Party members at different locations in the very large riding. It takes over an hour to drive from West Vancouver to Squamish, another 40 minutes to reach Whistler, while Pemberton was another half hour beyond. Except in West Vancouver, the audiences were small and media interest was minimal. In Pemberton, the local farmers and ranchers made up in interest and enthusiasm what they lacked in numbers.

I found these nomination meetings a good training ground for the all candidates' meetings during the election campaign. Peter Wearing and two other former students rented a video camera to get a record of my performance at the Whistler meeting.

Trying to keep the interest of large classes of teenage students had been a good training ground for me. I especially had learned to read audiences and react to disinterest quickly by changing topics and the delivery. It was obvious that except for Furk, the other candidates did not have an equivalent background.

During the nomination campaign I also had to raise some funds for what turned out to be relatively minor expenses. This was done mainly through meetings with constituents at coffee parties. I found the audiences friendly and ready to embrace the principles of Reform. But I was not good at 'closing the deal' and asking for money. Fortunately, Wearing had no such troubles and we collected enough money to cover expenses.

Getting Nominated for the Reform Party
The nomination meeting

The Reform Party nomination meeting took place on November 17, 1992 in a large auditorium at the West Vancouver High School, from which my daughter had graduated in 1983. The 400-seat auditorium was filled to capacity. Another 150 to 200 people listened to the proceedings in the hallway leading to the auditorium. Some representatives of the print media were there but none from the electronic media. I am sure that the other parties had sent observers. I knew several Party members who had come all the way from Squamish, Whistler and Pemberton. This meeting was a major event in the community.

The air was filled with electricity. All the candidates had tried to get their supporters out to the meeting and nervously circulated among them. The betting was that either Furk or I would win the required 50 percent majority on the second or third ballot, unless Thompson or Cant would deliver barn-burner speeches.

Lots had determined the order of speaking and I was third. A referee had been appointed to enforce the time limit of 10 minutes on speeches, with two minutes on the introduction of each speaker. It was quite a formal setup, as a yellow light went on one minute before the time limit was reached and the microphone was turned off when it had run out.

Thompson and Cant performed reasonably well. Furk did an outstanding job and clearly was a better candidate than the other two.

When my turn came I was introduced by Peter Stursberg. Among West Vancouver seniors Stursberg is a celebrity. They still remember his distinctive voice that used to come over the radio during the war, when he was a CBC correspondent in Europe. Stursberg took some interest in my campaign and to my delight agreed to introduce me. He did a superb professional job.

During the nomination campaign I often started my talk with a little humour. "Canada's fiscal crisis is much like a fire on a ship about to sink. Imagine how the traditional parties' leaders would react to such a fire. Jean Charest, the leader of the PCs would say 'No need to be concerned. Our technical experts have taken all measures required to bring the fire under control.' Audrey McLaughlin of the NDP would say, 'What fire?' Jean Chretien of the Liberals would say, 'Elect me quickly, I will use lots of loonies to smother the fire.' Only Preston Manning would say 'There is a serious fire threatening to sink this ship. All people to the pumping stations.'"

Strict time constraints did not permit me to use this introduction. Instead, I delivered the following speech.

Address to Reform Party members of the Capilano Howe Sound Constituency Association on the occasion of the election of a candidate for the 1993 federal election.

Chapter 7

"Fellow Reformers:

"You and I are all here today because we are concerned about the troubles faced by Canada as a result of the policies of the traditional federal parties; the mounting debt and intractable deficits; the persistently high unemployment rates; the levels of taxation that punish those who work hard, invest and take risks; the proliferation of spending programs that discourage effort and create dependency; the threat to our health care system which cannot survive without proper incentives for patients, doctors and hospitals; the octopus of regulations and subsidies which strangle our economy and rob us of our personal freedoms; the flood of bogus refugees that burden our budgets and school systems; the unfair shifting of government offices and civil service employment to Quebec; the arrogance of the élite that designed a flawed constitution and then tried to buy our 'yes' votes with our own money. I am sure that you could easily come up with many additions to this list of grievances. However, there is one general one, which deserves special mention. We are disgusted with the traditional parties' failure to deliver on their election promises, with the ways in which they disregard our views as citizens and instead cater to special interest groups to gather votes.

"I will not be such a politician! — and I am convinced that Preston Manning and the Reform Party also are different. I have no difficulties accepting and defending practically the entire Reform Party policy positions and recommendations. In particular, regardless of the outcome of the plebiscite on the Charlottetown Accord, I will fight for policies which will make our system more democratic: a genuinely triple E senate to assure the protection of the resource-rich provinces from exploitation by the majority in Ontario and Quebec; public referenda on major policy initiatives, including the opportunity for the public to initiate referenda; public recall for sitting legislators whose voting in parliament contradicts their election promises; the commitment of elected representatives to canvass the views of their constituents and to vote according to them.

"However, it is well known that elected representatives cannot canvas their constituencies on all issues. Nor is it clear that you want to be asked your views on every issue and vote that comes up in parliament.

"For this reason it is important that you know more about me, so that you can trust me to make the right decisions when your advice cannot be obtained. In this spirit, let me face head-on a question that appears to arise in many peoples' minds. Why does Grubel want to become a politician? The reason is definitely not that I am running away from my present job. I am a tenured professor at Simon Fraser University. There are great rewards in helping to shape the minds and values of Canada's young, who will be the leaders of tomorrow. I am happy to have learned from some of you here that your sons and daughters have learned a lot in my classes. I also much enjoy writing and publishing, which is an integral part of the work of a professor. My services as an economist and teacher are demanded

Getting Nominated for the Reform Party

widely. I have the honour of being a member of Preston Manning's official group of economic advisers. The financial rewards of an MP, together with the extra costs of maintaining an apartment in Ottawa, will mean a reduction in my income.

"So, why do I want to become a politician and go to Ottawa? The answer lies in my personal background and values. Some of these you can discover through my publications in the library and newspapers. But you should also know that I was born and raised in the home of a small shop keeper in Germany. Much like Mrs. Thatcher's, this background and work in the store at a young age has shaped my most fundamental attitudes towards work, honesty and respect for other people.

"A German high school and management training in Frankfurt taught me valuable business skills of a different type. My university education started at age 22 when I worked my way through Rutgers University in New Jersey, playing varsity soccer and meeting all of my financial needs through part time and summer work. As a result of my poor English I started on the night crew cleaning the floors of the university cafeteria. It did not take me long to become a cashier and supervisor.

"My formal training as an economist was at Yale University, but my true education came with a teaching position at the University of Chicago, where I had the opportunity to become a friend of Milton Friedman with whom I have played tennis and whom I have guided down Harmony Bowl runs at Whistler. There is nothing I like better than being called the Milton Friedman of British Columbia.

"I gained more understanding of business through teaching at the Wharton School in Philadelphia. A job with the government in a research position at the U.S. Treasury taught me unforgettable lessons about the working of bureaucracies. After living four years in Philadelphia I had no trouble understanding the joke that the first prize in a contest was 1 week and the second prize three weeks in Philadelphia. This is why in 1971 I came to SFU, Vancouver and Canada.

"But I did not just flee Philadelphia. I could have found work in many other places of the world. I chose this country and province because I like the environment, the mosaic of people from around the world and how under the free market system and personal freedom, they have been blending into a successful society that built the great city of Vancouver and world class ski resort of Whistler out of a rain forest at the edge of civilization. It is out of my love for this great country that I have decided to join the Reform Party and enter politics and fight for the preservation of the freedoms and market economies which are threatened by the traditional politics and politicians.

"During my 30 years as an academic my world view has also been influenced greatly by stints of teaching and research in Canberra, Oxford, Nairobi, Cape Town, Singapore, Berlin and others. These experiences have made me truly a citizen of the world, proudly Canadian.

Chapter 7

"In Vancouver, my and my family's life has been focussed on SFU, tennis at the Hollyburn Country Club and skiing at Whistler. My association with the Fraser Institute as a member of the Board of Editors and a frequent contributor to its publications is an important source of pride for me. I have put many needles into the sides of left wing politicians with my studies of marketing boards, unemployment insurance, cross-border shopping and many others.

"You can readily see that with this background I have no trouble embracing the political and social philosophy of Preston Manning and the Reform Party. I am sure that you can also understand that I feel the need to repay some of the debt I owe to the society which has allowed me to enjoy such a rich and rewarding life.

"I want to serve you as your representative in Ottawa. I want to become involved in shaping government policies, to bring to parliamentary debates and votes the principles of the Reform Party, my economist skills and knowledge and, importantly, my basic values, which I am sure are the same as yours.

"I hope that you will find me worthy of your support. With your help I will carry the Reform Party banner into the next election. I will fight to the best of my ability for victory over the old style politicians and, once in Ottawa, for a Canada in which we will be proud to see our children grow up and have a happy and successful life."

West Vancouver, November 17, 1992.

My speech was interrupted frequently by applause from the audience. They liked it and my candidacy. The first ballot gave me a clear majority of the votes cast. Furk came in second with about 25 percent of the total. The other two candidates split the rest among them.

It took some time to sink in what had happened that fateful evening. I had become the candidate for the Reform Party in the election expected within the coming year. I would have to fight an election campaign, talk to hundreds, raise money and deal with the media. I had the new challenge I had been looking for.

CHAPTER 8

The Election Campaign

AFTER officially becoming a Reform candidate in November 1992, preparations for the federal election campaign began slowly. Peter Wearing and I had worked well together during my nomination campaign and I was impressed by his skills and great ability to get along with people. I was very pleased when he agreed to continue working with me to serve as my campaign manager. He knew from experience exactly what had to be done to fight an election.

Assembling an election team

Wearing designed a detailed plan for the many things that had to be accomplished. He worked closely with the directors of the Constituency Association, assembling a team of leaders responsible for fund raising, poll organization, telephone services, publicity, the distribution of campaign literature and other important tasks.

Most members of the election team were experienced campaigners. Some had worked in provincial elections for the Socreds, others had worked for the federal PCs. Some had helped Neil Thompson when he had been the Reform candidate in the preceding federal election. All these campaign leaders were driven by their desire to bring about changes in federal policies. Some were 'political junkies' who like the excitement and camaraderie of an election campaign. I was extremely lucky because all the campaign leaders were highly educated, had much managerial experience and were dedicated to Reform. I mention a few of them here to express my appreciation for their contributions and to illustrate how well qualified they were. The aforementioned Brice MacDougall remained as constituency association president. David Dyke had had a similar career to MacDougall's, in the accounting profession. Dr. Philip Alderman and Dr. Ron McAdam were physicians; Deana Peitsch was a PR expert; Al MacDonald was a retired executive; Peter Stursberg had been a top CBC journalist; Bent Oxtholm had been a fighter pilot and colonel in the Air Force; Darrell Frith managed his own investment company; Ron and Isabel Banner of Squamish ran their own transportation business; and Nancy Greene of Whistler had been, as someone described her, 'Canada's darling' as a champion skier. Some women, like Hazel MacDonald and Diana Ball, put to work the managerial skills they had developed as mothers.

The work done

There was much to do even before the election was called. Poll organi-

Chapter 8

zations had to be set up and staffed. Their job was to contact voters by telephone and through material delivered to residences. A campaign office had to be found, furnished and equipped with communications facilities. Financial contributions had to be solicited and administered. Donors needed to be thanked and given tax receipts. Signs and campaign literature had to be designed and ordered. An ever-active line of communication with Party headquarters in Calgary had to be monitored and often required the passing on of information and many types of action. I needed to be exposed to the media and the general public through all candidates' meetings with service organizations in different locations, coffee parties and appearances at community events.

All this work went smoothly. Within a few days of the writ being dropped in mid-September 1993, campaign signs sprouted from lawns in the riding like flowers in spring. The media noted this fact and read it correctly as a sign that Reform was well organized and had much grassroots support. Immediately we had that intangible but important element of momentum. Volunteers, the foot soldiers in election campaigns, came forward in large numbers. The previous organizational work paid off handsomely as they were put to effective work immediately.

Financial support was coming in slowly but steadily even before the election call. Contributions accelerated thereafter and were sufficient to allow spending up to the legal limit of about $55,000 and permit significant contributions to the national campaign.

During the campaign it finally became possible to pay Peter Wearing a small salary, which he deserved for the full-time job he was doing. Over 90 percent of the contributions came in as small donations from private individuals. The biggest financial donors to the traditional parties, the banks, corporations and unions, largely ignored Reform.

I was spared the task of asking for money. After meetings at which I had spoken Peter Wearing, Bent Oxtholm and others did the job for me. I also never saw the list of contributors. This practice is designed to assure that there is not the slightest impression of influence-peddling. Reform candidates were asked to be sure to adhere to this policy.

MacDougall, in his capacity as the president of the constituency association, firmly insisted that no money could be committed to any project unless it was in the bank. In this he followed directions from the Reform head office in Calgary. The policy was designed to make sure that the party would not end the campaign with any debt. Reform was going to be different from other parties in the management of its own finances as well as those of the nation. I supported this policy, though in practice it caused problems.

Some spending projects needed a lengthy lead time, like the printing of signs and pamphlets, and during a campaign time is of the essence. As a result, the timing of some campaign initiatives was off schedule.

The Election Campaign
Candidate responsibilities

My own job as the candidate started slowly after the nomination in late 1992. I still had to teach a course at SFU in the spring of 1993 and had to attend and give papers at conferences in Italy, Germany and California. A major job involved the completion of a very long questionnaire about my background. All candidates had to complete such a questionnaire and obtain a criminal record check from the RCMP so that people with unsuitable backgrounds and records could be prevented from officially becoming candidates for the Reform Party.

Unfortunately for Reform, background checks for candidates did not work perfectly. In Ontario one person became an official candidate even though he had a history of association with groups advancing ideas of white racist supremacy. The candidate was very personable and articulate in meetings with a search committee; as a result, he was endorsed. The questionnaire made him look acceptable. As a result, Manning signed his papers and he became officially a Reform candidate.

In the middle of the election campaign the media obtained an inflammatory and politically incorrect pamphlet authored several years previously by this same candidate. The uproar that followed did much to feed the effort of the traditional parties to brand Reform racist and extremist. Some observers believe that this episode reduced the Reform vote in some ridings where the vote was very close. It therefore probably prevented the election of several more Reformers in Ontario whose victories would have given Reform the status of official opposition in the House of Commons.

There were several candidate briefing sessions in Calgary and Vancouver. They were time consuming and I did not learn anything that Peter Wearing had not taught me before about the mechanics and organizational challenges of an election campaign. However, the meetings were useful in getting to know fellow candidates and sharing their enthusiasm and excitement. Just before the election, one candidates' meeting was held in Ottawa. It was an inspiring affair. On the last day we gathered on Parliament Hill and listened to Manning's stories about previous reformers who had come to Ottawa and brought important changes to the political system of their times. Then we visited the House of Commons and were encouraged to select the seat we would occupy after the next election.

One of the meetings of candidates in Calgary devoted considerable time to the discussion of the election platform. The economic policies had been worked out in some detail by a team under the leadership of Stephen Harper and the direction of Manning and Cliff Fryers, the Reform Party chairman. Harper has a strong background in economics and was studying for a PhD when he entered politics a few years earlier. He was ably assisted by Dimitri Pantazopoulos, a young economist who, after the election, worked in the Reform Party research department for a year or so before leaving for greener pastures in Washington, D.C. The fiscal plans

Chapter 8

had obviously been given much thought and I found little to disagree with. However, the meeting left me with the feeling that I was an outsider who was being asked to endorse policies rather than work on their design. Little did I know at the time that this pattern would not be much different after I had been elected and taken on the position of finance critic in the shadow cabinet.

Campaigning

The campaign began in earnest in the middle of September after the writ had been dropped and the previous parliament had been dissolved. I had taken a leave of absence without pay from SFU for the fall semester and devoted myself full time to campaigning. Basically I stayed away from the day to day operation of the campaign. Wearing and his team appeared to be in complete control and I did not consider it wise to interfere. I basically did what I was told to do, namely things only the candidate could do. The main job was to meet as many potential voters as possible, to get out information about the Reform platform and to deal with the media. Not all candidates believed in as much delegation of responsibility as I did, but the strategy worked well for me.

There were numerous coffee parties in private homes where Reform supporters invited neighbours and friends. These meetings went very well. The setting was pleasant and the audiences of five to 25 people were interested in my ideas for fiscal policies and I learned a lot from listening to their concerns. I attended rallies organized by Reform and circulated at local festivals; I addressed public service clubs and spoke at local schools. There were media interviews and appearances on talk shows.

I was in my element, talking about economic policy and fielding questions on the subject. At the same time, I was uncomfortable introducing myself to strangers and making political small talk. I soon learned that it was necessary to have simple positions on complex issues. All my life had been dedicated to the careful analysis of such issues, trying to understand all the pros and cons. I found it difficult to change during the campaign and later in Parliament. I admire those who can simplify, politicize and communicate effectively without violating the truth and denying complexity.

Some of the events during the campaign represented an implicit endorsement of me and my Party by influential members of the community. In West Vancouver 'Budge' Bell-Irving, a former B.C. Lieutenant Governor, organized a well attended reception. Nancy Greene hosted an open house at Whistler on a weekend from noon until the evening. Many more people than showed up probably read in paid local advertisements about the event and Nancy's support.

As an academic I had been sheltered from the general public all my life. But in my new role I was very interested in and learned a lot from making contacts with many Canadians from all walks of life. Perhaps my experience was conditioned by a process of self selection, but I encountered very few people who disagreed with my analysis of Canada's fiscal problems and the need to take strong action to save the country from bankruptcy. If anything, campaigning strengthened the views that I held already and I acquired a large stock of real world examples of fiscal mismanagement and economic disincentives. I also learned much about the way in which the general public thinks about fiscal issues, helping me make my case more effectively. The audiences often brought up other topics important in their own minds, forcing me to keep a healthy perspective on fiscal issues.

Door-knocking and a campaign video

During the briefings of Reform candidates, we were urged to do as much door to door campaigning as possible. I followed these instructions for a while but found the work frustrating and inefficient. At least half of the time I rang a door bell, there was no answer. Yet at least a minute was wasted waiting for someone to respond. When a door was opened, at least half of the time the person responded politely but with body language suggesting annoyance at being disturbed. I felt guilty whenever the door was opened by a mother with a baby in her arms, trying to block the door for other children and a snarling dog trying to get out. There was little communication with such constituents. The exchange of greetings was perfunctory and I doubt that it produced many new voters for Reform.

Most of the other half of the people who opened the door were Reform sympathizers. It was pleasant enough to shake hands and introduce myself, but I did not feel that this gained many new voters either, since they were already on Reform's side. When I asked them what they wanted me to fix once I got to Ottawa, nothing new came to light, though presumably the question itself showed my interest in their opinions. The rest of those coming to the door were strong partisan supporters of traditional parties. Some were angry ideologues of the Left, spouting standard distortions of facts found in NDP platforms. I could not help myself and often wasted a lot of time arguing over the proposition that Canada did not have a fiscal problem, that higher taxes on the rich and business and more government control over the Bank of Canada and interest rates were the only changes needed to eliminate the deficit.

Later in Ottawa I discussed my experience with door knocking with caucus colleagues. I learned that I probably should have had an advance team of helpers get people to the doors and limit myself to brief greetings and handshakes. But I have doubts that such brief contacts mean much to the kind of sophisticated people who live in my riding.

Ted White, the Reform candidate for the adjoining riding of North Vancouver, shared my doubts about the efficacy of door knocking during election campaigns. We talked about our experiences and decided that we

Chapter 8

would use videos as an alternative method of introducing ourselves and the Reform platform to constituents.

We each wrote scripts for a seven minute video recording and for joint use found a team of professional filmmakers with access to editing facilities. Within three weeks White and I had several thousand copies of the new campaign instrument at the cost of about $2.50 per tape. The script required me to talk about my professional and personal background against clips of myself lecturing at SFU, talking to students, jogging in a familiar public park and shopping with my wife. The main part of the video presented Reform platform highlights with shots of campaign literature and graphics interspersed with pictures of me talking. The tape ended with an appeal for votes and help.

Flag-waving, rousing music and similar props used in professional advertising were omitted. We tried to strike a good balance between a professional appearance and the message that this video was done by the candidate of an upstart, financially-strapped new party.

The video turned out well. How well I learned when in 1995 someone told me it had been shown to provincial Conservative Party candidates in the Ontario election campaign in an effort to persuade them to produce videos of their own. Most of them did, and according to some Members of the Ontario Legislative Assembly I have met, they attributed much of their success to the use of this campaign tool. Ted White has reported similar assessments of the value of video tapes from as far away as New Zealand. In that country Ian Revell, a Member of Parliament used videos while the rest of his party's candidates did not. Revell significantly increased his majority while his party as a whole lost support.

The video also was a success because it was popular with campaign workers. Most had found it difficult to knock on doors, talk about Reform and hand out campaign literature. It is a job which requires much self-confidence and psychic energy. In comparison, the distribution of the tapes was much easier. Campaign volunteers only had to put into mailboxes or hang on door knobs a transparent bag containing the tape and some other printed material. Instructions were included to leave the tapes in the mailbox for pickup a few days later or to bring them to the campaign office.

A significant proportion of tapes were not returned. It is not difficult to envision what a strong supporter of another party was likely to do with the tape. But a large proportion of the tapes were recovered and distributed to other addresses. Some tapes were returned with the enclosure of financial contributions to the campaign. On the day of the election practically all 5,000 tapes were in the homes of constituents.

I personally had a number of encouraging remarks from individuals who had found the tape interesting and informative. On one occasion I knocked on a door to ask for the return of the tape when the resident asked whether he might keep it for another week since he was having a party to show it to some people from other ridings! Ted White felt so positive about the use of a video in campaigning that in the 1997 election he again used one.

All-candidates' meetings and the 'racist' label

The best-attended campaign meetings were arranged by Chambers of Commerce, churches or similar organizations at which all candidates were present. Unfortunately because of the large number of representatives of minor parties like the Libertarians, the Greens and the Natural Law Party, all of us had very little time to develop positions or engage in debate. It was quite obvious that at such meetings most people in the audience consisted of strongly partisan supporters of individual candidates. Only a relatively small number of uncommitted voters was present to learn about the candidates and party platforms.

Some of these meetings were telecast by the local community cable stations. As a result they were probably seen by many more people than were in the audience. At some of the all-candidates meetings the local print media attended and publicized positions taken by individual candidates.

One all-candidates meeting in North Vancouver early in the campaign took place in a small room and was crowded with partisans from other parties and very few Reformers. It was going to lead for me to one of the most difficult experiences of my life and one that would shape the rest of my campaign.

The subject was immigration. All candidates discussed it within the prevailing spirit of political correctness of the day. Immigration is good economically and the multicultural society that defines Canada and so on. The more immigrants, the better. I took a different line on the economics of immigration, based on empirical evidence on the performance of immigrants which I had learned from academic papers and seminars: historically, immigrants (on average) have earned higher incomes, paid more taxes and made fewer claims on social services than did the average Canadian-born population of the same age. However, during the last 20 years the margin of better performance of immigrants has been shrinking and, if trends continue, will, before too long, reverse.

The explanation of this development is found in changes in the selection of immigrants. Until the 1970s Canada admitted only people who met tough standards for education, training, health, age and language abilities. In the 1970s the number of these so called 'economic' immigrants decreased as a proportion of the total and became less than one half in the early 1990s. This development was caused by new laws which facilitated the entry of refugees and permitted people to be admitted only if they joined relatives already in Canada. These 'self-selected' immigrants almost by definition did not have the same personal characteristics as

Chapter 8

those admitted historically as economic immigrants. They tended to be older and less healthy and have less education, training and language ability. I argued that the government should examine the merit of the policies which encouraged the growth in the number of the self-selected immigrants.

I had only two two-minute segments to summarize this information, which I had written and lectured about many times before. So I am certain that Pete McMartin, the PC candidate for North Vancouver, was wrong when he immediately attacked me for having asserted that all immigrants to Canada were a burden on society. He issued a press release to this effect, branding me a racist. A government-financed Centre to Fight Racism followed with a nationally circulated press release with the same message. The media picked up the refrain and soon innumerable reports linked me, racism and Reform. Unfortunately, there were no video or voice recordings of what I had said and so it was my word against that of McMartin and representatives of immigrant groups in the audience. I tried to fight the racist label by asking journalists to read the articles and books I had written on immigration, including a contribution to the *International Encyclopedia of Education*. I gave the names of a dozen PhD students from developing countries who asked me to supervise their doctoral work, hardly something they would have done if I were a racist. None of this helped and instead seemed to produce more vicious attacks.

I had no previous experience with the media and politics but soon learned how stories grow from a remark into a national media storm. After the first report of my alleged remark, for days journalists elicited comments from individuals and groups with an interest in either immigration or the defeat of the Reform Party. The size of my alleged transgression magnified as the comments elicited more stories and distorted my remarks even further. On October 15, 1998 the front page of *The Vancouver Sun* carried a story with the headline 'Anti-racist group targets two Reform candidates.' The story reported that Alan Dutton, the secretary of the B.C. Organization to Fight Racism, had demanded Preston Manning dump me as a candidate for my allegedly racist views on immigration.

None of this media uproar would have bothered me as an academic. The people important to me in that position knew my writings and had attended my classes. They knew my true position. In my new role as a candidate for a seat in parliament my main concern was the potential damage to the Reform cause I might have caused. I suffered from anxiety and many sleepless nights. It did not help that no one from the Party called to reassure me or advise me on how do handle the affair. Reform and Manning did not have the resources for such consultations which are routine with established parties.

A large number of constituents thanked me for raising the issue of immigration which had been prohibited in previous elections under the unwritten code of political correctness. In retrospect it is ironic that in fact many people in Canada supported Reform precisely because I and other candidates raised issues silenced by this code and enforced by the media. The media campaign of vilification of my alleged remarks and the implicit racism may well have helped me and Reform to the unprecedented election success in 1993.

Opposition candidates

The PC candidate in Capilano-Howe Sound was Mary Collins. She had been elected twice and had been the Minister of Health. Mary was a real lady during the campaign. She was partisan in her remarks but refrained from personal attacks.

Political scientists claim that about 70 percent of votes received by a candidate are due to the popularity of the party's leader and platform. While Kim Campbell, the Prime Minister and leader of the PCs entered the campaign with a high level of public support, her popularity soon dropped precipitously as the campaign progressed. In my riding Collins' support fell along with that of Campbell and the PC Party. In public meetings Collins exhibited less and less enthusiasm and fighting spirit as the campaign progressed. I suppose the polls had told her she had no chance of winning.

I had one confrontation with Collins. In one of my speeches, reported in the media, I had asserted that she had voted against the death penalty in spite of surveys showing strong support for it among her constituents. She had in fact voted for the death penalty. She asked me to apologize for this misrepresentation of her voting record. With some embarrassment, I promptly did so.

The Liberal candidate was Audrey Sojonkey. She was a woman in her fifties with no previous experience in federal or provincial politics but a good record of service with charities. Her husband was known as an important fundraiser for the Liberals and probably had lots of experience in political matters that he shared with her. She was sincere and the well-financed Liberal campaign machine kept her well briefed. She was fair and to the point in debate. She worked hard. Her campaign organization produced a good number of lawn signs and volunteers. But she had an uphill fight, since the Liberals had not been popular in Capilano-Howe Sound for a long time.

The NDP, Greens, Libertarians and Natural Law Party fielded candidates who used up a lot of time in all-candidates meetings that could have been better used for debate among candidates of the major parties. These candidates were obviously sincere, but their presentations and answers to questions tended to be emotional rather than well-reasoned and factually correct.

There was no personal animosity between me and any candidates from the other parties. It was as if we met periodically to do a job that was required of us, respecting each other and the opinions we held. However, some dirty politics did take place. At some of the all candidates' meetings constituents found on their chairs a list of quotes from academic publications of mine. They were out of context and obviously designed to suggest that I was an extremist.

One of the quotes was something like 'Government support for single mothers has produced more single mothers and more children than would exist otherwise.' This quote was from a paper in which I had discussed the moral hazard effect of social insurance programs. The focus was on the way in which unemployment insurance had induced changes in behaviour and institutions which raised the unemployment rate. In the conclusion of the paper I had suggested that similar incentives for changed behaviour exist in the case of support for single mothers.

I never found out which party was responsible for the assembly and distribution of such quotes from my writings and remarks from speeches of other Reformers. I suspect the PCs and the NDP. As the party in power the PCs had large government resources for such projects. They also had a lot of money through donations from large business and from loans which in the end left them deeply in debt. The NDP has the support of many intellectuals with strong ideological commitments to the Left. They were the ones most likely to have read my publications and collected quotes that disturbed them.

Polling

Reform did not have the resources to commission local polls. As I learned later, having access to the results of such polls is not all positive. They produce emotional ups and downs. It takes great effort to keep down the elation coming from good news and retain an even keel when it is bad. We relied on published polls financed by others to get a sense on how we were doing.

One of the best polls was implicit in the UBC election stock market run by some professors in the Business School. Under this system one could buy bets on the election outcome with real money. It works as follows.

Assume the market price of Reform shares is 15 cents and will be paid to the holder of a share if the party wins 15 percent of all seats. Someone convinced that Reform would win 20 percent of the seats could buy shares at 15 cents. If that hunch was right and Reform actually won 20 seats in the election, this investor would have made a profit of five cents per share.

If enough others shared the view that Reform would get 20 percent of the vote, the price of the share would rise to this level. Therefore, at any time the share prices for the different parties represented the views of the public about the most likely outcome of the election. The market for the shares was deep enough so that no one group of people could help shape the outcome by buying shares to establish an inflated value for their favourite party. Moreover, such tactics were unlikely to receive enough publicity to create a significant band-wagon effect among voters.

As it turned out, the forecast of seats won by individual parties implicit in the UBC election stock market was more accurate than any other public poll. Of course, I did not know that this would be true until the election outcome was known. But my understanding of financial markets persuaded me to take seriously the prediction that Reform would do well at times when other polls were much less favourable. (Incidentally, I also made a whopping 20 percent on my $50 investment. Sometimes it pays to have strong convictions!)

Polls during election campaigns are best used for finding out public reactions to positions taken by a party, its leader and candidates. We obviously did not have the benefit of such information and largely focussed on issues and presented positions adopted by Reform Constituent Assemblies in preceding years. Unfortunately, however, most of the time the campaign issues and public debate were driven by the media.

Media harassment

The media have an important role to play in the political process and elections. Candidates and parties are apt to put forward positions and policies that make them appear in the best light. In doing so they tend to distort and hide facts. The media are there to dig out the truth and make sure that the public is well informed about candidates, parties and policy platforms. The media also force candidates to perform under pressure. As a result, the public gains important information about the personal strength and character of candidates. The media exposure of candidates' weaknesses resembles the actions of wolves circling a herd of animals. The wolves harass the entire herd but they are able to kill only the weak, assuring that only the strong and healthy survive and reproduce. The media assure that only the qualified enter public service as politicians.

However, it is impossible to know whether certain actions of journalists are designed to perform this socially useful function during elections or whether they are driven by other motives. Surveys have shown that most journalists support parties on the Left. The following personal experience is consistent with the view that in 1993 at least some of the media were motivated to damage the cause of the political right, as represented by me.

Frances Bula, a reporter from *The Vancouver Sun,* went to Simon Fraser University to find out about my background. She visited Professor John Chant, the chair of the department of economics. As he told me later, he started to tell her about my record of publications, ratings by students and service to the community, matters he was prepared to document. The reporter quickly cut him off and said: "Thank you, but this is not what I am after," and left.

Chapter 8

She eventually found someone in the Womens' Study program, and a well-known supporter of left-wing economic and social causes, Professor Marjorie Cohen of the Political Science Department, to go on record that they were afraid of my opposition to spending on special interest programs, especially (radical) feminists. Cohen was quoted as saying, "He out-right wings the right wing . . . He's outrageous in his anti-feminism and he's a dangerous man with his view on minorities." The headline in the October 15, 1993 edition of *The Vancouver Sun* on page 3 for the story written by Bula covered the width of the page: 'Candidate: objective economist or extreme right-winger?' Positive comments about me and my work by Wearing, a former student and my campaign manager and Mike Walker, executive director of the Fraser Institute, were summarized in one paragraph, while critical remarks took up 13 paragraphs.

One CBC reporter played a dirty trick on me. After an all-candidates meeting she asked me to stay on for a private interview. She posed some routine and easy questions. At the end I was moving away when she called me and said she had another question: "I know someone who was present when you denied the Holocaust. We have no other evidence on this but would like your reaction." The camera was there to record my every word and expression.

As I have learned since, the technique of posing difficult questions when a person has begun to relax is used widely for the purpose of using the surprise element to get at the truth. It also has its risks. Someone with a clear conscience might react in ways which might make him see guilty. I felt trapped. The dice was loaded against me. I have a German accent which gets worse under pressure. Previous media accusations of racism and extremism made the question seem reasonable. How should I react? Indignant, thoughtful, angry? What body language was appropriate? Should I just turn away with a shrug? Did it matter what I said? I answered truthfully. I knew that the Holocaust had taken place and never discussed the subject publicly.

That night my wife and I hardly slept. We cried in each others' arms and I regretted the day I had agreed to enter politics. We knew from recent experience how taped interviews could be edited to suit a media agenda. What would the next day's headlines be? Would they destroy Reform's election chances and the agenda for fiscal reform in which I believed so strongly? As it turned out, no such story was broadcast. I must have said the right thing with the right facial expression, body language and tone of voice to have appeared credible in my denial of the rumour.

Media bias?

The media influenced the election campaign not just by its focus on Reform and its candidates as racist and extreme, but by not reporting in depth on the general public dissatisfaction with the fiscal mismanage-

The Election Campaign

ment of past Liberal and PC governments. They dismissed the issue by taking the NDP line. There was no problem which could not be fixed by higher taxes and lower interest rates. It was easy to find people with this view and feature them in story after story. The media rarely lie or distort the truth. They just decide what the truth is and make sure the public gets a regular diet of it by airing the views of those who agree with their positions.

The media also failed to take seriously Western alienation over Quebec's special status in the federation. The implicit message was that the rednecks of Reform did not understand Canadian history and the need to keep Quebec in the federation through fiscal transfers and other special treatment. The Western alienation stemming from the National Energy Policy was brushed aside by media largely based in central Canada as an unreasonable complaint over a policy enacted long ago and serving the national, that is, central Canadian interest.

The media also ignored or vilified views on immigration held strongly by my constituents and a large majority of Western Canadians. These views were questioning the wisdom of Canada's policy of having 300,000 immigrants per year, a disproportionately large share of them settling in British Columbia. My constituents blamed them for high real estate prices, unemployment, high school taxes due to the cost of English as a Second Language courses, congested medical facilities, diminished membership and vitality of their places of worship and other bad effects on their lives. Rational discussion of these issues was prevented. Anyone expressing a view was attacked immediately as a racist; there was no scarcity of individuals and organizations willing to have such views appear in the media.

It was easy to make the link between immigration and racism since almost all of the recent immigrants to British Columbia had come from Asia and the Indian subcontinent. But this is not a legitimate link. The cost of immigration imposed on communities, in the short run, would exist whatever the national origin of the migrants. People have a right to discuss these costs without fear of being branded as racists. They were glad to be able to talk to me rationally about the costs and benefits of migration. I am sure many voters turned to Reform because the party was willing to break the code of political correctness. The media treatment of the subject only strengthened their determination.

However, I found it difficult to deal with the distorted media treatment of my position on immigration, which had been given much publicity by Pete McMartin and the B.C. Organization to Fight Racism. One evening my son called me from Toronto. He had just heard a rebroadcast of Peter Gzowski's radio program *Morningside*. During this interview Preston Manning had twice been asked why he was not firing that "well-known racist, Herb Grubel."

The media treatment was much the same with respect to another important topic, government policies towards Natives. Again, the issue was and remains important in many parts of British Columbia, including Capilano-Howe Sound. Native land claims, large transfer payments, privileges for Natives based on race and conditions on reserves are problems of great concern to my constituents. They want them to be discussed publicly, not hidden behind a veil of political correctness and stopped by the threat of the 'racist' label. My constituents were glad to be able to talk to me about the subject rationally. Again, I believe that the media treatment of the Native issues backed by the traditional parties drove many voters to Reform.

Finally, there was the issue of Medicare. Students of the subject know that the fundamental problems of all public health care systems are that individual users do not pay anything for an expensive and useful service and physicians who are paid on the basis of how many patients they see do not care about costs. The result of these perverse incentives is over-use and costs rising at an unsustainable rate. Every such public system in the world faces the need to ration the supply of the free service. In Canada this takes increasingly place through rationing and waiting lists for services. This is one more subject for which the media have a code of politically correct topics, phrases and words which discourage genuine discussion of the basic problem and alternative solutions. Many of my constituents were pleased to talk to me about these Medicare problems, free from the superficial rhetoric about U.S.-type two tiers and the moral superiority of universality of access.

I cannot conclude my discussion of the role the media played in the election campaign without mentioning Trevor Lautens, a columnist for the *North Shore News* and *The Vancouver Sun*. He interviewed me for a couple of hours early in the campaign. All the while the tape recorder was running. We had a good conversation. He was interested enough in some of the ideas I had developed in academic publications to ask for copies of them. I think he actually read some of them! He did his homework, and for this I applaud him. He was consistently fair in his commentaries on the controversies and the racist label which had enveloped my campaign, and for this, again, I thank him.

To victory

On election night the Constituency Association had rented a large hotel room in North Vancouver for what we hoped would be a victory celebration. Some national TV crews had announced that they would be there and we interpreted this as a sign that they expected Reform to win.

My wife and I were too tired and emotionally drained to care very much about the outcome of the election. A return to teaching, the contemplative life of an academic and a continuation of our good family relations looked very attractive should I lose the vote. As is the tradition, I was asked by the campaign team to stay at home and watch the election returns on television.

The Election Campaign

Never before or since did the TV coverage of the election campaign mean so much to me. I was shocked by the decimation of the PC and NDP parties in the East, the gains of the Bloc Quebecois at the expense of the PCs and Liberals in Quebec. By the time the coverage had reached Ontario it was clear that the Canadian political scene was being shaken to its roots. The large Reform vote in the largest province was elating but, disappointingly, had produced only one Reform seat. The returns from the Prairie provinces suggested that my party might after all have a significant number of seats in the next Parliament.

Buoyed and optimistic by these results from the West, I watched with some trepidation as the results for Capilano Howe Sound were tabulated. The first numbers showed Sojonkey and the Liberals winning by a large margin but soon the picture changed. The early results had come from retirement and nursing homes and were not representative of the general population. About 90 minutes after the polls had closed, I was declared a winner by the network computers.

When I arrived at the hotel, I was greeted by a happy bunch of well-wishers. After all of the hardships of the campaign, the celebration was a great relief. It was fun giving a victory speech, thanking my team, the volunteers and the voters. It was not difficult to congratulate my opponents on their fine effort and thank them for the fairness of the campaign. I happily took congratulatory calls from Sojonkey, the Liberal and Collins, the PC candidate.

The celebrations went on much after my wife and I had left for home and a long night's sleep. It would take several days before the reality of what had happened sank in completely. In my riding Reform had received 19,259 votes, or 42 percent of the total. The Liberals were second with 31.8 percent, the PCs third with 17.7 percent and the NDP a distant fourth with 3.3 percent of the vote. Candidates from seven other parties gathered together 5.2 percent of the vote. (The election results are from Munroe Eagles et al.: *The Almanac of Canadian Politics,* 2nd edition, Oxford University Press, 1995, p.587.) We had won about 90 percent of all polls. Importantly, I was going to be a member of a 52 member Reform caucus in Ottawa.

Immediate tasks

The next week I closed my office at SFU. My books went to the library and interested students. The archives wanted my correspondence. It will be interesting to see the usefulness to future historians of letters stored only on electronic disks and in obsolete program languages! Graduate students under my supervision found other advisers. The University readily granted me a leave of absence without pay for the length of the Parliament. I would be able to return to my professorship at the end of the Parliamentary term, but not if I chose to win reelection.

Chapter 8

The House of Commons arranged promptly for the newly elected MPs to learn about their responsibilities and privileges. The Parliamentary pay of $64,400 per year started the day after the election. At the same time, I received an annual tax-free expense allowance of $21,300. The after-tax value of this pay package was just about the same as my salary at SFU. The main difference in my basic financial position were that I would have major additional expenses in my role as a politician. I would have to keep an apartment and vehicle in Ottawa. There would be extra costs for clothing, food and recreation. The university's regular contributions to my retirement plan ended. Those made by the House of Commons were worth nothing if I did not seek and win reelection for a second term.

It is interesting to note that the media were very interested in my change in financial circumstances, wanting to know precisely whether it had been improved or worsened. A couple of articles were written on the subject but the public reacted with a big yawn. I do not recall that the media in previous elections had engaged in the reporting of such issues. Why did they do it? The topic of pay for MPs was never raised in my campaign.

The House provided me with an access code to the government's long distance telephone network. It permitted free phone calls any time, anywhere. A budget of $180,000 was available for hiring assistants in Ottawa and in the riding, to pay rent and insurance for a constituency office and a host of other expenses. My wife and I could take 60 free flights a year within Canada. The telephone and travel privileges seemed like perks at first, but it soon became obvious that they were essential to the work that was expected of me.

Within a short time after the election I hired Lynda MacKay as my executive assistant. Lynda had been recommended to me by John Reynolds, who had been her first employer in Parliament when he was an MP in the 1970s. Since then Lynda had worked for several PC MPs. As a result, she had a large amount of experience and seemed to know everyone and every institution in the House. She also had important, long standing work relationships with many government departments.

I entrusted Lynda with the task of getting my offices operating in Ottawa and West Vancouver. She looked after my budget, hired staff and kept from me as much of the administrative work as possible. Many of my caucus colleagues chose to bring trusted campaign helpers and committed Reformers to run their Ottawa and constituency offices. They distrusted all people who previously had jobs with PC MPs.

Of course, there were no qualified people with experience as parliamentary assistants who had worked for Reform before. So the choice was either hiring an inexperienced person or someone with experience gained in the employ of another party but who gave the impression of having a good professional ethic which made party loyalty a non-issue. I never regretted the decision I made. Lynda was extremely competent and loyal. Her administrative and political experience were a useful and treasured

The Election Campaign

asset I used all the time. I am glad that John Reynolds, who won the 1997 election in my riding for Reform, has again hired Lynda, probably for her last job before retirement.

Lynda also took primary responsibility for responding to constituents. Requests for dealing with Customs, Revenue Canada, Immigration and other government departments on behalf of constituents were handled promptly and efficiently by Lynda in Ottawa and Anita in the West Vancouver office. In four years I never received a single complaint relating to this aspect of my staff's work. Lynda also answered all letters concerning current political issues. We had a standard letter for certain issues which reflected my views; she personalized them to fit special cases.

After the election in October and before the new Parliamentary session started in January, I had to make several trips to Ottawa for caucus meetings. We discussed mainly administrative matters and political strategy. Policy issues were far down the agenda and received very little attention. To my disappointment, this pattern would change little during the next 40 months.

CHAPTER 9

Caucus Life and Question Period

CAUCUS DISCIPLINE! Caucus solidarity! Caucus power! These slogans evoke an image of mystique and importance. In fact, the weekly meetings of the elected MPs in caucus were routine and accomplished little of real importance. They provided, much like Parliament itself, an opportunity for MPs to talk. But the topics discussed were limited and determined by an élite. The time individuals were allowed for their contributions to debate was normally very restricted, a minute or two, regardless of how important a topic was. Real power in Reform, as in all other parties, lay elsewhere.

Routines

Of course, when I attended the first meeting of the Reform caucus in January 1994 I had no idea what it was all about. My seat was on one long side of a huge open rectangle seating 52 members. The door to the caucus room was thickly padded to keep out sounds, and was watched by a uniformed guard on the staff of the House of Commons. His job was to keep out media and other interlopers. Access to the room was allowed only to MPs and a small coterie of personal staff, mainly from the leader's office. We often received requests from outsiders for the opportunity to address caucus on some cause or the other. This was never permitted.

The media were kept at a safe distance from the door to the caucus room. A rope in the middle of the corridor allowed us to pass by. As we did so in the morning and sometimes after closing at noon, the TV cameras and notebooks were out. Normally the journalists were interested only in talking to Preston Manning, Deborah Grey and a few others who were sure to give them good 15-second sound-bites. Occasionally they would stop someone who was involved in a controversy or they might ask a question of a commoner like me in the hope of getting me to say something controversial. The media knew from experience where the power was and real news was made.

The caucus room was physically imposing, large, with high ceilings accentuated by tall windows on two sides. The window-glass was dirty and went unwashed during my three years in there. From my seat on one side of the table I had the view of an embankment, on the top of which was a 19th century statue of Queen Victoria. Her expression never changed, even when the temperature was 40 below! From the other side of the table the view was of a courtyard that seemed full of blowing snow most of the time. Ottawa is the second coldest capital in the world.

On the first day in caucus and every meeting thereafter, I forced myself to remember the strategy I had designed for myself: speak only on financial and economic topics; pick your fights carefully and limit them to just a few issues. I knew the importance of having good relations with my colleagues, with whom I would have to live and work for approximately the next four years. I resolved that I would not irritate them by giving opinions and facts on every subject on which I had some expertise due to past research or other scholarly involvements.

Randy White, an outspoken, bright, highly experienced and ambitious colleague from the Fraser Valley at the end of the first year told me, without prompting: "Everyone had been expecting you to be a stuffed shirt with irrelevant academic opinions. Now they respect you and pay attention to what you have to say because you are likely to be a step ahead of everyone." White may have been giving his own opinion rather than that of many others, but he surely helped my self confidence that day.

Members and solidarity

On that first day in caucus, as I looked around the table at all the expectant faces, I wondered what my colleagues would be like. They had come from a wide range of backgrounds. Here are some basic statistics about them. (To put them into perspective I also provide data on the Liberals, a much more traditional party than Reform.)

There were six women in caucus, representing 13 percent of the total (women in the Liberal caucus were 20 percent). Eighty five percent of Reformers had a college or university education (Liberals 94 percent). Ten percent of Reformers were older than 60, and 14 percent younger than 40 (Liberals in these age groups were 13 and 12 percent, respectively.) However, there was a very significant difference in the occupations Reformers held before the election. Reform had only one lawyer (Diane Ablonczy) representing two percent of the caucus (in the Liberal caucus were 40 lawyers, representing 23 percent of the total). Other professions in Reform were: business 23 percent (Liberals 14 percent), medical professions six percent (Liberals two percent), farmers 19 percent (Liberals three percent) and professionals in real estate, accounting and economics six percent (Liberals four percent).

The quality of the caucus discussions was excellent almost all the time. Interventions tended to be short and to the point — a refreshing difference from academia! On almost every issue discussions improved my understanding and appreciation of significant complexities and ramifications of proposed policies. The wide range of backgrounds brought breadth to the deliberations. Many members had much contact with their constituents and spoke with obvious authority about public opinion in their ridings. On balance, there were few caucus decisions I disagreed with.

Every caucus meeting started with the singing of the national anthem. Preston Manning reported on his work and important events of the week.

Chapter 9

There were reports on media relations. The legislative agenda was presented and individuals responsible for the field made recommendations on how the caucus should vote. In the rare cases where principle was involved and some individuals could not go along with the majority, long and heated discussions took place. In the end, we agreed that caucus solidarity could be broken only if MPs had documented evidence — telephone or mail surveys — of a majority of their constituents opposing this position. However, on some issues, it was impossible to obtain such information in time. What to do under those circumstances was never resolved completely.

A few times I voted with the government and against caucus. It was never easy, since without caucus discipline on votes, the parliamentary system cannot function. Perhaps the Parliamentary system should be changed for one more like that used in the United States. However, this is difficult and controversial subject. In my view, reform of a system which has worked reasonably well should not be undertaken lightly. There is no perfect system of democratic government. In a widely-publicized case the Liberal John Nunziata voted against the budget. He was thrown out of his caucus and in the 1997 election had to run as an independent and against an official Liberal Party nominee. He sits as an independent in the 36th parliament. Reform never imposed any sanctions on members who did not vote with the caucus.

Perhaps we could afford this luxury because our votes mattered little in practice except as a record of where we stood. My own votes breaking caucus solidarity involved principles important to me but not important for most of my colleagues. For example, one time I voted against the ban on cigarette advertising and other restrictions on the tobacco industry. This government bill was supported by the majority of caucus. As much as I think that smoking is a deplorable habit, I deplore even more government's growing reduction of personal freedoms and private markets.

In my view, people should have the right to mistreat their bodies in any way they wish. The reduction in freedom cannot be justified on the grounds that smokers, through the free medicare system, cause unnecessary costs for society. This justification can easily be used in the future to prohibit the advertising of fat foods or participation in risky sports: all these activities are addictive. The justification also makes no economic sense. The early deaths of smokers save society large public pension payments, savings at least as large as the cost they impose on medicare.

As it turned out, caucus never took me to task for my vote. The media did not make anything out of it and I had only one enquiry from the general public asking me about my reasons for the stand I took.

In the case of the gun control legislation, the caucus principle on dissenting 'free' votes was applied with much more passion and watched carefully by the media. Caucus members who strongly opposed the legislation insisted that MPs in favour of the bill produce documented evidence that their constituents supported the legislation, prior to giving consent to this breach of caucus solidarity. In the end, Ian McClelland, Jim Silye and Ted White produced such evidence and voted with the government.

Caucus secrecy

Caucus secrecy was taken very seriously. Speaking to the media about proceedings was strictly prohibited. Cellular phones had to be turned off. House security guards regularly swept the room for listening devices. Whenever the door opened, all conversation stopped. Occasionally TV crews took background shots for some stories. To prevent TV cameras from taking pictures of documents, we were asked to put them all face down. Apparently at least on one occasion journalists had obtained embarrassing and confidential information from another party by taking pictures of documents left on desks.

The secrecy code cannot be enforced readily on people who talk to the media confidentially. We had some members who engaged in this activity as was obvious from media reports on caucus proceedings. These individuals were never caught. How the caucus media relationship works was brought home to me after the publication of the book *Double Vision: The Inside Story of the Liberals in Power,* written by Edward Greenspon and Anthony Wilson Smith. The authors tell about how David Dodge, the Deputy Minister of Finance, a noted economist and the top civil servant in the Department of Finance, one day tossed on the table in front of Paul Martin a copy of the standard Canadian income tax forms with the words: '"I don't think you have ever seen one of these." He then spent two hours guiding Martin through its labyrinthine complexity' (page 129).

The day after I had read about this episode, during an administrative pause in the activity of the House of Commons, I crossed the floor and said to Martin with a smile, "I hear that you like filling out income tax forms so much that from now on you want to do your own." He smiled back and noted he could not understand how the media were able to get such confidential information. Sometimes he found the media with information which only an hour earlier had originated in a confidential caucus or cabinet meeting.

A few days later I asked Greenspon about the difficulties of obtaining such information. He replied with this account. "After the publication of the book some people asked me how I had obtained a specific, juicy piece of information. It was ironic that sometimes I had obtained it from the questioners themselves. They had just forgotten about our earlier conversation."

The caucus chair: Deborah Grey

From the first to the last day Deborah Grey was the caucus chair, an

Chapter 9

important and influential position. She had been the sole Reform MP in the preceding Parliament and therefore had much practical experience in parliamentary matters. She is a colourful, big woman with a strong voice, quick wit and biting tongue. She loved to refer to certain people as "potlickers." Whenever she did so her voice, inflection and body language left little doubt she was using the word in place of ones which would get her thrown out of the House for unparliamentary language. Before the by-election in 1989, which brought her to office at age 37, she had been a high school teacher in a rural area of northern Alberta. One of the subjects she taught was diction and speech. She either has a natural talent or taught herself well because she was one of the most articulate and effective speakers in caucus.

In her role as the chair she set the agenda, keeping debates on topic and allocating fairly the limited time to those who wanted to speak. In my view Deborah did her job exceedingly well and I rarely heard criticism of her work. She used good humour and played no favours in the allocation of time. However, she was not interested in ideas and aspects of issues without immediate relevance to the political fights at hand. Most of the time when I spoke she rotated her hand suggesting that I should hurry up and finish, often after I had just stood up to speak.

She used this hand signal rarely with others and at first I resented her attitude towards what I might have to say. But eventually I accepted that caucus was not the place for the discussion of ideology, the long run, unexpected consequences of policies and the similar matters of concern to me as an academic. I simply spoke less and less frequently and the few times I addressed topics I thought were of fundamental importance, I simply ignored her gestures and insisted that my time be equal to that given to others.

In 1994 Deborah got married for the first time. I met her new husband Lew a couple of times socially. Each time he shared with me at length his views on the lazy life and undeservedly high pay of academics who had never done an honest day's work. I did not bother to probe for the origin of his views and simply avoided him thereafter. Nevertheless, I wonder how much influence he had on Deborah and her tendency to be impatient about my interventions.

The House Leaders

One of the most important positions in caucus is that of House Leader. The job involves setting the House agenda, deciding the priority of bills for debate and passage and dealing with Parliamentary manoeuvres of the opposition. During the last parliament, Herb Gray was the government's House Leader. His long service in Parliament, past experience as minister, age and accumulated wisdom made him the obvious choice for the job.

Preston Manning appointed Elwin Hermanson as Reform's first House

Leader. Hermanson, a bright and articulate farmer from Saskatchewan, was 31 years old at the time, and had been active in Reform Party politics and organization from the founding of the party. Through this work he obviously had impressed Manning with his abilities and vision, but what he was lacking in was Parliamentary experience. Though he was a fast learner and did a credible job, he was replaced after about 18 months by Ray Speaker, when a major reassignment of caucus responsibilities occurred. Speaker should have been House Leader from the very beginning.

Speaker was the only professional politician in caucus. He was a teacher who, at the age of 27, had first run for office in the Alberta legislature for a Lethbridge area constituency. He won that election and every other one he contested during the next 30 years. When he switched to federal politics in 1993 and came to Ottawa he had experience as a member of the Alberta Legislative Assembly and as a minister in Ernest Manning's and Don Getty's cabinets. At one time he headed (and dissolved) the Social Credit Party of Alberta. He knew all about Parliamentary procedures, strategies, tactics and shenanigans, and had developed outstanding skills in interpersonal relations.

Speaker and I became quite close as, coincidentally, we lived in close proximity in Ottawa and often walked home together after late evening sessions in Parliament. Sometimes we discussed very sensitive party and sometimes even personal matters. In the process, I learned much about politics and how to get along with people.

If he agreed with a position I had taken, he would not just say "I agree." He would always give his own reasons for holding the same opinion. He was very gentle and apologetic when he disagreed with me, but stuck to his opinions without pressing them. He had a caucus reputation of never saying no to anyone or anything. It obviously pained him to do so. But this reputation had a flip side. Some colleagues thought that he could not be trusted because they thought he had supported their position and then he did not take the action expected of him: they did not know about his peculiar way of saying 'no.'

As the official House Leader, Speaker ran the parliamentary strategy and tactics effectively, with the help of an able staff of young and skilful assistants. In addition, he dealt with many conflicts among MPs and staff. I am not sure this work automatically comes with the official position of House Leader, but the delicate touch and firm hand it required came naturally to him. Reform lost much when he decided not to seek reelection in 1997, though he is certain to remain involved in Party affairs.

The Whip

The Caucus Whip's main job is to assure that MPs fulfill their responsibilities toward the party and the House of Commons and to use disciplinary measures to make sure that they do. The Reform caucus was not

Chapter 9

ready and willing to have itself disciplined in this traditional manner. Rosters for mandatory attendance — the weekly House duty rotation — were drawn up by the Whip. There were assignments to work on House Committees. But some members of caucus did not take these obligations very seriously and the Whip did not have any effective instruments for disciplining them. At its core, the job consisted of drawing up schedules, assigning responsibilities and keeping statistics on attendance.

However, there were some other interesting aspects of the Whip's job which made it attractive. It carried some extra pay and staff, a large office in the desirable Centre Block and, perhaps most interesting, serving as the Reform representative on the House Internal Affairs Committee. This Committee made up and administered the budget of the House of Commons amounting to many millions of dollars for its own operation. It decided on House staffing, budgets and procedures under the chairmanship of the Speaker of the House. Its deliberations were confidential and the recommendations often controversial.

Reform saw a succession of Whips. Initially Manning appointed Diane Ablonczy, a petite, friendly and hard working woman who had trained as a lawyer — the only lawyer we had in caucus. She had a long record of working for Reform and had impressed Manning with her abilities and commitment. However, Diane was not the right person for the job. She was too nice and not forceful enough. I sensed that she did not like the job very much herself.

In a shuffle of caucus officers and with the help of some pressures from caucus members in September 1995, she was succeeded by Jim Silye. In my view Silye was ideal for the job. After graduating from the University of Ottawa, where he starred on the football team, he played professional football for a number of years with the Calgary Stampeders, and thereafter had a successful business career. His personal achievements were reflected in the self-confidence with which he approached all decisions and issues. Articulate and unafraid to speak his mind, he had the quick jokes and repartee athletes acquire in locker rooms. His good looks and expensive clothes contributed to his election twice as the "sexiest male MP" by votes from the staff members of the House of Commons.

When another shuffle of caucus officers took place, he decided not to seek the office again for reasons he never spoke about, but I suspect were strictly personal. He was succeeded by Bob Ringma who, in his late sixties, had been retired from a successful career in the military as a three-star general before entering politics in 1993. He ran the office in the tradition of the logistical branch of the army where he had worked for 30 years. His record-keeping was meticulous and extensive, but he kept a low profile.

When taken to task by the media over some politically incorrect statements about homosexual rights, Ringma resigned and was succeeded by Chuck Strahl, a successful logging contractor when elected at the age of 26. Strahl has a sonorous bass voice, quick wit and is a genuinely nice guy.

I would be surprised if he ever had enemies. He is also a quick learner, articulates ideas well and delivers them very effectively. During the last year of the parliament he developed into a star performer in Question Period and gave a high profile to his position as the Whip in the House. In the 1997 election he won with the largest majority of any Reformer. I would not be surprised if in the future he were to become a major force in the Reform Party.

The Administrative Committee and Chief of Staff

The Caucus Chair, House leader and Whip were members of the Administrative Committee, which met every Monday at 5 pm. The other six members of the committee consisted of Manning and MPs who appeared to have been chosen on the basis of a long working association with him. During these meetings a conference call provided a link with Party headquarters in Calgary. Most of us in caucus who were not in this committee were curious about its work and function.

We were invited to attend meetings any time. I attended once and sensed that I was an intruder in a closed shop. I guess, the committee was the equivalent of cabinet of a government. Like cabinet, it separated those who were inside the power circle from those who were out. Having been an outsider for four years in this respect made it easier for me to decide against seeking office again in the 1997 election.

The Chief of Staff is the manager of a budget of more than a million dollars provided by the House of Commons for the Leader and Party. The Chief of Staff looks after the personnel and functions of the offices responsible for communications, research and the big job of responding to letters written to the Leader. Manning was slow in appointing a Chief of Staff and caucus became curious about the use of the relatively large sums of money available to the Leader for managing the parliamentary affairs of his party. Randy White became the leader of a group of caucus members demanding the establishment of a clear mandate and line of responsibility for these operations.

White had been a successful manager of a school district in the Fraser Valley before his election. In this position he had control over personnel decisions, the spending of millions of dollars and labour relations. He was very unhappy about the lack of a proper business plan for and control over Reform operations in Ottawa and administrative and financial links with party headquarters and the Party executive in Calgary. His unhappiness was not reduced when Manning appointed Stephen Greene as his first Chief of Staff.

Greene had been an unsuccessful candidate for Reform in a Nova Scotia riding in the 1993 election. After that election he returned to his position as an executive with one of the largest fish concerns in the Atlantic provinces. At the same time he remained actively involved in party affairs. Through this work Manning knew and trusted him. In my personal dealings with Greene I found him to be well informed and open to ideas and suggestions. However, most members of caucus did not have this experience. Many considered him to be incompetent with a poor management style and ability to deal with employees.

Greene invited Ray Speaker and I for dinner one evening at his house to meet Peter Nicholson, a friend and past working associate of his. Nicholson was an economist, high level executive with a Canadian bank and an incisive thinker. Paul Martin had asked him to come to Ottawa on leave from the bank and write an independent assessment of Canada's fiscal woes and how they could be solved. I have very pleasant memories of that dinner at Greene's home. I found Nicholson intelligent, insightful and remarkably open. As economists, we had much in common. Our conversation ranged widely and penetrated deeply into Canada's fiscal problems. Not too long after I had this memorable conversation with him, Nicholson's report was published in 1994 by the Department of Finance under the title *Agenda: Jobs and Growth, A New Framework for Economic Policy.* I agree with almost all of the analysis and policy prescriptions set out in this report. Martin's subsequent budgets reflected the report's main recommendations and brought a balanced budget about four years later. I never saw Nicholson again to congratulate him on his achievement. He had returned to private industry not long after he had completed his report.

After much pressure, Manning agreed to the formation of a committee headed by Speaker with Randy White and Jim Silye as members to design the equivalent of a business plan for the Reform party and especially its operation in Ottawa. Working with some members of the party's executive, the committee produced a lengthy document. It laid out an excellent structure for the organization and responsibility. Unfortunately, as is the case with many plans of this nature in all organizations, it was only partially implemented. Those who had spent much energy in fighting for and over it turned to other things.

I was never consulted about the business plan and was quite sceptical about its likelihood of success. From what I knew of it, it was designed to take away some of Manning's discretionary powers over appointments and the spending of money. I could see that Manning would never let this happen, because by this time I knew how he handled such matters. He let White and his friends exhaust themselves with their work, present its results with pride and then implement only recommendations that interfered minimally with his authority.

Question Period

Question period, in principle, is a highly desirable opportunity for opposition MPs to ask Government ministers questions about policies and keep

Caucus Life and Question Period

their feet to the fire. This institution is unique to Parliaments in the Westminster tradition. Members of the U.S. Congress are said to be envious of Canada and wish they had the opportunity to ask daily questions of their cabinet secretaries, who are the equivalent, albeit unelected, to ministers in the Canadian parliamentary system.

Since the advent of television, QP has become a bigger circus than it has ever been. Promptly at 2:15 (11:15 on Fridays) a speaker for the official opposition, most often the Party Leader, rises and asks a series of three questions of any minister he wants. The House cameras are aimed at the speaker and surveys have shown that on average at least 100,000 Canadians are watching on television in their homes. Sometimes big media hitters sit in the press gallery to observe, but most often the media are alleged to follow QP on television in their offices.

The Bloc Quebecois, as the official opposition, was also permitted a second question every day. Thereafter came questions from Manning (or a Reformer in his place when he was absent), as the head of the third largest party in the House. While these first three questions each day could have long pre ambles and take more than a minute, all subsequent questions and one follow up had to be very short. They were given in rotation to the Bloc and Reform, interspersed with some from Liberal backbenchers and about four times a week, to the NDP and Jean Charest as the leader of the two person caucus of the once-mighty Progressive Conservative Party.

Some of us were quite unhappy with the questions allowed by the Liberals. Typically, they were prompts for ministers to praise some new policy development which they had initiated. This practice flies in the face of the original intention of QP. If the ministers had some information for the public, they could always issue press releases and hold press conferences. On the other hand, it is understandable that the government would use its clout with the House Speaker to give its own backbenchers a rare moment in the limelight and at the same time reduce that given to the opposition.

We resented this, and protested loudly about Charest's opportunities to ask questions which were quite disproportionate to the size of the PC caucus. It is difficult to know whether the Liberals gave Charest this exposure out of a sense of fairness and in recognition of the long history of the PCs or whether they were just serving their own interest. After all, anything that generated publicity for Charest and the PCs increased the chances that in the next election there would be another split of the conservative vote between Reform and the PCs.

Once the subject of the question became obvious, the ministers responsible for answering it opened thick briefing books to look up the responses they were coached to deliver. Only Prime Minister Chretien appeared to reply completely off the cuff. His answers were almost always examples of his legendary tendency to make unintelligible pronouncements. The media

Chapter 9

are known to have meetings after press conferences during which they try to reach a consensus on what he had said! The political advantage of his jumbled syntax is that Liberal supporters in the public can read into it whatever they like. At the same time, Chretien was always good at delivering basically empty political rhetoric. Sometimes he was so good, his caucus gave him standing ovations.

Shortly after I arrived in Ottawa I went to the library to find some scholarly analysis of the Question Period practice. There were some articles dealing with its role in keeping the government accountable; my judgement was that it did in a very limited way. As an economist I missed any mention of the cost at which this accountability is achieved. I shudder thinking about the resources required in every ministry to prepare briefing books and coach the ministers on the contents of questions and, even more important, the style and potential sound-bites used in delivery.

There are other, sometimes very significant, costs. In the previous Parliament a heated debate once took place over the merit of the Goods and Services Tax. The Liberals, in opposition, argued that it would have very harmful effects on the poor. In response, Prime Minister Mulroney replied that the GST would not be applied to basic groceries. This statement allegedly was made without full debate in the PC caucus and against the recommendations of Finance Minister Michael Wilson and the tax experts in the department of finance.

As a result of this commitment, made in the heat of Question Period, the flood-gates opened for the exemption and special treatment of a wide range of other goods and services. The GST became an administrative nightmare and the rate had to be about two points higher than it could have been without the exemptions. Five donuts are taxable, six are not, to mention just one example. The GST operating in New Zealand is applied to all goods and services and levied at a much lower rate. Opposition to it is much less than it is in Canada. Besides, Mulroney could have just said that low income earners would be fully compensated for the higher cost of taxed food through the system of GST rebates already announced, but under the pressure of the QP spectacle, he gave in to an idea advanced by the opposition.

Accountability of ministers on issues of real substance raised in QP is extremely limited. The ministers use a simple and obvious ruse to get around having to reply to questions that raise important and potentially embarrassing policy issues. Paul Martin, the Finance Minister, was vulnerable on the disproportionate burden his fiscal restraint put on the provinces. Allan Rock, the Minister of Justice, was weak on his justification of the gun control legislation, refusing to obtain independent estimates of benefits and costs of the registration of rifles.

These ministers simply ignored what they knew were reasonable questions to which they had no reasonable answers. Instead, they attacked alleged Reform attitudes and policies. Such attacks were delivered with great rhetorical theatrics and often produced rousing applause from government backbenchers. The louder the applause, the more the question implied embarrassment on the substance of a policy. Sad to say, I am sure that if and when Reform is in power, its ministers and caucus will behave in the same way.

Reform Question Period strategies

Much effort was devoted to the preparation of the questions by Reform. There was a strategy meeting at eight every morning, the latest news developments being summarized by staffers, and a conference call involving Ron Wood in Calgary and Steve Green in Nova Scotia taking place. These individuals had checked local newspapers and summarized items of potential interest to the meeting. Those topics most likely to hold the interest of the media (and likely to embarrass the government) were selected. MPs with relevant knowledge and good delivery skills were assigned the task of writing up appropriate questions, often with the assistance from communications staff. At one o'clock the questions were rehearsed, under the scrutiny of communications experts and other MPs.

I discovered from my research that the value to a party of asking good questions was not to be found in the replies from the ministers but in the questions themselves, especially in the case of scandals and controversial policies which the government had attempted to hide or could not justify on reasonable grounds.

Questions repeated often enough would eventually attract the attention of the media, who would then put to work their enormous resources to flesh out the facts and provoke a public reaction. However, in practice, Reform strategy wavered between the use of a long series of questions on the same issue and the use of questions based on news already in the media. The latter approach was reactive but regularly led to interviews, which meant publicity for Reform's positions and success in the neverending quest for media 'hits.'

However, knowing that most often what counted was the question and not the answer did little to soothe my frustration and that of my colleagues when we had asked a penetrating and potentially embarrassing question, only to be subjected by the responding minister to misleading or factually incorrect counter attacks, with no opportunity for a come-back. The minister always had the last word and responses were always planned so that misinformation came at the end when there was no opportunity to respond.

A Reform MP who asked a question sometimes was interviewed by the media to obtain the party's official view on controversial issues. It rarely happened to me, and I never was sure why. I suspect that financial issues are too difficult to deal with in the usual news format. Probably I also was too scholarly and factual and thus not very good for the short clip in a newscast. Only Don Newman, the host of *Newsworld,* interviewed me

Chapter 9

regularly on special occasions like the release of the Budget or Finance Committee reports.

I went through a frustrating cycle in the delivery of questions. Initially I followed my own instinct and preferences, delivering questions in measured tone and very limited and disciplined gestures. This prompted the young Reform 'communications experts' — really recent graduates from university with majors in political science or journalism — to urge me to use more emotion. I followed their advice reluctantly but was rewarded with their and my colleagues' praise.

About a year after my change in style, Line Maheux joined the Reform staff as a mature and experienced professional media consultant. She promptly told me that the emotional style and gestures I had adopted were successful with the live audience in the House — and probably my classes in university, but they were inappropriate for the large TV audiences watching QP proceedings. I had no difficulties returning to my original style of delivery.

I also had some problems with the contents of questions. The media paid little attention to the often complex issues I tried to raise. Paul Martin sometimes simply ignored my question and went on one of his emotional and often factually incorrect attacks on Reform. Doug Fisher, a respected columnist once noted that the frequent Martin theatrics did not enhance his chances for becoming the leader of the Liberal Party. Aspiring leaders could not afford to become known as buffoons and for their rhetorical excesses.

In QP strategy sessions we were frustrated by our inability to stop Martin's repeated misrepresentations of our policies. We felt, rightly or wrongly, that if the media heard the misrepresentations often enough, they might accept them as the truth. After some discussion it was decided that we would react with periodic references to Martin's wealth and the foreign registration of the ships he owned. These facts were known to have hurt his leadership chances in the past. With appropriate hints about the correlation between his misrepresentations and our personal attacks, he might be more inclined to limit his answers to dealing with the substance of our questions.

When this strategy was adopted, I refused to weave the personal attacks on Martin into my questions. Monte Solberg was given the task instead. Martin obviously became very irritated by our technique and I wrote him a note explaining the correlation between the quality of his answers and our personal attacks. I never received a reply and he did not change his theatrics.

During the last few months of Parliament I had several quotes from Martin recorded by *Hansard* in my files that I was prepared to document to the media as being misleading or factually incorrect references to Reform's fiscal policy platforms. I was prepared to call Martin a liar in the House and have myself ejected for the use of unparliamentary language. On such occasions the media pay attention and would afford me to set the record straight. As it turned out, I never had the opportunity to use this strategy. The declaration that I would not seek reelection was accompanied by my demotion from the role of Finance Critic and the opportunity to ask questions.

Question period strategies were very divisive and damaging to the morale of caucus. Appearing on QP was one of the few ways in which a backbencher in an opposition party could get any public exposure important for self esteem and relationships with constituents. I was surprised how often constituents told me that they had seen me on TV asking questions. On the other hand, most of us did not have the talent or skills to write and deliver effective questions required to maximize the benefits of QP for the party.

Some Reform MPs had no trouble going without questions, but a substantial number were very unhappy and quite outspoken about the unfair treatment they received. The QP coordinators, Monte Solberg for the first two years and Ken Epp thereafter, had the unenviable job of dealing with this problem. Towards the end of the Parliament the complaints diminished: a small stable of QP stars had emerged. I was not one of them. Like others, I had come to realize how limited were the personal benefits from asking questions relative to the psychic and time cost of preparing and delivering them. The realization that I did not have the required talent for this work was another reason why I decided to return to academic life at the end of the Parliament.

Social life

There was surprisingly little interaction among members of caucus outside of occasions where our work brought us together. There were no officially organized and sanctioned occasions for social meetings among MPs. The traditional Christmas parties and organized sports like softball and ice hockey were poorly attended by MPs and served mainly to raise the morale of staff.

There were a few of us who occasionally went out to dinner together. I do not know whether other such groups did the same. The few meals I attended were enjoyable and informative. I got to know about the personal life of some of my colleagues as well as learned about their political interests and concerns.

Shortly after the new Parliament began sitting, it was decided that the traditional break for lunch should be abandoned. To permit MPs on House duty to remain near the chamber and get to eat lunch, food was brought in daily. As a result, there always were several MPs sitting around a large round table in the lobby to the House, talking. I found this occasion very useful for keeping up with developments, even though we had to keep an eye on the TV showing proceedings in the House. Sometimes we had to drop everything and run onto the floor to stand for a motion that otherwise would have been passed to the advantage of the government.

Perhaps the lack of social interaction is inevitable. The time spent on committees, other meetings and on the floor of the House tended to leave one exhausted and talked out. There was no regular quitting time. Some MPs worked late into the night on their own, others had meetings or tried to get some exercise. On days around weekends we tended to go the airport at different times.

Perhaps a greater effort by the Whip or some other caucus officer should have been made to facilitate such informal gatherings of MPs. I had found such affairs very useful in my career in academia. And, as I read recently in a book on the habits of successful people, one should never spend a meal alone and waste time that could be used for the exchange of information. And perhaps even more importantly, such affairs could ease the loneliness that many of my colleagues and I often felt when going home at night to an empty apartment, with our families thousands of miles away.

CHAPTER 10

The 'Racist' Label

THE 1993 Canadian federal election results were like a major earthquake, dramatically changing the political landscape. The traditional 'right-wing' Progressive Conservative Party (PC) lost all but two of the 169 seats it had held in the preceding Parliament. The traditional 'left wing' party, the New Democratic Party (NDP) fell from 43 seats to only nine, while the 'centrist' Liberals more than doubled their seats in Parliament to 177. This number represents 61 percent of the total of 291 seats, allowing them to form the government.

The beneficiaries of the loss of support for the PCs in Quebec were the Bloc Quebecois, which moved from nine seats to 54. As the second largest party in the House, they became the official opposition. The political background and motives of the Bloc were unique. The traditional ideological labels like right, left and centre were not applicable. Its members were dedicated to using the federal parliament in hastening the creation of an independent Quebec. This motive overrode what under normal circumstances would have been serious ideological differences of its caucus members, which became obvious as its policy positions on non-Quebec issues were neither predictable nor prominent.

The main beneficiary of the PC and NDP losses in the Western provinces was the Reform Party. Mainly through a strong showing in Alberta and British Columbia, the Reform Party went from one to 52 seats in the House. Reform was the only other official party besides the Bloc.

Under the existing rules of the House of Commons, the number of members elected under the NDP and PC banner was insufficient to qualify them as official parties. As a result, they lost substantial financial benefits, status on committees and rights to participate in the question period and debates in the House. Reform enjoyed all of the benefits of an official party. However, these were considerably less than those available to the Bloc, which as the party with the second-largest number of seats was designated to be 'Her Majesty's Loyal Opposition.' Reform's role as just an ordinary party in opposition was galling to all Reform MPs. Reform had missed being the second largest party by only two seats. In addition, it seemed ironic to both Reform and many Canadians that the official opposition status should be conferred upon a party whose avowed goal was to gain independence for Quebec and break up the country.

Reform, a populist party

The unprecedented election results and the distribution of power in the

Chapter 10

House of Commons gave rise to much soul-searching and anxiety among the media. The old rules which treated the official opposition as the government in waiting were no longer valid. The media's biggest problem stemmed from the Reform Party's rise from a regional political movement into a strong representation in Parliament. Was Reform the successor of the PCs on the right, or was it a party with an extremist and racist agenda, as had been alleged during the election campaign? Was there a permanent realignment of parties in Canada or was Reform the product of a regional protest movement that would disappear in the next election?

The media found it difficult to obtain answers to these questions about Reform. The party leader, Preston Manning, in a book titled *The New Canada,* described himself and his party as 'populist,' which simply means that it is a party without a basic ideology but with a deep commitment to representing the wishes of 'the people.' One of Manning's favourite ways of putting the matter is: 'Reform is like a hockey team. We have left- and right-wingers and centres. All play together for the benefit of the team.' Professor Tom Flanagan, a political scientist at the University of Calgary, has written a scholarly history of the Reform Party, *Waiting for the Wave,* in which he analyzes the opportunities and pitfalls of such political populism. The following owes much to his analysis. Populism's main pitfall is the possibility that a majority of people want a government policy which is financially unsustainable or has other serious detrimental effects in the longer run. How would a populist party treat such a public demand? Would it give up its commitment to populism or would it enact policies that could ruin the country?

Leaders of populist parties in the past, including Manning presently, defend populism by asserting that the people are always right. Their demands may *seem* to result in policies that are bad for the country, but it will always turn out in the end that the policies were for the better. The truth of such a fundamental belief can be established only through empirical evidence. The history of populist parties reveals that they either disappear soon after their initial success or turn into parties with an ideological base.

The reason for this history is simply that a populist party's success inevitably evokes responses in traditional parties which remove the public's discontent and the populist party's base of voters. This is not inevitable. A populist party could ride a succession of waves of discontent with a series of different government policies. In his book, Flanagan notes Manning's great success in doing so. Or the traditional parties could fail to respond properly to the public's mood. Nevertheless, history shows that it is one thing to ride waves of popular discontent and quite another to turn such a parliamentary presence into a majority and form the government. It remains to be seen whether Reform will remain populist or adopt a more ideological base, whether it will disappear or become a permanent fixture of the Canadian political scene. The election results of 1997 brought

The 'Racist' Label

Reform the much coveted status as the official opposition and suggest that Reform was not just a symbol of popular dissatisfaction based on some special circumstances.

Populist sentiments and the media

Whatever the future may hold, in 1993 Reform's populist ideology resulted in the media finding plenty of material for their continued efforts to paint Reform as a dangerous party of extremists, rednecks, radicals and racists. Someone pointed out to me at the beginning of the new parliament that the media were so successful in persuading themselves that Reformers had these characteristics that they almost literally expected us to arrive on Parliament Hill riding horses, wearing cowboy hats and boots and shooting guns in the air. Where did the media get information for use in their campaign to discredit the Party? The Party had no record in parliament. Its leader and members were political neophytes without a public history. The scholarly analysis of Manning and Reform by Tom Flanagan had not yet been published. The only comprehensive study was by Murray Dobbin, whose book, *Preston Manning and the Reform Party* (1991) revealed his strong socialist leanings and an obvious, hateful bias against Western populism. This state of information about the Reform Party made the media turn to the history and public pronouncement of individual Reform members.

I have already described how in my case they did some 'yellow journalism' at Simon Fraser University and how, with the sole exception of Trevor Lautens of *The Vancouver Sun* and the *North Shore News*, did not study what I had actually said in my many publications. They preferred the much easier method of finding people who disagreed with the positions I had taken. For more general information about the Reform Party the media turned to the record of the party's bi-annual General Assembly of members, mostly again through secondary sources like published newspaper reports. These assemblies represent populism at its best. Local constituency organizations elect delegates for the meetings. At the Assembly, days are spent discussing policy positions which had been generated and discussed previously at the constituency level. Resolutions binding on Reformers in Parliament must be passed by a majority of delegates. In addition, to prevent domination of the voting process by the large numbers of delegates from the large provinces, resolutions are approved only if they are passed by six out of 10 provincial delegations.

I had been very impressed with the level of common sense and wisdom of the majority of delegates at these conventions in general. I also had a specific experience strengthening this view. I was able to speak about a number of financial policy resolutions and the flat tax proposals at the 1996 Vancouver convention. From the dynamics of the discussion and later comments made by delegates, it was clear that my arguments had

Chapter 10

strongly influenced the final vote on these issues. Obviously, I think it was a good thing that the facts and analysis I presented won out over more emotional arguments.

However, it is clear that in a genuine grass-roots, populist party assembly everyone has a right to speak, and this right is taken very seriously by all delegates. In such an environment the media had no difficulty in finding individuals expressing views which fit the media's definition of extremist, radical, racist and so on (one of these was West Vancouver columnist Doug Collins: see page 113 ff.). Now that Reform had gained its election success, all the news reports about past Assemblies could be mined for evidence to reinforce the extremist label.

For the media it did not matter that views expressed by individuals at these Assemblies were not shared by the majority of delegates and were not reflected in resolutions passed. Nor did it matter that some of the views considered extremist and racist by the media are not considered to be so by the majority of Canadians. Nor did it matter that Manning violated the populist principles so close to his heart and put conditions on Doug Collins' candidacy which were almost certain to be unacceptable to him. Collins in fact withdrew as a candidate for Reform in the 1988 election.

For the media it did not matter that John Beck succeeded in getting himself nominated as the Reform candidate for the Ontario riding of York Centre in a meeting at which very few party members attended. It later turned out that Beck held outrageous views on immigration and was prone to making racist remarks. He was quoted as having said 'immigrants bring death and destruction into Canada' and 'It seems to be predominantly Jewish people who are running this country.' It did not matter that such views are not held officially by Reform and that Manning withdrew Beck's official right to be a Reform candidate the day he found out about Beck's views.

What mattered to the media was that they had material which allowed them to make a link between extremism and racism and the Party, its leader, ordinary members and MPs. They did so in a time-honoured fashion designed to make them seem to be objective reporters of events. They did not comment on such remarks themselves. Instead, they asked others to do so.

The commentators they selected typically were unelected, self-appointed and often government-financed guardians of the 'public interest' — as they themselves define it. Reliably they would condemn Reform. With the help of editors, these condemnations would be given large newspaper headlines or prominent spots in television broadcasts. During the election campaign and the first few years of Parliament the media spared no effort in using this technique to paint Reform as the party of extremists and racists.

Many observers suggest that this media behaviour was designed to discredit Reform policies on the deficit and debt, the size of government, influence of special interest groups, criminal justice, gun control, immigration and other similar subjects. Reform positions on these issues are distinctly different from those promulgated by the traditional parties in power during the post-war years. Members of the media felt a need to fight these ideas because they were also in conflict with their personal ideologies.

Studies have shown that most Canadian journalists and editors had strongly supported the left-wing policies of Canadian governments during the preceding 30 years. I know, for example, that until quite recently most journalists and editors accepted as valid the economic models championed by the NDP and the left wing of the Liberals. For this reason they praised government deficits for job-creation and argued that government debt does not matter because 'we owe it to ourselves.' By the time of the 1997 election, these views were no longer considered valid by most economists and journalists. In 1993, however, they were for all practical purposes the conventional wisdom held by the Canadian media.

During the 1993 election Reform candidates in a number of Ontario ridings came in second. Some were defeated by Liberals by very small margins. There has been much speculation about the effect which the John Beck affair and its media treatment has had on this outcome. During a visit to the Stratford festival in the summer of 1994 I talked to the owner of a Greek restaurant about his political views on Reform. This person's accent suggested that he was an immigrant and his strong and immediate reply was that he did not vote for Reform because of the party's position on immigration, even though he supported strongly its views on fiscal responsibility. This person obviously had formed his views on the basis of the media reports which made so much about the non-representative views of ex-candidate John Beck and quotes falsely attributed to me. It is quite conceivable that in the absence of this media treatment Reform would have won more than the one seat it did and, as a result, would have been the official opposition and would have been in a much better position to gain additional seats in the 1997 election.

I cannot reminisce about these matters without being hit by the irony of it all. Once the Liberals were in power they lowered annual rates of immigration, much like Reform had recommended. In addition and much more important, they imposed a fee of $1,000 on persons applying for immigration abroad, allegedly to help cover the administrative cost of dealing with the applications. This amount of money is an important deterrent for potential immigrants from the poorer regions of the world and much less so from the United States and Western Europe. The media did not deal with these policies in the manner they used during the election campaign. Routinely as an MP I received mail from immigrants' interest groups condemning these policies as racist, in the tradition of the election campaign. But the media never followed up on these press releases and unleashed a barrage of criticism based on quotes from the leaders of these groups.

Chapter 10

Reform and Political Correctness

The media treatment of Reform described above was actually part of a much larger agenda best captured in the concept of 'political correctness.' Politically incorrect topics involved Natives, immigration, unemployment insurance, welfare, the feminist agenda, abortion, the death penalty, gun control, homosexuality, official language policies and others. Anyone presenting factual, historical or analytical arguments which questioned any aspect of government policies or the alleged public consensus on these subjects would face a barrage of attacks. These attacks were designed to discourage others from violating the code of political correctness.

I have discussed the methods used in launching these attacks above. They involve predictable condemnation by commentators kept in the public eye by government grants and media exposure for just this purpose. The justification for this media agenda has been that such politically incorrect views would stir up resentment, hurt an obviously delicate public consensus and retard the development of a social democratic or socialist society in Canada.

I know, from first-hand experience, much about the methods used by the media for punishing someone in violation of the code of political correctness. In Chapter 8 I discussed my experience during the election campaign when I raised some questions about the net benefits of immigration for Canadians. I will discuss some others below. I know from my experience that such media attacks have strongly influenced my willingness to express my views on certain subjects. I know others who have had similar experiences.

There are indications that the Canadian public is fed up with the media's role in enforcing the code of political correctness and the left-wing policies it supports. In the 1990s the CBC was subjected to repeated, severe budget cuts. The minimal public protest over these cuts was attributed by a number of observers to the public's dissatisfaction with this government-financed broadcaster's editorial and programming policies. Many of my constituents were in favour of these cuts to the CBC on the grounds that they were fed up with much of the organization's support of politically-correct causes and the stifling of genuine public debate of the issues.

It is interesting to speculate that public dissatisfaction with the media's handling of political correctness may actually have helped Reform's electoral success in 1993 and 1997. Voters were attracted in large numbers to Reform by the media's refusal to permit a full public debate on issues of great concern to them. Reform promised to discuss these subjects publicly and in Parliament.

Natives and South Sea Islands

I raised a number of politically incorrect subjects in Parliament. The most important of these involved government policies towards Natives. (Readers will note that I will refer to them by this term, rather than the politically correct 'First Nations,' a term invented by spin-doctors and designed to appease, or by the more traditional terms 'North American Indians' or 'aborigines,' both of which are imprecise since they neglect Inuit and Metis, respectively. There is obviously no perfect name). Here is my tale.

I had been in Parliament only a few months. To prevent a repetition of my experience with the immigration topic during the election campaign, I had been very careful to write out all of my speeches. In spite of the media's close attention to everything that I and all of my colleagues said in debate, we had largely avoided giving them fodder for their extremist and racist cannons. On the morning of the day that this condition changed profoundly I was carefully preparing a talk on Native policies for delivery in the afternoon. I was about half done when the Whip approached me in a panic. A Reformer scheduled to speak in 20 minutes could not do it. Would I please take his place? I said yes, and gave a speech 'from the heart.'

The message of my speech can be summarized in five simple points. First, Canada's policies towards Natives have not served them well: these policies have caused unemployment and created welfare dependency and many social problems from alcoholism to family violence and a lack of self-esteem.

Second, it was not appropriate to spend more money on programs that had created these problems.

Third, we need a new approach to help Natives. While I did not have a well-developed program of new approaches, as an economist I knew that such a program would have to face some realities. The most important of these was that remote and small reserves had no chance whatever to become economically viable, let alone prosperous.

Fourth, the right ideological approach to government policies on Natives was 'tough love.' This love would foster self-reliance and build the self-confidence of Natives. It would rely on personal freedom and free markets as dominant institutions. Paternalism and socialism had been tried and had failed; it was time for a change.

Fifth, discussions over the history of mistreatment of the Native people are not productive. They only strengthen the already paralysing culture of self-pity. We need to look forward and set policies which improve conditions for Natives from now on.

Here is some financial background which I did not present in my speech but which is important for understanding the origin of the views on economic issues I presented. The Government of Canada spends about $10,000 *per Native* or $40,000 *per family of four* annually. To put this figure into perspective consider that the average Canadian working full time in manufacturing enjoys an annual income of only about $25,000. This income is used to *support the typical Canadian family*. The income of the

Chapter 10

Natives, received through government, whether in transfers or in kind, like housing, is not taxable. The ordinary Canadian's income is subject to income and excise taxes. So, it seems that the Government of Canada spends enough money and gives sufficient other concessions to bring the living standards of Natives up to those of other Canadians. To me, it remains a big puzzle why this has not happened — why, in fact, we see so much poverty among Natives.

The preceding data are based on figures found in the 1997 *Canada Year Book,* which shows that in 1991, Canada was home to about 365,000 North American Indians, 75,000 Inuit and 30,000 Metis. Annual spending by the federal government was more than *$5 billion* in 1995 (the precise figures are difficult to establish because, for example, while the Department of Indian and Northern Affairs alone spends $4 billion, many other Departments like Housing, Fisheries and Oceans, Housing and Health have special programs for Natives which are not shown separately). Experts put the value of these programs at over $1 billion annually.

To put these figures into perspective, it can be noted that about five percent of total federal program spending is going to about 1.6 percent of the population. The official explanation for this extraordinarily high spending on Natives and the persistence of poverty is that the remote location of many reserves makes it very expensive to deliver services. Others note that a large part of the money is absorbed by bureaucracies in Ottawa, the provincial governments and tribal councils as well as the lawyers, accountants and other advisers who constitute the 'Indian industry' in Canada.

The debate in the House that day concerned a treaty with Natives in the Yukon. It proposed granting huge amounts of land to the Natives and more money grants, all without provisions for a reduction in existing transfers. I opposed this legislation for reasons already stated in general terms and obvious from the financial information just presented.

During the delivery of my speech I was carried away by my passion and concern for the welfare of Natives. I used dramatic language and gestures to describe the conditions under which Natives live. My wife had, in her medical practice, a number of Natives from a nearby reserve. Several times she had described to me how she had treated Native women with battered faces and, most horrifically, in one case, the marks of burning cigarettes on her arms. As I was speaking I held out an arm and pointed at imaginary burns. This scene was televised on the national news reports repeatedly for a number of days while critical comments by Natives were given.

As a teacher, I have always tried to see the other side of an issue, so I raised the question of why Natives like welfare programs, even though these have had such a detrimental effect on their lives. I answered my own question by saying all human beings have a basic longing for financial security and freedom from the need to work, while cautioning that such financial security tends to bring serious problems for those who actually experience it. To illustrate this point, I told a story about a group of people who, having received large inheritances from a rich uncle, moved to a South Sea Island paradise to enjoy the indolence they had dreamed of. Soon, however, most of them left because they became bored, having discovered the truth that life without work holds no meaning.

I suggested that the Government is much like the proverbial rich uncle and that it encouraged a life for Natives on reserves without work or meaning. After the reports on my speech had passed through a number of stages, I was quoted as having said that 'Native reserves are like South Sea Islands.' This quote was used to elicit enraged comments from many who were familiar with the deplorable living conditions on reserves. If I had been asked by someone to comment on this statement, I too would have declared it uninformed and misleading. To this day, occasionally, friends laughingly greet me with the question 'How is your rich uncle in the South Sea Islands?'

Reactions by Manning and others

When the media assault started and Preston Manning was contacted for comments on my speech he immediately distanced himself and Reform from my position. I do not know whether at that time he had read what I had actually said or simply reacted to what he had learned from the media. He called me and arranged a time and location where I could be reached for instructions on how to minimize the damage my remarks had done to Reform.

In the meantime I went into hiding and refused all media interviews. At no time during this stressful period did I think I said anything that was racist or designed to create divisions among Canadians. My greatest regret was that my speech hurt Reform's basic agenda of restoring fiscal sanity to Canada's finances and generally offering a conservative alternative to the left-wing politics of the traditional parties.

Later that day I met with Ron Wood, Manning's press secretary, who had extensive experience in the media as a journalist in Ottawa and elsewhere. Presumably on instructions from and with the help of Manning, he had prepared for me a short statement in which I apologized for any distress I had caused Natives through my remarks. The statement came close to but did not say that I regretted having made my speech or that I had said things that were wrong. Bewildered, after some soul-searching and under much emotional pressure, I decided that I could live with the text. A press conference was arranged, and in front of a dozen cameras and a national audience I read a prepared statement, but refused to answer further questions.

In the wake of these events I received at least 100 messages by telephone, fax and mail. Nearly all of them suggested that I had been right in bringing up in Parliament the issue of the detrimental effect of govern-

Chapter 10

ment policies on the lives of Natives, and that it was about time a debate took place on the issue. Several positive communications came from Natives; a Native social worker on a reserve even offered to back up everything I had said and offered to provide me with more examples if I needed them. Out of the blue (so to speak) came a handwritten note from Don Cherry, written on the back of a picture of himself in the pose that is his trade-mark on the CBC *Hockey Night in Canada* TV broadcasts, encouraging me to keep up the good work. All these communications helped restore my self-confidence.

During a Parliamentary debate, one Liberal MP was summing up the nature of the speeches made by his party and other politicians; when I brought to his attention the positive comments I had received from the public, he said: 'These comments come from racists, and you should not be proud of their support.' The Minister of Indian Affairs asked for my resignation. NDP MPs received the opportunity for media attention that had eluded them for many months, and made the most of it. While condemning me, they promised to 'give away the shop' to Natives if ever they were to come to power.

The most hurtful comment, in a way, came in an unsigned editorial published in the *Vancouver Province*. It suggested that, as a racist, I should be forced to resign my seat and to 'go back where you came from, Herr Grubel' — totally missing the irony that such a reference to my German background was not entirely free from racism on the part of the editorial writer!

Someone in a position to know told me that for a substantial number of months Manning received more correspondence on my speech about Native policies than on any other subject, much of it coming from party members. Almost all this correspondence chastised Manning. These members had supported Reform in the expectation that we would raise politically incorrect subjects.

When I had finally delivered on this expectation, the Leader distanced himself from me and made me apologize. They suggested that he should have supported me instead and used the opportunity to bring to the public's attention Reform policies on Natives.

In the September 18, 1998 edition of *The Globe and Mail*, Edward Greenspon reported on a lengthy interview he had with Prime Minister Jean Chretien about his years in politics and the highest office. In a separate box entitled *No Regrets*, Greenspon quotes Chretien saying that ". . . politics means never having to say you're sorry." The text in the box goes on: "'Then he [Chretien] recalled one time he did apologize. It came after an April, 1994 speech in Toronto in which he suggested that unemployed people shouldn't sit around drinking beer. The next day in the House of Commons, he said that his words had been taken out of context, that he'd been discussing the dignity of work but if I offended anyone, I apologize.' Now he wonders whether he should have. 'You know the problem

The 'Racist' Label

is, faxes came in by the tonnes. 'You said the truth, Chretien, goddamn it . . .You tell the truth, and then you apologize!'"

Faxes did not come to me by the tonnes, but I can understand Chretien's sentiments. I wonder how Manning would react to the affair now.

About six months after my speech, the bi-annual Reform Assembly took place in Ottawa. A large number of delegates whom I did not know shook my hand, thanked me for bringing up the subject and criticized Manning's handling of the affair. The Leader's barn-burning speech before the traditional vote on his leadership at the Assembly contained no reference to individual MPs, except me. Humorously he noted that the Peace Tower on Parliament Hill was under repair and that I had requested replacement of the traditional time clock with a clock broadcasting the growing national debt. In my view, through this remark and by singling me out for mention, Manning sent a message to the grass-roots that in fact all was well with our relationship.

Many caucus members were very supportive of my being in trouble with the media and Manning, knowing that some day they too might say something politically incorrect and end up 'in the soup,' and were critical of Manning's handling of the affair. Ray Speaker and Stephen Harper, the promising, bright young Calgary MP, suggested that Manning should have used the media attention to explain the Reform position on Native issues to Canadians. This could have been done quite simply by having me coached on how to deflect media questions and turn them to issues of more substance. I am confident I could have handled such an assignment.

After the media attention subsided, I wrote a short paper entitled 'How to handle foot-in-mouth disease,' which contained a description of how the disease hits without warning and great force, how it can be contained by appropriate behaviour by the afflicted and Party doctors, and how it could be turned into an advantage for Reform. I proposed the establishment of a 'crisis team,' which would spring into action at the first sign of the disease. I thought it important that the majority of members of this crisis committee should be caucus members, mainly because they were likely to be trusted by the member afflicted by the disease. Some spin-doctors on the committee would provide technical advice; specialists in relevant fields would develop the best way of presenting the official Reform position.

Many caucus members agreed with my recommendation for the creation of such a committee. However, I had no chance to get it discussed officially in caucus or approved by Manning and his inner circle. When I pushed some members of that circle for reasons why the committee was not created, I received the answer that "Reformers do not like to be told by anyone what to say and do. There were other, more appropriate contingency plans in place to handle future problems. As it turns out, these plans were inadequate for handling the second major media feast over politically incorrect statements by members of caucus.

Chapter 10
The speech on Natives, in retrospect

I want to present a few retrospective thoughts on the events following my speech on Natives. It was a harrowing affair, personally. My background had not prepared me for dealing emotionally with the massive assault by the powerful and skilled national media. When it was at its peak, I attended the annual meetings of the Canadian Economics Association. In the corridors, several acquaintances approached me with the information that about every 20 minutes the CBC news channel showed excerpts from my speech on national television. I smiled in response, but inside I was worried — about the damage I might have done to Reform, a movement whose basic goals I strongly support; about my reputation as a professional economist and writer; about the troubles I had caused for Manning, especially with respect to his relationship with grass-roots members who had criticized him for making me apologize and distancing himself from me. Worries like these do not make for good sleep or the ability to concentrate on other matters!

I did not feel I had sent a bad message. I had told the truth as I saw it, and could support my arguments with factual evidence. I thought I had done Natives — and all Canadians — a service, by raising issues which needed to be discussed publicly and which ultimately might result in better government policies on native issues. If, coincidentally, my remarks had caused suffering among some natives who felt that they had been victims of racist stereotyping, I had in fact apologized to them. But I still believed that this bad aspect of my speech was outweighed strongly by the potential benefits of starting a rational discussion of the issues. At the time, I was convinced that I had made a major mistake using the inappropriate analogy involving rich uncles and South Sea Islands.

I know now that I should not have worried as much as I did. The affair strengthened the Party; my reputation was not damaged among people whose views I value, and Manning masterfully handled his relations with the grass-roots. Ironically, I now realize that if I had carefully written out my speech and delivered it non-emotionally and without the offending analogies, it would not have been noticed and given such a wide national exposure by the media. Under these conditions, the battle over political correctness would not have been joined as well as it had. Serious and factual discussions over native issues might still be avoided in Parliament. Grass-roots Reformers would have been disappointed with their MPs and, as they like to put it, their capture by the Ottawa political and media establishment.

I now know that on all of these issues I can never be an objective judge. I comfort myself with the thought that, however the public judged me then and will judge me in the future, I have a clear conscience on my motives. I had wanted to advance the cause for new government policies to better serve the interests of Canada's Natives in the longer run. I stuck my neck out because I cared for their welfare, not in order to stir up hateful or racist sentiments.

The bill giving Yukon natives property rights to land and natural resources of unprecedented magnitude and without any corresponding reductions in existing transfers and subsidies was passed quickly. In 1997 the Government of Canada still had policies in place which gave Natives welfare benefits, free medicare, educational services, housing and infrastructure facilities under one important condition: *they had to remain poor and stay on their reserves.*

Like other recipients of such free government services and under such conditions in Canada and elsewhere in the world, Natives are caught in the classic 'welfare trap,' and it becomes more difficult for each new generation, that grows up knowing nothing else, to escape it.

Views of two Native leaders

A few months after my experience, I attended a luncheon address by Mike Cardinal, a Native who had grown up on an isolated reserve in northern Alberta. At the time he was Minister of Social Services for the Government of Alberta. In his speech he recalled the village in which he grew up. Everyone had a job in what was a reasonably affluent subsistence economy. The women raised their families and worked to supply food for their tables, while the men maintained the housing, provided wood for the stoves, obtained meat by hunting and raised a little cash from selling furs. In the 1960s, the Government of Canada changed all that. With the best of motives (of course), it provided money which could be used to buy food, fuel and many other consumer goods in modern supermarkets. Cardinal concluded that with the inflow of this money came all the social problems of excessive leisure, unemployment, family violence, suicide and alcoholism which now plague his village. 'Welfare has to go!' was his final message. The identical message was given to me a few months later by Ovide Mercredi, Chief of the First Nations. Appearing before the Finance Committee of the House of Commons, Mercredi was lobbying the government to grant rights over land to Natives. As a member of that committee, I had a chance to question him about his plans for the use of this land. He declared that it was to be used to make reserves economically independent. I then asked him about details of this strategy. He replied that it would permit Natives to export the riches of the land they owned, like fish, wood and minerals. I agreed that this strategy had a good chance for success in cases where the reserves were on rich land, but what would happen on remote, small reserves where the land was not so productive? Mercredi responded that the Natives on these reserves could build their own housing and staff the stores which rented out videos. I made it clear that such activities would not produce anything for export and thus the means to pay for the imports needed for genuine economic independence. Did he have any specific

Chapter 10

ideas about what these reserves might produce to *bring in* dollars? His reply was, "Services for tourists, arts and crafts . . ." and then his voice trailed off.

After the end of the hearing, as Mercredi shook members' hands, I said to him privately: "I do not think you are doing many of your people a service by suggesting that tourism and arts and crafts can make them economically independent."

He looked me in the eyes and responded with conviction in his voice: "You and I can agree on one thing. Welfare must go."

I suppose agreement on the need for this course of action is an important first step in getting to a solution to the native problem. Unfortunately, there is much less agreement on what this solution should be. Land claims settlements may help some Native bands, but probably fewer than is widely expected. The economic surplus from natural resources is very small in today's world with many competitors and strict environmental standards. Just ask the existing fishing, mining and forestry companies everywhere in Canada. Except during a few exceptional boom years, their profits are low and they often incur large losses.

Mercredi obviously believes that to solve the problem by the granting of a large amount of wealth — land, mineral rights or cash — is the best approach. There is little evidence that such wealth would solve the current problems besetting the Native population. Reserves with large amounts of income (from sources such as oil and gas royalties, as on the Stoney Reserve in Alberta, or from land, such as the Squamish Reserve outside Vancouver) remain troubled by many social problems. My own solution is as simple as it is disliked by many Natives, but even more so by the 'Indian industry': *move to where the jobs are, and become Canadians in every way.* And that includes holding on to your Native culture and identity in families and associations, just as the Italians, Chinese and Germans have done for generations in Canada (and the Sikhs have begun to do). *Let your offspring decide the extent to which they want to continue with their Native traditions and cultures* — the freedom to choose is one of the most important things you can give them.

Chapter 11

Employment Equity, Homosexual Rights and Internal Dissent

THE media campaign to label Reform as a party of racists and extremists was fed not only by my speech on Natives reviewed in the preceding chapter. It also feasted on a number of other events. The most difficult of these involved statements about employment discrimination and homosexual rights by Bob Ringma and David Chatters. Probably the most damaging to the Party were Jim Silye's and Jan Brown's remarks to the media about extremists in caucus. They were brought on mainly by relatively minor instances of political incorrectness by Art Hanger on the subject of refugee claimants and corporal punishment, Jack Ramsay on gun control and Randy White and Myron Thompson on criminal justice. Here is my story of these events.

Employment equity and homosexual rights

Employment equity and quotas are highly controversial political topics. Add to them the issue of the rights of homosexuals and you have a volatile cocktail of issues. Expose this cocktail to a media determined to discredit Reform and you have all the ingredients for a major explosion. All you need is a politically incorrect quote from a couple of inexperienced politicians to provide the spark, and the explosion takes place.

Reform MPs Bob Ringma and David Chatters were the two inexperienced politicians who provided this spark. At the time, Bob Ringma was a 67-year old retired Major-General of the Canadian army, representing the semi-rural Vancouver Island riding of Nanaimo-Cowichan. A stocky man, he did not look his age. He spoke French fluently and had the demeanor of the successful leader that he was. He held firm views but expressed them cautiously; he got along well with people. At the time of the event, in the spring of 1996, he was the Reform Whip in the House.

David Chatters, a 50-year old farmer, represented the rural Alberta riding of Athabasca. He had a quick smile and was rather shy, rarely speaking up. On the infrequent occasions he did speak up in caucus he always was right on the mark and advanced the issue being debated. He is the kind of solid person I would like to have on my side in any battle. I have come to know both these men very well and am completely convinced that they do not hold any racist sentiments.

On the day in question a debate was raging in the House over a Liberal

Chapter 11

bill to extend the prohibited grounds of discrimination in employment to include sexual orientation, amending the grounds already on the book which are race, religion and gender. Peter O'Neil, a reporter for *The Vancouver Sun*, had obtained the copy of a story in a Nanaimo newspaper which in 1994 had headlined Ringma's politically incorrect views on homosexuality. He interviewed Ringma on the telephone, leading off the interview with references to this story. He then asked a clever 'hypothetical' question, which went roughly like this: "Consider the owner of a store who is confronted with the fact that his cashier has declared himself to be homosexual. This information spreads quickly through the community and business drops off, as many bigoted customers decide to take their business elsewhere. How should the owner of the store react?"

In reply, Ringma said something like: "I could understand it if this owner would move the cashier to the back of the store where he would have no contact with the public." Chatters was interviewed separately and rose to the bait of a reporter. He went on record as supporting this point of view.

The media quickly made an analogy out of the back-of-the store expression and the infamous back-of-the-bus policies of the racially segregated Southern states of the U.S. and the hated system of apartheid in South Africa. Mercilessly they rounded up comment after comment on this remark by a wide range of politicians, the leaders of special interest groups and other self-appointed guardians of the public interest who could be counted on to express outrage over such a quote with the desired intensity. Editors gave these comments prominent time on radio and TV and space and headlines in newspapers and magazines. The media coverage was very intense and lasted for weeks.

The reaction by leaders of the Reform Party was swift and decisive. A committee consisting of caucus members Ray Speaker (the House Leader), Deborah Grey (the deputy leader and caucus chair) and the party official Rick Anderson (chief political adviser to Manning) met with Ringma and Chatters.

It should be noted that unlike in my debacle over Native issues, Manning was not directly involved. Ringma was asked to resign his position as Whip. Both Ringma and Chatters were urged to apologize for what they had said. Both agreed, but only after a very long session in which it was established what actually had been said, what the words meant and the fundamental problems associated with the government's policy initiatives. All of this took place with the knowledge that the media were waiting like hyenas ready to devour the wounded MPs once they came out of that meeting.

Finally, after many hours of discussion in the committee, Chatters and Ringma read to the media a prepared statement expressing regret over any emotional problems they had caused homosexuals. Chatters made the mistake of staying on after this event to answer questions by reporters. I know from my own experience that this is not a good idea; one's emotional state and hour-long grilling by caucus and party officials interfere with rational thinking.

Chatters promptly got himself into even deeper trouble. He essentially reconfirmed his basic position and contradicted the statement he had just read. Ringma resigned his position as caucus Whip. Both he and Chatters were suspended from caucus for a number of months. All these events fed the media frenzy for some time. Many thought that the affair would damage irreparably the reputation of Reform, but this did not happen.

Chatters had very strong support from his constituents which was communicated to him by mail, faxes and telephone calls during the crisis. In 1993 he had won his seat after receiving 47.07 percent of the total votes cast. In the 1997 election he was reelected with by an absolute majority of 54.61 percent of the total.

Ringma was similarly backed strongly by his constituents. He informed me that he received large amounts of mail from the rest of Canada, much of it from people who noted that they were not members of the Reform Party. About 80 percent of that mail was either supportive or understanding of the position he was alleged to have taken. Knowledgeable observers believe that he could easily have won re-election in 1997 if he had not declined to run again for personal reasons. His Reform successor, Reid Elly, won the riding with 44.97 percent of the vote, up from the 41.22 percent received by Ringma.

It is more difficult to assess the damage the affair had done among the general electorate, the crucial Ontario ridings in particular. However, the fact is that the affair and views expressed were nowhere a major election issue. In my view some damage, again as in the case of the affair of native policies, was inflicted upon Manning in his relationship with the grass roots.

Ringma and Chatters were seen by many to have been set up by the media and deserved their leader's support, not punishment. Many also believed that the basic issue should be discussed and not swept under the carpet by the consensus on political correctness.

My view

It is easy to criticize Ringma and Chatters. When the reporter asked his question they should have just said, "I do not answer hypothetical questions like this," and walked away. Not giving an answer to the question would not have made a story. This strategy would have been especially appropriate given that the focus was on the rights of homosexuals. This is an issue on which Canadians are deeply divided and where there are many outspoken bigots with strong feelings. There are also many people who become very emotional on this subject for very profound and respectable religious and ideological reasons. Such outspoken antagonists exist on both sides, for and against increasing the rights of homosexuals.

Chapter 11

I know some of these people on both sides and would not call them unthinking bigots, but thoughtful people, who take seriously their religious beliefs and views on the culture that they want to live in and leave for their children.

Whatever anyone says on this subject provokes strong reactions and heated debates. There are never any winners from such emotional clashes. It is difficult to construct a scenario under which the political careers of Ringma and Chatters or the interests of Reform could have been advanced by any conceivable, substantive reply to the question.

For me, the affair had a positive effect. It forced me to listen to long debates on the issue in caucus, the House and in the media. I formed a strictly personal view which is not shared universally by members of caucus. On a number of occasions I was tempted to share it with the media but wisely, in retrospect, never did. I adopted the practice of entering and leaving the House through corridors off limits to the media. I simply did not trust my ability to resist engaging in a debate with reporters and leave them with sound-bites that would only further feed their frenzy. However, I want to take this opportunity to set out my views on this very complex issue. I know that I do so at some risk, though it is much smaller than it was when I was a member of the Reform caucus. So here are my views, condensed and with only limited reference to relevant empirical evidence. I will first discuss the issue of discrimination generally and in relation to employment equity legislation. This discussion sets the framework for dealing with the homosexuals back in the store issues.

The economics of discrimination

In my view, major studies have produced a very strong case for the proposition that the rights of individuals for equal and non-discriminatory treatment are best protected by a free and open market. Here is the reasoning for this conclusion, originally developed by Nobel laureate Gary Becker, an economist teaching at the University of Chicago. Consider a country originally free from discrimination: whites and blacks earn exactly what they deserve in terms of their education, training, age and productivity. Now assume that a substantial number of firms adopts the policy to employ only whites, even though there are better trained and more productive blacks available to do the job. This policy drives wages of the blacks below those of the whites, the kind of condition which underlies the demand for government remedies. But it is clear that such wage differences cannot persist in a free society with competitive enterprise.

Because the blacks are now earning wages below their productivity, it makes good economic sense for non-bigoted entrepreneurs to hire them. These workers will produce high profits for their employers, since for every hour worked, the output of blacks is greater than their wage. These successful entrepreneurs can expand their business by charging a lower price for the product than their bigoted competitors, since, in a free market, consumers do not care who produced the goods they buy as long as the price and quality are right. As the business of these non-bigoted entrepreneurs expands (some might be themselves members of minorities discriminated against), more and more blacks are hired and their wages rise until they properly reflect their true level of productivity. In the end, the competition from the profitable firms drives the bigoted employers out of business or forces them to earn less on their investment than they could if they engaged in non-discriminatory hiring!

Losses or lower than normal returns suffered by these bigoted entrepreneurs may be seen to be the price they pay for their behaviour. In the view of many, in a free society, people should be allowed to pay such a price to indulge their preference for certain types of association. However, it is unlikely that entrepreneurs, known for their desire to maximize profits, permit such losses to become large or last for a long time. Sooner or later they change their policies and hire on the basis of merit, not racial or other criteria. Ironically, such behaviour is more likely to come from large employers like corporations. These institutions, so disliked by the Left, are driven by their many shareholders to maximize profits and to instruct managers that they must refrain from indulging in economically damaging policies. Perhaps most importantly, bigotry does not matter to materially-affected blacks, since they have employment opportunities with non-bigoted firms. It is easy to dismiss this reasoning as 'ivory tower' and irrelevant to the real world.

However, a number of empirical studies have confirmed its validity. Space limitations allow me to mention just two of the most important. The first was done by Professor Tom Sowell, a black economist teaching at Stanford. He found that historically in the U.S., some minorities, such as the Japanese and Jews, while subject to strong discrimination, have enjoyed higher average earnings than whites! His research is well-documented and unquestioned. He concludes that the observed lower earnings of blacks in the U.S. have been due to reasons other than discrimination in the market. Many of these reasons are historic, like slavery and the racist policies of the governments of the South. These government policies prevented the forces of the market from operating in the way discussed above. In recent times, a more important factor has been government policies that have provided (and continue to provide) *wrong* incentives for education, work and self-reliance of some minorities. He believes that legislation for pay equity, affirmative hiring and quotas not only restrict personal liberties, but in the longer run are counter-productive — for those they are designed to help!

A second study examined the earnings of women in Canada, which on average tend to be lower than those of men with equal schooling and age. This study notes something already widely known. On average all workers are more productive and therefore earn more the older they are and the more experience they have. Now compare women and men with the same education at age 40. The women, on average, have less experience and therefore will be less productive than the men. The reason is that at least some of the women have taken time away from formal employment in order to raise their children. Under these conditions, the higher earnings of men are due to their higher productivity, not discrimination. This proposition is confirmed by Statistics Canada, which finds that women in Canada who have never been married and had no children, earn on average the same as men of the same age and with the same schooling. It is important to note in this context that whereas a free market and society automatically and anonymously provide individuals with effective protection against discrimination, historically the most serious and persistent discrimination has been that created and enforced by governments.

Outstanding examples of this in history are the 20th century policies of governments in the southern U.S. and South Africa (against blacks) and in Germany (against Jews). On the basis of this reasoning and empirical information, most economists see pay-equity legislation and hiring quotas as a coercive method for redistributing income. This is so since the policy does not increase the total national income of a country. Giving more to minorities like blacks or women means that less can go to the rest.

The slippery concept of 'fairness'

It is ironic that such policies are unfair, or in the language favoured by the politically correct, they are racist for Canadians who do not belong to protected minorities. These policies do not treat individuals according to their personal characteristics but according to unalterable characteristics of the group to which they belong, in recent years mainly white, Anglo-Saxon males. It is even more ironic that the Charter of Rights, which prohibits such racist discrimination, does not protect them. There is a clause in the Charter which explicitly permits exemptions to the basic rule as long as the policy is deemed to serve 'the public interest.' Many Canadians who do not belong to favoured and identifiable minorities resent this racist policy aimed against them by the State. They are resentful that they and their children often do not get hired or promoted, even though their qualifications are superior to those who get the jobs they covet. They resent being singled out to bear individually the burden of government policies (allegedly) designed to serve the public interest by creating more equal opportunities for all. For them, clearly, the legislation has tilted the playing field and made opportunities *less* equal.

In my view, the kind of discrimination and special treatment of individuals resulting from employment equity legislation is involved in the example of the store owner whose cashier declares that he is a homosexual. The store owner who loses bigoted customers can do nothing to *make* them deal with the homosexual cashier. However much the storekeeper supports the creation of a Canadian society free from racism and discrimination against homosexuals, he cannot get back the customers. Ultimately he loses his livelihood – unless he does what Ringma and Chatters said he would be expected to do: find work for the homosexual that keeps him away from contact with the public. If the store went out of business, his homosexual employee would also lose his job!

The answer given by Ringma and Chatters reflects the sentiment held by many Canadians who are not members of minorities. They resent being innocent victims of policies initiated by elites in Ottawa and the big media centres, elites that are out of touch with the realities of life in the rest of Canada. Reform promised to give these victims a voice in Parliament. Ringma and Chatters merely delivered on their promise.

I know from conversations that many Canadians feel extremely uncomfortable with the logic of the analysis in the preceding paragraphs. Many refuse to accept the empirical proposition that in Canada a shop owner ever has to face the loss of customers. Projecting their own attitudes, they assert that in Canada "no-one cares about the sexual preferences of a cashier." That may well be true, but it is also misses the point about the inherent injustice and racism aimed at individuals by employment equity legislation. Peter O'Neil's question about the homosexual cashier brings out the issue most clearly and effectively. If innocent individuals were never impacted by employment equity legislation, the question would be meaningless and would not have been asked.

Others I know are willing to accept the proposition that customers will be lost. However, these people then tend to assert that the shop owner should be happy not to have to deal with such bigots and carry on with his business. This reaction misses the point that fiscal reality may not give this option to shop owners and others affected by the policies. They might go bankrupt.

In many states of the U.S., affirmative action (the equivalent of Canadian employment equity legislation) has gone even further than that in Canada. It explicitly sets out employment quotas; in California it requires State-financed universities to accept students in proportion to their percentage of the total population. This university quota system has resulted in outrageous and well-documented examples where black students with C grade averages were admitted to Berkeley, while Caucasians with Bs and worst of all, Orientals with As graduating from the same school were not. The public outrage over such official, racist policies has resulted in the passage of a public referendum prohibiting quotas — in spite of the powerful opposition of many minority groups for whom very much was at stake.

Canadians upset with employment equity legislation cannot use referenda to end them. The next best thing has been for them to vote for the Reform Party, which had promised in its platform to fight against legislated employment equity and the racism it implies. It is for this reason that my caucus colleagues and I opposed the employment equity legislation in general and its extension to sexual orientation as a prohibited ground for employment discrimination in particular. We spoke at length about the injustice of reverse discrimination and a number of other undesirable consequences of the policy. These speeches were ignored by the media. They had all been heard before and could be written off as irrelevant opinions of people who were considered to be either racist bigots or ideologues with visions rejected by Canada's elites. And then came the Ringma-Chatters affair with much publicity for Reform. There are many indications that Reform constituents appreciated it and increased their support for the party. The 1997 election result is at least consistent with this fact.

It is clear to me that in spite of my attempts to analyze the issues rationally and introduce empirical information, there are many who will remain unpersuaded by the preceding analysis. They will say that Ringma and Chatters *are* racists, that my analysis is a sophisticated justification for racism, that Reform supporters *are* bigots and racists, and that employment equity legislation must be enforced and strengthened until Canadian society has eradicated all traces of racism. These people are entitled to their opinions. We live in a complex world. I hope that there are not too many such people and that the media will not give them attention out of proportion with their numbers. However, most importantly, I hope that the discussion of the issues raised by personal and state-initiated discrimination will continue in a spirit of tolerance and rationality and that the media will promote such discussions rather than kill them through their almost coercive measures of punishment for those who are seen to hold politically incorrect views.

Gun control and criminal justice

Government policies on gun control, the treatment of criminals and refugee immigrants during the last fifteen years also have become icons of left-wing ideology, to be protected by the code of political correctness. It was to be expected that Reformers would bring up these subjects in Parliament. The reaction was predictable, causing me and my colleagues much grief. Here is my story of what happened and the background to each issue.

In 1994 the government introduced gun control legislation. I must confess that I knew virtually nothing about existing laws in this field. As a result it came to me as a great surprise to find out that Canadians under laws existing at that time could not own automatic weapons, sawed-off shotguns or handguns. Special rules existed for collectors of arms. They may be said to be highly effective. To the best of my knowledge, no major crimes had been committed using weapons owned by a collector.

Most surprising to me was the fact that hand guns could be owned only for target shooting and law enforcement. Extremely rigorous conditions are attached to the ownership of hand guns for target shooting. For example, the guns can be transported only in vehicles if they are disassembled and then only between a person's home and the shooting range. Besides law enforcement officers, only very few people are allowed to own hand guns for self defence.

For example, I was surprised to learn the following facts from the owner of a jewellery store in a large Canadian city. About twice a month at night the alarm system in his downtown store goes off as a result of attempted burglaries or other events. He is required to turn off this alarm personally. For self-protection during this night work he would like to carry a gun to protect himself in case he runs into a burglar still on the premises, but police authorities have steadfastly refused to grant him a licence to do so.

There is also strong legislation regulating the ownership of rifles and shotguns. Canadians wishing to buy such weapons for hunting or target shooting must attend a training course, get a license, police clearance and provide a host of personal information to the seller of the weapons. The owners of such guns, including collectors, are subject to strict regulations concerning storage and safe-keeping of weapons and ammunitions.

Many Reformers and I support this legislation, even though it obviously has not eliminated the use of firearms in the commission of crimes and causing death. Criminals about to commit a crime that might lead to life imprisonment are not normally deterred by existing regulations. In fact, homicide through the use of firearms during a criminal act in Canada is relatively rare.

Many will be surprised to learn that in 1995, 1,100 people died of gunshot wounds. Of those deaths from gun shots only 13 percent stemmed from homicides, while 81 percent were suicides and six percent were due to accidents or unexplained causes ('Use of guns dropping in homicides,' *Globe and Mail*, June 24 1995, page A3). Guns are used only in two percent of all violent crimes in Canada ('Firearms figuring less in violent crime,' *Toronto Star*, June 24 1997, page A2). All these figures should be seen in the light of the fact that in 1995, 1,529 people were killed in Canada by alcohol-impaired drivers.

The new legislation introduced by Justice Minister Allan Rock extended the already costly and tough gun control legislation by mandating the registration of long guns. I could not and still cannot understand the rationale for this policy. Very few crimes are committed using these weapons because they are almost impossible to conceal. The proposed registration of the guns' serial numbers and their owners' name does not make it possible to trace either the gun or the owner, should it be used in a crime and a bullet was found.

The legislation cannot prevent crimes committed by mentally unstable individuals like Marc Lepine, who killed 14 women at the University of Montreal December 6, 1991. The proposed registration is expensive both for the government and the owners of rifles and other long guns who have to pay costly fees and spend time filling out forms and dealing with a bureaucracy.

Chapter 11

Many of these owners need rifles in their occupation (farmers, hunters and trappers, for example) and some for protection (surveyors and wilderness guides). For many Natives, guns are essential to their lifestyle and culture. For these people, the registration is nothing but a new and discriminatory tax on their tools.

Need for a cost-benefit analysis

In my view, the merit of registering long guns cannot be assessed rationally without an estimate of the cost and benefits it brings. I have heard some people argue that costs are irrelevant when lives are at stake. But this is not a rational argument, and public policy must consider the alternative use of the cost of registration. As an example, consider that the registration costs nationally $500 million and that it results in the saving of 10 lives per year — for a cost of $50 million per life saved. This cost must be compared with the lives that could be saved if the same money were spent on medicare for pregnant mothers or more ambulances, for example. In the absence of such information I found it impossible to either support or oppose Rock's proposed legislation. I asked the Minister in the House (and through a personal letter) to make information available to Parliament about the cost and benefits of the registration of long guns. He promised me he would, but never delivered on his promise. I think I know why.

An independent researcher, Professor Gary Mauser at Simon Fraser University, prepared a study showing that the cost of registration *alone* was projected to be about $500 million. He also assembled data about the likely number of lives saved, the essence of which is captured by the figures about the number of non-suicide deaths by gunshot wounds provided above. In the absence of official estimates, I accepted Mauser's well-documented results, concluding that the registration of long guns made no sense. There are too many other, more important and socially valuable projects on which the government could spend this money. I joined my caucus colleagues in opposing it in the House debates.

Two of my caucus colleagues, Jack Ramsay and Art Hanger, were retired police officers from Alberta. Ramsay, in his late '50s, had a distinguished career in the RCMP, where he successfully fought the establishment to gain rights for the rank-and-file: on his resignation from the force he courageously published an article titled 'My case against the RCMP,' in *Macleans* magazine (June 1992). Many believe that it contributed much to the decision to establish a Commission of Inquiry into RCMP operations. The findings of the Commission confirmed as valid most of the criticism Ramsay had made in his article. He has a good sense of humour and shows much passion arguing his cases. He is very much in touch with the Reform grass roots and probably reflects the views of the bulk of his former RCMP colleagues.

Employment Equity, Homosexual Rights and Internal Dissent

Hanger, in his early '50s, was tall, with the typical manner of the detective featured in crime movies. Like Ramsay, he was 'on the beat' for many years, dealing with criminals and seeing the victims of crimes. Such experiences gave both Ramsay and Hanger an air of well-earned authority on this subject. Ramsay and Hanger opposed the new gun legislation on populist grounds, as well as the large costs relative to benefits. As official Reform Justice critics, they received much attention from the media. Their speeches were scrutinized carefully and they were interviewed frequently. Of course, the media had no difficulties in painting them as rednecks and extremists. Their views were described as going against the public interest and being totally out of touch with public opinion.

Surveys had shown — convincingly — that Canadians wanted more gun control legislation. I encountered such sentiments in my own riding. However, after a number of discussions it became clear to me that this demand for gun control was based on a serious lack of information. Hardly anyone knew what the existing legislation was, nor what the new legislation proposed to do. There is also an asymmetry between costs and benefits for most people. They do not own nor do they ever use guns. Therefore any legislated restrictions or added costs on owning them is of no concern to them. On the other hand, they know that guns are dangerous things, are used in violent crime and represent a threat to their own security and that of their children. So however small the possibility that new legislation will reduce this threat, they support it. For them, the benefit/cost calculation comes out right. They do not even have proper incentives to inform themselves about costs or the size of benefits. The costs and inconvenience imposed on legitimate owners of long guns are of no concern to them.

The most important aspect of the public controversy over the merit of the proposed mandatory registration of long guns was that it permitted the media to use it once more to link Reform to extremism, using the techniques described above. Giving quotes from Hanger and Ramsay to prominent persons in favour of the legislation, they obtained many stories and headlines condemning Reform for its lack of caring and redneck attitudes. Again, as in the case of policies on natives and employment equity, this campaign helped Reform. Many of our supporters live in rural areas of the West, where guns are a way of life and used in work. For them, the cost of the proposed registration was real. The benefits, if any, in terms of reduced violence and crime in the big cities, was worth nothing. They welcomed our opposition to the legislation.

Hanger, immigration and criminals

Hanger attracted a 'racist and extremist' label from the media on two other occasions, the first occurring when he was the Reform critic on immigration. As a retired police officer, he had the confidence of his

Chapter 11

colleagues still working in law enforcement; they regularly supplied him with information about the criminal abuse of the immigration refugee system. He presented data on crimes committed by such groups as Asian gangs containing many refugees (which information could not be kept officially, since law enforcement officials are not allowed to collect information on race and other potential minority characteristics of criminals). This meant, according to the media, that he was guilty of three violations of the code of political correctness. He had questioned the merit of immigration and refugee policies, and he mentioned "refugees" and "Jamaicans."

The latter act involved racism, since it noted group characteristics. By so doing, Hanger was alleged to have unjustly injured the reputation of all Canadian Jamaicans and refugees who were law abiding citizens. No-one ever explained how it is possible to discuss the merit of Canada's refugee policies without bringing up facts about the criminal record of refugees in comparison with the rest of the population. For the media it was enough that they could once again accuse a Reformer of racism and get all the headlines to condemn him.

It is ironic and important to note here that a report on the refugee system prepared by a government-appointed board of inquiry: 'Not just numbers: a Canadian framework for future immigration' (1997) suggested major changes be made, which noted many witnesses they had listened to identifying facts of the sort produced by Hanger (page 2 of the report). Reportedly, a high proportion of criminals and welfare recipients were among refugees; there were excessively long delays in the deportation of bogus refugees and those found guilty of criminal activities. There was also a lack of professionalism among politically-appointed judges in courts adjudicating refugee claims.

One of the most interesting statements made in the report (page 4) is directly relevant to Hanger's activities, my own experience with immigration (and Native) issues during the election campaign discussed above and political correctness in general. I quote: 'One of the flaws in Canadian politics . . . is the difficulty in dealing with subjects such as immigration, as if to raise the issue itself were tantamount to questioning its benefits, the place of immigrants, or the value of a certain category of immigrants. This kind of unspoken censorship has been a chronic problem for both journalists and politicians.' I agree with the sentiment of this statement but I disagree with the supposition that journalists have a chronic problem. *They are* the chronic problem. They seek out and give great publicity to those who condemn all rational inquiries into the merit of policies on immigration (as well as Native policies).

The second issue on which Hanger was chastised occurred when he was one of Reform's justice critics. He had announced that during a parliamentary break he was going to travel to Singapore to watch the public caning of a criminal and determine its effects on public attitudes. Importantly, he was going to use his own money to finance the trip. At that time the public had discussed intensively the merit of the method of punishment because it had been meted out to an American teenager who had been convicted of vandalizing an automobile in Singapore.

The media seized upon Hanger's plan and created a major furore. They had no difficulties finding commentators willing to express their horror at even the thought that a Canadian might find caning an acceptable method of punishment. The media had once again succeeded in managing to link Reform with extremism.

Hanger received much support for his idea from Canadians. In my own riding, many constituents thought that caning was a good idea and should be considered as a method for dealing with vandalism by youths. A scholarly discussion of the subject of what is known as 'shaming' of criminals has been published by a Professor at the Law School of the University of Chicago. He believes that the publication of the names of people convicted of drunk driving, bankruptcy, petty theft, which is practised in Canada, is an effective deterrent to crime. He also believes that the public shaming aspect of caning, rather than the pain inflicted, is the main deterrent of this form of punishment.

The same issues are also addressed in a book by Albany University Law Professor Graeme Newman, *Just and Painful: A Case for Corporal Punishment of Criminals* (London:Collier MacMillan, 1983).

More generally, Hanger's views reflected a strong public resentment of what many believe is the soft treatment of criminals and the justice system's disregard for the victims of crime. They see excessive concern about the appropriate punishment for youths who vandalize property. No-one appears concerned with the cost and inconvenience inflicted upon the owners of such damaged property. The issue of the coddling of criminals and lack of concern for the rights of the victims of crime was also taken up in many speeches and public rallies by caucus members Randy White and Myron Thompson.

White, then in his mid-40's, was a former Secretary-Treasurer of a large school board, and represented the riding of Fraser Valley West in British Columbia. His riding holds a number of prisons and there are many prison guards in his constituency. He often brought up the opposition to existing criminal laws by his constituents, who lived daily with its consequences and had intimate knowledge about the operations of prisons.

While presenting details on how the government spends taxpayers' money on conveniences for prisoners, White enraged many people by noting that one of the prisons in his riding had its own golf course. Most prisons had modern gymnasiums with the latest, most expensive workout equipment. He reported about the horrors felt by victims of crime, relating the fears of people who were stalked by prisoners on early parole. By doing so very effectively and forcefully, he became very popular with the public and journalists in his own riding.

However, the national media did not like him or his messages, which were considered to be politically incorrect. How dare he question the wisdom of policies based on the belief that prisoners are themselves victims of our social and economic system? He had no right to raise doubts about the notion that criminals can readily be rehabilitated through counselling. It was improper to question the early release on parole of criminals who had given signs that they had regretted their acts and were ready to return to a productive private life. White became another symbol of Reform extremism.

Myron Thompson, in his late '50s, was a former high school principal. Representing the rural Alberta riding of Wild Rose, he was first elected in 1993 and reelected in 1997 with one of the largest majorities of any Reformer. The name of his riding fitted the image he cultivated. Big, strong and athletic, in spite of his age (he was once a professional baseball pitcher), he regularly wore cowboy clothing. He spoke like, and bore the manner of a rancher as portrayed in Western movies, though behind this front is an intelligent and thoughtful man with a university education and much experience as a school administrator.

Thompson's main interest was criminal justice, the coddling of criminals and neglect of victims. He cultivated contacts with the grass roots where he was a popular speaker who could arouse the anger of people. More than anyone else in caucus, he was, for the media, the prototype Reform redneck with no place in a civilized Parliament. They often used his image and quotations, which he supplied liberally, in their quest to paint Reform as a party of extremists.

The Brown-Silye affair

It was one thing for the media to pick on quotations from Reformers to build a case that the party was made up of racists and extremists. But they had a credibility problem: Canadians were becoming increasingly sceptical of the comments made by their favourite, politically correct sources of opinion. It was quite another thing to have members of the Reform caucus themselves say publicly that they were disgusted about the racist and extremist attitudes of their colleagues. How better informed and more reliable could sources be?

Well, early in 1996 Jan Brown and Jim Silye served journalists these information gems. They were quoted as having said that their Reform caucus colleagues were racist and extremist. The media had another major feeding frenzy. Caucus was in an uproar. I was very, very unhappy over the entire affair.

Jan Brown, in her late forties, was elected for the first time in her life to a political office, representing the urban riding of Calgary Southeast. She has a masters degree in communications and is a very skilled professional. Her last job before the election was serving as the Chief Executive Officer/General Manager of the Potato Growers of Alberta (1987-92). She was

Employment Equity, Homosexual Rights and Internal Dissent

always elegantly dressed and perfectly made up and groomed (she was also a bit of a flirt). Twice, at least, she was voted the 'sexiest female in the House.' After one of these votes she had herself photographed for the *Hill Times* in a suggestive pose, reclining on the hood of an exotic sports car.

Brown was obsessed with the need to have good relations with the media. She courted them and fed them good quotes and ideas. In return, the media made her into a star. For at least a year, no one in caucus, except Manning, was mentioned more often in the media. However, she did have some problems.

First, she did not understand policies well. One morning in the House lobby she told me excitedly that the evening before she had had dinner with Don Newman, the popular host of *Capital Report,* a daily program on the CBC News Channel. She then proudly said to me: "Don told me that I should spend less time on appearances and more time on the substance of issues." I have since talked to Newman about this dinner with Brown and he confirmed having said this to her. I think that this episode tells almost all there is to know about Brown and her role in Ottawa. A dinner alone with Newman symbolized to her the public relations success she was. She needed to make me appreciate it to the full by reporting on the conversation she had had, and the expression of interest in her by a member of the media elite. Apparently she had no idea how disparaging Newman's remark about her lack of understanding of issues of substance was.

The second problem was that Brown became very intimate with the media. I can just imagine the conversations she had with journalists, talking about her feelings and ambitions, as she did with me and other members of caucus. I can also imagine how in her need to make herself look good in the eyes of such journalists she passed on information about her colleagues that was both privileged and potentially damaging.

Here is how Brown brought about an unsettling episode in which she involved all Reformers. A Calgary journalist with whom she was very close interviewed her about the positions caucus members had taken on employment equity, homosexuals, immigration, refugees, gun control and criminal justice. I have described these positions in the preceding paragraphs. She denounced them as 'racist' and 'extremist.' The familiar pattern of comments by 'authorities,' breast-beating by politicians from the government and the NDP followed, all reported prominently in the media. There was great jubilation among the opponents of Reform. They now had incontrovertible proof that their past accusations were correct!

Jim Silye's comments to the media, in the same vein, reinforced the ferocity of this campaign. Silye is a charmer. A sharp dresser, he was, at least twice, voted the 'sexiest male in Parliament.' Of relatively short stature, he was fit-looking, with the broad shoulders and big chest of an athlete. In his youth he was an all-star football player with the University of Ottawa and later won a Grey Cup ring playing with the Calgary Stampeders.

Chapter 11

After his football playing career ended, Silye became a successful entrepreneur. He radiated the self-confidence that comes with success in business and had the self-deprecating humour that helps one survive the fierce ribbing of the athletes' locker room. Articulate and freely expressive of his views on issues of concern, he is always good for a laugh.

Like Brown, Silye also became intimate with the media and, like Brown, was often mentioned favourably in the newspapers, on radio and TV. During one intimate conversation with a reporter he revealed his unhappiness with the 'racist' and 'extremist' views held by some members of the Reform caucus. This information hit the headlines and was milked by the media for all it was worth. The leader and caucus took Brown and Silye to task for their indiscretions. We had all known about Brown's unhappiness with the likes of Ramsay, Hanger, White and Thompson, the views they held and the image they projected. I was never a direct target of her criticism directly, but I knew that if Native policy issues ever became prominent again, I would also be considered as one of those caucus 'racists.'

Her criticisms in caucus meetings were accepted graciously. Like everyone else, she was entitled to her opinion and it was her right to express her disagreements and stimulate discussion of the ideas. The problem was that she often went to the media with her views, breaking the rules of caucus confidentiality and the need to present a united front to the world, hurting all of us.

I know Brown well enough to form the view that she meant well; she wanted Reform to succeed. She believed in Reform's fiscal platform and program for direct democracy. The trouble arose basically from her belief in left-wing causes concerning criminal justice, the right of homosexuals and other special interest groups, employment equity, immigration and a host of similar social policy issues.

But her liberalism on social policies was not enough to get her into trouble. She also had an over-arching desire to be a 'media star.' She succeeded and it went to her head. She thought she was so influential and so important to Reform that she could succeed in forcing caucus to change and accept her views on these issues of social policy. Of course, she did not succeed in this, but only made all of us very unhappy. One Saturday morning, during a drive to the Gatineau Hills on a warm fall day, my wife Hélène and I listened on the car radio to an interview Brown was having with Jason Moscovitz, the host of the popular CBC radio program *The House*. Essentially, she was arguing that since she was such an obviously compassionate person with the proper views on social policies, all of us in caucus who disagreed with her *must* be extremists and racists! The memory of this interview spoiled, for Hélène and me, a delightful outing.

In caucus, Silye showed his full understanding of the damage his interview had done to Reform. He explained how he had been quoted out of context but acknowledged that he had become too intimate with some journalists. In the end he apologized for what had happened. That day after

Employment Equity, Homosexual Rights and Internal Dissent

caucus he was interviewed by the media pack hovering outside the caucus room. He lost control and shed some tears over the mistakes he had made. He had my full sympathies and I forgave him in my own mind. The episode affected him profoundly. He chose not to seek re-election as a Reformer in 1997 and has returned to the world of business.

Brown remained defiant about her right to criticize Reformers collectively and publicly, continuing her public denunciations in the self-righteous belief that we all needed her to keep us from the political wasteland of extremism and racism. When it became clear that Manning would ban her from caucus as a punishment for breaking caucus rules, she resigned from the Party and sat as an independent MP in the House. After that event I rarely saw her and never spoke to her again.

As a final act of defiance, in 1997 Brown left the riding where she had been elected in 1993 as a Reformer and ran as a Progressive Conservative candidate against Manning in his own riding. In her public pronouncements she implied that she would win against Manning because his constituents were fed up with the 'extremism' and 'racism' of Reform and its leader. She received only 8,617 votes, or 17.9 percent of the total in the 1997 election, while Manning received 27,912 votes, or 57.99 percent.

I wish Jan Brown well in her pursuit of a career in the media and as a public relations consultant.

CHAPTER 12

The Leader, Preston Manning

LEADERSHIP requires vision, intelligence, discipline, drive and stamina. Successful leadership also requires luck, being 'in the right place at the right time.' I believe that Preston Manning has all of these leadership qualities and a lot of luck, at least until now.

Manning also has some limitations. His management style is inappropriately centralized, causing him to get too much involved in trivial decision making. He is a very private person, controlling his emotions very effectively, and therefore appears to be aloof. He is loyal to a fault, relying heavily on friends and advisers of long standing to the exclusion of others he does not know well. His vision is limited by adherence to the principle of Populism.

In this chapter I will present my very personal views on Manning's leadership and personal qualities as I formed them through my experiences as a member of his first caucus in Parliament. These tales will obviously be coloured by my own experiences, not all of which were happy. I had stood for election in the hope that I would have the opportunity to work closely with him on the formulation of economic and financial policies; my hopes were never fulfilled. Even the titular role of Finance Critic escaped me for nearly two years. I never became a member of his inner circle, which worked out major policies, managed Parliamentary and party strategies and dealt with the important daily problems of putting out fires in caucus and the House. I did not come close to him at a personal level. Many of my caucus colleagues had similar experiences, becoming disappointed about their lack of influence on policy-making and the management of caucus and party affairs. None became personally close to Manning.

I believe that these conditions played an important role in convincing the most able and experienced members of caucus, Ray Speaker and Stephen Harper, not to seek reelection in 1997. They certainly influenced my decision not to run again.

Vision and dreams – power to the people

Manning's vision, like that of all great leaders, reflects the aspirations of the public. In democracies, this ability to express public concerns often brings electoral success. The aspirations of the public were shaped by conditions during the late 1980s and early 1990s. Canada was in economic and political turmoil. The Progressive Conservatives had been fiscally irresponsible in the extreme. Annual deficits had led to the accumulation of a huge debt; there was talk about the need for a bail-out by the International Monetary Fund. Spending on popular government programs was curtailed because of the ever-increasing interest cost of the debt. Ever greater deficits forced interest rates up, which caused a recession which, in a vicious cycle, deepened the deficits, causing higher interest rates and deepening the recession. Unemployment and bankruptcies were at record levels.

In Canada's western provinces, the public was resentful over the way past governments had disregarded or damaged their interests, particularly those governments under the leadership of the Liberal party. The two governments headed by Pierre Trudeau generated the deepest resentments. Trudeau's National Energy Policy, enacted in the wake of the world energy crisis, put unfair and discriminatory taxes on Alberta's natural resources; in British Columbia, tariff policies resulted in excessively high prices on many consumer goods. The natural north-south trade in such goods had been replaced by flows from the East, where producers prospered behind high tariff walls. Refrigerators, for instance, had to be purchased from eastern Canada instead of the western states of the U.S., which would have been cheaper due to lower transportation costs — were it not for the high tariffs.

The West also resented the way in which the political system had appeased Quebec separatist sentiments. Many Westerners believe that Quebec was favoured in federal spending and transfer programs. They were also unhappy about the cost of and social divisions caused by bilingualism and multiculturalism, which they continue to see as policies designed to prevent Quebec separation.

Perhaps most importantly, past Liberal and Conservative governments in Canada had enacted 'progressive' social legislation on abortion, the death penalty, gun controls, the treatment of criminals, immigration and refugees and others. These policies were not welcomed by the more conservative, more rural populations of the West. The people of this region felt that an arrogant, politically dominant central elite had forced moral and social standards on them that they disagreed with, and did not fit their lifestyles.

Preston Manning has a vision which meets the aspirations of Canadians and addresses their dissatisfaction with fiscal and social policies. He rhetorically asks audiences how it was that Ottawa governments could pass so much unwanted legislation. The answer he gives is that the Canadian system of government does not give enough power to the people. There are 'insiders' who prey on 'outsiders.' In speeches around the country he looks for people who consider themselves 'shut out' or 'disillusioned' by the existing parties. If people had more power over the political and legislative agenda in the past, he argues, the present problems would not have arisen. He then offers himself and the Reform Party as the agent for the creation of the 'New Canada,' which is also the title of a book in which he details his vision (MacMillan, 1992). Manning's vision for a New Canada rests on Populism, which has a long history in the West.

Populism postulates that 'The People are Always Right' (or that 'The

People are One'). Manning loves to refer to the reliability of 'The Common Sense of the Common People.' According to populists, political strife is created by the political system and the politicians. They gain personally from doing so. But, as Ken Boessenkool pointed out to me, such Populism has no room for ideology. The people Manning attracts into his party are united through their *unhappiness* with the existing system and policies. The reasons for their dissatisfaction are too diverse to fit into any ideological mould. For this reason, Manning has the tendency to dwell in his speeches on what is wrong at present and to offer only relatively vague alternative policies and none that are ideological and run the risk of offending an important segment of the discontented.

Manning's Populist solutions to existing problems consists of changes in political institutions and increased public information to reduce misunderstanding and conflict. He avoids offering specific solutions since, under populism, they are found by the people themselves. The agenda for populist innovations consists of a Triple-E Senate (Elected, Effective and Equal), binding referenda, free votes in Parliament and recall of elected politicians through citizen initiatives and votes.

These instruments for giving more power to the people have much appeal, but are also beset with difficulties.

The Triple-E Senate

A Triple-E Senate would be *elected*, to provide it with legitimacy. Under the present system Senators are *appointed* by the Prime Minister. The public sees them as political hacks rather than elected officials accountable to them through elections.

The Triple-E Senate would be effective by providing a check on legislation passed by the House of Commons, much like upper legislative chambers do in most modern democracies. The power of the U.S. Senate is often held out as the model for an effective Canadian Senate. The Triple-E Senate would be equal in the sense that all provinces (or regions) would have equal representation. In such a Triple-E Senate, all of Canada's regions would be able to protect themselves from the tyranny of the majority. Smaller provinces like British Columbia and Alberta could block policies of the sort which had disadvantaged them in the past. Or at least, they could demand modifications of policies proposed in the House of Commons where voting power is dominated by provinces and regions with the largest numbers of citizens.

The Reform Party's bi-annual Assembly has adopted voting procedures which achieve what Manning envisions for the reformed Senate. Resolutions binding on the party are passed *only* if they receive an overall majority of votes of the delegates, as well as separately majorities in provinces which constitute over 50 percent of the total. This rule effectively prevents the passage of resolutions that would benefit only Ontario and Quebec.

It is not enough that the number of delegates from the two provinces make up a popular majority. If the resolutions injure the interests of smaller provinces, they can block them because between them they make up more than 50 percent of all provinces.

The Triple-E Senate has much political appeal in the West, but much less so in the centre of the country. It is easy to see why. In effect the Triple-E Senate can block the will of the majority of Canadians. For this reason, many see it as profoundly undemocratic. Pragmatically, however, the Triple-E Senate also would mean that Ontario and Quebec would lose the privileged position they have enjoyed and benefited from for a long time.

There is an additional problem with the Triple-E Senate, arising from the great inequality of the size of provinces. The four Atlantic provinces have only 15 percent of the population; if every province in the Senate were given an equal number of votes, just like all U.S. states have two Senate seats, 15 percent of the population would hold 40 percent of the seats. Most people would agree that such an alignment of power in the Senate would create new types of inequities. I wonder whether even British Columbia and Alberta would be happy with such a power structure in the Senate.

The obvious solution to this problem would be the creation of an Atlantic region, to include all four provinces and holding the same number of seats as each of the other historic provinces. But this solution would not likely be very popular with the Atlantic provinces. Another solution might be to give seats in the Senate according to the size of each province. The disadvantage of this solution is that it would replicate the power structure of the House of Commons.

By listing the problems associated with the Triple-E Senate I do not mean to suggest that the principle is bad, or that with much good will solutions can be found for the problems. I only wish to suggest that Manning will need much skill in persuasion, find many good compromise solutions and much luck to persuade Ontario, Quebec and the Atlantic provinces to agree to changes which reduce the power they enjoy under the present system. But one never knows, more unexpected things have happened: the Liberals became fiscal conservatives and abandoned the universality of social programs! And we know that we will never get anywhere unless we know where we *want* to go. That is the merit of Manning's vision for a Triple-E Senate.

Binding Referenda

The second component of Manning's vision for getting power to the people is the use of binding referenda. Under this scheme, groups of individuals can initiate policy resolutions which are placed on ballots and voted on at regular intervals. Experience with such referenda in Switzerland and several U.S. states has been generally positive, but there are many devils in the details. The system for binding referenda must prevent the

Chapter 12

formulation of too many questions. For example, in in recent Californian elections, referenda by the hundreds were on ballots, producing what is called 'ballot overload.' The public does not have the incentive or the interest to get fully informed on all the issues.

As a result, two forces have gained strength. On the one hand, well-financed special interest groups use mass media ads to suggest that the passage of the referendum would provide benefits for all. In reality, the referendum would benefit mainly the special interest groups concerned.

On the other hand, the public has reacted by simply voting against initiatives — the 'naysayer' phenomenon. In Switzerland, where referenda have been used for a long time, they have done much good. The key ingredient of their success has been the small size of the population and geographic region involved. Both facilitate public discussion of the issues, creating interest among a well-informed public.

It is also important to note that the Swiss referendum tradition was developed before the age of mass media and transportation. Under these conditions, the public's attention could be attracted much more readily than it is today. The Swiss are reluctant to give up the tradition which has served them well for such a long time.

Finally, political scientists have long opposed referenda because they can lead to the tyranny of the majority over minorities. Referenda were used by Napoleon and Hitler to sweep into power and trample traditional democratic institutions and rights. In most countries, legislatures protect the rights of minorities through Bills of Human Rights or similar constitutional clauses. In addition, there are checks and balances between legislative, executive and judiciary branches of government. 'The People,' acting through referenda, face no such restraints (in principle).

In recent years, in California and elsewhere, the judiciary has nullified initiatives passed by majority votes in referenda, doing so to protect the rights of minorities. Important political battles are being fought over the right of the judiciary in these instances to thwart the 'will of the people.' The preceding is designed not to dismiss the increased use of referenda in Canada but to show that it brings many difficulties and dangers of its own.

I have found that many strong supporters of referenda are not aware of them. I have never heard Manning refer to them in his speeches. Ted White, the Reform MP for the riding of North Vancouver, has worked out how the shortcomings and dangers of referenda can be dealt with. I hope that Manning will take note of this work if and when the time comes to put his vision into effect.

Free votes

The third leg of Manning's strategy to give more power to the people is the greater use of free votes in the House of Commons. Under such a system, constituents could lobby their MPs to vote in certain ways, and punish them at the next election if they failed to carry out their instructions.

A system of free votes in the House of Commons has much popular appeal. Many people like the power of legislators in the U.S. House of Representatives and Senate, which on crucial votes are sometimes called by the President. Often they can curry favours for their constituents in return for their support of certain legislation. But many students of the system also warn of its problems. Legislative gridlock, wasteful spending brought on by legislative compromises and the excessive lobbying needed to persuade individual legislators are serious disadvantages of the U.S. system.

In the end, this system works because of the power of the President. He can veto legislation which proposes unreasonable spending or taxation; he can afford to act responsibly, because he is accountable to the country as a whole in direct elections.

The balance of power in Canada is different. Under a system of free votes, MPs would be tempted to vote for spending increases to curry favours with their constituents. They would be much less likely to vote for higher taxes to pay for this spending, since it would make them lose favour with their constituents. Such a system would be biased toward over-spending and deficits, and the Prime Minister could not prevent these biases, because does not have the President's veto power and independent electoral base.

Other difficulties associated with the concept of free votes raised their ugly heads early in our Reform caucus following the 1993 election. Manning could not afford to have Reform MPs vote unpredictably on all issues and present a picture of a divided party to the public. Therefore, caucus adopted the principle that MP voting in the House would normally be determined through majority ballots in caucus. Before such votes took place, critics in the area of the legislation, such as health care or the environment, would present a position paper and recommend voting with or against the government. Most critic recommendations were accepted without debate and there was no opposition to all MPs voting the same. However, on some contentious issues like gun control, or affirmative employment policies, the caucus was divided. There were the normal discussions about principle, and the causes and effects of legislation. Members who took their commitment to populism posed a serious stumbling block to party unity when they insisted that they be allowed to vote according to the wishes of their constituents.

These members faced the problem of providing evidence of their constituents' wishes, an issue which was never completely resolved. Some insisted that voluntary communications by constituents to the member's office were enough, while others asserted that it was necessary to have scientifically-designed random sampling through the use of unbiased questions. In addition, there were questions about timing; on some critical votes there might not be enough time to poll constituents scientifically.

Reform's commitment to free votes was put to the test by the government's gun control legislation. Jim Silye, Ted White and Ian McClelland provided evidence that they had polled their constituents, who had instructed them to vote with the government. These three Reform MPs voted accordingly and faced neither resentment in caucus nor punishment by the Leader. I voted a couple of times with the government on issues involving fundamental principles like personal freedom and responsibility without having first polled my constituents. The issues were of minor public interest and did not attract any attention from my constituents or the party leadership. In one case only, one person contacted me to ask for the reasons that made me vote with the government.

Perhaps Parliament could be made more responsive to the will of the people through free votes on non-budgetary legislation only. Such rules would deal with the problem of potential voter alliances leading to irresponsible spending and deficits. However, there are problems with this approach as well. All social and regulatory legislation has some fiscal implications. One would expect to find more MPs willing to vote for social and regulatory laws than willing to vote for the taxes needed to pay the costs they entail.

One of the most difficult problems associated with free votes surrounds social policies like abortion and the death penalty. Public feelings on this subject run deep, and MPs themselves are likely to have strong personal preferences. The chances are that legislation proposed in these sensitive areas would elicit very large pressures from the public and may expose MPs to serious conflicts with their own conscience. For this reason, Manning favours binding referenda rather than votes in Parliament for dealing with these issues. In this context he always hastens to add that during campaigns before such referenda, individual MPs are free, if not morally obligated, to speak out on the issues according to their personal convictions and attempt to influence the outcome of the referendum.

Recall

The fourth leg of Manning's strategy of giving more power to the people is to recall legislators who do not carry out the will of the people (or who engage in criminal or morally reprehensible activities). Recall has enormous popular appeal. In principle, it gives constituents real power. It provides an outlet for the energies of people who are enraged by unpopular government actions.

However, again there are many devils in the details of how such a system would operate. How soon after an election can recall procedures get under way? If there are no time limits, in close elections, recall petitions can be used essentially to have another round in the election fight a short time after the last one ended. What exactly are grounds for recall? What methods must be used for documenting cause? How long and costly can recall campaigns be? What is the voter base for recall?

These have turned out to be important matters in a recent recall initiative in British Columbia. Voter lists had become obsolete because so many voters had moved away.

Again, Ted White has done much research on optimal rules for recall. I hope that they will influence Reform policies on this issue, but I have my doubts about the merit of recall legislation on the basis of a very fundamental problem — which I believe cannot be overcome by institutional arrangements.

The PC government, under Brian Mulroney, passed two pieces of very contentious legislation, the Goods and Services Tax (GST) and the North America Free Trade Agreement (NAFTA). In my view as an economist, both of these legislative programs will serve the interest of Canadians very well, in the long run. The Liberal government under Chretien soon discovered this fact after it came into power in 1993 and failed to deliver on its election promise to scrap the GST and renegotiate the NAFTA.

Yet, under the leadership of the Liberal opposition in the House, passionate ideologues, helped by eager left-leaning media, inundated the public with false and misleading information. As a result, public sentiment was strongly against this legislation. Had recall initiatives been possible this media blitz might have provoked recall campaigns. I doubt that under these conditions the government would have been able to get these important programs passed. It will be interesting to see how Manning will handle the problems created by recall legislation if and when he is Prime Minister and the threat of recall endangers passage of laws that he knows are unpopular at the moment but good for Canadians in the longer run.

Presumptive merit of existing institutions

My views on Populism are probably strongly coloured by my academic background and strong conservatism. I am very sceptical about panaceas. My conservatism stems from fundamental Darwinian principles applied to human institutions. These principles can best summarized by the question: 'If the proposed political, social and economic innovations are as good as their proponents argue, why do they not exist now?'

For me the answer to this question is the following. Presumptively these innovations have been used before or elsewhere but have been found wanting. They did not survive the competition with alternatives. As in the case of mutated species in Darwin's natural world, they lost out. For this reason I believe the burden of proof about the superiority of innovations is on those who propose them. It is up to them to show why the shortcomings of the past or in application elsewhere are no longer relevant in the context where they want to revive them and claim that they are progressive and new.

Chapter 12

It is possible that the proponents of new institution can show that technological developments, a better educated public and more wealth have shifted the balance in favour of new approaches. It is also possible that for a time inferior institutions exist, like the totalitarianism of the Soviet Union and a return to older institutions represents an improvement.

Evolution and the selection of the best institutions take time and do not move on a straight line of improvement, but I do not think that present institutions in Canada represent such a temporary exception to the rule. Nor do I think that changes in technology and education have swung the balance in favour of these populist innovations.

The preceding analysis is incomplete and I retain an open mind on the subject of the presumptive merit of existing institutions. Perhaps I am wrong, and populist institutions will make Canada a better place. But I need more theoretical and empirical evidence to be persuaded.

In the meantime, I ask the convinced populists among my colleagues like Ted White, Preston Manning and other Reformers, not to neglect the costs and risks of making large-scale experiments with political institutions. Almost certainly it is not wise to present populist changes to the political process as panaceas to Canada's present of future problems. Such promises, like those about the use of Stornoway, the traditional residence of the Leader of the Opposition, and about the acceptability of 'excessively rich' government pensions by retired MPs, may turn into a public liability.

In 1998 Reform experienced this problem when, contrary to promises made during elections, Manning moved into Stornoway and a number of MPs decided to accept the parliamentary pensions they once had fought against so vigorously.

Manning is a master in talking to general audiences about the benefits of policies designed to give more power to the people. He has found very effective ways to make his points and create enthusiasm for them in crowds. One of his most effective presentations involves hauling onto the stage a seat which once served members in the House of Commons. He deplores the prevailing attitude that this chair 'belongs' to the elected politician. In fact, he argues, it belongs to the people who elected the member of parliament. He then asserts that free votes and recall would assure that the elected member would always act accordingly.

However, in my view, Manning is not entirely honest when he talks about the virtues of populism. He rarely if ever mentions the difficulties and risks just discussed; I think he has a moral obligation to do so. I think he also would benefit from it because it would raise his credibility with those who are familiar with the problems.

Finally, such a policy would serve his interests if and when he is the head of a Reform government. At such a time he will either have to give up his populist reform agenda or change it significantly to deal with these problems.

The Leader, Preston Manning
Intelligence and discipline

Manning is intelligent, well educated, is widely-read and has good recall of what he has read. No ghostwriter penned his own manifesto, *The New Canada*. He writes most of his own speeches. He inserts into these speeches references to historic events, drawn mainly from memory. He knows analytical and factual details about every major field of government policy. He used to read every memo I wrote to him on financial matters. I know, because he always sent me his personal comments. Manning's intelligence was driven home to me when one day we had dinner together. We sat in conversation at a remote table in the Ottawa Delta Hotel dining room for about two hours. The tone and contents of the conversation was set with his opening statement: 'I have asked you to have dinner with me so we can review the current fiscal situation and Reform policies in this area.'

During this conversation Manning displayed to me an astounding depth of factual knowledge and analytical understanding of Canada's fiscal policy. Any graduate student with such qualifications would have earned an A+ in my course at Simon Fraser University and other institutions of higher learning I have been associated with. I am sure that he is equally well informed about almost all other policy areas. Manning is also a man of integrity. Many caucus discussions and personal conversations I have had with him allow me to make this judgement. I am convinced that he would never enrich himself at the expense of the general public. He appears to have a strong inner compass of what is right and what is wrong, where he is, has been and wants to be.

Not everyone who knows Manning well shares my views. I have been given hints by a number of people about 'inappropriate behaviour.' The stories were disturbing: where there is smoke, there may well be fire. But the information given to me about Manning's alleged lack of integrity was not strong enough to make change my mind.

I do not know what determines a person's integrity. Some have speculated that Manning's is built on his strong religious beliefs. I have no information which allows me to judge the merit of this speculation. The subject of his personal religious beliefs never came up in any conversation, and he never used it in defence of any policy position. I never probed him on this matter.

Related to this integrity and strong inner compass are his mental and emotional discipline. I never saw Manning lose his temper or emotionally display his displeasure. Even on occasions when he used strong words, his voice and demeanor did not fit the message. It seemed that he was uncomfortable delivering messages of criticism, though there were many opportunities for him to do so. Members of caucus often made mistakes or revealed poor judgement; other parties often took unfair pot-shots at him, his behaviour and policies, and the media often distorted his positions or told outright lies.

Chapter 12

His reactions to new topics were never impulsive nor did they stray from his populist world view. He avoided open personal conflict and was a master of verbal *jiu-jitsu*. Users of this technique show great understanding of the often strongly held views of their antagonists. As a result, the opponents of the users of verbal *jiu-jitsu* are often pleasantly surprised and become open to the rational exchange of views on the subject. At this point the practitioner calmly and rationally brings up reasons for holding a different point of view. Often this technique calms stormy feelings and a genuine dialogue begins. Sometimes, however, this technique fails. Under these circumstances Manning tended to defer decisions to another meeting or asked a committee to resolve the conflict.

During part of his life Manning was a management consultant. One of his areas of special interest was conflict resolution. In his writings he is a strong proponent of the view that all conflicts can be resolved if people communicate properly, that in the end all serious conflicts are based on mutual misunderstanding. I believe that this principle guided many of his actions as the leader of the Reform Party. It is also an essential ingredient of Populism as a political system which can in principle replace the adversarial system of parliamentary democracy and which is such an important part of Manning's vision. I think that Manning is correct in this view about the nature of some human and political conflicts. There often exist solutions which bring benefits to both sides. Such solutions are often referred to as 'positive sum' games. But there are also many conflicts which involve 'zero sum' games: if you get a little more, I will get a little less. Some other conflicts are 'negative sum' games in which both parties lose. Unfortunately, many political disputes are 'zero' or 'negative sum' games. The government taxes some to give benefits to others. There are losses in income and well-being for both sides. The taxed work and invest less to avoid some of the taxes. The recipients of benefits are induced to change their behaviour, become more needy and get more benefits.

In spite of the existence of many solutions to conflicts it is important to devote resources to the exchange of information among antagonists; as a result many seemingly zero and negative sum games can turn into positive sum games.

However, such a basic approach raises the question about the amount of resources one should devote to such information exchange. Often it may be optimal simply to accept that conflicts are a necessary part of governing and leadership. Decisions that might benefit many, for example, could hurt a vocal few. The unwillingness of politicians to make such decisions is criticized by many as one of the serious shortcomings of modern governments. In economics and political science this tendency is explained through the theory of public choice, which subject has come up in other contexts in this volume.

I am not sure that Manning fully appreciates the need for political parties to make unpopular decisions for the public good, even if they result in opposition which cannot be won over by proper explanations. His dedication to Populism and his basic belief in the power of reason stand in the way of accepting this proposition. I think that this makes him a less effective leader than he could be.

Drive, work ethic and stamina

Manning is driven to better the life of all Canadians through helping the passage of proper government policies. He wants to be Prime Minister so that he can carry through on his vision. He derives satisfaction from the fact that through his party's electoral success he already has influenced government policies to move in what he considers to be the right direction.

I do not know the origin of Manning's drive. Perhaps he is driven by his desire to emulate his politically successful father who for many years was the very popular premier of the province of Alberta. Perhaps his religious beliefs are important. However, I do not think it is important to dwell on this issue. What counts for me and should count for all Canadians, in the end, is what kinds of policies Manning and his party favour and how they affect the welfare of the people.

Drive is not enough for success. One also needs a willingness to work and make personal sacrifices in pursuit of the goals set by the inner drive. In addition, willingness to work has to be backed by stamina, the physical and emotional resources needed to keep at the job. And finally, success requires psychological hardiness to get on with the job in spite of inevitable setbacks. Manning has an insatiable appetite for work, seemingly unlimited stamina and much psychological hardiness.

The work load of the leader of a political party is so great that, having observed Manning closely, I wonder why anyone wants to assume that role. Manning has to deal regularly with five main groups of people: The leadership of the Party, the rank and file members, caucus, the general public and the media. All five groups are the sources of many conflicts, most of which require Manning's personal attention.

The leadership of the Party consists of the Executive and Constituency association officers. These people are the body of the party; the Leader is the head. They need each other, and must interact frequently and intensively. This interaction often involves conflict over vision, finances and individual ambitions. The leader has to deal with these conflicts very carefully since the executive and other party officers are volunteers and can very easily leave their positions.

The executive and association officers are recruited from the large body of rank-and-file party members. These foot-soldiers of the party are essential to the success of elections though financial contributions and work with candidates in the ridings. Manning has to keep in frequent contact with

Chapter 12

this rank and file through mailings and appearances at meetings and rallies, providing the inspiration to keep them committed to the cause. He also has to spend much time dealing with conflicts among ambitious and headstrong individuals, especially during elections.

The third group of people requiring much attention from Manning is caucus. All members of caucus have substantial egos. Without a good dose of self-confidence they would not have stood for election, and fighting and winning an election strengthens it. They know that without them, the Leader and Party would have no presence in Parliament. At the same time, caucus members know that they owe much of their election success to the work of the Leader, the party officers and workers. Caucus and the Leader need each other.

As in all human organizations, the work of caucus gives rise to many conflicts. Manning has to dedicate much time to dealing with them sensitively to avoid resentments. In addition, he has to inspire members and provide leadership on policy issues. Manning's work with caucus consumes much time and energy. During my membership in caucus he handled these difficult tasks quite well.

However, there was one way in which he was not very successful. Caucus members, in spite of their often blustering self-confidence, have some very common personal and psychological needs which only a leader can satisfy. They need to know they are doing a good job, that they are liked and that the leader supports them when they are in trouble with the media or their constituents. Manning went through the motions of praising our work and of saying how much he appreciated it, but his remarks were too mechanical. They occurred at the beginning of each caucus session, and for reasons I cannot explain, for me they never quite did the job. I will return to this subject later.

One of the most important problems in Manning's relationship with caucus arose out of his lack of public support for those of us who got into trouble with the media. I have already discussed in the preceding chapter the episodes involving my own remarks on native policy issues and the opinions voiced by Hanger, Chatters and Ringma. Manning seriously damaged caucus morale by not defending us publicly. He could have done so even if in caucus he criticized us heavily. I do not know why he behaved in such a manner. Perhaps he saw opportunity for personal gain with the media and other Ottawa powers; perhaps he did not realize the damage he was doing to us and the rest of caucus. Some day he, too, will write about his years in Ottawa and we will learn the true facts.

The biggest problem facing any leader, including Manning, is how much time to devote to courting the general public directly, through speeches, rallies, intimate dinners with community leaders and similar affairs. Such activities bring in new voters, financial support and manpower for the next election, while consolidating the existing base.

Courting the general public is a very strenuous activity. Campaign swings mean covering large distances, living out of a suitcase, getting up emotionally for speeches and much concentration on interpersonal communications. Typically, such campaigns are interrupted by frequent returns to Ottawa for caucus meetings and other parliamentary business. Since the Official Opposition status was attained following the 1997 election, such return trips to Ottawa sometimes are necessitated by the need to meet with visiting foreign dignitaries, who by protocol are required to interact with the official 'government in waiting.'

The media offer a very efficient means to communicate with the general public. TV clips, radio interviews and newspaper articles reach many more people than personal contacts ever can. But use of the media is fraught with dangers and uncertainties. Coverage often is negative, however well-prepared the briefings are and how positive the basic message might be. The personal touch is absent. I have been to many dinners and rallies where critical audiences left as enthusiastic supporters of Reform even though they had come as sceptics or out of curiosity. Close personal contact with Manning, seeing his body-language, voice and demeanour captured their sympathies in ways media images could not.

Manning spends much time dealing with the media. Reporters with cameras and microphones line up in front of the door to weekly caucus meetings both when they start and end; regular scrums are held after question period. Special press conferences are held when major policy initiatives are launched or responses to government policies are required. Manning gives special interviews on request to individual journalists, participating in TV panel discussions and guesting on radio talk shows. He is superbly effective in his dealings with the media. They scare me, and I wonder how he has managed to become such a master of the art (much of it is probably due simply to experience). Giving lectures to large groups of people no longer scares me the way it did when I began my career as a university lecturer, but there is more to it than that. Manning is always well-prepared, knows his material and can handle the toughest questions without showing irritation, rudeness, talking down or, most important, providing sound bites that can be spun into damaging stories. Perhaps he is just a great talent.

Psychological hardiness

In my career in academia I have met many brilliant people who never became successful professionals. What they lacked was the ability to deal with adversity, which takes the form of students complaining about lectures and their grades, editors or colleagues giving negative comments on their research and writings, or the denial of promotion and tenure. Everyone, in every walk of life, faces analogous criticism and setbacks. But only those with what I call psychological hardiness learn from their mistakes, change some of their ways and stay with others because they know they are doing the right thing. These types of people become successful. Those who do not have psychological hardiness never reach their potential. They worry too much about the mistakes they have made and what they imply about their basic abilities. They often try to please everyone and end up pleasing no-one. They question their own inner compass.

Like all successful leaders, Manning has plenty of psychological hardiness. His inner compass serves him well. He knows that setbacks are inevitable. He gives the impression that he always sees the glass half full, not half empty. Through his example he inspires others.

The problems raised by social conservatives

One of the most difficult problems facing all so-called 'right wing' parties is conflict among members about social policies. It turns out that many Reformers are fiscal conservatives who want balanced budgets and a smaller, less intrusive government. But Reform has also become the party of choice of a substantial number of social conservatives who focus their political ambitions on the role of the state in setting and enforcing social and moral standards. These social conservatives fight against legalized abortion, the permissiveness of laws on pornography, the 'rights' of homosexuals and laws which discriminate against the family. Unfortunately for Reform (and the harmony and power of right wing parties in all countries), fiscal conservatives often strongly disagree with social conservatives.

David Frum, in his book *Dead Right* (New York: Basic Books, 1994) discusses the nature and seriousness of these conflicts between the two types of conservatives. Fiscal conservatives want a smaller State and more freedom, responsibility and self-reliance for individuals. The social conservatives want the State to expand its role by setting and enforcing social and moral standards. In the process, individuals lose freedom, responsibility and self-reliance. The two positions, in principle, are irreconcilable. Experience in many countries has shown that conservative parties dominated by social activists and corresponding platforms tend to lose voter support. They are deserted by many fiscal conservatives and they never attract the ideologically non-committed voters who like fiscal conservatism but cannot stomach social conservatism.

This lack of broad electoral support comes as a surprise for many people. The reason is that social conservatives tend to be motivated by strong religious and moral fervour. They are very vocal and well organized, giving the impression that they have more support than they do. It is tempting to suggest that social conservatism causes troubles for the Right much like Communists do for the Left.

Manning has been able to minimize the damage social conservatives could do to Reform. He avoids committing the party to the most controversial of their causes by recourse to his populist strategy. He insists that once in power, Reform policies on abortion and the death penalty will be decided through binding referenda. He downplays his own social conservative beliefs on these issues but has committed himself to fight for them in referendum debates. He also encourages all social conservatives to do the same. At the same time he asserts his commitment to accepting the verdict of the majority and have his government enact policies accordingly.

Until now Manning's strategy has succeeded in keeping peace in caucus and the party. Social conservatives may not like the lack of strong commitment to their causes by the Leader of Reform, but they have no other place to go. Reform at least promises referenda on the issues. It therefore is better to vote for Reform than to stay home and help elect a party which opposes all social conservative policies. These pragmatic views on social conservatism appear to motivate publisher Ted Byfield's editorials in *Report Newsmagazine,* which is widely read by both fiscal and social conservatives in the West.

Caucus had a number of members who were strongly committed to the somewhat less controversial social conservative issues surrounding the family. Manning allowed these MPs to form the 'family caucus' and most caucus members had no objection to their activities. Under the leadership of MP Sharon Hayes from Coquitlam, the family caucus developed positions for discussion and possible adoption by the full caucus. The positions they developed tended to be rich on rhetoric and short on policy recommendations. In spite of this fact, the full caucus always refused to vote on the family resolutions and sent them back for further study and refinement. In effect, the Party escaped the danger inherent in even these less controversial aspects of social conservatism by letting supporters have their say but stopping them short of committing the party to specific policies.

The taxation of child support payments

I had one personal clash with the social conservatives in caucus. The government had given in to a strong feminist lobbying effort, introducing a bill forcing fathers to make child-support payments to their former spouses out of after-tax income. This new policy was demanded by women who under the old policy had been forced to pay taxes on their former husbands' child support payments. They erroneously believed that through this policy they would end up with higher net incomes, being wrong on two counts.

First, working fathers tend to have higher incomes than their former wives responsible for raising the children, and they therefore are subject to higher marginal tax rates. A shift of the income tax obligation from the mother to the fathers therefore reduces the total pool of after-tax income available for distribution to the children. In fact, the new bill was estimated to result in an increase in annual government tax revenue of $410 million at the expense of the family units.

Second, discussion on the bill revealed the government's clear expectation that judges setting the level of child support payable would do so in the light of the total resources for distribution. On average, therefore, the proposed bill would lower the amount of money going to mothers as child support.

In Finance Committee hearings, long after the bill had been passed, groups of women who had begun to realize this outcome began lobbying for the restoration of the old provisions.

In the caucus meeting at which the party's vote on this bill was established, I argued that we should oppose this government bill on the grounds that it would damage the well-being of children. In addition, since Reform stood for freedom of choice, I argued that families in divorce proceedings should be allowed to choose between having the support payments taxed in the father's or mother's tax return (it turns out that this was the existing policy, but we could emphasize the element of choice in the public defence of our vote). I was outvoted by a small margin; I still remember my disappointment over the fact that both Preston Manning and Ray Speaker voted against my motion.

What carried the day with the social conservatives in caucus was the argument made by Sharon Hayes in the name of the family caucus. Under the existing system, a family in which *only* the father works, total tax payments are higher while the marriage is intact than if there is a divorce and child support payments are made, the reason being that child support payments are taxed at a lower marginal rate than if the same money is included in the intact family income. Logically, it therefore follows that the possible taxation of support payments in the returns of the mother represents a subsidy to divorce. The existing policy represented a tax on families; as such it encouraged the breakup of families.

I argued that divorce is a gut-wrenching, difficult matter which no-one enters into lightly; there must be very strong causes for it to be undertaken, especially should younger children be involved. Therefore, the slight monetary incentive was likely to influence only a very small proportion of all divorces.

Debate on the issue showed that conservative caucus members shared this empirical judgement. They voted in favour of the new bill — on principle. They would never vote against a bill which removed a tax on staying married. After that vote I understood more than ever the motives of social conservatives; this increased understanding did little to endear them to me.

Homosexuality

Social conservatives also have strong views on homosexuality. They favour active government policies to suppress it. The majority of Canadians do not favour such policies and Reform has not embraced this agenda of the social conservatives. However, in recent years homosexuals have lobbied not just for tolerance but legislative activism for their cause. The most important of these is to have it made illegal for employers to discriminate against homosexuals and to give equal rights to homosexual partners in a marriage as are granted to couples in a traditional marriage. While it is difficult to know with certainty, it appears that most Canadian oppose such legal activism in favour of homosexuals.

Reform has taken the position that government should treat all people equally before the law and that all distinctions based on race, colour or creed be eliminated. Under this principle it makes no sense to identify homosexuals as a group equivalent to these others. Nevertheless the subject remains a difficult one for Reform and other parties. The Ringma-Chatters affair discussed above shows just how difficult it is.

The Manning era

Manning is a leader with a strong vision, the intelligence, drive, stamina and psychological hardiness to lead a major political movement. He also has been lucky. The time for his vision to lead to success was right in the early 1990s because of past governments' fiscal irresponsibility, injustices in the treatment of the West, problems with Quebec and the pursuit of a social agenda which was too 'progressive' for many. He has been able to handle well the problems stemming from social conservative initiatives in the Party and caucus. His personal characteristics and luck brought him in 1997 to be the Leader of the second largest party in the House of Commons, serving as Her Majesty's loyal opposition. All this was achieved within a very short time and in the face of formidable opposition by established parties and the media. The Manning era is sure to merit a chapter in future books on the history of Canadian politics, whatever happens in the next decade.

What will happen? Will Manning and Reform reach the ultimate prize in politics? Will he be the Right Honourable Prime Minister, heading up a Reform cabinet and a majority caucus? The answers to these question is possibly to be found in two fundamental problems associated with his vision and management style.

The trouble with the populist vision

The following owes much to Tom Flanagan's incisive analysis of the nature of populism, *Waiting for the Wave,* and conversations I have had with fellow MPs Ray Speaker and Stephen Harper. I have touched on this theme before but because of its importance, I will again outline it here.

The very future of the Reform movement will depend on how it resolves the conflict between Populism and Conservatism. The success of populism depends on public contentment or discontent with government and political parties and the political agenda they have pursued while in power. In the early 1990s public discontent with fiscal irresponsibility, the treatment of regional interests, including Quebec, and an excessively 'progressive' social program was very high. Manning identified this discontent and exploited it. He offered to balance the budget and modify some social programs, providing a vision for democratic reforms to end regional inequities and address the problem of Quebec separatism.

The most basic and inevitable problem with the populist vision in general is its reliance on strong public discontent with existing government policies. Once this discontent has disappeared, the main reason to vote for the populist party has also ended. When people vote during more normal times, they want to know what a leader and the party stand for, what they are likely do when in office. Will they expand government or shrink it? Are they in favour of high or low taxes, progressive or proportional rates? Will they act paternalistically or encourage self-reliance? Will they use coercive instruments of persuasion or rely on moral leadership to deal with problems of economic and social injustice? Will they listen to the people through the use of referenda or will they insist that it is their responsibility to provide 'leadership' in advancing contentious issues? How open will they make the country to immigration? How will they approach the problems of unlimited needs for medical care, education, support for low income earners in the face of limited resources and taxation capacity? What will they do about the burden on future generations stemming from the debt and obligations under medical and pension plans? How much money will they spend on the military?

The answers to these and many other questions define the political orientation of a party and its leadership. The answers also determine voters' preferences in the absence of major crises and discontent. But a party and leader which really stand for 'The People know Best' *by definition* cannot have positions on this multitude of issues because they believe that they must be determined through referenda, free votes cast by representatives who have been lobbied heavily and the threat of recall in case they do not take their directions.

How will Manning and the Reform Party respond to this challenge inherent in Populism and the basic nature of democratic politics? Flanagan suggests that Manning sees no need to abandon his populist model, that he believes he can ride some yet unborn waves of discontent to future electoral victory. Flanagan credits Manning for having anticipated such waves successfully in the past. The big question is whether such waves will come his way again or whether, by his own leadership, he can create some.

I share Flanagan's doubts that new waves of discontent large enough and geographically well enough distributed will rise to permit Manning to ride them to victory. The very existence of the Reform party and its platform have led the Liberals to enact policies which have calmed the waters of public discontent. Even the NDP has embraced fiscal responsibility in its platform.

My own experience as a member of caucus and in private conversations with Manning lead me to share Flanagan's view that Manning is a convinced Populist. He has shied away from discussions of political principles other than Populism when, I believe, they were in order. Such occasions arose in caucus when the party's position for upcoming votes and House debates were outlined by individuals who had researched them. Occasionally, in my view, these proposed positions were not consistent with conservative ideology (even though they had much popular support), because they involved such non-conservative measures as increased government paternalism, regulation, spending or benefits for special interest groups.

When these policies were brought up for discussion and vote I opposed them on those grounds; Manning never supported me in these debates. He never himself made arguments related to his party's positioning on the political spectrum. Discussions of broad principles in caucus were always very short and certainly never on the official agenda. The process of determining resolutions on policies ratified by the bi-annual Party conventions and binding on caucus is also consistent with Manning's populist convictions. These resolutions come from the grassroots, where they are formulated by groups of interested Reform members. Draft resolutions are collected and, in a tedious and often contentious process, are consolidated.

Finally a manageable number is selected for open debate at the convention by a committee whose members are also supporters of populism. A number of such resolutions debated and ratified at the Assembly remain inconsistent, in my view, with conservative principles. In caucus debates, these binding resolutions are taken seriously and occasionally brought up in debate. It was particularly galling to me that they were used to defend populist motions inconsistent with conservatism, but that they were disregarded if they did not fit the present populist sentiment. On such occasions, it was allegedly all right to disregard them on the grounds that 'conditions have changed' or 'the resolution was based on misinformation.'

Perhaps I, and possibly Flanagan, are too academically inclined. Perhaps for this reason we falsely believe in the need for the Leader and the Party to position themselves clearly on the right and to offer voters a true conservative party platform. Perhaps we are wrong in asserting that the Party's internal debate should be over the strength of the conservative positioning, not whether conservatism is a viable alternative to populism. These doubts arise in my mind because in practice, Manning and the Party have carved out a conservative position. This may more or less have happened by accident. As Ted White pointed out to me, it may also have happened because the majority of the Reform grassroots are conservative. All of the major populist issues in the 1990s involved 'conservative' platforms: fiscal responsibility, smaller government, getting tough on crime, support for the traditional family, a reformed and partially privatized social security net and the decentralization of more government functions which would meet the demands of Quebeckers for more autonomy. Therefore during the 1990s populism and conservatism were the same. As a result the public, by and large, sees Reform as the party of the right.

Manning could have his cake and eat it too. He could with a clear conscience insist that he is a populist and win the votes of the supporters of this ideology. At the same time he could win the votes of those who wanted more conservatism in Parliament.

An important political development in 1998 was the push for the merger of the PC and Reform parties in the wake of Jean Charest's resignation as the leader of the PCs. During the debate over this merger Reform was considered to be clearly a party of the right. The issue of Manning's and Reform's commitment to populism never came up. Instead the main issue was the exact positioning of a united party on the right of the political spectrum.

Only future developments will reveal the extent to which Manning and Reform are truly conservative. The test will come when the wave of public discontent with the policies of the left has ended. Will Manning and Reform then embrace populist demands for left-wing policies in line with their commitment to Populism or will they stick with conservative policies of the right?

During the 1970s, Ray Speaker had been a member of the Alberta legislature (well before the founding of the Reform Party), and had a working relationship with Manning, often discussing political issues. Speaker remembers that at that time Manning was a strong social conservative but, in the light of the prevailing populist sentiments of the times — liberalism and the hippie movement — was anything but a fiscal conservative. He changed his basic views once. Will he do so again, as popular views change?

The personal image

Perhaps Manning's biggest problem after the 1993 election, and later, was his 'image' and lack of 'charisma.' It is difficult to pin down the determinants of these intangible qualities of a public figure. Some believe the image is created by such things as body language, voice and speech patterns and appearance determined by the style clothing, eyeglasses and haircut. Charisma comes from having a vision for the country and being able to present it to the public engagingly and convincingly. It took Manning several years in Ottawa before he accepted advice and changed his appearance. He has had laser surgery and now does not need glasses; his haircut and clothing were made more stylish. He has worked on his diction, body language and how they affect TV viewers, in particular. Manning always had the basic ingredient of charisma, a vision for a more democratic country through parliamentary reform and more power to the people. The trouble has been that he has not been able to get out the message to the public charismatically – or perhaps Populism itself is at fault since it prevents the Leader from taking any strong positions on any principles for government, other than that 'The People are always right.'

Taking strong positions on specific policies opposed by many is not enough to instill in the public the kind of confidence which translates into 'charisma.' The media made much of the changes in Manning's appearance and style, but it appears from public polls that these changes have not made much difference in his public image. Even getting the mantle of the Leader of the Opposition after the 1997 election did not help.

I wish I knew what it takes to make things better for Manning and Reform. It is unfortunate that the public is influenced in its views about the merit of a leader and party by superficial personal characteristics and the intangible 'image' and 'charisma.' What *should* count are the policies they propose and enact. However, this is a matter which has haunted politics and politicians for a long time. Chretien's popularity in Quebec is alleged to be much diminished by his speech defect. On the other hand, Trudeau's electoral successes were enhanced by his image as a youthful man of the world. My sympathies are with Manning and all the other public figures fighting with this problem.

Managing people

In my view, Manning's biggest personal problems stem from his interpersonal relationships and his management style. These may be related to the lack of image and charisma in the eyes of the public; almost certainly, they limit his potential for success. I have always seen Manning act properly and say the right things in interpersonal relationships, whether in dealings with me or with larger groups like caucus or political audiences. The problem seems to stem from a lack of personal warmth when dealing with people; he gives the impression of being aloof and distant. His management style is autocratic and involves him in too much detail. He does not delegate authority enough and does not always give credit where it is due. Here are a few personal observations in support of these judgements.

About six months after Reform had first arrived in Ottawa, someone in caucus let go with a cry from the heart, saying, "My constituents often ask me 'What is Preston like? What makes him tick?' To my embarrassment, I have to tell them that I do not know him any better than they do." Others in caucus, myself included, echoed this view.

Again, on at least two different occasions in the House, two different seatmates at the beginning of Question Period called my attention to the way in which Chretien gave some personal attention to the members of his

Chapter 12

caucus. On the way to his seat in the front row he would stop at desks to chat with rank-and-file members. He would put his arm around a shoulder and there was some bantering, accompanied by a broad smile. I have personally experienced this 'stroking' by Chretien on a number of occasions. It does not matter whether Chretien's behaviour towards others comes naturally or is part of a deliberate strategy to be popular. The fact is and the reason why my colleagues called attention to Chretien's behaviour was to contrast it with that of Manning. The Reform leader typically gets to his seat for question period by walking through the lobby of the House and down the aisle at a fast pace, without stopping or looking at anyone. He then sits down and reads the questions he is about to ask. After question period he hurries off to meet the media. He never stops for small talk or stroke the troops the way Chretien does.

A third illustration involves Stephen Harper, who speaks French fluently and has an outstanding grasp of Quebec politics. He had taken over the Unity Portfolio to prepare a written document setting out the Reform position on Quebec, and had worked very hard for many hours and days in the production of a document entitled '20/20.' In it he listed 20 sources of costs and risks which Quebec would face if it were to separate. He also spelled out 20 changes to the present federation which Reform pledged to undertake to meet Quebec's aspirations while it remained in confederation. The analysis was brilliant and perceptive. The document left no doubt that a rational consideration of costs and benefits makes staying in Canada superior to separation.

Harper eagerly anticipated the publication of the document. He had expected to hold a press conference where he could deal with the Quebec media in French. This would have helped Reform's cause in the province. It also would have enhanced Reform's image in Ontario, where the public views the party as regional, elected on a platform of opposition to Quebec and therefore a danger to unity.

As it turned out, Manning launched Harper's document at a press conference in Ontario. Harper was not present and was not given a single word of credit for the work he had done. The proceedings were in English only. It is easy to see that Harper was extremely disheartened by Manning's action.

The next two stories are very personal. On a number of occasions I walked side by side with Manning for about 10 minutes from the House after late night sittings to our residences, which were quite close together. On the occasion of the first few walks I tried to start a conversation involving topics that were not work-related. My efforts did not succeed. Thereafter I deliberately tried a different strategy. I did not say anything, wondering what topics Manning would bring up to close the conversational vacuum. Most of the time the vacuum just stayed until it was broken by someone else joining us. Once, after a long time of silence, he said how much he appreciated me giving up the good life as an academic to come to Parliament in Ottawa. That was as much as he ever volunteered any personal recognition of me or my work.

The final episode involved a two-hour dinner alone with Manning, as already mentioned above. The structure of our conversation during this period was unforgettable. As soon as we sat down, he announced the purpose of our get-together: he wanted to talk about the financial policy platform of the Reform party, and immediately plunged into the substance. There was no light talk about the weather, the family, holidays, sports or innocent gossip about colleagues. Only at the very end of the dinner, when dessert was served and he had completed his brilliant discussion of fiscal policy issues did he change the subject, turning to the topic I had wanted to discuss when I had requested a personal meeting with him: his choice of a Finance Critic.

Stephen Harper, the only other economist in caucus, had resigned the post to devote his full energies to the Quebec file. After Harper had announced this shift, Ray Speaker, the House Leader, had arranged a meeting with me, and had informed me that I was unsuitable for the position of Finance Critic. He stated repeatedly that this was not because I was not qualified professionally but because he had concerns about the manner in which I would handle the responsibility. He thought I would be too dogmatic and unwilling to work with others.

Of course, I was disappointed about this assessment of my ability to handle the responsibility of Finance Critic and decided to request a conventional 10-minute private meeting with Manning to discuss the issue. He responded by arranging for the dinner instead.

During the almost two hours of the dinner I had been nervously waiting for this topic to be brought up. When Manning finally turned to it, it became quickly obvious that he had no idea on how important this position was for me. In my view it indicated the party's symbolic choice for Finance Minister if and when it gained a Parliamentary majority. To have a chance to occupy this position was one of the reasons I had stood for election, even though I knew that in no way did it guarantee membership in cabinet if Reform would form the government and certainly not the position of Minister of Finance. I also noted that he was not aware that as the Deputy Finance Critic during the preceding two years I had compiled a good record. There had been no complaints from any source that I am aware of. I had made one political rookie mistake in my 'South Sea Island' speech on natives discussed above. But since then and importantly on fiscal policy issues I had not given the media any cause to embarrass Reform and me, even though there were many opportunities to do so.

I had attended all meetings of the Finance Committee conscientiously and gained the respect of members from other parties. I had been told many times how much they appreciated having an economist in their ranks who could question witnesses on complex issues of finance. A leading Liberal member of the Committee told me how much he had learned

Chapter 12

from me to appreciate the many risks and unintended consequence accompanying government intervention in the market.

I also had concerns about how the public would interpret Manning *not* appointing me Finance Critic. Would the business community and other economists interpret it as a signal that my resolute stand on fiscal responsibility was not shared by Manning? How could I explain his action to my constituents? After I had presented to Manning these reasons for wanting to be the next Finance Critic, and why it was in the interest of the party to appoint me, he replied: 'I did not know you wanted that position. I thought you wanted to devote more of your time to policy formulation.' Dessert was eaten and we went home.

The next day Ray Speaker ceased to talk about his concerns about my personal suitability for the job. A few days later, in a long-awaited shuffle of the shadow cabinet, I was appointed the chief Finance Critic. After a few months Speaker told me how pleased he was with the good job I was doing in consulting with my colleagues on fiscal policy issues. He also confided in me that his earlier job of preparing me for not being chosen for the position as Finance Critic had been one of the most difficult of this life. That is really something to say for someone who had been in elected politics for 25 years and had to make many unpopular decisions as a minister. To this day I do not know the extent to which earlier he had acted for Manning rather than expressing his own views on my lack of suitability.

I think this episode shows clearly the problems which arise from Manning's lack of interaction with people. How could he not have known what this position meant to me and to the party's image with a knowledgeable public? It was because he does not interact enough with people at the personal level. It was because he often used other people to do unpleasant work involving interpersonal relationships.

Manning is aware of this problem. After the caucus session mentioned above he instituted a procedure which he thought would deal with his lack of contact with caucus members. Periodically, he would spend ten minutes alone with every member for an unstructured conversation. This effort was not successful. The sessions were too official an event. The time was too short to establish a personal rapport and for many to work up the courage to bring up what was really on their mind.

I can understand that Manning faces serious problems in improving his personal relationships with caucus and other colleagues. These problems haunt all people at the top of organizations. First, there is the lack of time since he has many other responsibilities.

Second, he must be sure not to create jealousies and divisions by spending more time with some people than others. From remarks made in caucus it is clear that he is very concerned about this problem intrinsic in personal contacts.

Thirdly, he cannot get involved in time-consuming petty disputes among individuals and he cannot be a nanny to those whose expectations for success exceed their qualifications.

I do not put much weight on the argument that Manning's deficiencies in personal relations are due to a lack of time. Many of us would have liked to have Manning join us for the occasional informal lunch or dinner — he has to eat anyway! At such meals he could have had contacts with many people at the same time. None of us were heavy drinkers, nor did we want long sessions. Short chats in the lobby or on the way to or from his seat in the House would have been even less time-consuming and much appreciated.

Work as an MP in opposition is a lonely and stressful business, with few rewards. A little pat on the shoulder from the Leader would have helped morale very much. Perhaps Manning thought that his regular practice of giving praise and thanks to us in caucus was enough. It was in fact a very imperfect substitute for the occasional stroking of the sort Chretien demonstrably used almost every day in front of our eyes.

There remain the other problems of having to avoid favouritism and staying out of petty conflicts. Other leaders have successfully done so and I think he could have found ways if he had tried.

The inner circle

From the beginning in Ottawa, Manning chose as his closest working associates people with whom he has had much previous contact. Some had helped found the party, others had been on the party executive. The rest of us had little chance to show what we could do.

It is difficult for me to write about this problem of the inner circle because of the possibility that my views are biased through my own exclusion from it. However, I know that others felt as I do about the lack of opportunities to get involved and show what one could contribute. My evidence on this matter comes not only from contacts with caucus colleagues but also from Manning himself. On a number of occasions he addressed the issue in caucus directly. He noted that it had been brought to his attention that some people were unhappy about their lack of involvement with the so-called Administrative Committee. It meets every Monday at six in the evening, is attended by a small group of people selected personally by Manning and makes many administrative and strategic decisions affecting the operation of the party in the House and in its public relations. In response to this discontent, he invited caucus members to attend the meeting as observers any time we wanted to and downplayed the role of the committee. I attended a couple of times to observe the proceedings, but it was quite clear to me that my comments and involvement in affairs under discussion were not welcomed.

Upon reading a draft of this manuscript, Ray Speaker explained to me that there was a group of people who met regularly and made certain decisions. This group consisted of caucus officers and Speaker was a member of

Chapter 12

it in his capacity as House Leader. According to Speaker, this group was preoccupied with administrative matters and setting the caucus agendas; Manning never asked the group to make any strategic or political decisions.

Manning's reliance on people he knew from prior working relationships came to the fore most strongly in the context of the appointment of the first House Officers. The House Leader and Whip play very important roles in a difficult environment. It would have been good to have in these positions persons with experience in politics and management. Ray Speaker was the only person in our caucus with such prior experience in parliament. He had spent over 20 years as an elected member of the Alberta legislative assembly, and had never lost an election. During this period he had been a cabinet minister (in Ernest Manning's last cabinet), House Leader of the Official Opposition (the Representative Party of Alberta, with two members). He had been elected Leader of that party in November 1984. In 1987 he became involved with the Reform movement and in was asked to run as a Reform candidate in the 1988 federal election, but Don Getty, the Premier of Alberta asked him to run in the 1989 provincial election and he opted for this alternative. However, in 1991, he resigned his cabinet seat in the Alberta government and devoted himself to run the upcoming federal election in 1993. Manning had strongly encouraged Speaker to take these actions with the words 'I will welcome you' (information provided to me by Speaker).

So, with Speaker available and his vast experience ready to be used, whom did Manning appoint as his first House Leader? He appointed Elwin Hermanson, aged 42. Hermanson is a very intelligent, articulate, hard-working, person with a good sense for politics. He was a successful Saskatchewan farmer before the 1993 election. He made a decent House Leader, but obviously lacked the experience Speaker would have brought to the job. I have asked myself many times why would Manning appoint him rather than Speaker as the first Reform House Leader.

One possibility I considered was that Speaker had conflicts or disagreements with Manning. Speaker assures me that his was not the case. In fact, he had resigned his Alberta cabinet seat specifically to run in the Lethbridge riding after having been asked by Manning to do so. He had accepted the challenge hoping to be able to use his great experience to help Reform in Ottawa. He was very disappointed when the job he was most qualified to fill went to a political neophyte instead.

The only reason I can think of why Hermanson was chosen was that the two men had worked together from the beginning of the Reform movement and Hermanson had done good work organizing the party in Saskatchewan.

It is interesting to note that Hermanson lost the 1997 federal election, the only sitting Reformer to do so. The loss was undoubtedly due to a redrawing of the borders of electoral districts in Saskatchewan, which severely fractured the riding in which he was first elected. Since his 1997 defeat he has helped found, and has been elected the leader of a new provincial party, the Saskatchewan Party. Its goal is to unite the divided right wing interests in the province in an effort to unseat the NDP and end its long dominance in provincial politics. I am sure that Hermanson will have a distinguished career in politics, be it at the provincial or federal level.

Ray Speaker eventually replaced Hermanson as House Leader. After he had decided not to seek reelection in 1997, Chuck Strahl took over from him. The first Whip appointed by Manning was Diane Ablonczy. She was the only lawyer in caucus, petite, soft-spoken, articulate, considerate and intelligent. But she does not have the personality to be the 'boss' of 50 MPs. The Whip's job is to assign and monitor House duty. This task is needed to assure that every day a minimum of eight Reform MPs are on the floor of the House or nearby to speak on issues being debated and, most importantly, to be present when procedural manoeuvres by the government require votes or roll-calls. Numerous other jobs of the Whip, like automatic membership in the powerful Committee for Internal Economy, require forceful and assertive personalities.

As in the case of the House Leader, there were in caucus a number of individuals whose professional backgrounds and experience would have made them into superb Whips. In private life, Randy White was a successful manager and negotiator. He has a strong personality. He was elected House Leader after the 1997 election and has done a superb job in this position.

There were others like Bob Ringma, who had a distinguished career as an administrator in the military, and Jim Silye, who was a successful athlete and entrepreneur with outstanding organizational capabilities. All three men had the respect of caucus members.

Why did Manning choose Ablonczy over the other three more suitable persons? The only possible reason is that Ablonczy had been working with Manning on the creation of the Reform Party from the beginning. He had confidence in her judgement and was loyal to her in return for the support she had given him during the early struggles of the Reform party.

Manning also had to appoint the Caucus Chair, choosing Deborah Grey. This appointment was not controversial and there was no-one better suited for the job. She was universally liked and respected for her rhetorical skills. She also had been the only Reform MP in the preceding House and therefore had a better sense of politics than most. However, she never took leadership roles on any matters, her loyalty to Manning being very strong.

Manning's selection of House Officers was discussed widely and criticized among Reform MPs in private and more publicly in caucus. We were not happy with his selections, and demanded the right to elect House Officers in the future. Manning resisted our demands, but eventually relented and accepted a compromise. Caucus would elect the House Officers but he had the right to veto their appointment.

Chapter 12

No Shadow Cabinet

Prime Ministers in Canadian politics are all-powerful, virtual dictators. But they cannot know or do everything necessary to manage the largest enterprise in Canada. To gather basic intelligence they rely heavily on the Privy Council, a body of technical and political experts. In Parliament they rely heavily on ministers and their collective, the cabinet. To the disappointment of many ministers there is typically also a smaller circle of trusted ministers holding important portfolios who work with Prime Minister more closely than does the larger cabinet. Both the large and smaller cabinet permit the Prime Minister to receive advice, share responsibility for decisions made and monitor or control the execution of policies.

Chretien has said publicly that when he was Finance Minister in Trudeau's cabinet, on several occasions his decisions were overruled by Trudeau. For this reason he exercises much less control over his cabinet. He will not consult with individual ministers unless they get into trouble. He trusts them explicitly to do a good job and relies on cabinet and the Privy Council to assure that their policies are consistent with overall party strategy. When he sees them alone it is mostly because they made a mistake and may have to be replaced.

Opposition parties traditionally have organized themselves in parallel with the government. They create a shadow cabinet with individual MPs responsible for watching over and criticizing government ministers and policies falling into their area of competence. They are also responsible for the development of policy positions, all in cooperation with and under the watchful eye of the other members of the shadow cabinet, caucus and influential party advisers. The party leader exercises effective control as the chair of these shadow cabinets, as tightly as is consistent with their leadership styles.

In 1993 Manning decided to break with this long-standing tradition. He did not appoint members of a shadow cabinet. Instead, he appointed what he called 'clusters' of individuals with special interests. There were the social policy, finance and industry clusters. I was a member of the finance cluster and shared responsibilities with a number of other MPs like Ray Speaker, Jim Silye, Stephen Harper and Charlie Penson.

Interestingly enough, Harper, an economist and person with considerable experience as an aide to two elected officials, attended these meetings only sporadically. He did not like the cluster system and absence of clear lines of responsibility associated with a genuine shadow cabinet. The finance cluster elected Ray Speaker as chairman and gave him the primary responsibility for finance.

I ended up as a member of the House Finance Committee. My personal experience illustrates the difficulties caused by the cluster system and Manning's unwillingness to pick a shadow cabinet. At the first meeting of the Finance Cluster, we all expressed our interest in different areas. Natu-

The Leader, Preston Manning

rally, I said that I was very interested in being the Finance Critic because my professional background would help me to be effective. In response, Jim Silye said that as a successful businessman he was the right man for the job. 'Knowledge in economics is not necessary. Expertise in economics can always be hired,' he said. I bit my tongue and smiled in response, knowing that I would have to live and work with Silye for a long time. But it is clear that this experience did not do much for my morale and my longing for the life in academia.

In the absence of a clear line of responsibility and regular meetings of a shadow cabinet, the process of policy formulation was confused and without the direction necessary to make it effective. I felt left out of the process of designing responses to the Finance Minister's budgetary and taxation policies. I had no responsibility for the design and modification of Reform policies on finance. My only clear responsibility was to attend meetings of caucus and the House Finance Committee. I took both of these jobs seriously, but did not find them fulfilling. I will discuss further in the next chapter the process of policy formation by the Reform party.

On my own initiative I wrote position papers on several financial issues confronting Canada, but because I had no regular contacts with Manning or a shadow cabinet as a sounding board, my papers died unheroic deaths. Manning responded to almost all my memos, but I was working in an even greater vacuum than I worked in as an academic. Then, at least, I had my professional colleagues and conferences providing guidelines and setting standards.

I know that other qualified and eager members of caucus had the similar experiences to my own. The cluster system was a waste of talent and did not produce the results that would have helped Reform's standing with the public and the media. The system did not allow the development of any one person who could rival Manning in public recognition or influence over policies. I think that this was and remains an important issue with the public.

My view on the need for a higher profile for other caucus members and prospective members of a Reform cabinet was formed as a result of an interesting luncheon meeting with David Radler, Conrad Black's relatively low-profile partner in the ownership of the newspaper empire. Radler lives in Vancouver and has a long standing interest in party politics (for example, the B.C. office of the federal PC Party is in the basement of his office building). Radler had complained to a leading Reform supporter that the party did not have any people in caucus intelligent and experienced enough to be effective ministers. It was suggested to him that he meet me. That is how the luncheon came about.

I do not know whether our conversation made him change his mind, but the food was good and I learned a lot about newspaper empires! We had another luncheon together a year later.

I do not know why Manning chose to go with the cluster system rather

Chapter 12

than the traditional shadow cabinet. During my last year in parliament he had agreed to the formation of a shadow cabinet, but it was not the real thing. It was headed by Ray Speaker and Manning attended none of the meetings. The main agenda was administrative. The shadow cabinet never functioned in the traditional way of providing for interaction with the Leader on policy formation and monitoring. After the 1997 election a shadow cabinet was formed immediately and I have been told that it performs more of a traditional role now.

Caucus colleagues and I have speculated about the reasons why Manning chose to break with tradition and form the cluster system. His own explanation was that he did not know the qualifications of the members of his caucus. The cluster system would allow him to let them develop and come to his attention. If this is the true reason, it shows Manning as a poor manager. A little work looking at the experience and investigating the reputation of individuals could easily have pointed to the best candidates. If after their appointments they turned out to be unsuitable or made too many mistakes, they could have been replaced by other eager people, much like Prime Ministers do with their cabinets. Manning also hinted at the fact that the cluster system was more democratic than the traditional method of appointing ministers. Under the traditional system the bulk of caucus members are frustrated and disappointed for having been omitted from cabinet. However, in my experience, there were many members of caucus who knew their limitations and never had any ambitions to be in the shadow cabinet.

Furthermore, in 1993 the number of Reformers was so small that a full cabinet of ministers and their deputies would easily have exhausted the pool of eligible people. If we take Manning's explanation for the use of the cluster system at face value, in retrospect he was either incompetent or naïve. In my view, he could have avoided the mistake he made on either ground if he had discussed the matter with more experienced people. One would have expected him to consult with Ray Speaker and Stephen Harper, for example. He might have elicited input from caucus, but he did neither. He certainly revealed that he does not believe in the Darwinian process of evolution of institutions which suggests that institutions like shadow cabinets have existed for a long time because they are successful. But perhaps Reformers are by their very nature inclined to disdain this view.

There are more sinister interpretations of Manning's use of clusters and non-use of the shadow cabinet. Some caucus members believed that Manning likes to be in control and have as much autonomy as possible in is own decisions, basically because he does not trust others.

Others thought that Manning does not want to give status and public recognition to anyone who might become his rival as leader of Reform. Manning wants no competition for his vision for a Canada run by the people through populist institutions.

I do not know how to handle these interpretations of Manning's motives.

It makes him sound more Machiavellian and power-hungry than I think he is. On the other hand, I do not know him well enough to reject the hypothesis entirely. He did not interact with me sufficiently to form a strong view. But neither did he interact well with those who judge him to be Machiavellian and power-hungry. Here is another reason why his lack of personal contacts may limit his party's success.

Similarities between Manning and Reagan

In conclusion, I want to put an historic and international perspective on my views on Preston Manning the Leader expressed in this chapter. The book *Ronald Reagan: How an Ordinary Man Became an Extraordinary Leader* (New York: The Free Press, 1997) was written by Dinesh D'Souza, one of his personal advisers in the White House.

D'Souza's description of Reagan's personal relationships reminds me strongly of Manning's. According to D'Souza, no-one 'knew' Reagan the President. In dealings with individuals, Reagan was always charming and open. But beyond these superficial dealings, everyone always encountered a wall of extreme privacy. He never bared his inner feelings — according to D'Souza, not even to his children or his wife Nancy. Yet, as it turns out, Reagan has been a very successful President. During his regime the Cold War ended, inflation was terminated, the economy boomed and Americans regained the self-confidence they had lost through the Vietnam war, the Watergate scandal, economic stagflation, the expansion of Soviet imperialism and the humiliation administered by the Ayatollah of Iran.

D'Souza argues convincingly that Reagan was personally responsible for most of the important policy successes of his tenure in the White House. In many instances Reagan went against the advice of his closest associates and certainly against the views of the chattering classes of intellectuals in universities, foundations and the media. In the end his judgement turned out to have been right.

There are many important differences in the personalities, management styles and other personal characteristics between Manning and Reagan. What both have in common is a strong wall against intruders into their inner being and feelings. What is important is that this personal shortcoming is not necessarily a barrier to political success and the ability to create a better government. It may be something which brings success. D'Souza's story also shows that great leaders can succeed even if they are opposed by intellectuals in universities, foundations and the media. It is important that such leaders have a strong and consistent vision which they cling to in the face of opposition from brilliant establishment experts. Reagan did.

Manning, from the beginning of his political career, has been opposed by the majority of the Canadian Establishment. His ideas for fiscal responsibility, populist reforms of democratic institutions, decentralization of government functions, equality of Quebec and other provinces in dealings with the federal government and many others were out of touch with reality as the establishment perceived it. Manning shows great strength of character and conviction that his vision of reality is superior and consistent with the aspirations of most Canadians.

Many of Reagan's critics from the chattering classes refuse to give credit to his policies for the successes of his regime. They claim that Reagan succeeded in spite of himself and the bad ideas he brought to policy-making — he was simply 'lucky.' The Soviet Union was ready to self-destruct; inflation was not a problem; tax cuts favoured the rich; increased military spending and Star Wars were a waste of precious resources.

Much the same has been said about Manning's success in taking a new political party to become the Official Opposition in parliament in two elections. He was lucky that Mulroney and the PCs self-destructed, that other political leaders failed to grasp the seriousness of the fiscal crisis in the early 1990s, that Quebec separatism stirred up regional sentiments in the West and so on. I think it unfair to give so little credit to Reagan and Manning for noting and seizing upon the political opportunities in their environment. Of course, all great leaders need some luck in timing, in finding conditions fertile for their vision.

What will the future bring?

As an economist, I have always stayed away from the temptation to predict the future of the stock market or the economy. I will also not attempt to predict what will happen to Manning and Reform. However, I am always willing to analyze what will happen if certain policies are followed. So here are my views on the actions which will increase the chances of Manning and Reform to form the government:

Firstly, Reform should stake out a clear position as the 'conservative' or 'right wing' party of Canada. The most important and simple ingredients of such a position are a commitment to fiscal responsibility and a smaller and more decentralized government. The latter policy will automatically bring lower taxes, less social security spending and increased self-reliance of individuals. It will reduce government interference in the lives of Canadians and, very importantly, improve the chances that Quebeckers can fulfil their cultural and economic aspirations as members of the Canadian federation.

Secondly, Reform must play down its commitment to sweeping democratic reforms and populism and come clean when discussing the pitfalls of such reforms. Perhaps Canadians *are* willing to embrace a Triple-E Senate, referenda, recall and free votes as risky innovations which could turn out better than the present system. But these goals will not be attained by downplaying the risks and problems brought on by such innovations. Opinion makers will not support a party which does not deal honestly with the public on important issues.

The Leader, Preston Manning

Thirdly, Reform must find an accommodation with the Progressive Conservative Party to unite the Right in Canada. This is a difficult task. In most ridings of the West Reform's electoral successes virtually wiped out the PCs, leaving only rumps of official organization staffed by dedicated veterans. In Ontario and elsewhere Reform did not have such electoral success and it is doubtful that they will come. In these regions accommodation has to take place at the constituency levels. This process requires PC organizations to get rid of Red Tories, members who are ideologically close to the Liberals. Reform will have to modify its commitment to populism and embrace the conservative agenda to attract the genuine Conservatives in the Progressive party. Attempts to forge a formal merger between the two parties, most likely under a new name and possibly with a leader other than Manning, should be pursued, even if the probability of success is small.

Fourthly, Manning will have to find the magic formula, change his image and acquire more charisma. I have no views on how he can achieve this, but I hope he can. If he does not succeed, he should consider stepping aside for another leader. The Reform Party is a formidable organization. It has an important role to play in Canadian politics. By stepping down as leader and thus bringing electoral success to the party, Manning would serve his country well. It would make his place in history even more secure than it already is.

CHAPTER 13

Designing Policies

I HAVE spent my entire adult life as a professional economist researching, writing and teaching about economic policies. I agreed to run for office in 1993 with the expectation that as an MP I would have the opportunity to use this professional background and experience. I had hoped to help make sound Reform policies and well-grounded critiques of government policies. My hopes were not fulfilled. For the most part I was inside the party caucus but outside the policy formulation process. Politics based on rhetoric rather than substance dominated the criticism of government fiscal policies and had no use for my expertise.

My professional experience had taught me that the influence of economists on policy formulation is justly limited. Input by politicians is at least of equal importance. Economic analysis can only point to the losses and gains made by different groups of people. Politicians have to decide whether the losses incurred by some are less important than the gains made by others. The main role of the economist is to make sure politicians and the public know of the size of both the losses and the benefits.

I also did not expect to have my way all the time on technical economic analysis. The results of this work are often contentious and I know from long experience that one's own background and narrowness of vision can be a problem.

I have often changed my mind about economic issues as new facts and analytical tools were brought to my attention; I certainly was willing to do so in Ottawa.

Perhaps I am too pessimistic about the influence I have had on Reform policies. Many caucus colleagues have told me that my views were always taken seriously and that I had more influence than I realized. Obviously I cannot be objective on this issue and invite readers to judge for themselves from my account of the formulation of economic and fiscal policies of the Reform party 1993 - 97.

My account will show that Reform suffered from interference by the leader, top-down directives from a charmed inner party circle and, on some issues, benign neglect and lack of direction. I think that the following account of my experience with policy formation of Reform should be seen in context. The leader, his inner circle, caucus and I had no experience in this line of work. We were all learning. I know now that I could have been more tenacious in pushing for ideas and projects.

Too 'hands-on'

In February 1995, the Reform Party published its 'Taxpayers Budget,' which presented a program of spending cuts which would eliminate the deficit in three years. The Taxpayers Budget was welcomed by the business and financial community and was considered to be better than the government's budget presented a few weeks later. The Liberals decried the Taxpayers Budget as 'slash and burn.'

Ray Speaker was the head of the Finance Cluster and therefore had full responsibility for the development of the document. Speaker appointed a committee to develop the basic outline of the budget. It included Dimitri Pantazopoulos, who had been deeply involved in the first budget exercise of Reform (called 'Zero-in-Three') leading up to the 1993 election; Ken Boessenkool, Speaker's legislative assistant and a number of other legislative assistants of MPs. Stephen Harper, one of the main authors of the Zero-in-Three budget, was consulted heavily.

This committee worked out that the Taxpayers Budget needed to make cuts worth $25 billion, equal to 21 percent of program spending. They also worked out how these cuts should be distributed among the different ministries, and individual critics responsible for these ministries were then invited to approve these cuts. This task was undertaken conscientiously through examination of individual spending programs, though the amount of information about each at the disposal of each critic was rather limited.

After much talk and some negotiations, minor revisions in the proposed cuts were undertaken. Throughout this process Manning remained on the sidelines and did not intervene.

After Pantazopoulos left Ottawa to move to Washington, D.C. for personal reasons, Ken Boessenkool led the budget effort with minimal direction and interference by Speaker, who believes in the delegation of responsibilities. Boessenkool was a bright and energetic young man in his middle 20s who now works for the C.D. Howe Institute as an economist and at the same time is enrolled in a program to obtain an MA degree in economics. He had been one of Speaker's close aides during the 1993 election campaign, and had an undergraduate degree in management, with majors in finance and philosophy. He consulted with me privately, and willingly took my advice on a number of issues. The most important of these was to include in the document a discussion of the causes of Canada's high unemployment, which drew heavily on the OECD Jobs Study and implied that spending cuts would not have a major impact on unemployment. However, Speaker never consulted with me or asked me to participate in the determination of the overall size of the cuts or the negotiations he had with critics.

About three months before the scheduled release of the document, the draft was passed from Boessenkool and his group to the Communications Department. At this point, Manning became involved and unilaterally changed some of the numbers. Speaker was no longer involved in the process.

Chapter 13

About a week before the scheduled release of the Taxpayers' Budget I was given a draft for comments. This draft was disappointingly rough. By my standards it was very poorly written and organized. I also disagreed with some major points of policy. I began to rewrite the document but my editorial work for the most part was wasted.

One point of disagreement on policy involved Medicare spending cuts and the proposed devolution of responsibilities to the provinces. It is worth telling my experience with this issue, for it shows clearly how Manning manages the affairs of the party. The draft stated in a paragraph that the federal government would retain control over national standards, in spite of the fact that under the proposed withdrawal of funding and it therefore would have lost all financial levers to enforce such national standards. As I learned later, Manning had insisted on the inclusion of this paragraph because in his travels and contacts with the public he had discovered that the majority of Canadians liked a national medicare program which provided the same standard of care everywhere in the country.

At one of two meetings on the budget document I had with Manning, I brought up the problem his government would face trying to enforce national standards without a financial lever. Manning explained that he was not thinking of the traditional top-down approach to the creation and enforcement of national standards. Instead, he envisioned national standards set through voluntary agreement among the provinces, encouraged and enforced by the federal government with the full agreement and cooperation of the provinces. I was still sceptical about the merit of this approach, but trusted Manning's judgement that such a process of voluntary agreement was feasible. I rewrote the relevant section in the document to reflect this position.

It was Thursday afternoon and the document was to be released on Monday. I was still editing it when Manning announced that he would do the job himself. He took the document away and 24 hours later it went into production for type-setting, printing and binding. The time-schedule was very tight. Nevertheless, it was ready on Monday. I had been given the task of explaining to the media the main features of the Taxpayers Budget at a press-conference in Vancouver. The document arrived by courier at the same time as the media. Journalists spent some time reading it, I made my prepared statement and then responded to questions.

The first question was 'How did Reform expect to maintain national standards in health care if it stopped all federal payments to the provinces for this purpose?' I looked at the relevant paragraph and discovered that Manning had taken out the explanation of the voluntary nature of the agreement on standards and substituted his original, own and unqualified assertion. I was forced to defend a position I had previously thought indefensible. It was not easy doing so while the TV cameras were rolling.

The same scenario developed with respect to a major theme in the document which I consider to be indefensible in terms of economic theory. Manning was and still is in love with the slogan 'Lower taxes to create jobs.' He obviously found it resonated well with the general public. When I asked him to explain the process by which lower taxes would result in more jobs his answer was: 'People will have more money in their pockets and they will spend it more wisely than the government.' This might sounds good on the political stage, but it makes no sense economically.

There are two possible scenarios. One, taxes are lowered without cuts in spending. This policy had fallen into disrepute because it resulted in deficits which in the recent past had caused a fiscal crisis and done little to reduce unemployment. The alternative is that taxes and spending are lowered simultaneously. The reduced spending, be it on such things as roads or medicare, throws out of work at least as many workers as are hired as a result of increased private spending made possible by lower taxes.

Economic analyses suggest that cuts in unemployment insurance benefits and payroll taxes have a positive effect on job creation. I included this point in the text to qualify the general assertion about the effect of lower taxes on job creation. However, again Manning deleted my amendment.

Upon receipt of the document, Peter O'Neil of *The Vancouver Sun* promptly confronted me with the question: "You are an economics professor. Could you please explain to me how lower taxes and spending will create jobs?" This episode of the design and launch of the Taxpayers Budget in 1995 reveals the extent to which Manning involved himself in details and disregarded advice.

This episode did not help my morale, especially since after the event Manning complained in caucus about the fact that he personally had to put the finishing touches on the document at the last moment. Eventually it dawned on me what he meant by this. Any document which did not reflect his positions perfectly, by definition, was unfinished.

Too 'top-down'

The preceding episode already showed that Manning and his inner circle held a very tight rein on economic policy formation. The Taxpayers Budget episode was not an isolated incident. There were many others, but the most important of all occurred in the design of the budget which was used in the 1997 election campaign. In the fall of 1996 Reform's preparations for an election in 1997 kicked into gear. The basic outline and first draft of the election budget was prepared by Manning working together with Rick Anderson, his chief political adviser, and Cliff Fryers, a Calgary lawyer and long-time close associate of Manning. I was not involved in this process.

Late in 1996 this first draft of the election budget was made available for reading and comment by members of caucus and the party executive. Much effort was devoted to assuring its confidentiality, which complicated even internal discussions. Most importantly, the document was

Chapter 13

accompanied by instructions that we should not be too critical of the basic plan and focus on positive comments. Ray Speaker noted that after his many years in politics he recognized the strategy behind such an admonition. At the end of the consultation process the original authors of the document can claim that there was no important opposition to the proposal.

The basic fiscal initiative outlined in the draft document was a $15 billion cut in program spending, a key figure since it represented government outlays on all programs other than interest on the debt. This cut was to come on top of the $11 billion cut already undertaken by the Liberal government, and would bring the annual level of spending to $94 billion, down from $120 billion in 1993.

I thought that such a large, additional cut was politically unwise because the Canadian public had begun to feel the bite of the Liberal cuts and did not like it, particularly in Ontario, where hospital closings, higher university fees and many other belt-tightening measures had taken their toll.

The initial opposition to the Liberal spending cuts was muted by the public understanding that without them the country might go bankrupt. But, as Ray Speaker pointed out to me, the political acceptability of cuts was limited and the time for more cuts had run out. The cuts were also economically unnecessary. Government revenues were rising rapidly and the budget was expected to be in balance in 1998/99; there was no need for further cuts to restore fiscal responsibility. However, this fact put Reform into a bind — the most important part of the 1993 platform had lost its punch. So what was left to make Reform different from the Liberals and PCs? Manning and his advisers decided it would be Reform's advocacy of smaller government and tax cuts it would allow.

I agree with a Reform platform advocating smaller government and tax cuts. The problem I had with the proposal presented in 1996 was the timing and tactics of getting there. A smaller government could have been achieved through spending freezes and the passage of time. Increases in population, prices and incomes would automatically reduce real spending per capita by about four percent annually. As a result, a spending freeze in the course of an electoral mandate would have cut the real size of government by 16 percent.

My preferred strategy would have had several advantages. Economically, it would have avoided the dislocations and personal hardships brought about by outright cuts in spending. Tax cuts could still have been promised, because after the budget was balanced in 1998/99 large surpluses were expected. Politically, it would have avoided confronting especially Ontario voters with the choice: 'Vote Reform and we will double the pain you have just experienced. Vote Liberal and the pain will be over.'

I do not know why my reasoning was not accepted, but I have some ideas. Rick Anderson was probably most influential in the design of the fiscal strategy. He is a very creative and original thinker and has Manning's full confidence. He wanted Reform to offer Canadians tax cuts of a very precise magnitude and at a distinct point in time, with the thought that this precision would make the promise more credible and different from the promises offered by the political opposition. So, he came up with the slogan '2000 in 2000' – a cut of $2,000 in taxes for every family by the year 2000.

In a number of caucus presentations he revealed his deep attachment to this slogan. The trouble with it is that it required deep spending cuts in 1997 and 1998 to prevent the creation of a deficit. In some conference calls involving Anderson, Fryers, Monte Solberg (the deputy Finance Critic) and myself it was made quite clear that the '2000 in 2000' slogan was untouchable and that therefore, the spending cuts needed to keep the budget balanced were not to be challenged.

I had only one face to face meeting with Anderson to discuss the issue, which took place over lunch and was entirely unplanned. On that occasion Anderson asserted that the election successes of Ronald Reagan and Harris in Ontario were entirely due to their promises to cut taxes. I promptly sent him information about exit polls taken at the Reagan and Harris elections which showed that the promise of tax cuts played a very small role in voters' decisions. Anderson never responded to this information. Reform failed to win even one seat in Ontario in the 1997 election, in spite of a massive campaign effort. That failure was due to many factors and I have no information on exit polls. However, I am convinced that the Reform fiscal platform could not possibly have helped persuade Ontario residents to vote for the party. How many people were driven by the thought that if they voted Reform they would increase the probability of even more hospital closings, increases in university fees, reductions in unemployment insurance and welfare benefits and other social services?

Anderson's strong views on the public's desire for tax cuts had another consequence. He ruled out the use of fiscal surpluses to pay down the debt and none were planned for in the first draft of the election budget. Through contacts with constituents and reading of polls I had come to the view that Canadians were very concerned about the debt and wanted it paid down. Most preferred debt reduction over tax cuts. I argued strongly with both Manning and Anderson to take account of these public views in the election platform. At that time a number of public polls supported my position and after a long struggle the election platform was changed. It promised to make 'a first down payment towards the national debt.' However, there was no commitment as to the size of that payment. It could not be fitted logically into the '2000 in 2000' strategy.

During the election campaign Anderson's favourite slogan never played a big role; I watched out for it in advertisements and in public discussions. I do not know what caused it to get so little play, but it seems that its value did not make up for the risk and cost associated with building an entire election budget around it.

Chapter 13
Benign neglect of flat tax and pension reform

The preceding episodes describe the excessively hands-on and top-down process for the formulation of some important fiscal policies. I now want to turn to the description of how Reform developed its policies on the flat tax and pension reform. Manning had no special interest in these policies, as far as I could tell. Or, if he was interested in them, other priorities crowded them out of his schedule. However, these two important policy issues were on the Ottawa agenda because they had been proposed through grass-roots procedures at Reform Assemblies. In addition, serious U.S. discussions about a flat tax and Liberal proposals for changes to the pension system required that Reform come up with policy positions on these issues.

Since Manning's priorities prevented him from getting involved in the formulation of these policies, the process suffered seriously from his benign neglect. No-one with any competence was in charge. I did my best to assure that the policies would be rational and defensible. Unfortunately, the proposals which saw the light of day were defective in a number of ways. They gave Liberals huge targets to shoot at and criticize for the lack of consistency. Opinion-makers in Canada who know about taxation and pensions were turned off Reform for producing such shoddy policy proposals. For me, the mishandling of these policies were a major source of frustration.

The flat tax

Canada's tax code is very large. It occupies several feet of shelf-space in libraries and every year several hundred more pages are added. It is also complex (as everyone knows who ever filled out an income tax return). Revenue Canada, which is in charge of enforcing the tax code, is a huge and costly bureaucracy with few friends among Canadians.

It has been estimated that the cost of compliance with the code is about $12 billion annually. The system has deleterious effects on work effort, investment and risk-taking, thus slowing economic growth. Reformers at several Assemblies have passed resolutions binding the party to a significant overhaul and simplification of this complex and costly tax system.

In 1989 a party task force headed by Jim Silye recommended the adoption of 'a flat tax that is simple, equal and visible and has one objective: raising funds to pay for federal programs.' It envisioned personal returns fitting onto one page and consisting of just a few lines which give the filer's income from wages, salaries and pensions and information to claim personal exemptions. There would be no taxes on capital gains or dividends; no incentives aimed at social engineering through personal deductions or special tax concessions. Tax returns for business would be equally simple. The flat tax would be perhaps as much as 50 percent lower than the current top marginal tax rate as it is applied to a broader tax base.

When I arrived in Parliament in 1993 I recommended against Reform working out detailed proposals for a flat tax. I realized that the basic idea had much populist appeal, but as an economist I was also very much aware of the risks and costs of fundamental tax reform. It would have enormous implications economically as it would alter incentives, destroy financial wealth and create chaos in international dealings. Politically it would be a hard sell because it would inevitably result in winners and losers. The winners from tax reforms are happy but unwilling to do much to help the party which provided them. Losers, on the other hand, are prepared to fight very hard against anyone responsible for their allegedly unjust reduction in income.

Occasionally governments engage in tax reform, as Canada did in 1970, when the top marginal tax rate was lowered to 70 percent and again in 1980, when it fell to 60 percent. These tax reforms were designed by commissions working for years, drawing on the country's best economists, accountants and tax lawyers and involved lengthy hearings and studies to assess the impact of proposed changes on all affected parties. Even after that, politicians still had to decide who would win and lose.

Those reforms simplified the tax code, but soon after they had been put into effect it became complicated again. The reason was that the government wanted to be fair to everyone, adding special clauses to the code to accommodate individuals and firms to cover special circumstances not envisioned in the original design. About 20 percent of the present code consists of 'transition rules,' providing fair treatment for those who had made decisions based on the old code and would lose under the new one. Codes have to be added constantly as foreign tax regimes change and cause inequities for Canadians.

Over half of Canada's tax code deals with issues of valuation and timing of capital gains. They were made necessary because of the complexity of peoples' financial affairs. I am certain that an initially very simple flat tax code would similarly expand rapidly to prevent injustices to Canadians.

Developing a Reform version of the flat tax

For nearly 18 months after the 1994 election, Reform did not work on a flat tax proposal. However, two events then took place. In the U.S. the Republicans gained a majority in the House of Representatives and they began a serious inquiry into flat tax reform. They drew heavily on work done by Robert Hall and Alvin Rabushka, academics from Stanford University (*The Flat Tax*, 2nd edition, Stanford: Hoover Institution Press,1995). They also found strong support from some Washington think tanks.

A study commission was set up and worked out details. Jim Forbes, seeking the nomination for President, made the flat tax one of the central themes of his campaign and generated a wide public debate about its merits. Pundits considered it a real possibility that the United States would soon adopt a flat tax.

Chapter 13

Jim Silye had resigned his position as Reform Whip in the House in order to dedicate himself to pushing for a flat tax. Manning appointed him Revenue Critic and he began a big media campaign to get his ideas before the Canadian public. I read a number of newspaper articles outlining and commenting on his proposals. I was horrified. He promised a flat tax at such a low rate that it would have doubled the size of the deficit. He claimed that the deficit would be wiped out quickly, because the flat rate system would stimulate economic growth and bring increased tax compliance from participants in the underground economy. I noted that he was not familiar with the details of a flat tax nor did he understand the economic arguments of Hall and Rabushka. I felt that the publicity he generated would do great harm to Reform's reputation with knowledgeable accountants, lawyers and economists. Liberals would be sure to use his statements to embarrass Reform in the House and during the next election.

After one particularly embarrassing report about the Reform flat tax proposal I offered to work with him on working out the technical details of a flat tax for Canada. He agreed, and we became partners. The Fraser Institute agreed to arrange a conference of experts in Toronto to discuss detailed economic, legal and accounting implications of a flat tax. Top experts from the Toronto business community, specialists from the Department of Finance, a U.S. representative and speakers from the Liberal and PC parties spent a day discussing a wide range of arcane and difficult subjects associated with tax reform.

Ken Boessenkool, Jim Silye and I had prepared a paper with some specific proposals for a flat tax for Canada. We drew heavily on the academic work by Hall and Rabushka and on the U.S. discussions. In one of the sessions, our paper was discussed by experts. One of them was Satya Poddar, a former Assistant Deputy Minister of Finance who had been in charge of the design of the GST under Mulroney. At the time of the conference he worked as a private consultant and advised national governments throughout the world on tax policies. He is an economist and like most other economists, he is a strong advocate of taxes based on spending rather than income. He endorsed our proposal on the grounds that it was almost equivalent to a pure expenditure tax except that it used income rather than purchases as the base for the calculation of taxes due.

Other experts were quite critical of all flat tax proposals. Robert Brown, a partner in a large management consulting firm, and one of Canada's most distinguished tax lawyers, had spent his life finding tax loopholes for his clients. He said he already could envision a number of schemes through which his clients could take advantage of foreign reporting and investment opportunities if the flat tax were adopted. He noted that the Department of Finance would eventually close these loopholes, but that this would require many new provisions in the code and that in the meantime he would have found some new ones.

Designing Policies

He suggested that the simplification of the code trough a flat tax was not likely to be large or last long. The same view was expressed by a top official from the Department of Finance, who had supervised the introduction of many changes to the tax code. He noted that he had been the author of the original code for the system of Registered Retirement Savings Plans. The first published version of this code was one paragraph long. Today it covers hundreds of provisions, all aimed at special circumstances in which taxpayers find themselves. He predicted that the flat tax would require a large number of such changes to deal with inequities generally and especially those arising from the proposed broad changes under the flat tax proposal.

Senator Lowell Murray presented a paper on the politics of tax reform. He was a Conservative from Ontario with a long and distinguished record of service in federal politics. Drawing on his experience, he outlined the vociferous opposition a flat tax would draw from those who would have their tax burden increased. He concluded that tax reform was politically feasible only if it was accompanied by an overall reduction in government revenue so that every group in the country paid fewer taxes. There also were discussions of the merit of removing the double taxation of dividends, which was very important in some U.S. flat tax proposals and has the support of many economists as an efficiency and growth enhancing policy.

The Hon. Maurice McTigue, High Commissioner for New Zealand and former Minister of Finance, reported on how his government had finessed the political problem associated with such a change. Corporations in New Zealand continue to pay taxes on their income but along with dividend checks they issue certificates to stockholder showing that the tax had been paid for them. Therefore no more personal taxes were due on dividends received. This New Zealand system is unlike the Canadian, where corporations pay an income tax on their earnings, distribute as dividends what is left over to their stockholders who then pay taxes on the dividends again.

For my work on the Reform flat tax proposal one of the most important discussions involved estimates of the flat rate needed to raise the same revenue as the present system. This revenue neutral rate was about 21 percent for the federal tax alone, 25 percent if the GST were eliminated. This is in contrast to the 29 percent top marginal rate currently and much higher than the one Silye had been using in his dealings with the media.

The discussions also provided some realistic assessments of the dynamic changes which a flat tax might create. These dynamic changes would be stimulated through improved work and investment incentives as well as incentives to move economic activity out of the underground economy. Experience in other countries has shown that such changes would increase tax revenues but not nearly by as much as Silye had been predicting.

As a result of the information gathered at the conference on the flat tax, I considered myself ready to develop a logically and empirically sound

Chapter 13

proposal for a flat tax which then could be adopted by caucus and ultimately the Assembly. However, these goals were never reached.

Working with Jim Silye

Silye simply refused to accept the need to give realistic estimates of revenue neutral flat rates. I had many frustrating discussions with him about this subject. A few weeks before the end of the parliament and after both of us had announced that we would not seek reelection, we had a long conversation reminiscing about our experiences over the last four years. Silye surprised me by saying that he had learned at lot from me about the need for intellectual honesty, which had been a hard struggle for him. For a long time he had paid no attention to what I had been saying about the need for having a flat tax rate that was revenue neutral. By the time he made this confession the discussions about the flat tax had died both in Canada and the United States. But, in my view, Silye had done a lot of damage to the reputation of the Reform party in the eyes of opinion makers and community leaders who knew more about the nature of the flat tax than populist slogans. He had also raised unrealistic expectations in the minds of many Reformers and other Canadians who thought that through the magic of tax reform their tax burdens could be made to shrink by 50 percent.

At the 1996 Reform Assembly in Vancouver at a special session devoted to the flat tax I found many who were fervent supporters of it because they believed the numbers Silye had publicized for such a long time. Silye also disagreed with the treatment of investment income and deductions which the experts at the conference considered to be essential to get the full economic and administrative benefits of a flat tax. He insisted on the continuation of the double taxation of corporate income and the deduction from income of contributions to CPP, UI and RRSP programs. He called his version the 'Proportional Flat Tax' for reasons I was never able to fathom. As was pointed out to him many times by several people, this proportional flat tax would bring the worst of both worlds. It would bring many of the administrative complexities and damaging incentives of the present system. It would also lower the tax burden on the rich and increase it on the low income earners, a fundamental and serious criticism of all flat tax proposals.

Because of Silye's advocacy of the proportional flat tax, after the conference we always had two Reform flat tax proposals, Silye's and mine. As a result, caucus, the public and grass roots members of Reform were confused and divided. The party struck a special committee of experts to decide which of the two versions should become official policy. The head of the committee and a majority favoured my proposal, but a vocal minority sided with Silye and blocked an effective agreement. Several efforts had been made to get caucus to endorse one or the other version of the flat tax.

Each time the issues were too difficult to be understood fully and voted on in the time allotted to the discussion. No vote was ever taken. Eventually, interest in the flat tax died.

In the United States a similar rift developed between advocates of different versions of the flat tax and contributed to its demise. In the preceding chapter I described the power Manning wielded when it came to policy issues that interested him. It was clear to me and everyone else that the official adoption of any policy depended on his endorsement.

In the case of the flat tax, Manning did not have enough interest to familiarize himself with the basic issues which required his decision. I had told him a number of times about the risks to Reform's reputation which arose out of Silye's indefensible statements about the flat tax. I had also urged him to decide whether Reform should go with the pure flat tax or Silye's proportional tax. He stayed out of the fray and did nothing to limit Silye's public relations campaign.

My experience with the flat tax proposal illustrates the shortcomings of the Reform party decision making process in Ottawa. Manning should have taken the time to familiarize himself with the issues, choose one version of the flat tax and use his prerogative as a leader to keep Silye from making indefensible public pronouncements. Alternatively, he should have delegated responsibility for these decisions to someone in whose expertise and judgement he had confidence.

As it turned out, the absence of Manning's leadership on the flat tax issue had no serious consequences since the flat tax ceased to be a prominent public issue and never became a serious legislative program in Canada or the U.S. Unfortunately, the same cannot be said about the issue of pension reform, which was similarly without guidance and dominated by persons without the proper background.

Reform of the Canada Pension Plan

The Canada Pension Plan (CPP) was introduced in 1966. Unlike a private pension plan, it was not based on the investment of premiums paid by working people. Instead, it relied on a 'pay-as-you-go' mechanism. Workers paid premiums sufficiently large to pay the pensions of the retired. Whenever workers became pensioners and collected benefits, new workers took their place to pay the premiums and so on without end. This system worked very well initially since the so-called elderly dependency ratio was low. People over 65 represented only 13 percent of the working age population at the time the plan was established, which implies that five workers financed the payments going to one pensioner. The system was expected to continue functioning well in the light of forecasts that the population would continue to grow rapidly for a long time so that the dependency ratio would remain constant or even fall.

It was only coincidental that at the beginning the pay-as-you-go system

Chapter 13

developed some surpluses. Everyone had to pay premiums immediately while the number of beneficiaries grew slowly. This state-operated pension system was expected to have several attractive features. Every generation of workers was larger than that of retirees. Therefore, premiums could be relatively low at all times. Since the system mandated participation by every Canadian, there were no sales costs as is the case with private pension systems. Similarly, administrative costs were low. Importantly, since there was no need for means tests to qualify for benefits, there were no costly incentives for people to arrange their affairs to appear poor.

By the 1990s the system was in trouble for a number of reasons. Most importantly, the growth in population had slowed. The post-war population boom was followed by a bust, which had serious effects on the dependency ratio. From 13 percent in 1960 it rose to 17 percent in 1990. With the retirement of baby boomers at its peak in 2030 the ratio will be a whopping 39 percent — by that time, only three workers will support each pensioner!

In addition, it had been expected that economic growth would help ease the real burden of those who paid the premiums. Much slower than predicted economic growth dashed that hope. Finally, since its inception, benefits payable were enriched several times through political decisions aimed at winning the votes of pensioners.

The net result of these unforeseen influences on the system can best be summarized in the following figures. In 1966 it was estimated that by the year 2030 the average worker would have to pay as CPP premiums 5.5 percent of the first $35,400 earnings per year. Now it is estimated that in 2030 the contribution rate would have to be *14.5* percent.

The Chief Actuary of Canada is required to estimate the present value of the promised future pension benefits minus the future premiums paid according to schedules embodied in law. In 1996 the present value of the unfunded liabilities was about $700 billion. That is a sum about equal to the debt of the Government of Canada.

Students of the CPP have known for some time that the system is unsustainable. It has turned into a pyramid scheme which has run out of suckers to pay those ahead in the chain. The cost to future generations has grown so much that it is unlikely they will agree to pay the 14.5 percent of eligible earnings as premiums. It has to be remembered that at the same time, these future generations have to pay the interest on the $1,000 billion provincial and federal debt and medical costs and Old Age Security benefits for the large number of people over 65! It has been estimated that the obligations on taxpayers due to these programs and debts in 2030 will require about $150 billion annually in today's dollars. This sum is about 50 percent greater than the total program spending of the federal government in 1998. All the while, of course, these future generations have to pay for the education of their own children, defence and the large range of other government services Canadians have begun to expect as a matter of 'right.' Because of the size of these future obligations many analysts believe that future taxpayers will renege on at least some of them. They certainly have a moral case to do so.

It was not fair that preceding generations used the political system to enrich themselves at the expense of people not yet born and unable to vote. Just like the previous generations used the political system and their voting power to rob future generations, these future generations can use the same political system to get even and lower their tax burden. Therefore for the sake of inter-generational equity and to assure the payment of adequate pensions to coming generations of retirees, CPP finances have to be put on a sound basis.

Reform's alternative: Super RRSPs

One method for putting the CPP system on a sound footing involves its partial privatization. This approach has been adopted successfully by a number of countries like Singapore, New Zealand and Chile. Under this method, individuals own fully-funded investment accounts. At the time of retirement, this investment must be turned into an annuity bought from private insurance companies, which assures that every person has a secure income until death. The state remains in the picture by mandating premiums at rates which result in a socially desirable level of pension, and by making rules to protect the value of the investments.

Such a private system, mandated and regulated by the state, has a number of advantages. The premiums paid out of before-tax income earn interest making it possible to keep premiums low. Many Canadians who own Registered Retirement Savings accounts know about the financial benefits of such arrangements. The pension funds are owned outright by the contributor. Therefore, if the owner dies before retirement, the funds go to heirs after the payment of taxes. Under the CPP system, heirs receive no benefits from the premiums paid by a deceased relative other than some 'death benefits' which are small and designed to cover little more than the cost of a funeral.

Investment of the funds in financial markets through private investment managers assures returns free from the control of government and the political process. The system also increases a country's supply of savings which encourages investment and growth and reduces indebtedness to foreigners.

However, these private, funded and government-mandated pension systems also have disadvantages. The private placement of funds for retirement involves risks of default and costs of administration much greater than those of a pure, public, pay-as-you-go system. Most important, the system does not guarantee a specific level of benefits, as does the CPP program. The level of benefits is uncertain, since it depends on the unpredictable market yield of the investments; however, these disadvantages

Chapter 13

can be limited through government actions. Thus, through strong prudential regulation of investment firms, risk of default can be minimized.

A system of insurance with the government as the ultimate backer can protect against the risk of catastrophic financial panic. The uncertainty of returns can be minimized by unlimited opportunities for the diversification of holdings. Economies of scale will result in low administration costs. A socially desirable level of retirement benefits can be approached through periodic adjustment of the mandated level of premiums if they are endangered by disappointing investment returns.

Reform Assemblies have passed resolutions committing the party to the adoption of a private, government mandated pension system. Modeled after those in Chile and New Zealand, the proposed system has been named the SuperRRSP in reference to the existing, smaller RRSP program in Canada.

However, there are many 'devils in the details' of moving to such a new system. Overshadowing all is the problem of how to pay for the overhang of unfunded liabilities which are due to people already in or near retirement. The importance of this problem can be seen readily by considering what would happen if tomorrow all CPP premiums ceased to go to the government and instead were invested in private accounts. Under these conditions the government would have no more revenues to meet its obligations to Canadians in or near retirement.

Jan Brown in charge

At an early stage of the last Parliament, Preston Manning gave the responsibility for developing the details of the SuperRRSP policy to Diane Ablonczy. The plan had been subjected to some critical analysis under Ablonczy, when the name SuperRRSP was adopted.

Ablonczy's work had been complicated by a Reform motion adopted by several Assemblies that all social programs, including the CPP, Unemployment Insurance and Medicare, should be privatized. Individuals should be forced to make contributions into a tax-sheltered private fund from pre-tax income. This private fund would then be used to meet private needs in case of unemployment or medical emergencies.

It is clear that such a major overhaul of Canada's social programs could not possibly be planned in any detail by a lawyer, which was Ablonczy's profession. Nor did Reform research have the skilled manpower for such a task. For a long time, with Ablonczy in charge, the entire project languished. The work that was done concentrated on cosmetics, such as what to call the fund and the description of the desired outcome.

In September 1995 Manning appointed Jan Brown as Social Affairs critic and charged her with the development for and publicity of the SuperRRSP. In this context, it is interesting to note that the Liberal government decided to have the CPP reform project handled by Paul Martin and the Department of Finance, rather than by Lloyd Axworthy in the Department of Human

Resources Development Canada, a New Age name for what traditionally and in most countries is known as Department of Social Welfare.

If Manning had also considered pension reform to be a financial issue, I would have been responsible for it in my capacity as the Finance Critic.

Brown's professional background was in public relations and she was without any expertise in the field. She worked on a proposal with Scott Reid, a member of the Reform research department (with Brown in firm control of the agenda at all times). Brown and Reid worked out and circulated a policy document which was used by Brown in her work with the media. This document spelled out the merit of a private pension system at a very general level. Rolling the UI and Medicare system into the same Super-RRSP program was no longer mentioned.

The main focus of the document was on provisions designed to assure Canadians that they would get their pensions whether they were already retired or about to retire. The document did not deal in any depth with the problem of how a Reform government would finance these promises, nor did it address any of the operational problems noted above. Vague references were made to the use of what in Chile was called 'recognition bonds' to compensate people for their past contributions to CPP, but it was not acknowledged that these bonds had to be paid off with revenues collected from future generations, so that in effect they did not alleviate the problem of inter-generational inequity besetting the present system.

As in the case of the flat tax, I was appalled by the poor quality of the Reform proposal presented to the public. It reduced Reform's credibility with a knowledgeable public, raised unreasonable expectations and provided the Liberals with powerful ammunition to attack us. Therefore I decided to get involved in producing a better proposal. Once again I thought that the Fraser Institute could provide an important public service by organizing a conference at which foreign experts would discuss the experience of their countries with their privatized public pension systems. The presence of Canadian actuaries, government officials and politicians from all parties would help the evaluation of these programs in the Canadian context.

A Fraser Institute conference on pension reform took place in Toronto in the Spring of 1995, featuring experts from Singapore, Chile and New Zealand. In preparation for the conference, Brown, Reid and I prepared a short paper in which we outlined a privatized pension system and our thoughts on how to deal with the unfunded liabilities. During the session, when I was summarizing our paper and the assembled experts were reacting to it, Brown left the room to speak to the media. Later she asked that her name be removed from the paper as an author, claiming that she did not agree with the proposal that the age of mandatory retirement be increased to help finance the unfunded liabilities. It was also apparent to me that she was not interested in the 'nitty-gritty' of pension reform. Dealing with the media was her thing; the media loved dealing with her.

Substance of policy issues was not important to either of the two parties in this love affair.

In our paper we proposed some methods for safeguarding the pension investments and for dealing with a number of other technical problems. All these proposals drew on the experience of other countries and did not give rise to much critical comment. Some commentators expressed their concern over the social merit of switching to a system which specified premiums and left benefits uncertain, suggesting that the general public appears to prefer a government system with guaranteed levels of benefits over one which leaves them to the vagaries of private market returns.

The problem of unfunded liabilities of CPP

However, the focus of the discussion of both our paper and of others was on the problem of the unfunded liabilities. Unfortunately, we could not learn much about possible solutions from the experience of other countries. When Singapore introduced its system it had no unfunded liabilities at all. In New Zealand and Chile the liabilities were relatively small because inflation and other influences had eroded the value of pensions payable.

After the conference Brown continued with her campaign to publicize the SuperRRSP proposal she had worked out before, misleading and embarrassing as it was. I begged her to stop her media efforts until a more solid proposal could be worked out. She refused, telling me that Manning had asked her to get media attention for the SuperRRSP plan, so she was just following orders. The media generally reacted favourably to what she presented; only a few raised questions about the unfunded liabilities.

However, Martin began a campaign that would last for a long time and spilled over into the next Parliament. He would ask again and again how Reform was planning to deal with the unfunded liabilities, and never receiving a satisfactory answer.

After Brown had left the Reform caucus to sit as an independent in the House, Manning had an opportunity to copy the government's approach and give the responsibility for the SuperRRSP plan to Finance and myself. Instead, he gave it to Ian McClelland, the new Social Affairs critic. McClelland was a thoughtful, street-smart, successful entrepreneur from Edmonton. But there was nothing in his background which prepared him for dealing with the difficult issues of privatizing CPP and taking care of the unfunded liabilities. Reid had persuaded him to approach the Chief Actuary to make some statistical simulations about the present value of the unfunded liabilities under a number of assumptions. Paul Martin refused to let the Chief Actuary do these calculations for Reform. The money needed to have the work done by a private actuary was not available. McClelland realized the existence of the problem of unfunded liabilities but could not come up with solutions. He asked me several times for my views on the subject but I felt that he never understood them. The party leadership had no interest in resolving the issue and it languished.

In the Spring of 1997 the government proposed its own plan for dealing with the unfunded liabilities and the inter-generational inequities it implied. Reform criticized this plan and McClelland had no choice but to hold out the Brown plan as a superior alternative. A few weeks before the end of the parliament in the Spring of 1997 I had lunch with Edward Greenspon, the head of the Ottawa office of the *Globe and Mail*, a specialist in financial matters and the co-author with Anthony Wilson-Smith of the best-seller *Double Vision: The Inside Story of the Liberal Party in Power* (Toronto: Doubleday, 1996). He told me that he had given McClelland an ultimatum. If he did not come up in two weeks with a logical explanation of how the Super RRSP system dealt with the unfunded liabilities, he would 'blow the Reform plan out of the water.' Other important developments and the dissolution of parliament intervened and Greenspon did not publish the threatened exposé.

In the fall of 1997 the new parliament again debated the Liberal plans for changes to the existing CPP system. On this occasion Martin and the media launched a strong attack on the Reform plan, which still was basically the one prepared by Brown. The attack became so strong and pointed that Manning was forced to admit that more work had to be done, promising to report on the solution to the problem of the unfunded liabilities at some future time. The world is still waiting.

Ablonczy, once more in charge of the issue in the new Parliament, produced a glossy pamphlet touting the merits of a privatized pension plan but short of solutions to the problem of unfunded liabilities. Manning could have avoided this embarrassing retreat and the loss of confidence it caused with many Canadians. I had been asking since late 1996 for an opportunity to discuss with caucus the alternative methods available for dealing with unfunded liabilities, all of them involving difficult political judgements and requiring a collective decision. Here are the alternatives I would have presented to caucus if the leadership of Reform had given me the opportunity.

Dealing with unfunded liabilities

First, the age of normal retirement can be increased. Actuarial calculations show that such a policy can eliminate a very substantial proportion of the unfunded liabilities under the present and the proposed Super RRSP systems. To understand the magnitude of this effect, consider that before the 1998 reforms, CPP premiums were scheduled to rise by 2016 to a maximum of 10.10 percent of qualified earnings. At this rate, the revenues raised in the year 2030 would have been equal to 3.8 percent of national income. With the normal retirement age at 65, the bill for pensions that year would have been 6 percent of national income. The unfunded difference between the annual income and expenditure of the system would have been 2.2 percent of national income (to make up for the difference, the premiums would have had to be 14.5 percent, as noted above).

If the age of normal retirement were raised to 67, annual pension payments in 2030 would have been only 5.1 percent of national income. At the unchanged 10.10 percent contribution rate, the gap would have shrunk from 2.2 to 1.3 percent of national income. If the age of normal retirement were higher than 67, the gap would shrink even more and could be eliminated altogether if it were 70.

The case for increasing the normal age of retirement is very strong. In 1966, when CPP was created, life expectancy at age 65 was 15.3 years. Today it is 18.4 years and in 2030 it is expected to be 20 years. Even if people retired at 67 in 2030, on average they could look forward to a much longer life than people who retired at 65 in 1966.

In addition, older people are much healthier than they were in the past due to advances in medical technology and changes in life styles. An increase in the normal age of retirement does not imply that everyone has to retire at the specified age, any more than it does now. The public tends to confuse the provincial and private firm rules for mandatory retirement with the rules determining the age at which maximum pensions are available. Under the proposed as well as the current system, earlier retirement can be taken by accepting a smaller government pension. Presently in Canada, many people retire early; the average age of people going into retirement is 62.5, even though maximum benefits are available only at 65.

One objection to increasing the age of retirement is that it would raise unemployment among young people, because the older people continue to occupy the jobs they need. This analysis is false. Given Canada's demographics, by 2030 Canada is likely to suffer from a shortage of labour because there will be relatively few people of working age. More generally, the people working longer have a higher income which they spend on goods and services produced by labour. Job opportunities rise correspondingly.

There is another important advantage to a higher age of normal retirement. It would also lower the burden of the OAS system financed out of general revenues and paid for by future generations. This burden presently is just as large as that stemming from the unfunded CPP obligations.

Overall, the logic of the case for higher age of normal retirement is overwhelming. For this reason, other countries like Sweden and the United States have adopted plans under which the age is raised by a month annually until it reaches 67 and higher. Unfortunately, Martin's reform of the existing CPP system does not include an increase in the age of normal retirement. Neither does the plan advocated by Brown and McClelland.

I have searched for reasons why Canada has ruled out increases in the age of normal retirement. The most plausible answer I could find was that public opinion surveys and focus group studies have revealed great public hostility to such a plan. I find it irresponsible to use this reason for failing to act on such an appealing policy alternative, especially since the tests of public attitudes took place without any explanation of the facts surrounding the issue.

A second appealing alternative for dealing with the unfunded liabilities I would have presented to caucus is the following. Consider that under the present system the average Canadian pays premiums all his or her working life which, upon retirement at 65, will provide a pension equal to 25 percent of the last year's income. Under the alternative privatized system the average Canadian would invest these same premiums but earn interest on the growing fund. If the return on investments were five percent a year, at retirement the sum available would allow the purchase of an life annuity equal to 40 percent of income at 65.

These calculations suggest that a person switching to the proposed private investment plan would enjoy a large windfall gain. I think it would not be inappropriate to ask such a person to devote some of these gains to help with the elimination of the unfunded liabilities of the old system. It would be possible, for example, to institute a temporary tax which would divert one quarter of premiums paid to such a purpose. Under these conditions, the premiums going into the private fund would yield a replacement of 30 percent of income at 65. These pensions would still be 50 percent higher than those paid by CPP. Eventually the unfunded liabilities would be paid off and premiums could be reduced or higher income replacements could be paid.

The OAS system in Canada currently supplements the CPP and for the average Canadian pays a pension approximately equal another 20 percent of the income at age 65. This pension is financed from general revenue and the right to it does not 'belong' to individuals. For example, Canadians who have moved abroad and given up their citizenship have a right to CPP but not OAS pensions. Canadians pay lifetime general taxes to finance OAS benefits. These taxes, though not earmarked for the purpose, are strictly equivalent to the CPP premiums the other half of retirement benefits.

It is possible to privatize the OAS and amalgamate it with a privatized CPP system by the following arrangement. Personal tax rates would be lowered by an amount equal to present CPP premiums. Individuals would then be required to deposit these sums into their private retirement Super RRSP. Assuming that the enriched fund earns five percent per year, the annuity the accumulated funds could buy upon retirement would be equal to 80 percent of income at age 65.

Retirement benefits equal to 80 percent of income are too high for most people. They come at an age when needs are relatively low. The money needed to build them up could have been used better at the stage in life when the cost of raising children is high. For this reason, rates of replacement of income at 65 at 40 to 50 percent might be more appropriate. If a target of 50 percent were accepted, 30 percent of the annual premiums

Chapter 13

that would go into private investment funds could be diverted for a limited time to pay off the unfunded liabilities of the CPP and OAS system.

The preceding analysis is rough and tentative. I had asked Brown and McClelland to have professional actuaries determine the exact outcomes of the different scenarios just discussed. Unfortunately, the work was never done, except for the figure quoted that CPP premiums invested privately would yield an annuity equal to 40 percent of the income earned by the average Canadian aged 65. However, I am quite certain that the basic methods to finance the unfunded liabilities are sound economically. They do not involve some confidence trick because the funds set aside every year are invested productively and yield a true return. The system takes advantage of the power of compound interest.

There is a final, appealing method to reduce the unfunded liabilities of the present CPP system. In 1996, benefits paid out under the CPP plan came to about $20 billion. Of these, $3.3 billion or 16 percent were payments to disabled persons. For historic reasons not entirely clear to me, this burden of financing federal disability payments has fallen on the CPP system. In my view, disability payments should be part of the country's general social security system. This system is designed to take care of the needs of the unfortunate members of society unable to look after themselves, regardless of their history of work. If disability payments were taken out of the CPP budget and paid for out of general revenue through the Department of Human Resources budget, 16 percent of the unfunded liabilities of the CPP system would be eliminated.

It is important to note that this approach would not open a floodgate for future demands to finance pensions out of general revenues. The switch is logically defensible and can even be seen as a correction for a bad decision taken in the past. It should be clear from the preceding analysis that all of the methods available for dealing with the unfunded liabilities of CPP in the process of switching to a privatized system involve political risks. People dislike change and fear the unknown. They prefer to stay with systems they know. In any change there are some winners and some losers. If I had been given the opportunity to present the preceding analysis to caucus, my colleagues at the very least would have understood the problem of unfunded liabilities brought on by a Super RRSP system of private pensions. They would have been forced to consider the merit of the three alternative methods for dealing with the problem.

I do not know what the outcome of such a meeting would have been, whether there would have been a vote to go with some or all of the available solutions to the problem. Perhaps there would have been demands for more rigorous actuarial studies, which I would have welcomed. Perhaps many other problems associated with CPP and Super RRSPs would have been brought up and seen to require solutions. All I know is that because of decisions made by Manning and others, the caucus meeting I demanded never took place.

In 1998 the Super RRSP plan was an embarrassment for Reform and raises questions about the party's readiness to govern. Diane Ablonczy's effort to produce a solution to the problems of unfunded liabilities since the new session of Parliament resulted in glossy brochure full of political rhetoric and questions for the public. It did not lead to any financially sound plans.

Liberals and the unfunded liabilities

In conclusion, a few remarks about the change to the CPP system adopted by the Liberals, which involves simply an increase in premiums to 9.9 percent in 1999. The revenue generated by this policy is much greater than the benefits paid every year until 2023. As a result, the CPP system accumulates a surplus fund which may go as high as $200 billion, including the earnings from investment. After 2023 the revenues generated by the 9.9 percent premiums are less than the pensions paid and the fund is drawn down. Importantly, the fund is expected to be large enough to see the system through the demands of the baby boomers in retirement without the necessity for higher premiums.

The change reduces the unfair burden which otherwise the system would have put on future generations. In effect, baby boomers pay premiums while they are working which are set aside to pay for their own benefits upon retirement; their children are relieved of the burden of paying all of these benefits from their own pockets. The large CPP fund will increase the supply of funds for investment.

The plan has been hailed by experts in Canada and abroad as politically courageous and financially sound. The plan is not perfect and can be criticized on several grounds. Ideologically it entrenches the government in the provision of pensions. They will remain a battleground for political manoeuvres as special interest groups fight for better deals, typically not for the betterment of society as a whole. Practically, the change has missed the opportunity to move towards a higher age of normal retirement. It will be difficult in the future to effect such a change unless another crisis develops, in spite of the intrinsic merit of later retirement and other countries' commitment to it.

Finally, the administration of the surplus fund gives rise to some difficult problems. It has to be kept free from political interference, but its managers are accountable to no-one. They do not face punishment by the market place because the money is owned publicly. If they are made accountable to parliament, the door is opened for political interference.

There are additional problems arising from the fact that the fund is required to limit its foreign investments to 15 percent of the total. As a result, the massive funds will have great influence on equity markets and at the same time will be exposed to risks from stock market and bond price fluctuations caused by other economic factors. Investments by the fund

Chapter 13

managers can seriously influence the fortunes of individual companies and industries. For these reasons the limitations on foreign investment should be eliminated.

The sizzle and the steak

Every day Reform asks questions of the government during question period in Parliament. The basis for these questions are government policies and the results they produce. Often the opportunity is used simply to criticize the government or the actions of individual ministers. However, the opportunity is often used to advertise Reform's policy positions. Such questions offer a good opportunity to inform the public about Reform's ideas, especially if the media take up the issues.

When I decided to stand for election, I had hoped to be able to participate regularly in the formulation and asking of questions. I thought in this task again my professional expertise would come in handy, but my expectations were not fulfilled.

After the election in October 1993, one of my first activities was to speak with people who had been in government as politicians or bureaucrats. I asked them for tips on how to be a good MP. The most important and most frequently mentioned suggestion was that I should not be too partisan, that I should acknowledge it when the ruling party had done the right thing. Such a policy would raise my and the party's standing with the public and the media. It would also increase the credibility of the criticism of policies that I would make. It was suggested to me that part of this strategy was the avoidance of rhetorical excesses and personal attacks on ministers.

I was not given much opportunity to follow through on this strategy in question period. Substantive, critical questions in economics and finance often tend to involve statistics and dry facts, which did not fit into the theatrical atmosphere of question period. The media paid scant attention to them. I also decided from the start that I would deliver all questions in a calm and measured way appropriate for the message, but again, this did not fit the atmosphere. At one point I was coached to be more dramatic, modulating my voice and gesturing to emphasize points. Later another coach thought that this style was not appropriate for the many thousands who watched question period on TV and I reverted to my old way of asking questions.

Manning had promised during the 1993 election that Reform would change the style of question period from partisan and personal attacks to reasoned criticism, delivered calmly. This approach was used for a while and I got to ask more questions than the average Reform MP. But soon Manning and the administrators of question period changed their mind. Questions became more aggressive and personal. My role in question period diminished correspondingly and towards the end it was non-existent. I had refused to go along with the shift to dramatics and personal attacks. To illustrate, at one point it was decided to use preambles to questions in finance to attack Martin on the grounds that he was a millionaire and owned freighters that were flying foreign flags to escape Canadian regulations. I refused to ask such questions. Solberg, the Deputy Finance Critic, did so with relish.

Manning had a strong hand in the design and execution of all of these question period strategies. They were a disappointment for me. Many others in caucus shared my views. But in discussions it became clear to me that in question period, like in almost all politics, the sizzle was more important than the steak. Perhaps this fact is inevitable in parliamentary democracies. Nevertheless I fault Manning and the party leadership for not trying harder to use more steak than sizzle, even if it would have changed the 'theatre' atmosphere of Parliament.

Conclusions

My experiences with the Reform policy formulation process just described were not very positive. I had stood for election in the hope that being in Parliament would allow me to be closer to the policy formulation process than I was as an academic. It was not to be, for a number of reasons. One was that for a long time I did not have any explicit responsibility or authority to work on financial policies, Ray Speaker and then Stephen Harper being the Finance Critics. To the extent that I worked on details of policies, Manning in several instances changed what I had written, even though in discussions he had agreed with my reasoning. Even after I had finally become Finance Critic, major policy strategies were decided by Manning and an inner circle of advisers who had great political instincts but knew very little about economics and finance.

It gives me little satisfaction to know that my criticism on some aspects of the policies designed by this inner circle was valid even politically. In question period I found similarly that the substance of policies was distinctly secondary to the rhetoric and delivery of questions.

The design of policies on the flat tax and reform of the CPP required exactly the kind of professional expertise I possessed. Manning gave the responsibility for these policies to others who had better communications and political skills but knew nothing of the subject. In spite of my intense efforts to develop good policies and get them accepted officially, I was stymied. It was a great source of frustration to watch how the poor design of Reform policies on the flat tax and pension reform hurt the party's image and opened up lines of attack by the government.

In conclusion I want to note that my unhappy personal experience with policy formulation may be due to my personal inadequacies, genetic and acquired through 35 years of life as an academic. It is possible that my values, styles and strengths did not match those of Manning. It is also

Chapter 13

possible that both Manning and I were new to the business of designing financial and economic policies for an opposition party in the Canadian parliament. It is up to readers to judge these matters. Whatever they may be, I hope that my account will be of some use to those interested in Reform policies, Manning and the role academic economists with my background can be expected to play in such an environment.

CHAPTER 14

Committee Work and Relationships with other Parties

THE Finance Committee of the House of Commons holds hearings on legislation, the budget and a wide range of other issues important to government activities affecting the economy. I was fortunate to be a member of that committee for the four years I spent in Ottawa as an MP. For two of these years I was the ranking representative of the Reform party. Work on the Finance Committee was a very positive experience. It was almost like attending university seminars. Witnesses presented short papers and the members of the Committee acted like faculty, asking questions. I always learned from the presentations and discussions. The learning broadened my understanding of the complexity of society, the many injustices handed out by nature and the many ways in which people expected government to come to their aid.

Personal relationships

The members of the committee from all parties behaved very collegially. We learned from each other and respected each others' point of view. Good-natured bantering eased the fatigue which sometimes overcame us after many hours of sitting. Once a year, we travelled to different cities and suffered together through many trials of an exhausting schedule. These shared experiences created a comforting bond between the members. The work helped me better understand what motivates politicians from different parties, Liberals, NDPers and members of the Bloc.

The Committee consisted of thirteen voting members, seven Liberals and three each from the Bloc and Reform parties. This balance of members assured the government a voting majority. The government used this majority to pass reports on hearings presented to parliament. Reform usually voted against the government and inserted a minority position in the report.

The working climate in parliamentary committees is determined largely by the chair's handling of procedural matters and the cooperative spirit of the members. The chair determines when and for how long members can question witnesses, when votes are taken, how much input members have on the agenda and so on. The Finance Committee of the 36th Parliament was chaired by Jim Peterson, a veteran politician and brother of the former Ontario Premier David Peterson. A tax lawyer by training, he is very articulate and politically astute. He ran the affairs of the committee fairly, efficiently and civilly. There were very few procedural disputes, except when

Chapter 14

Yvan Loubier occasionally used the committee selfishly, to advance the Bloc's political agenda. These tactics tested my and everyone's patience severely, but Peterson was always civil, courteous and accommodating.

I enjoyed my working and personal relationship with Peterson. He allowed me to ask more than my fair share of questions of witnesses, especially if I was likely to uncover how their positions and demands were self-serving and harmful to the public interest. To this day I am not sure to what extent he used me in the process. My tough questions did not endear me and Reform to these witnesses and their constituents. By contrast, Liberals could appear more sympathetic. On the other hand, his Liberal colleagues or Peterson, himself, often followed up on the issues I had raised. Occasionally, in private, he congratulated me for the questions I had asked. To my puzzlement, a number of times he told me that he had learned a lot of economics from me. As a result he understood better than ever before that 'government messes with markets at great costs' and that the ability of government to improve the welfare of people is much more limited than he had previously believed.

The agenda and witnesses

The topics considered by the committee were formally decided by the executive committee on which Reform had one member. Peterson invited me to submit subjects for hearings. In one case he took up my suggestion and we invited a number of witnesses to discuss the large difference in the unemployment rates in Canada and the United States. The subjects for nearly all other hearings were determined by the government's legislative program, which in turn relies heavily on input from the Department of Finance and was controlled ultimately by Paul Martin as Minister of Finance.

I was unable to determine the process by which the committee decided on the witnesses invited to testify. Peterson issued a formal invitation to Reform and the Bloc to submit the names of potential witnesses, but in the end it seemed we always heard from an almost unchanging set of persons, who for the most part represented the major lobby groups headquartered in Ottawa for just this purpose. These groups also provided general information to government departments. I am sure that the Committee Clerk had a list of those lobbyists. There probably exists an unwritten agreement with the government that they would be able to testify on all affairs of interest to them.

At one point I was lobbied by a well-known economist from the University of Toronto. He wanted a chance to testify on the budget, as he had done regularly during the Mulroney era. Peterson declined to invite him on grounds that seemed to me to be personal rather than professional.

The Committee had a competent and friendly staff looking after logistics; they faced quite a formidable set of tasks. Witnesses had to be invited, submissions duplicated, distributed and translated (the Bloc made a big political issue out of the occasional absence of a French language version of material used by the committee). Notices of meetings were sent out, rooms booked, simultaneous translation and sometimes TV coverage were put in place. The transcripts of the hearings were typed in both languages, sent to MPs for correction and then published officially. Whenever the committee went on the road, the staff arranged transportation, meeting rooms, advertising and hotels for the members. The committee also had a permanent staff of two researchers assigned by the Library research department, to provide background information on topics under discussion — on many occasions they supplied us with penetrating questions to ask of witnesses. They were very competent economists with advanced degrees. I had very good relationships with them and they told me about their pleasure of having a professional economist serving as a member of the committee.

Any real function for the committee?

Parliamentary committees are often criticized for a number of shortcomings. They have no real power. Unlike committees in the U.S. Congress, they cannot block legislation by failure to report to the legislature. They are creatures of the government and, in the Canadian parliamentary system, carry out its agenda. Cynics suggest that committee work is given to keep government backbenchers busy and to make them feel important. I agree with these criticisms to some extent. The committee work certainly kept me busy and gave me some sense of accomplishment. But committees also perform some other important and useful functions. Hearings provide an opportunity for the public to express its concerns about pending legislation. Groups of people affected by legislation feel that their views are heard. As a result they have much reduced incentives to take to the street or use some other less civil methods to voice their concerns.

In this Canadian system testimony is rarely given by 'average' citizens, but well organized special interest groups. The existence of a wide range of such interest groups assures that a broad spectrum of the population is represented.

The testimony of witnesses influences legislation in subtle ways. I used information obtained in the committee hearings in question period and speeches in the House. A representative of the Department of Finance always present at hearings passes information on to officials responsible for the design of the relevant legislation. Often, the media are present and report on proceedings. Unfortunately, these reports focussed more often on hard-luck stories of individuals rather than basic facts relevant to the legislation. When important subjects are discussed, the meetings are televised nationally on the cable network called C-Pac. Some feedback from constituents suggests that such broadcast attract some interested viewers.

Chapter 14
Effects on legislation

On a number of occasions the hearings revealed some flaws in the legislation proposed by the government. As a result, the laws were modified. The most memorable of these incidences involved financial regulations. The proposed legislation would have made it more difficult for foreign banks and other financial intermediaries to compete with Canadian banks. For example, a foreign bank had planned to establish an ordinary Canadian corporation to market credit cards to special clients selected through an innovative computer program. These clients would pay lower interest rates than those charged by Canadian banks. This credit card corporation would not take deposits or make loans and therefore by commons standards would not be considered to be a bank. However, the legislation before the committee proposed that this corporation be treated as if it were the subsidiary or branch of a foreign bank. As such, it would be required to meet a host of regulations so costly that it would be unprofitable. The legislation would thus have prevented the creation of a business clearly in the interest of Canadian consumers.

The testimony by the corporation wanting to issue credit cards brought out all of the preceding facts. The representatives of the big Canadian banks argued in favour of the proposed legislation. They were not persuasive and it was obvious to the members of the committee that the legislation was introduced as a result of their lobbying. It would have protected the banks against competition. As a result, members of the committee strongly urged the government to change the proposed legislation. Eventually our recommendation was accepted.

Another law on which the committee had some important influence was the taxation of charitable contributions. After some initial representations from charitable organizations during routine hearings on the budget, it had become clear to me that the law needed to be changed. I subsequently urged Peterson to hold some special hearings on the subject; he agreed readily and made the project his own. Here are the issues we discussed.

Harvard University has the largest endowment of any public U.S. institution. It was worth over $4 billion in 1996. Other U.S. universities, museums, hospitals and similar charitable institutions have correspondingly large endowments. By comparison, equivalent Canadian charities are poor. The main reason given for this discrepancy is the taxation of charitable gifts in the two countries. In Canada a donor of a block of real estate or corporate shares has to pay the government a capital gains tax on the appreciated assets at the time it is given to the charities, but in the United States such cash payments on capital gains would not be necessary. In addition, the proportion of the gifts deductible from income is greater for American than Canadian donors.

Peterson arranged committee hearings for a blue-ribbon panel of experts on charitable giving. The experts included a former Lieutenant Governor of Ontario, the President of the University of Toronto and some of the country's top tax lawyers. Their testimony was very persuasive. Undoubtedly it had some important influence on new legislation which was brought to the House of Commons some months later. It removed some of the existing tax disincentives to charitable giving in Canada.

The testimonies of Minister Paul Martin and Governor Gordon Thiessen

In the fall of every year the Finance Committee had an important special meeting at which Paul Martin outlined the state of the economy and talked about the forthcoming budget. On this occasion he presented a set of questions regarding the budget on which he wanted input from the Canadian public.

For example, during the time of large deficits in 1994-96 he asked for recommendations on the size and nature of spending cuts. These questions were the main theme for the Finance Committee hearings in the fall and the months leading to the budget presentation in February. Martin's pre-budget presentations attracted much media attention.

Manning always used the opportunity to get exposure for himself and asked the first question of the Minister. His questions were always well prepared and to the point (he never asked me for any input). His knowledge and instincts were excellent and earned him good coverage in the media.

All members of the Finance Committee were also allowed to ask a question of the minister. The Bloc used the occasion to advertise the separatist agenda. The Liberals tended to ask questions which permitted Martin to elaborate on the points he had made in his initial address, and in 1996 Martin made much about the reduction in the deficit he had achieved. I knew that most of this reduction had been due to increased government revenues and another large share resulted from cuts in transfers to the provinces, while government spending cuts had been relatively small.

I asked him to tell the people of Canada the exact figures on these sources of deficit reduction. To my delight, he did not have the numbers and had to consult with David Dodge, his Deputy Minister, and even then gave a rather unsatisfactory answer. The facts were obviously embarrassing to him.

However, most of the time Martin handled questions effectively and with obvious ease. Greenspon and Wilson-Smith in their book on the Liberals in power noted that Martin had spent much time preparing for this meeting with the Finance Committee, and it showed.

Gordon Thiessen, Governor of the Bank of Canada, also met with the Committee once a year. His testimony attracted much less general media attention and Manning was never there. Thiessen is a very personable gentleman who deals patiently with even the silliest questions about

Chapter 14

money and finance. It was pointed out to me that this was in great contrast with the behaviour of his predecessor, John Crow. Crow was reputed not to suffer fools gladly and had many run-ins with Paul Martin (at that time Finance Critic for the Liberals, who were in opposition).

Thiessen knew always to expect me to ask a question about the quantity of money the Bank had created. The issue of the money supply had been given great prominence by Milton Friedman at the University of Chicago. Friedman's research in the postwar years had shown that excessive increases in the money supply inevitably create inflation. This result was in conflict with conventional wisdom, which held that monetary policy did not matter and that central banks should manage interest rates rather than the money supply.

The double-digit inflation of the 1970s had created much interest in Friedman's work; as a result, central banks changed their approach to making monetary policy, making the money supply grow at a non-inflationary rate and paying scant attention to interest rates. However, this strategy resulted in large fluctuations in interest rates and was eventually abandoned. Central banks, including the Bank of Canada returned to the old strategies of setting interest rates.

Yet the relationship between the excess creation of money and inflation still exists and is an ever-present danger. Friedman's basic criticism of managing interest rates is still valid. Consider the question of whether a 20 percent interest rate reflects easy or tight monetary policy. Most people would say that a 20 percent rate is evidence of a very tight policy. Yet, if inflation is expected to be 25 percent, the monetary policy producing the 20 percent interest rate is very easy. Money can be borrowed at a negative rate of five percent per year. In other words, if someone borrowed $100,000 at 20 percent interest to buy a house and could sell that house one year later for $125,000, he would have earned five percent per year on the money he had borrowed. Under these conditions borrowers will be eager to get their hand on loans, buy goods with them and feed the inflation. For this reason, Friedman suggested that central banks should not manage interest rates but the money supply.

During the 1970s the inflation experienced in the U.S. and Canada was accompanied by relatively low interest rates and very large increases in the money supply. By 1980 Paul Volker, the Chairman of the Federal Reserve, finally grasped the policy nettle, accepting Friedman's prescription and severely restricting the growth in money supply. As a result, U.S. interest rates rose to unprecedented levels. As the supply of money dwindled, money became more and more expensive to borrow (the rarer a commodity, the greater the demand for it, the higher its price).

The Bank of Canada copied Volker's policies. Many people will never forget the bankruptcies and large economic upheavals brought on by mortgage rates over 20 percent which existed in 1980-81. Inflation was stopped, but at high cost. I think that the experience of the 1970s and that of many countries require the Bank of Canada to keep a close watch over the growth in money supply.

Thiessen never mentioned growth in money supply in his opening remarks, even after it had been very high during 1996 and had prompted a critical analysis by David Laidler, William Robson, and Ken Boessenkool entitled *Devils in the Details: Improving the Tactics of Recent Canadian Monetary Policy,* published by the C.D. Howe Institute. But, in response to my questions, he assured me that the Bank was paying attention to the money supply figures and that the money supply was being watched especially closely after its recent rapid growth. However, I was disappointed to know that money supply figures play no systematic role in assessing the state of monetary policy.

The exchange with Thiessen on this subject and some others were fun for me. Academic economists do not often have the chance to ride their hobby-horses and ask questions of the Governor of the Bank of Canada about them. But issues which interested me had little appeal for the media and were never covered.

Obnoxious witnesses

Occasionally witnesses were obnoxious. Maude Barlow of the Council of Canadians and a couple of her associates at one session harangued the committee about the inadequacy of the government's policies, which she saw as hurting social welfare and Canada's independence. As always, I listened attentively to the presentation. I had to take many deep breaths to control my impulses to interrupt the flow of what I considered to be logically or empirically indefensible arguments. I then had a chance to ask a question of Barlow. While I did so she talked with her associates, giggled and paid no attention to what I was saying. I stopped my question and asked her to extend to me the same courtesy that I had extended her. Peterson took my side and criticized her behaviour. Fortunately, or unfortunately, the proceedings were not televised so no visual record of the incident exists.

On another occasion a witness in Nova Scotia made me leave the hearing room in protest. I am told that people there still talk about this incident. The topic under consideration was the report of a Liberal task force on government support for the handicapped. I asked one of the co-authors of the report how the responsibility for spending was divided between federal, provincial and local authorities. This is an important issue since, in my view, the administration of support for the handicapped is carried out more efficiently the closer the government is to the people. Instead of replying to my question, the witness went into a diatribe and accused me and Reform of a lack of compassion for the handicapped, at which point I lost my cool and left the room.

At a committee hearing in Montreal a number of radical students attacked the government on its fiscal policies, which they alleged were responsible for high tuition fees for university students. They recommended raising taxes on the rich to balance the budget. I knew that it made no sense to argue with young political activists of the sort who were present that day. However, after some earlier experience I thought it might be useful to raise some questions about the real world, which might at least have the effect of teaching them some facts.

In this spirit, and in a neutral tone of voice, I asked one student whether he knew at what level of income a person belonged to the top ten percent of all income earners in Canada. Earlier that year the head of one university student federation, who was lobbying me in my office, thought that people in the top ten percent of the income distribution all earned well over a million dollars. In fact, individuals with more than $50,000 are Canada's rich, by this definition. In a follow-up question to him, I asked what percentage of all income taxes was paid by this top ten percent of income earners. He had replied it was perhaps 20 percent or less, "since the rich have so many ways of cheating on taxes."

In fact, Canadians with the highest ten percent of incomes pay *50 percent of all income taxes collected by Canadian governments*. I never got to the second question during the hearings in Montreal. The student interrupted me. In an angry tone he said that he and his friends were not here to answer questions, but to tell us what to do! His behaviour raised memories of student radicalism in the 1960s and I felt great sympathy for my predecessors who suffered greatly at the hands of such politicized student activists.

Professional economists as witnesses

In the fall of every year the committee heard from a panel of economists working at universities, for financial institutions, left- and right-wing think-tanks and unions. These witnesses addressed questions about expected economic conditions, the merit of spending cuts, the appropriateness of monetary and tax policies and other topics related to the upcoming budget.

These meetings provided me with an enjoyable opportunity to talk with professional colleagues I had known from other occasions. The testimonies presented at these meetings revealed much consensus on the policies the government should pursue. However, there were always dissenters, representing unions and left-wing think tanks. It never ceased to amaze me how these people could spin the facts and argue that policies clearly beneficial to their constituents should be adopted because allegedly they were also in the interest of the general public.

At the same time I was surprised by the sincerity of the motives and the depth of conviction of these economists. The experience was a useful reminder of the fact that economics is not a science and political economy is largely sophisticated politics.

Committee Work and Relationships with other Parties

Travelling with the Committee

The work on the Finance Committee was very time-consuming and tiring. During certain times in the legislative calendar the committee's approval was needed to move legislation into second reading and votes. This meant meetings running from 10 am until 10 pm, with a short break for lunch and question period. Sometimes, sandwiches were brought in for supper while the hearings continued.

Once a year the committee travelled to the ten major cities of Canada to listen to local views on the budget and related issues. To ease the burden on members, two teams were formed. One travelling west was headed by Barry Campbell, a distinguished lawyer from Toronto, with whom I also had a good personal relationship. Over Christmas 1996 he and his family visited Whistler and we had a good time skiing together. The second team, headed by Peterson, travelled east; thus we were able to cover the entire country in a week.

The schedule for these meetings was gruelling. Anyone who believes that such trips are an enjoyable perk are seriously mistaken. Hearings started at 9 am and lasted until four or five in the afternoon. Often there was no lunch break and we ate a sandwich 'on the fly.' At the end of the hearings we were off to the airport. We would often arrive late at night in the city where the next day's hearings were to take place. Depending on the length of the flight, the food served on the plane was usually the dinner. After an often restless sleep in a strange hotel, and without the benefit of any exercise, the daily routine was repeated. There was no time to see any sights or meet locals. The meeting rooms typically had no windows.

However, the regional meetings of the Finance Committee served a useful purpose. I gained many insights and found refreshing the testimony of locals who were different from the professional lobbyists we saw regularly in Ottawa. They spoke from the heart, confirming to me that many problems cannot be solved from distant Ottawa. Canada is too large and diverse for simple, centralized solutions to local problems. The atmosphere of Ottawa and the very professionalism of the lobbyists make it easy to forget these facts.

My involvement with the Finance Committee was an important source of satisfaction. I learned much about economics, finance and taxation from the many witnesses who were top experts in their fields. The lobbyists representing many diverse interests opened my eyes to the complexity of economic and social problems. Colleagues on the committee from all parties were cordial, worked well together and appeared to appreciate the contributions to the discussions I could make as a professional economist. Most important, I was able to participate effectively in a few but important efforts to change pending legislation so it would better serve all Canadians.

Chapter 14

The Speaker of the House

I was and remain an admirer of Gilbert Parent, the Speaker of the House. He is a member of the Liberal Party but, in my view, has been an excellent referee in the often heated discussions in the House and on other matters affecting the functioning of Parliament. His job was not easy. The House was populated with political novices and full of passion.

Parent tried to make Parliament a more interesting place for MPs. He initiated a program of bringing distinguished Canadians from sports, the arts and sciences to Ottawa for special day-long visits. These visitors attended the House, sat in on question period and were honoured with speeches at receptions open to all MPs. Through this program I had the privilege of talking to Nancy Greene, the champion skier, a former resident of Whistler and a supporter during my election in 1993. I also spoke with Michael Smith, the Nobel laureate in chemistry from UBC, with whom I had skied a number of times at Whistler. The largest crowd of MPs was attracted to the reception of the legends of Canadian hockey like Gordie Howe, Rocket Richard and Howie Meeker. I am certain that these distinguished Canadians from different fields of endeavour enjoyed these affairs. I certainly enjoyed myself and the interruption it brought to the dreary routine of being an MP.

Parent also encouraged socialization and culture. Every fall he held a barbecue at his official residence in the Gatineau hills, which had been one of the three private residences of Mackenzie King. It was a treat to take a guided tour of this historic building.

Parent also brought to the House of Commons an all-female string quintet from Cuba, which he had heard playing in a church during his visit to that country. Early one evening they played a mixture of European classics and contemporary Cuban composers. It was an enchanting experience, but unfortunately, only a handful of MPs attended the performance.

After I had announced my decision not to seek re-election, I was surprised by the reaction from several Liberals. Paul Martin said 'I wish you would run again.' At a reception, three Liberal MPs with whom I had never spoken before said 'We will miss you,' and the following day, Parent said the same. I asked him why these things were said to me. His reply was, 'We appreciate quality in MPs.'

NDP Members of Parliament

Understandably, Manning reacted differently to my decision to retire from politics. He promptly appointed Monte Solberg as Finance Critic and moved me from the front to the back row in the House. As a result, I sat next to the small contingent of NDP members. During votes, while we had to sit idly in our assigned seats, we had many discussions. I purposely brought up some issues which are important to NDP ideology. For example, on welfare policy I suggested provocatively that it created dependence and in the longer run harmed the well-being of many who enjoyed short run benefits. To my surprise, they shared my concerns and readily supplied examples of welfare dependence they had encountered. Similarly, they shared my concerns about the abuse of the unemployment insurance system and the damage done to the self-esteem of natives by the generous support provided by the government.

I found these NDPers' views surprising, having never heard them speak in public about the negative consequences of social insurance programs. They almost always ask for more generous benefits, easier access or new programs to deal with social ills not yet covered by the security net.

I had one bad experience with Svend Robinson, an MP who had been reelected several times for the NDP. His militant stance on left-wing issues have made him a celebrity with some Canadians and many journalists. I had agreed to be with him on a panel to discuss the problems of the Canada Pension Plan. The meeting took place in East Vancouver, a working class neighbourhood and strong base of NDP support. The meeting started late and every speaker was given 10 minutes to present his party's position.

I spoke first, Robinson last. He used almost his entire allotted time to comment on the Reform plan for privatizing the CPP (see chapter 13). All his statements about the Reform plan were false and designed to stir up fear in the minds of older people and pensioners. I do not know whether he had failed to study our proposal or whether he was lying deliberately.

After he was finished I asked for a brief opportunity to set the record straight, but the chair of the session refused my request. Robinson sneeringly said to me something like, "That's politics." I had been taught an important lesson. Do not engage in political discussions with a pro like Robinson on his home turf where he controls the agenda.

Paul Martin and the IMF meeting in Madrid

In the fall of 1994 the annual meetings of the IMF and World Bank were held in Madrid. Paul Martin sent an invitation to Reform and the Bloc to send along an MP each as observers and official members of the Canadian delegation. Ray Speaker, who at the time was the Reform Finance Critic, graciously allowed me to go to Madrid as the Reform representative. I was very happy for this opportunity.

As an academic I had written papers and a best-selling book on the IMF, and during the 1980s I had sat twice in IMF Directors' chairs at the Washington headquarters as one of a small group of academics invited to discuss the future of the institution. In 1970 I had attended the annual meeting in Washington as a member of the U.S. delegation while I worked as an economist in the U.S. Treasury Department. So, naturally, I was thrilled to attend the Madrid meetings as a Canadian member of Parliament.

Apparently, an opposition MP had never before been on the government's official delegation to such meetings. When I asked Martin why he had chosen to set a new precedent, he replied that I knew more about the international monetary system than anyone else on the delegation and that he welcomed my input. As it turned out, there was no opportunity for me to get involved in the official business. Most of the routine work of these international organizations is carried out in committees staffed by their civil servants. Work involving inter-governmental relations are staffed by delegates from member countries. There is no room for politicians and outsiders at these levels of work. The Ministers of Finance have some public meetings where nearly all of the proceedings have been orchestrated beforehand by national and international civil servants. The real work at these IMF-World Bank meetings goes on behind the scenes and in private meetings with very restricted attendance.

After the Madrid meetings I wrote a letter to Martin to thank him for the opportunity to attend the affair. In this letter I also noted that I had felt lonely and useless during the meetings. I suggested that if and when he again invited opposition MPs to attend such affairs they be given some official work involvement. To the best of my knowledge, no invitations have been issued to opposition members to attend IMF-World Bank meetings since 1994.

It was fun talking to a number of delegates I had known through my academic work and travels; some had taken up positions of great importance. Jacob Frenkel, a former colleague at the University of Chicago, was Governor of the Bank of Israel. Michael Mussa, whom I knew from academic conferences, was the Director Research of the IMF. Alexandre Kafka, with whom I had met a number of times while I worked at the U.S. Treasury was the longest serving Executive Director on the IMF Board. Gerry Helleiner, a class-mate from Yale, was an articulate spokesman for the interests of developing countries and non-governmental organizations in Madrid to lobby the IMF and World Bank.

A number of former students and university colleagues attended the meetings working in some official capacities. The trouble was that there was no time to meet with these acquaintances. They were always running to some meeting they had to attend.

A dinner with Paul Martin

The most interesting and useful event during my trip to Madrid was a reception at the Canadian Embassy, followed by a private dinner hosted by Paul Martin in a fine restaurant. When we left the embassy reception, three cars were waiting to take us to the restaurant. I witnessed official protocol at work; everyone waited for Martin to choose a car and companion before they entered their vehicles. Only after Martin said "Herb, why don't you accompany me and my wife in my car?" did the other two cars fill quickly and we were on our way.

Committee Work and Relationships with other Parties

On the half-hour drive I had a good conversation with Martin. We broke the ice with talk about people we both knew. He knew my wife's parents and had played tennis with my sister-in-law and her husband in Montreal, but the conversation quickly turned to business and politics. He said he needed me and Reform to demand very drastic spending cuts to eliminate the deficit. These demands would allow him and his rather substantial cuts to seem moderate by comparison. They would help him in his fight with members of cabinet and caucus who thought these cuts were not needed, or should be much smaller.

Perhaps to get this message to me was his main and real purpose to have me along to these meetings at the IMF. If it was, I do not mind it. To help restore fiscal sanity to the federal budget had been my main motive for entering politics. If this could be achieved by letting the Minister of Finance appear moderate while he took strong action, that was alright with me.

I told Manning about our conversation. It did not change Reform's strategy on fiscal policy. It already had been as tough as was feasible economically and politically.

The dinner was attended by Martin and his wife, his personal assistant, Karl Littler, and two senior civil servants from the Department of Finance in Ottawa. We sat at a round table away from other diners and had an intense conversation, which he dominated. He started off by saying to me, with a laugh, "You might be Minister of Finance some day, God help us, so listen to this conversation carefully." He then launched a strongly worded attack on the Finance officials present for not advising him better on the size of spending cuts in his first budget in 1994. He was so direct and aggressive that his wife nudged him a couple of times and said, "Paul, watch what you are saying." I do not know whether she was concerned about the feelings of the civil servants or whether she was afraid he was saying things in front of me that I could leak to the media.

Martin obviously thought of the second concern because he said to me that if any of our conversation that evening got to the media, I would be 'dead.' I think that since 1994 enough time has elapsed for me to tell about that evening's conversation for the record. Besides, the most important points have already been made by Greenspon and Wilson-Smith in their book *Double Vision: The Liberals in Power.*

In response to Martin's accusation that they did not push him hard enough into the adoption of a tougher budget, the civil servants offered the following explanation. They had presented Martin a selection of three alternative budgets. One was tight and would have cut spending quickly and by large amounts; the second was very easy and increased spending slightly, while the third was in between these two extremes. The civil servants added that they did not know Martin's views. As politically neutral civil servants they were required only to set out the choices available. It was Martin's task as the political boss to make the political decision.

Chapter 14

Martin disagreed vehemently. He had wanted them to push more strongly for what by then he knew would have been the correct choice, a tougher budget with more cuts than he had presented in the spring of 1994. He went on to suggest that the civil servants should have known his mood on the crucial day when the budget document had to be finalized. He had been ready to fight with cabinet, caucus and the Prime Minister for a budget as tight as necessary to restore Canada's fiscal health. To their surprise, he said that when he took the budget to Chretien for final approval, he was prepared to resign as Minister of Finance if Chretien vetoed it. This was heady stuff and I wondered why he exposed me to it. Was it his plan all along to have me come to Madrid so I would hear this information without the media even knowing about our meeting? What, politically, had he hoped to gain by it? How could I help his cause other than continue in my role as a strong advocate of fiscal restraint?

I have found no satisfactory answers to these questions. During the next three years Martin and I met only for brief chats in the corridors or on the floor of the House. People noted that he always took notes when I asked questions of him during Question Period. I was told that he had left instructions that anything I wrote to him would be passed on immediately. Karl Littler revealed later that he kept close track of what I was saying publicly for Martin.

Other dealings with Martin

The following brief meeting with Martin was coincidental but very interesting to me. In February 1995, the Mexican currency crisis was rampant. In its wake, the Canadian dollar was under attack, interest rates were being raised significantly, unemployment rising, growth slowing and the deficit had once again begun to increase. I knew that Martin was in the last stages of preparing the 1995 budget and, when I met him in the corridor, expressed my sympathies for the troubles the recent developments must have caused for his budget process. He smiled and waved his hand, suggesting 'yes and no.'

It was clear that the crisis had provided him with a lever to tame the big spenders in cabinet and caucus. On one occasion I asked him a question in the House which I anticipated correctly he would answer in a certain way. My follow-up question pointed out clearly that his answer was inconsistent with a certain policy position he had defended strongly a short time before. It was the first and only time he stammered an incoherent reply. After he sat down and the cameras were no longer on him, he gave me a broad smile and a thumbs up. He had appreciated my successful debating trap and held no grudge.

On another occasion I questioned the interpretation of some labour market statistics Martin had presented in the House. He defended his view vigorously but agreed to consult with his staff. After I had returned to

Committee Work and Relationships with other Parties

academic life he told me that after my question he had asked his officials for clarification. He said felt the blood drain from his face when they told him I had been correct in my criticism. The matter was not important in any sense, but it reveals how seriously he takes his work and public image. In my lengthy official speech in reply to his 1995 budget I jokingly gave him an A- for the work he had done.

The budget for the first time since the end of the Second World War had actually reduced the number of dollars spent on government programs. It set a fiscal course which would eliminate the deficit within an expected four to five years. As it turned out, the economic prosperity and low interest rates achieved this goal a short three years later.

I thought that this budget was courageous and statesmanlike, especially since it was so inconsistent with the ways of the Liberal party. I am sure that he had to overcome much opposition from his colleagues in cabinet and caucus to get it accepted. I am also sure that he was very uncomfortable cutting into some of the spending programs his father had initiated in more prosperous times.

In this context it is also worth noting that without the leadership style of Jean Chretien, Martin might not have been able to produce this important, tide-turning budget. Chretien has often talked about his experience when serving as Trudeau's Minister of Finance. Sometimes Trudeau would overrule his decisions, and, on occasion, would make an announcement affecting the Finance portfolio without prior consultation. Chretien thought such behaviour inappropriate and damaging to his effectiveness as the Minister of Finance. For these reasons, he is strongly committed not to interfere with ministerial decisions.

It is interesting to speculate whether Chretien would have allowed Martin to present a much tougher budget in 1994. At that time many Liberals in cabinet and caucus had not understood the severity of Canada's fiscal crisis. Their lobbying might have led to the confrontation Martin had talked about at dinner in Madrid. It was only the Mexican currency crisis and its effect on Canada which brought home the seriousness of the fiscal crisis and enabled Martin to formulate the path-breaking budget of 1995.

Martin appeared pleased by my favourable remarks about his budget, though on several occasions he made it clear in the House that he and I were far apart ideologically. Manning was not pleased with my favourable comments on the 1995 Martin budget. He suggested that I was too close to Martin, was naïve for not recognizing that he had used me for his purposes and that my remarks would come back to haunt me and Reform. I disagree with Manning's views on this subject. Far from helping Martin, my remarks caused him some trouble with his left-wing colleagues in cabinet and caucus. They were sure to argue that a budget praised by a well-known conservative like Grubel could not possibly be a true Liberal budget.

In the Fall of 1997 I had resumed teaching economics at Simon Fraser

Chapter 14

University. The subject was Canadian Economic Policy. When I left Ottawa Martin, Manning and Bill Blaikie, an NDP MP, had suggested that I invite them to address this class. Only Martin managed to come to Burnaby Mountain for a lecture. He spoke to a sizeable audience which included not just my class but many graduate students and faculty. My economist colleagues were very favourably impressed with his analytical skills and knowledge in economics. They also liked his visions for the future. He was embarrassingly generous with his praise for my work in Parliament.

Observations on Chretien and other ministers

I had few personal contacts with Chretien, occurring only in social situations like the annual Press Ball. He appeared to have a good time talking to my wife, who was born and raised in Montreal. He also commented favourably about my presence at parliamentary social affairs boycotted initially by Manning and other Reform MPs. I thought that these boycotts were silly and resulted in missed opportunities to acquire knowledge useful for being an effective MP and critic of government policies. Besides, they were fun.

For a long time I sat in the House opposite Doug Young, the Minister of Transportation. I admired him for the cuts he undertook in regulation and spending. Under his regime, the budget of his ministry fell by two-thirds. I also liked the straight and honest answers he gave in question period. I told him privately that if it were up to me, there would be a statue on the Hill in recognition for the record downsizing he had accomplished.

However, he did a very poor job in the privatization of the air navigation system. He granted a full monopoly to AirNav, a private company, with the full right to set the fees airlines have to pay for the use of Canadian airspace. This monopoly position, and the right to charge airlines, will foster the development of a very militant union and large pay increases for the employees of AirNav. I predict that in a few years these employees will have the highest salaries for comparable work in all of Canada.

Of course, we will have expensive public relations experts repeat at every opportunity that the stress facing these workers justifies every cent of the high income they earn. Young should have known that privatization without competition is no better and, because of the absence of political control, often is worse than public ownership of an organization providing a service like air navigation. He should have made sure that AirNav did not have a complete monopoly.

Lloyd Axworthy is a career politician with very liberal instincts. The failure of socialism has left him bewildered. He was not very happy that Chretien had made him Minister of Human Resources with the responsibility for direct cutbacks in social programs delivered by the federal government. Chretien chose Axworthy for this task because of his strong credentials as a man who cares for the unfortunate. There would not likely be any credible challengers in cabinet and the Liberal caucus to program cuts he would undertake in his ministry.

When he took on the task of reforming and cutting back social programs he started a lengthy process of consultation with private sector interests. I could see his face every day during question period. He looked tired and depressed. He did not like the work. During the preceding 20 years in Parliament, his speciality had been the development of programs for increased spending on social causes; now he had to reform and cut back. Greenspon and Wilson-Smith obtained information from insiders and described how Axworthy had made a real mess of the consultations and ultimately the reforms. Inconsistent in the directions he gave, he antagonized many people while accomplishing very little. Canada's social programs, especially unemployment insurance, needed a major overhaul, but he tinkered, choosing symbolism over substance. For example, he was responsible for changing the name 'unemployment' into 'employment' insurance, a name change which makes no sense. We buy insurance against car accidents, not to stay out of accidents.

It is unfortunate that Axworthy let slip by a unique opportunity for substantial reforms in social programs. There is widespread agreement among academics and many politicians what these reforms should be. The problem in the past has been that existing programs have created a 'rights mentality' among its recipients. It is politically very difficult to confront this mentality. People about to lose what they thought were their entrenched rights put up a very strong fight. At the same time, the general tax payers who benefits from retrenchment gain so little that they are unwilling to provide support to politicians undertaking it.

In 1994-96 the fiscal crisis had changed this political calculus. Canadians were demanding fiscal restraint. They were prepared to take on those who thought their programs needed to be spared from cuts. What a shame that Axworthy did not use this window of political opportunity to push through fundamental reforms.

Axworthy was much happier after he had become Minister of Foreign Affairs. This position allowed him to indulge to the fullest his instincts for collective action to save the world. He smiled again and became more jovial. But many of his initiatives are not popular with the U.S. government which carries the burden of having to confront renegade countries militarily. Canada plays a token role in these affairs.

One of Axworthy's first major initiatives was to organize a renewed humanitarian intervention in Rwanda. He launched it in the House with pride. He was in his element. But then his program ran into problems: the refugees to be helped could not be found! Only countries with few resources committed to the effort backed it fully. The day the news came that his initiative had failed and made him look bad, he sat in his seat in the House with an expression in his face that made me think he would start to cry any moment. I crossed the aisle, put my hand on this shoulder and

Chapter 14

said, "I am sorry for what happened." He merely nodded his head, looking even sadder.

Since then he has been on a rampage with global initiatives which will assure him a prominent spot on the list of the world's most famous collectivists. He has been instrumental in getting a treaty aimed at a global ban on land mines. His dream of getting the Nobel prize for Peace eluded him, but it was a close call. He might yet get it if he succeeds with the initiative to create an international court of justice.

He has also been a strong supporter of the global agreement on greenhouse gas emissions at Kyoto, and happily signed an agreement which few believe was necessary, or that Canada can live up to. These global collective programs have noble goals. No-one can dispute that the world would be a better place if there were no more wars, crimes against humanity, poverty, sickness or degradation of the environment. The problem with these programs is that their goals are unrealistic and cannot be achieved. Failure to achieve these goals in itself can be damaging as raised hopes are dashed, and the process of trying to achieve them is costly.

Sometimes the programs have the opposite of the desired effect. For example, it is becoming increasingly obvious that the economic assistance programs to the Atlantic provinces have caused dependence and retarded development. (Fred McMahon: *Looking the Gift Horse in the Mouth: The Impact of Federal Transfers on Atlantic,* Canada, Halifax: Atlantic Institute for Market Studies, 1996). Substantial and lengthy support for developing countries may already have caused similar damage.

Another shortcoming of these collectivist international initiatives is that the world's most powerful nations like the United States, China and Russia have shown a great reluctance to sign on. These three large countries have not signed the treaty banning land mines. They will not permit the establishment of a permanent international war crimes tribunal. They are unwilling to risk that a collective of small nations which might be run by dictators of the right or left, will try their citizens on what might be ideological grounds.

For example, a number of small countries could accuse the U.S. Secretary of State of crimes against humanity because of its boycott of Cuba. The large nations of the world would agree to the establishment of such a permanent international court only if they have a veto over its agenda, much like they do on actions of the United Nations through the Security Council. But putting all of his energies and his ministry's resources behind these initiatives have allowed Axworthy to flourish and stay in the limelight.

There were several ministers whose work I thought highly of. Industry Minister John Manley strongly supported Martin's efforts to cut spending, reducing a number of subsidies to industry. Unfortunately, thereafter he initiated a new set of programs in support of research and development. There is little evidence that these programs yield a good return on average, even if they score some outstanding successes.

As Minister of Fisheries and Oceans, Brian Tobin rationalized the fishing industry to some extent, but was not willing to embrace the use of tradable fishing quotas. Such quotas, used in Iceland, New Zealand and elsewhere, are favoured by economists. They give individuals the right to catch a specified amount of fish annually for one or more years. The total catch allowed under this system is set to assure a steady, high yield for all, giving assured full employment to the holders of the quotas and bringing a steady flow of fish to processors, which can operate efficiently and without interruption.

By contrast, the Canadian system attempts to limit fishing effort through the issuance of a restricted number of licenses and permission to fish limited to a few days a year. Under this system, individual fishing boats have been made increasingly capable of catching large amounts of fish in ever shorter time. As a result, fish stocks have been depleted and processing facilities are inefficient, being shut down most of the year. Fishermen and processors in the Atlantic provinces receive unemployment insurance benefits every year equal to six times the value of the premiums they pay! In effect, the rest of Canadian workers are providing a very heavy subsidy to the fishing industry.

One day, after some particularly bad news about the depletion of fish stocks in the Atlantic was made public, I approached Tobin with the question of when he would introduce quotas as used by Iceland to limit catches. He obviously knew the economists' arguments in favour of them and about their successful use in Iceland. He replied, "Be patient, they will come eventually. We are not ready yet."

Marcel Masse, as the Minister for Intergovernmental Affairs and Minister for Public Service Renewal, has a low profile. Before his election in 1993 he had been a top civil servant. His task was to effect economies in the civil service and develop a plan for downsizing through consultation with individual ministries. He worked closely with Paul Martin and developed a very laudable plan for cuts. He and Martin should be given full credit for this achievement, though I retain some scepticism about the actual implementation of all of the planned reductions in staffing.

However, Masse did not initiate a plan for changing the incentive structure for bureaucrats as it had been implemented in Britain and New Zealand in recent years. In these countries the heads of some bureaucracies were given targets for output and cost as well as the power to make changes in operation and staffing to achieve them. If they were successful, they were rewarded financially. If they failed, they did not get bonuses and often were replaced. These systems in Britain and New Zealand have been very successful in lowering the cost and effectiveness of government programs.

I approached Masse with a question about the use of such systems in Canada. He was familiar with them but said, "In Canada we are not ready for such programs." What a shame — another opportunity missed! With

Chapter 14

the end of the fiscal crisis it will be impossible to impose such a system on the powerful civil service unions. They do not like having to be accountable in ways that can be measured and are in the position to prevent any reforms of the present system.

Allan Rock was the Minister of Justice. He always dressed impeccably and was in control at all times. He projected the image of the quintessential member of the Ontario (and therefore Canada) élite of corporate lawyers, and was very articulate and magisterial when answering questions. He was strongly committed to a number of causes, making him squarely a liberal on social issues, the most outstanding of which was the registration of long guns like rifles and shot-guns.

I have already elaborated on the issues surrounding this policy, arguing that the merit of a program for the registration of long guns rests on a benefit/cost analysis. How many lives could be saved and injuries prevented, and how much would the program cost? Such a calculation does *not* involve a callous disregard for lives, as Rock liked to argue. Society's resources are limited. If $100 million, for example, are required to save one life per year through the registration of long guns, it would be rational to consider how many lives could be saved if this sum of money were used to provide better medical care or improved highway safety.

I approached Rock several times, asking him to provide MPs with estimates of the cost per life saved of his proposed legislation. I promised him that if the estimate were favourable, I would break ranks with Reform and vote for his bill. He was very polite in response and promised to deliver such an analysis of costs and benefits, but he never did. I never figured out whether Rock's dedication to the registration of long guns stemmed from his personal commitment or whether he had been captured by the liberal activist bureaucrats of the Department of Justice.

David Anderson is a competent professional politician who speaks French and English. His experience made him Chretien's logical choice for member of cabinet from British Columbia. However, he was given a rough deal. His first portfolio was Minister of Revenue, a job in which one wins few friends. Then he was Minister of Transport, a lacklustre portfolio under strong fiscal restraint. Then he became Minister of Fisheries, an extremely difficult job. Fish disappear and the Department is blamed. Conservation measures are taken and the Department is blamed for hurting some too much and by others for not being tough enough.

The media love to report on stories of personal hardship caused by the crises and government policies. Self-appointed experts have unlimited supplies of advice, knowing that they are never held responsible if it turns out to be bad.

I had few contacts with Anderson, but one was rather memorable. Vaclas Klaus, the Prime Minister of the Czech Republic, was on a State visit to Canada in March 1997. Klaus is a professional economist with a conservative ideology. I had met him on a number of occasions, and had once had skied with him for a couple of days at Whistler. So I was invited to be a member of the Canadian delegation accompanying him on a visit to Banff, where he gave a public lecture attended by a large number of Canadians with a Czech background (there was also time for some skiing at Lake Louise).

David Anderson was the representative of the Government of Canada and official host for Klaus during his visit to Banff. On one occasion I shared a ski-lift ride with Anderson. Shortly before we got off the lift he said to me: "Now that you have decided not to seek re-election for Reform, how would you like to run for the Liberals in some other riding than yours?" I was so surprised by this suggestion that all I could do was mumble "I don't think so," before we had to jump off the lift.

I do not know what motivated Anderson to ask me that question. I do not know whether he acted on his own as the Liberals' head man in British Columbia in charge of preparing for the upcoming election or whether he talked about the issue with his colleagues in Ottawa. At any rate, I was flattered and got a deepening sense that I was more appreciated by the Liberals than by Manning and his inner circle.

The fights over perks

In closing this chapter I want to discuss the subject of perks for MPs. This subject was a serious source of irritation for me and many of my colleagues in caucus. It caused many frictions and, in my view, reduced the effectiveness of Reform.

During the years leading to the election in 1993, a number of books had been published which attacked the perks MPs were receiving in secret — or at least without the public being aware. The revelation of these perks resulted in much public discussion and indignation. Preston Manning sensed that the existence of these perks was a populist issue ideally suited to gather electoral support. He therefore committed himself and Reform to the elimination of them when in the position to do so and, in the meantime, announced that he and his caucus would not use them.

I always thought that the Reform policy on perks was populism at its worst. I rarely discussed the issue during my election campaign in 1993, and then only when it was raised by someone else. In my riding it was not an election issue, and I made no commitments about the personal use of Ottawa perks.

Nevertheless, I was forced as a result of caucus solidarity to give five percent of my salary to charity, which I did for the first year. I was also forced to surrender my right to a pension, for which I would have been eligible after a second term in office. Participation in some important and interesting parliamentary activities was considered taboo.

I disagreed with the judgement that I was overpaid. My monthly after tax deposits in my personal account were identical to those I had received as a university professor. My real financial well-being was lowered since I had extra expenses through the need to have a residence and car in Ottawa. I also lost the opportunity to earn extra income through consulting and royalties from publications; in addition, the work of a senior academic is much less stressful than that of an MP. For these reasons, I resented having to pretend that I was overpaid and to pay some of my income to charity.

Pensions

Pensions for MPs have to be more generous than those for people in the private sector. After one term in office and even more so after several re-elections, an MP's earning power outside politics is reduced considerably below what it was before. Some former MPs cannot find any work at all. I had a little taste of this process after my return to the university.

For over 20 years before going to Ottawa, I was responsible for teaching international economics and finance to both undergraduates and graduate students at Simon Fraser University. After my return, these teaching responsibilities had been given to another professor. I had to teach lower level courses in general economics which required much less specialized and current knowledge than international economics and finance.

I was glad for this change in my teaching responsibilities. After being four years away from the job, the failure to read the literature, attend seminars and conferences and write papers involving the frontier of the subject had left me feeling unprepared to teach courses that required being current with theory and real-world developments.

My experience is typical. Most people cannot further their careers and add to their occupational knowledge while in parliament. Their market value necessarily decreases. In addition, the political experience can have a separate, negative influence. Again, I can speak from experience. I was testing the waters on the possibility that after my retirement from politics I might be able to serve as a director on the boards of charities, public organizations and corporations, thinking that my professional and political experience might make me useful in such jobs. One distinguished individual who sat on the board of a number of Canada's largest corporations informed me that my political background would be an obstacle to such appointments, and not an advantage, as I had supposed.

For some former ministers of the crown, their political background appears not to be a problem, the reason being that they have demonstrated executive abilities and tend to have useful connections in ministries and with major party brass. In addition, they might have provided some useful service to their employers while they were in charge on ministries.

However, MPs from government back-benches, from the opposition and even former ministers holding minor portfolios typically find their political experience a barrier to private sector jobs. Most MPs lose elections or quit politics before they are eligible for retirement at the traditional age of 65. They therefore often end up in financial difficulties. They need pensions at an age deemed unreasonably young by people who do not know how badly serving in parliament affect earnings opportunities and capacities.

I think it was unwise to force members of the Reform caucus to give up their pension rights. Many will be at a serious financial disadvantage once they leave office. Initially, the average MP who had served for five years was eligible for pension benefits worth $6 for every $1 contributed. The Liberals gave in to pressures from Reform and the public and lowered these benefits to $3 for every $1.

Stephen Harper, who led the Reform initiatives on this issue insisted that the ratio be lowered to 2:1. The Liberals put the squeeze on Reformers by insisting that we had to accept the new conditions or irrevocably leave the pension system. All Reformers, except John Cummins, did so. Cummins, who was in his 50s, had lost his teacher's pension and had a young daughter. He simply could not afford to opt out. Manning and the Reform leadership did not take kindly to Cummins' action and I am certain that he has no future in caucus or the party.

For me, having lost the right to a pension was one of a number of important considerations in my decision not to seek re-election. It may well have played a role in the decision of some other Reformers who retired.

There are two ironic aspects to the Reform policy on pensions. Surveys and informal contacts revealed that the general public was not aware of the sacrifices Reformers had made by opting out of the pension plan.

Such information must be especially hard on Deborah Grey from Alberta. She had been the only MP in the previous Parliament. As a result, in 1995 she would have been eligible for a pension worth a great deal of money, yet she gave up all rights to it. Pensions generally and her great sacrifice were not an issue in the 1997 election and I doubt that they had any influence on the outcome. It is also ironic that in 1998 Reformers as individuals had sober second thoughts about the merit of their past policy stance. They voted, without a record of names, to accept legislation introduced by the Liberal government which raised their basic salaries and created a face-saving method for opting back into the otherwise unchanged pension system.

Subsidized food services

Perks in the form of subsidized personal services in Parliament were a red herring, even though they had attracted some public ire before the 1993 election because they were heavily subsidized. The prices for food in the Parliamentary restaurant and cafeterias were no lower than those at Simon Fraser University. I documented this fact with some comparative pricing. However, unlike the SFU food services, those in Parliament required large subsidies ultimately paid by taxpayers. The cause of this problem is

Chapter 14

quite obvious to economists. Whenever and wherever a business has a monopoly and there is the possibility that deficits can be recovered by hidden subsidies from taxpayers, unions are strong and militant, and face managers who are not overly concerned with efficiency. The access to the deep pocket of taxpayers' funds enables unions to negotiate high wages and the use of more workers than would be needed if they worked in a private firm in a competitive industry.

When Paul Martin's fiscal retrenchments were put in place after 1994, these subsidies for food services in Parliament were promptly eliminated. Prices rose only slightly because substantial increases would have resulted in massive losses of business to competing private restaurants nearby in downtown Ottawa. The main burden of adjustment fell on the employees, as they should have. Initially I obeyed the Reform caucus rule that we must not use the 'fancy' Parliamentary restaurant. Eventually, however, an atmosphere of tolerance developed among Reformers on this issue and I ate lunch there occasionally. By that time the media had ended its vigilance over Reformers who strayed from the approved path and my transgressions were never reported.

Perhaps I was just lucky, because in June 1998, Tim Naumetz, a reporter specializing in yellow journalism for *The Vancouver Sun*, wrote an article on the subject. He had seen Deborah Grey and Monte Solberg in the Parliamentary restaurant, and went on at great length about the cost of meals listed with flourishing adjectives in the menu, making them appear to be gourmet dishes. They may be served on fancy china adorned with the crest of Canada, but in my judgment, at least, they are far from 'gourmet.'

International travel

Another perk which received much publicity during the 1993 election campaign involved international travel. Reformers committed themselves strongly to not partake in such so-called 'junkets.' However, soon after arriving in Ottawa it became obvious to us all that not all such travel was equivalent to a holiday in a tropical resort in the middle of the winter at taxpayers' expense. Therefore we quickly developed a system under which MPs who wanted to travel abroad needed caucus approval. They had to demonstrate that the trip was not a junket and that it was important to their work.

One of those approved was my trip to Madrid as part of the official Canadian delegation to the meetings of the IMF and World Bank. Another such trip was taken by Charlie Penson, the critic for the Department of International Trade, who attended a meeting of ASEAN trade ministers in Singapore. Travel like mine and Penson's was opposed by some members of caucus on principle, but the majority realized that they were necessary if Reform wanted to develop the expertise needed to run the government at some point in the future.

Committee Work and Relationships with other Parties

Opportunities for travel existed also through involvement with parliamentary friendship associations. Such associations bring together legislators from Canada and different countries for informal meetings to exchange ideas and talk about important policy issues facing their countries. I joined the German and U.S. associations, and would have liked very much to accompany the Canadian delegation on a visit to Germany, where my background might have been useful and I would have derived much personal satisfaction from returning to my land of birth in my capacity as a legislator from another country. However, I did not even approach caucus to gain approval for this trip. It almost certainly would have been turned down.

Meetings with U.S. members of Congress take place once a year, alternating between locations in Canada and the United States. For that reason, they were not considered to be an international travel junket and caucus acquiesced to my participation. One meeting took place in early June at a resort north of Toronto. The second was hosted by the Americans, with Senator Murzankowski from Alaska in charge of logistical details. He obtained the services of an Alaskan Highways ferry, which had just been refitted and needed a shakedown before returning to public service.

The Canadian delegation arrived by scheduled airlines in Prince Rupert, while the U.S. senators and members of the House of Representatives arrived in special planes. The delegations included the spouses of legislators. The Americans brought a physician, a contingent of Marines for security and some personal staff; altogether we were a party of about 150.

The Canadian delegation consisted of six Senators, half of whom were Liberals and Conservatives, and 10 MPs. I was the only Reformer; the rest were Liberals (a second Reformer, Mike Scott, from British Columbia, missed the trip for personal reasons coming up at the last moment).

The ferry took us on the Inside Passage to Skagway, with a stop in Juneau, where we attended a reception by the Governor of Alaska. In Skagway we boarded a special train to the Yukon border and continued on by bus to Whitehorse. That same day the Americans were taken home by their special planes for important legislative work. Canadians used public carriers leaving the next day to return to Ottawa or their home ridings.

On occasions like this the food and drinks are good. The Alaska trip, which lasted three days, was pleasant. What did we accomplish? The official schedule had us meeting for three hours every morning and afternoon. The agenda for discussion involved policies of mutual concern: fisheries, tariffs, culture, Cuban relations, agriculture and a number of others. The Canadian delegation had been given a briefing book on these issues prepared by the Department for External Affairs, which I found very useful. The discussions were frank and often animated. They clearly raised personal awareness of the views and constraints which drove each country's policies.

I have been told that on some past meetings, powerful U.S. legislators

Chapter 14

intervened in ongoing disputes and speeded up settlements. In these formal meetings the Canadian positions were presented mainly by Liberals from the House and Senate, in effect representing the government. On many of the issues these Liberals took very liberal positions. Sometimes I felt compelled to intervene and say that not all Canadians adhered to these left-wing positions, offering more conservative Reform views on the issues.

When the Americans were boarding their planes in Whitehorse at the end of the trip, I shook hands with Republican Senator Connie Mack, from Florida. He said, "It was important that you presented the conservative point of view on issues. Keep up the good work." In my view, these words justified my presence at this meeting. It was good that the Americans should realize that not all Canadian politicians are strongly committed liberals.

There were also many other opportunities to interact through conversations over meals and other social functions. For over an hour I sat next to a member of the House of Representatives from the Virgin Islands. He was black, and a Democrat. He was very outspoken on how welfare was destroying his island's society. I was reminded of conditions in Newfoundland and found that his views coincided very much with my own. I noted that he sounded more like a Republican than a Democrat. In response he said that someone running under the Republican banner in his electoral district had no chance of winning, but that his tough views on welfare were shared by a majority of his constituents.

I also had a number of lengthy conversations with Sam Gibbons, who for a long time had been the Chair of the powerful House Ways and Means Committee of Congress. He had been in Congress for more than 30 years and until the Republicans gained a majority in the House held some of the most influential positions in the legislature. We talked about the need for tax reform, which was on the agenda of both the U.S. and Canada as a result of vocal demands for a flat tax. Gibbons had heard many experts' testimony on this subject for nearly a generation, and made many points that were new to me, which helped me improve Reform's position on the flat tax. Gibbons, it seems, was a strong supporter of a general national value-added or sales tax for the U.S., the implementation of which would make it possible to lower personal and corporate income tax rates, which in turn would be beneficial for creating incentives for work and investment.

At one formal session we were treated to a very heated debate between the Democrat Harry Johnson, a long term member of the House from Florida, and Senator Connie Mack and some other Republicans. The subject was the Helms-Burton Act, which was designed to penalize Canadian and other businesses which had dealings in Cuba. Johnson, like the Liberals in our group, opposed the law. He thought trade with Cuba was more likely to bring down the Communist regime than the existing blockade.

It was informative for me to hear the polished arguments of the antagonists in this discussion.

Senator Chuck Grassley of Iowa is a fiscal conservative Republican. We had many useful discussions about the conservative agenda in both countries. On the train from Skagway he was reading the *Wall Street Journal,* which on one of the front page articles was discussing his role in Congress. It made special reference to his demands for strict accounting for a program providing financial aid to special groups of university students. According to the article, the program was obviously very wasteful and did not achieve its objectives. However, the author had interviewed some people who thought the program was very good. One of these was quoted as saying that Grassley was a "skinflint." He showed me the article and asked whether his demands for accountability of this program made him a skinflint. I knew how he felt, having been called 'uncaring' many times for raising concerns about the negative effects of Canada's policies on natives, unemployment and welfare. I replied that I did not think he deserved such a label.

A final interesting aspect of the trip was getting to know three outstanding Canadian senators. John Buchanan, Gerry Grafstein and Bud Olson were old warhorses with impressive political records. Their stories often shed light on important events in recent Canadian history. Buchanan, who had been the Premier of Nova Scotia from 1978 to 1990, is a story teller of great distinction. Grafstein is a dyed-in-the-wool Trudeau style Liberal with whose views I often disagreed but respected for the depth of the commitment they revealed. Bud Olson, now Lieutenant Governor for Alberta, was an old fox whose contributions revealed his long experience in politics.

Some of the most interesting conversations among Canadians involved the problem of Quebec separation. While I did not hear anything new, I was impressed by the passion these political leaders had on the subject and how far apart they were on what they saw as solutions to the problem.

An assessment

I cannot rule out the possibility that there might be more useful ways for governments to spend the money that goes to meetings of friendships societies of legislators from different countries, but in my limited experience such meetings serve a useful purpose while providing an enjoyable break from the tedious routines of work as an MP.

The very existence of the personal benefits should not be seen as evidence that little of substance is accomplished at the same time. MPs in opposition are essentially getting ready for becoming members of government, some for roles as ministers. Such preparation requires getting familiar with many aspects of government. Learning from the experiences of legislators from other countries on important policy issues is important in this

Chapter 14

process, as is raising one's understanding of the problems affecting intergovernmental relations.

Manning and Reform have gradually changed their minds on the merit of what in 1993 they would have called 'perks.' Perhaps the most outstanding evidence of this process is Stornoway, the official residence of the Leader of the Opposition in the House of Commons. For a long time, Manning had argued that such an official residence was not needed and represented an unwarranted perk. A few years ago, when officials informed him that the building had no other use and could not be sold for technical reasons, he replied that it should be turned into a bingo hall for use by the public, but in 1997, after becoming Opposition Leader, he moved into Stornoway. I supported him in this decision in a private conversation, suggesting it was time for Reform to acknowledge that some of the past attacks on this and other alleged perks were not warranted. He agreed with me. As the Leader of the Opposition and in the process of getting ready to become the Prime Minister, Manning has to meet with visiting heads of state and perform many other official functions. It would not be appropriate to do this work in the hotel-room he used to occupy or in rented hotel facilities.

I am pleased that Manning and Reform have taken a more relaxed attitude towards so-called perks. I can understand that they were swept up in the public outcry over them in the early 1990s. Siding with those calling for changes fitted their image as Reformers, challenging the old ways of doing things.

In some instances such as pensions and food service subsidies, Reform's opposition has yielded positive results, of which they can be proud. On the issue of salaries and international travel they have modified their once rigid opposition.

Reform's successes on pensions and some other perks were achieved at some cost. Reformers in caucus are less prepared to run the government when they are elected. On the other hand, their relaxed stance on some issues, Manning's move into Stornoway, for example, has antagonized some core supporters who believe that Manning and caucus have been captured by Ottawa, and that they are no better than the other parties. It remains to be seen whether there is a price to pay at the ballot box.

CHAPTER 15

An Assessment and Look Forward

AS I LOOK back on my four years in Parliament, my memories inevitably come back to the fiscal problems which faced Canada in 1993. The budget deficit was very large and growing. The size of the debt had reached dangerous levels. The cost of servicing the debt had sky-rocketed and was increasingly financed by further additions to the debt. The resultant vicious cycle was about to create a fiscal crisis with severe consequences for the well-being of all Canadians.

The growing crisis in 1992

Underlying the fiscal problems was an overexpansion of government caused mainly by increases in social spending at rates greater than economic growth. Social spending had encouraged unemployment and contributed significantly to a wasteful unemployment rate of over 12 percent. There was another pressing problem: Quebec's demand for sovereignty. In addition, the West had grown in population and power to the point where it was ready to challenge the hegemony of Ontario and Quebec. The Reform Party, which had grown out of Western dissatisfaction, threatened to create political turmoil in the federal parliament.

Many Canadians knew about these troubles. They were worried about their well-being and that of the country if the problems were not addressed. I had written and lectured about the issues and possible solutions. The publications of think tanks like the Fraser Institute and the CD Howe Institute had produced analytically and empirically solid evidence on the nature and magnitude of the problems.

However, to my dismay, during the campaigns leading up to the 1993 elections, the traditional political parties made light of these issues. The deficit and debt were trivialized as temporary nuisances; Canada was and always would be the best country in the world. Only a little fine-tuning and the usual economic recovery from a recession were needed to solve all economic problems. The recent strength of the Quebec separation movement was seen as part of a long-term cycle of Quebeckers' rising and falling interest in nationalist goals. It was expected that granting a few more fiscal benefits and special rights of symbolic importance to Quebec would deal with separatist threats, as they had always in the past.

The promise of the Reform Party

Only the Reform Party under the leadership of Preston Manning had a

Chapter 15

platform based on the realistic assessment of the problems facing the country. This platform recognized that the fiscal imbalances required drastic cuts in spending. It argued for an overhaul of the social insurance programs, and advocated changes in the political system which would give greater power to Quebec and other regions of the country. It suggested the devolution of many federal powers to the provinces to satisfy their demands, thus reducing the appeal of separatists in Quebec and quelling unrest in the West. In my view, Reform had the answer to Canada's most pressing problems of the early 1990s. I was glad to be asked to join that team and help carry out its agenda.

The people of the Canadian West and my constituents shared my own and Reform's views. They elected me and 51 other Reformers. We went to Parliament to remind Jean Chretien and the Liberal government that the country needed some tough medicine to get things right. And the government got the message. The unprecedented election results were a wake-up call; the ideas of Reform could no longer be disregarded. My colleagues and I were there to keep them in front of the government and the people of Canada.

In large part, on most crucial issues, the Liberal government adopted the Reform Party's agenda because it was the only one which could solve the country's economic crisis. Fiscal policy in particular changed dramatically, in ways that had not been included in the Liberal election platform. A careful analysis if the spending reductions undertaken by the Liberals in four to five years shows them to be nearly identical to those proposed in Reform's 1993 'Zero-in-Three' election budget.

Paul Martin, the Minister of Finance, admitted that in his new position he had gained a full understanding of the seriousness of the country's fiscal condition for the first time, now realizing that the deficit would not disappear through general economic growth and some spending freezes.

Serious cuts were made in spending. Lloyd Axworthy oversaw a major overhaul of the unemployment insurance system. The future growth of the public pension system was curtailed through the introduction of the so-called Seniors Benefits, which better targeted spending on the needy and away from those in good financial condition.

This program has now been cancelled, officially because the fiscal condition has now improved so much that it is no longer needed. I suspect, however, that lobbying by the elderly has been fierce and that Martin has begun to fully realize the distortion of incentives caused by the withdrawal of benefits as family income has increased.

A number of ministers, particularly Minister of Transport Doug Young, privatized large parts of their operations and slashed subsidies to the private sector. Several ministries devolved some responsibilities to the provinces. Reduced transfers of funds to the provinces loosened the federal government's ability to dictate how provincial governments carried out some programs.

An Assessment and Look Forward
Giving Reform credit

It is difficult to know exactly how great Reform's influence was on these beneficial developments. Perhaps the facts confronting the Liberals when they took office were so clear that the adoption of the corrective policies was inevitable, Reform in opposition or not. But there is also the possibility that the Liberals would again have tried to muddle through, just like the PCs had before them. Certainly, if the NDP, instead of Reform, had made large gains in the 1993 election and had been the third largest and quasi-official opposition party in parliament, the policy alternatives presented for public debate would have been much different.

The NDP would have demanded more spending to solve the unemployment and debt problem, while Reform insisted on spending restraint. They would have demanded higher taxes on 'the rich' and corporations, while Reform insisted on unchanged tax policies; they would have demanded that Martin order the Bank of Canada to print money and cause inflation, while Reform insisted on the independence of the Bank and price stability.

Perhaps most important, Reform played the politically important role of giving the Liberals policy norms relative to which the fiscal restraint they adopted appeared moderate to the public and to the red Liberals in cabinet and caucus. Paul Martin once told me privately how much he needed Reform for these purposes and asked me to keep up my public demands for greater fiscal restraint.

My colleagues and I did not need this admonition. We certainly did not want to do Martin a favour; that is not how politics works. We simply continued to restate the positions we had taken during the election, making our policy proposals more precise through the publication of alternative budgets, which was an unprecedented and politically risky manoeuvre.

In the end, motives do not matter. What counts is that Martin and his cabinet colleagues *did* adopt policies that resembled very much those advocated by Reform. They *did not* go far enough at a sufficiently rapid pace, but they were on the right track, and eventually, they did the job. In 1998, helped by a strong U.S. economy, lower world interest rates and a general cyclical economic recovery, five years after a close call, the country's fiscal crisis had ended, the government is smaller, and separatism is at bay. The most important 'problem' facing the government has become what to do with the fiscal surplus which is likely to develop during the next few years if spending and taxation levels remain unchanged.

The Reform Party can be proud to have played an important role in getting in place the policies which so dramatically changed Canada's fiscal condition. I am proud to have been a member of this Reform Party and to have served as its Finance Critic.

Chapter 15

The unfinished agenda

At the time of writing (1998), Canada still needs to change a wide range of economic policies to assure Canadians a brighter future. The size of government in the economy has to be reduced through major tax cuts. Such policies would increase the disposable income of the public. Incentives to work, invest and take risks would be strengthened, economic growth raised. Less spending on social programs would reduce the dependence it creates for its recipients. There would be an increase in personal freedom, which many value for its own sake.

Projections made by economists in 1998 suggest that the government will enjoy growing, large fiscal surpluses in coming years. Some estimates put the expected surplus in 2002 at $40 billion. These projections are based on the assumption that the government will keep spending constant and does not lower taxes. In addition, the projections assume that economic growth will continue at its normal pace without interruption by major cyclical downturns and that interest rates remain at their present low levels. These projections offer unique opportunities to lower the size of government and finish the job of taking Canada into the new millennium in good shape.

In October 1997 the Fraser Institute held a conference in Ottawa designed to bring economists and politicians together to set out the ways in which the expected fiscal surplus can be used. I presented two papers and edited the conference proceedings for publication by the Institute. Several important conclusions emerged from the deliberations.

First, it is important that the government proceed cautiously with any changes in spending and taxation. There is a substantial risk that a recession or higher interest rates will invalidate the rosy forecasts. Unwarranted spending increases and tax-reductions under these conditions would again result in deficits and further additions to the debt.

Second, the impact of possible increases in interest rates on the fiscal balance is more serious the larger the outstanding debt becomes. A one percent increase in the interest rate will ultimately result in $7 billion additional annual spending to service a debt of $700 billion. If the debt is only $400 billion, the additional spending required would be only $4 billion. For this reason, it is highly desirable that some of the fiscal surplus be used to reduce the debt. It would seem reasonable to devote something like 30 percent of expected surpluses to debt reduction, though there are no solid economic models suggesting any particular figure.

Third, debt reduction is also desirable on the grounds that it lowers the burden of serving it now resting heavily on future generations.

Fourth, the government should hold constant spending on existing programs level, except in the case of programs where increases are mandated by legislation. Examples of such programs are pensions and the Indian Act, which require increased spending simply to keep up with the larger number of people eligible to receive benefits. By holding constant spending level on other programs and by not initiating new ones, there would be a continuous shrinking of the size of government in the economy, measured as a fraction of national income. This process is due to the fact that regular increases in population, real per capita income and the price level tend to increase national income at the annual rate of about four percent, or 20 percent in five years.

The following illustrative calculation shows how this growth diminishes the relative size of government if spending is frozen. Consider that government spending initially is equal to $300 billion, or 50 percent of the national income at $600 billion. Five years later, under the preceding assumptions about economic growth national income would be $720 billion. With spending at $300 billion, it is equal to only 42 percent of national income.

At the conference, researchers presented evidence from Canada and other countries that spending by all levels of government at rates greater than about 30 percent of national income has a serious negative impact on economic growth because of the deleterious effects it has on incentives to work, invest and take risk. Papers noted that higher spending did not produce better outcomes in terms of indicators of social wellbeing.

In a paper on Canada's experience, which I co-authored with Johnny Chao (an SFU student), it was estimated that Canada's optimum level of government spending is 34 percent and that the present level of 47 percent is 13 percentage points too high. To reach the optimum level of government, therefore, total spending in Canada as a fraction of national income has to fall by more than a quarter (i.e. from 47 to 34 percent of national income). The federal government presently spends about 17 percent of national income. To reach its optimum level it would have to fall to 12 percent of national income. If the economy were to grow at four percent annually, the optimum level of spending for both the federal and all levels of government would be reached in about six years.

Fifth, if spending is held constant, not only would spending as a percent of national income decrease rapidly, there would be another important benefit. The projected fiscal surpluses will be available for debt and tax reductions. Strong arguments were presented at the Ottawa conference for the use of well over half of the surpluses, perhaps 70 percent, for tax cuts.

The future of the Canadian economy depends greatly on the types of tax cuts undertaken. In particular, it was argued that there should be relatively larger than average cuts in payroll taxes like those going to the Unemployment Insurance Fund. These cuts in payroll taxes would lower the cost of labour for employers and thus encourage job-creation.

Another suggestion was that basic exemptions in the personal income tax be raised to help Canadians with lower incomes. High marginal tax rates should also be reduced in order to slow the 'brain drain' of the best and brightest to the United States, where tax rates are much lower. I would add that the capital gains tax, which in Canada is at twice the level it is in the U.S., must also be lowered in order to reduce the loss of venture capital and capitalists.

The Parties and the fiscal surplus

Media reports suggest that the Liberal party has found it difficult to agree on a plan for the use of the fiscal surplus. On the one side are many members of the Liberal caucus, who want to increase spending and initiate new programs. Others want to reduce taxes and pay down some of the debt. Paul Martin, the Minister of Finance, urges caution in making plans for the use of a surplus which may or may not develop. While I think it proper for Martin to be cautious about making plans for disposing of the surplus, I regret his unwillingness to lend his considerable prestige and sales talents to the advocacy of lower taxes and debt reduction. Mainly because of Martin's fence-sitting, I find it difficult to predict what the Liberal strategy will be. My best guess is that it will be in the long standing tradition of the party. There will be much compromising with a strong bias in favour of keeping, or even expanding, the role of government in society.

The NDP is on record as favouring increases in spending on a wide variety of social programs, the explicit redistribution of income and industrial strategies. The NDP appears determined to defend its commitment to bigger government in spite of world-wide evidence that such policies cause economic stagnation, unemployment and ultimately curtailment of the very social programs central to its platform. I am quite sure that the ideological position of the NDP is shared by an ever-smaller fraction of Canadian voters.

In the 1997 election, the PCs presented a platform in which they proposed to do the impossible: raise spending and cut taxes — in amounts which, in my view, are likely to create new deficits. I cannot find credible the predictions that the proposed policies would increase so much economic activity that the budget would remain balanced. The public will remain sceptical about the consistency of recommending tax cuts with the Red Tory rhetoric of wanting a 'compassionate' government, one that plays a much bigger role in the lives of Canadians than that of the U.S.

Only the Reform Party has a platform which basically reflects the ideas of economists presented at the Ottawa Conference. The party proposes to freeze spending on all programs except those which require higher outlays to service greater numbers of people. It rejects ideas for new spending initiatives, suggesting a lowering of taxation rates and structural changes to the system to increase efficiency and incentives, and using a substantial share of the surpluses to pay down the debt.

Because Reform has embraced this fiscal program, I believe that it continues to play an important role in the determination of Canada's economic and fiscal policies in the future. As long as Reform remains the official Opposition, its positions will influence the government's policies, much as they did following the fiscal crisis of 1993. Should the party form the government, its policies will create a more prosperous Canada for all the reasons given above.

Personal influence on Reform policies

I do not know how much influence I had on the formulation of Reform's fiscal policy platforms. As noted above, the 1997 election platform had envisioned large additional spending cuts. I argued against this policy because I believed that needed reductions in the size of government in the economy could be achieved at lower economic and political cost through gradualism, rather than drastic surgery. While I lost that battle, I remain convinced that the deep cuts promised did not help — and probably hurt quite badly — public support for Reform in Ontario in the 1997 election.

After that election, I was invited by Manning to comment on the development of a new platform. My recommendations were basically those which later came out of the Ottawa conference proceedings described above. After I had submitted my paper to Manning I had no further communications with him; there was not even an acknowledgement that the paper had been received. Nor was I consulted by Monte Solberg, who has been the Reform Finance Critic since my announcement not to seek re-election. All I know is that Reform's fiscal platform largely reflects my recommendations and those of the Ottawa conference. It is the best of all those presented by Canada's other parties. For this reason I hope, for the sake of the welfare of all Canadians, that Reform will win the next election or, at the very least, remain a vital force in Canadian politics.

Uniting the Right

During the 1993 federal election in Ontario, the Reform Party received the second-highest total of votes in about 70 of the province's 99 electoral districts. It has been estimated that if at that election the votes cast for the PCs had instead gone to Reform, the latter party would have won nearly half of Ontario's seats in parliament. Under these conditions, Reform would have beaten the Bloc Quebec and have been the official opposition in the 1993 Parliament in which I sat a member.

Basically, in the 1997 election, the 1993 election results were repeated. In Ontario, the Liberals won all 103 seats (the total number of seats in the Province had climbed to 103 because of population increases). If all votes cast for the PCs in Ontario had gone to Reform, it would have won at least 30 seats in that province.

A similar scenario existed in a number of electoral districts in the Prairie

Chapter 15

provinces, where vote-splitting among the two conservative parties helped propel several NDP candidates to election victory. Without the vote-splitting, the balance of power in the House of Commons would have been much less favourable for the Liberals. They would have been forced to take Reformers and the right wing agenda much more seriously.

Unfortunately, from my point of view, there is every prospect that vote-splitting will take place again in future elections, at least for as long as both the Reform and PC parties continue to offer themselves as 'right wing' alternatives to the 'left wing' Liberals. Canada can therefore look forward to a long period of Liberal rule in Ottawa, even if a majority of voters prefer a party to the right of the Liberals. To end the splitting of votes on the right, two different, basic approaches to uniting the right have been suggested. The first involves merging of the two parties through deliberate efforts of party leaders. The second is based on efforts to persuade grass-roots members to abandon their loyalties to one of the two parties on the ground that it has no chance of winning enough seats to form the next government. Both approaches are beset with serious difficulties. Let me deal with the second one first.

In effect, the 1997 election was fought on this basis. The Reform and PC campaigns were designed to discredit each other and to persuade the electorate that they offered the only true alternative to the Liberals. Reformers emphasized the poor record of the Mulroney government which was one of fiscal irresponsibility and disregard for popular opinion in the enactment of the GST legislation. Reform also made much of its populist program and bottom-up policy making commitment, attacking the PCs for their elitist, top-down tradition for policy formulation.

The PCs attacked Reform as a regional Western party whose success was largely based on the irresponsible exploitation of issues which divided the country. Reform criticism of the special treatment of Quebec and the Atlantic Provinces received by the federal government were the primary targets of the PC campaigns. In addition, the PCs insisted that Reform had a platform that would lead to the destruction of Canada's welfare system. Reformers were called 'extremists' while PCs emphasized their commitment to the strengthening of the unemployment, health and pension systems.

The second approach to uniting the right involves the top-down merger of the two parties. I do not expect this strategy to work. Officials at the constituency levels of both parties are very committed to the causes given so much prominence in the 1997 election. Almost none of them have been amenable to suggestions that they merge their organizations officially and create a new party with appeal to the core supporters of both Reform and PCs. There is simply too much animosity between the core supporters of the two parties. This animosity is likely to be strengthened even more through fights among MPs in the House of Commons and in future election campaigns.

An Assessment and Look Forward
Reform's fundamental problem in Ontario

The most important reason why the two approaches to uniting the right have not worked is a problem decisively rooted in history. Ever since Canada was founded, the people of Ontario and Quebec considered themselves to *be* Canada, in every sense. Theirs were the provinces of economic power and the national cultural identity. The rest of Canada was unimportant, except as a source of cheap raw materials and a captive market for manufacturing exports. These lesser provinces did not have the population and therefore representation in federal parliament to threaten the hegemony of the centre. For Ontario, Ottawa was most like a second provincial capital. In a complex interplay between Ontario and Quebec interests, the policy platform of two traditional parties, the Liberals and PCs, accommodated these geo-political ambitions and realities.

One method for accommodating Quebec has been to have prime ministers from that province. Under these arrangements, the centre thrived and outlying regions were without the power to affect the treatment they were given. Small bones were thrown to them to keep them quiet. These took the form of fiscal transfers through regional development agencies.

However, since the 1980s, the world has changed. The West — Alberta and BC in particular — has 'grown up.' Their population, economic power and cultural identity have developed to the point where they are ready to challenge the hegemony of Ontario and Quebec. Small bones are no longer enough. Reform's success in the West is both the result and symbol of these developments.

The big problem for Reform and, in a sense, for all of Canada, is that the people of Ontario have not realized the seriousness of the ambitions of the West or Quebec. Ontario remains committed to strong central government, which is dominated by their MPs and run for their benefit. They see no reason why the old formulas for accommodation with Quebec cannot continue to work. They do not want Ottawa weakened and their cozy arrangement disturbed by forces from the West. The Liberals know this and their platform promises to let Ontario continue this hegemony. Reform threatens it. Ontario voters know exactly where their interests lie. Why should they vote for a party which has had as one of its main slogans 'The West wants in'?

Eventually, Ontario voters will have to come to terms with reality and accept that economic and population growth in the West has significantly changed Canada's geo-political power structure. They will have to consider the demands of the West as well as Quebec for a less centralized federal government as legitimate. They will have to grant more autonomy to the West and Quebec, as demanded by Reform and the Bloc.

I have described above how this can be achieved, by letting the provinces design and administer their own social programs, and leaving Ottawa with the most important economic responsibilities, of assuring free trade, migration and capital flows within Canada. Once the people of Ontario have accepted this reality and consider Ottawa not their capital run primarily for their benefit, they will again vote for parties on the basis of the traditional right and left positions expressed in their platforms.

When they have reached this point, the people of Ontario may well choose Reform as the party most likely to bring a conservative government into power, the reason being simple. Reform has near-unassailable strength in the West, precisely because of its commitment to fight for Western rights. Reform thus offers both a conservative platform and a strong base which, with the help of Ontario voters, can bring a right-wing government to Ottawa.

By contrast, the PCs suffer from two handicaps. Firstly, the Red Tories have for a long time dominated policy formulation and, in most important aspects, the PC economic platform is liberal or left. The other handicap is due to history. The last three PC governments under Clark, Mulroney and Campbell primarily served the interests of Ontario and Quebec. The PCs knew that their election success was based on strong showings in these two provinces. They knew how to get it. But they also destroyed, for a long time, their chance of getting support in the West. They will find it very difficult to shed the image of being the party of Ontario.

Implications for Reform

The implication of my analysis for Reform are simple. It must cease to focus on its Western roots. It must become a genuinely conservative party for the country as a whole, one where the West is an equal partner to Ontario, Quebec and all other regions in a more balanced federation. It must offer a clear alternative to the *liberal* Liberals. The ideas and platform for such an approach are already in existence. They wait to be discovered and accepted by the people of Ontario — and Quebec. I am sure that this process will take place soon for reasons to be discussed below.

However, there is another serious problem associated with the need of Reform to become a genuinely conservative party. Manning continues to emphasize its commitment to populism at every opportunity. In Chapter 14 I discussed what I consider to be the problems associated with populism. There is nothing wrong with a mild form of populism which stresses the role of grass-roots input into policy formulation. Of much more doubtful merit is the strong version of populism based on the notion that 'the people are always right.' I believe that many Canadians like the weaker version of populism but that are distrustful of a party which promises to base policies on the outcome of the most recent public opinion polls.

The people of Canada want leadership with a vision. I therefore think the vision they want is of a conservative, right-wing one, to lead them out of the malaise in which the country found itself in the 1990s. This malaise, symbolized by the falling value of the dollar, high unemployment and slow economic growth, was caused by the left wing policies of the preceding 25 years. Moving the country out of this malaise means ending subsidies to regions and industries, diminishing the power of special interest groups, making social programs less generous, lowering taxes and undertaking many other changes that can easily affect adversely more than half of the population in one way or another.

For these reasons there was much opposition to the right wing policies introduced by Ronald Reagan in the U.S., Margaret Thatcher in Britain and Roger Douglas in New Zealand. It took strong leaders with a firm inner compass to see through the programs which were sure to turn against them all those whose interests were damaged. At the same time these programs would provide benefits only after the passage of some time and in a diffuse manner unlikely to make special interest groups rally to the support of the politicians responsible. In my view, no genuinely populist leader would have been able to do what Reagan, Thatcher and Douglas did for their countries.

Some risks would accompany Reform's increased emphasis on right wing policies with a national focus and the abandonment of strong populist principles. The party might lose the support of some Western regionalists, though it is not clear what party this group could vote for as an alternative. The party would also lose support from those who believe the populist rhetoric for its own sake, but this effect can easily be exaggerated. Populism once was the cornerstone of the NDP platform, along with its emphasis on socialist-inspired economic policies. Since the 1993 election these populists have voted Reform, the reason being that the NDP abandoned its commitment to populism. I see no reversal in this NDP stance. So, again the question is where would the strong supporters of populism cast their votes? Would they cast them for the NDP and the lost cause of socialism and its derivatives?

Ted White pointed out to me that all of the people in Canada responding to the populist platform of Reform, in his view, are strongly conservative. He points to the resolutions passed by successive Assemblies. He also notes that in California and Switzerland, the frequent use of public referenda has moved public policy strongly to the right.

If this is the case, the abandonment or the downplay of Reform's populist agenda would not result in a loss of the support of these people. It suggests that the support of Reform from the very beginning was due to the leftward drift of the PC policy platforms, that Reform supporters were and are in search of a true conservative party.

It is also possible to offer populists the assurance that Reform remains committed to a modified form of populism. The party's grass-roots assemblies can continue to be held, used to shape the broad outline of Reform policies and constrain the formulation of policies by party elites. The use of binding referenda on the most contentious issues like the death penalty can be retained.

Chapter 15
The United Alternative

In June 1998, Reform's Bi-Annual Assembly launched a new campaign to capture Ontario voters under the title 'The United Alternative.' The document outlining the policies that were expected to unite right-wing voters under the Reform banner is encouraging to those who believe in the merit of these conservative policies: fiscal responsibility, smaller government, greater power to the provinces, tough on crime and support for traditional family values. But it also emphasizes its commitment to democratic reforms, including the creation of a Triple-E Senate and, importantly, to a deep and broad populism. In my view, the latter part of the Reform platform for the United Alternative will doom it. The creation of a Triple-E Senate, as discussed above, raises the intractable problem created by the historic fact that Canada has 10 provinces, four of which are very small in every relevant sense. It makes no sense to have a legislative chamber designed to balance regional interests in which Prince Edward Island, with a population of 137,000, and Ontario, with 11.3 million, have equal voting power. The people of Ontario (and Quebec) will never agree to the creation of such a chamber for selfish reasons. Strong arguments can be made that such a relatively small federation of provinces with such very unequal provinces is unlikely to function efficiently.

Proposals to modify voting power in the Senate by basing representation partly on population, if carried far enough, would replicate the distribution of power in the House of Commons. The main problem is that all fundamental reforms of the Senate will require changes to the constitution. Such constitutional change is very difficult and wastes scarce political energies which could be used much more effectively on the negotiation for a more decentralized federation. The irony and a powerful argument against Senate reform is the fact that the proposed decentralization of power would meet the demands of the West and Quebec and therefore remove the need for Senate reform.

Chances of success for the Reform Party

Of course, I do not know whether and when the people of Ontario will accept the new geographical distribution of power within Canada, whether they will accept Reform as the new bearer of the conservative banner or whether, indeed, the Reform party leadership will share my vision and change into a genuinely conservative party.

It seems reasonably clear to me that if the current system is continued, the Liberals will keep on forming the government and leave its central power unchanged. Under these conditions the West and Quebec will continue to send regional party representatives to fight for their rights in Ottawa. The traditional method of keeping regional interests at bay through small targeted benefits like the regional development programs will continue to sap the country's vitality. At some point, Quebec may play the independence card in earnest.

However, I see some reasons for hope. Gordon Gibson, a former Trudeau adviser, leader of the provincial Liberal Party and columnist with the *Globe and Mail*, is now a Senior Fellow at the Fraser Institute. He has published a number of studies on the Quebec problem and how the separation threat can be diminished. He considers it essential that the federal government grant more policy autonomy to provinces. My analysis of the role of Ontario in the political future of Canada draws heavily on Gibson's views. He consults regularly with provincial premiers and governments, as a result of which he believes that the Ontario government and the people of that province are beginning to understand their crucial role in the country, how their unwillingness to share more equitably the power they have held for so long in Ottawa can easily result in the break-up of Canada. He has urged the Ontario provincial government to take the leadership in explaining the new Canadian reality to the public and to take leadership in forming a front of provinces united in their demand for greater decentralization.

There is some indication that this might happen. In August 1998 the annual Premiers' conference broke new grounds. In the past, their demands for the devolution of power were presented by Premiers deeply divided on the precise shape of such a policy. Some provincial governments were always dissatisfied with whatever proposal was agreed upon by the rest. As a result, the federal government found it easy to divide and conquer the provinces; proposals for power sharing never went anywhere. At the August 1998 meeting, the Premiers, for the first time in recent memory, presented a united front. Ontario was crucial in this role; historically it had opposed the devolution of power because it meant loss of its own influence for the reasons discussed above.

Gibson interprets Ontario's willingness to go along with the other provinces as evidence that its government recognizes the new reality. The threat to political stability and economic prosperity will not go away unless and until Ontario supports policies which meet the demands of Quebec and the West for greater autonomy. I hope the Premiers' conference of 1998 was the beginning of a trend, and that the federal government will agree to accept its recommendations. If Gibson's interpretation of recent political events is correct, Reform has a great opportunity to turn itself into a champion of the causes espoused by the premiers. They are a natural part of Reform's basic platform. Reform can ride the wave into office in Ottawa, if the main issue is not clouded by its commitment to populism, likely to turn off the voters in Ontario.

Preston Manning's future

Manning is a man of vision who embraced a conservative fiscal platform

Chapter 15

when it was wanted by many Canadians but the establishment parties rejected it. He also had the vision and skill to articulate the demands of the West for a more equal federation. I ran for office because I supported these causes, as well as some other traditional conservative policies adopted by Reform like smaller overall government and a greater role for the family.

I admire Manning's achievements in forming a party that so quickly became the official opposition and strongly contributed to the adoption of fiscally conservative policies. He may have similarly contributed indirectly to the increasing acceptance of having a smaller role for Ottawa and greater power for the provinces.

Unfortunately, Manning's personal vision also embraces democratic reform and populism. He refers to it in all of his speeches. For a long time he used an old seat from the House of Commons as a prop, asking rhetorically, "To whom does this chair belong?" The answer he provides himself, after much build-up, is "It belongs to you, the people. Vote Reform and you will get it back from the politicians who now claim it as their own."

Democratic reforms were featured prominently in the 1997 election platform, under the title 'A Fresh Start.' The context for their use was that Reform would introduce free votes and recall legislation, while referenda would provide the people with a guarantee that Reform would deliver on its election promises. There has been little progress in getting Canadians to see merit in these reforms and to act on them where it counts, at the ballot box. As I argued above, if anything, these policies may have contributed significantly to Reform's poor performance in Ontario during the 1997 election.

In my view, the future of Reform depends on Manning's willingness to downplay, or possibly abandon, his commitment to the strong versions of democratic reform and populism. He may be willing to do so; I am not in the position to evaluate his intentions, but the platform of the United Alternative suggests he is not. If I am correct in this 1998 interpretation of events, Reform is at a cross-roads.

If, with Manning at the helm, Reform continues on its old path, it is likely to fail. It will not win seats in Ontario in the next election and will languish as a regional party. It may ultimately be abandoned by its Western supporters interested in gaining real power in Ottawa.

The other path requires Manning to step down as the leader of Reform because of an inability or unwillingness to surrender his commitment to the strong version of populism and democratic reform. In his speech outlining his vision of the United Alternative to the 1998 Assembly in London, Manning hinted at the possibility of stepping down if his campaign for the United Alternative fails. If these conditions are realized, Reform will be able to focus its platform on genuine conservative issues and distance itself from a strong commitment to democratic reform and populism. In this event, my admiration for Manning would be even greater than it has been until now.

An Assessment and Look Forward

There are at least two individuals who could take over the leadership of Reform from Manning. Stephen Harper is committed to conservatism and has many personal attributes that would permit him to lead Reform to the ultimate electoral success. Stockwell Day, Treasurer (Minister of Finance) for the Alberta Government and a member of the provincial conservative party, gave a rousing address to the 1998 Assembly of the Reform party. He is articulate, a true conservative and an experienced politician. Both Harper and Day are fluent in French, which remains an essential attribute for anyone aspiring to be prime minister of Canada, but neither have declared any interest in seeking the Reform leadership. It remains to be seen whether they will do so once the opportunity presents itself; on such an occasion almost certainly several others not yet identified will throw their hats into the ring.

Manning's management style

In a preceding chapter I described some shortcomings of Manning's style of people management and the affairs of a multi-million dollar, complex organization. My stories speak for themselves. There is his unwillingness or inability to have close personal relationships and to cater to the needs of individuals to be praised for their efforts, his tendency to leave important projects languish under benign neglect until at some point he steps in to impose on them his personal stamp, often negating the careful analytical and political work done by people he had asked to do it. There is his tendency to rely for advice on people he has known for a long time and to appoint them to positions of responsibility, in disregard of others with superior qualifications and abilities available to do the job. There is his inconsistent treatment of people who violate caucus rules or who make honest mistakes in communicating with the media through the use of politically incorrect phrases and concepts. There is his lack of leadership by example, as when he moved into Stornoway in spite of having campaigned against what at the time he called a costly political 'perk,' while a few months later punishing MPs who opt into a pension plan, which they personally need more than he needed to move into Stornoway.

There is his acceptance of personal financial support from the Party through a process designed to hide it from public scrutiny, when one of his main political commitments is to honest and open government. Many of these shortcomings were exploited by the media and some of his personal antagonists, who identified them as fundamental flaws of Manning and, by extension, all Reformers. I have a more reasonable explanation and suggest that most of these shortcoming are those of a rookie, of a caucus and party organization without a tradition and seasoned standards. I also believe that Manning's seeming inability to cultivate good personal relationships are not a fatal problem. The similarities between Manning and

Chapter 15

former President Reagan are striking in this respect. Reagan was a great President. I am not sure that the public shares my benign views on the importance of Manning's problems with personal relationship and management style.

MPs, including myself, regularly receive communications from members of the party and even the general public suggesting that these characteristics of Manning are insurmountable obstacles to his ability to lead the party to victory and into government. The public is a tough task-master. They want to see another leader. For this reason the most important question is, in my view, whether Manning is willing and able to change some of these personal shortcomings. There is no reason why he could not delegate more management responsibilities, including the appointment of qualified people to positions where their skills are used optimally, or why he could not surround himself with good advisers who might prevent the development of inconsistencies and the appearance of double standards. Such people are also very capable in minimizing the public relations impact of errors, some of which will always occur.

But, much like Reagan, he probably cannot change his psychological make-up, and will probably always remain aloof, uncomfortable in social situations and disinterested in the details of people and what makes them function. The public should not expect him to change in this respect. The quality of the policies he would enact as Prime Minister does not depend on this matter. The public should instead focus on his policy positions. As I noted above, the issue they should be most concerned about is his total commitment to Populism and his unwillingness to offer a true conservative policy platform.

Personal experiences and plans

As I look back on my four years in Parliament, memories of my personal experiences are very ambivalent. I suffered some personal hardships due to the disruption of family life and of the comfortable routines of work and sports that had made my life enjoyable before. My health suffered. I missed my involvement in teaching and the many sources of satisfaction open to successful academic researchers. My living standard was basically unchanged.

All these negative memories are balanced to some extent by positive things that happened. I learned much about politics, economic policy formation and how the Reform party manages its affairs. I made the acquaintance of many politicians and gained the friendship of a few others. I will always value my working relationships with my office staff in Ottawa and some individuals in the Reform Research Department.

I got no kick out of having power, perhaps because I never had any. Perhaps, as an academic, I had no inclination to seek or use it. I never actively sought to be the chair of committees and none were offered to me.

Work on ideas and policies was more important to me than work on persuading others of their merit. I know that I was and remain much better at the former than the latter task.

Influences on policy formulation

My greatest disappointment was the lack of influence I had on the party policy platform. When I agreed to run for office, I had hoped that my professional expertise would be sought by Manning and the party leadership. It was not to be, for reasons that I still do not understand. Maybe I did not do enough lobbying, but others who were more expert at that and more dedicated to pushing their ideas similarly had little success. Perhaps our experiences were common in politics; perhaps they were due to the Leader and Reform's culture of internal politics. I am in no position to decide these issues. My experience has been too limited.

When I became involved with the party in 1993 the first election platform had already been worked out fully. The platform on fiscal policy owed much to the input from Harper and Pantazopoulos, both economists. Other people had been involved in this work as well, but not being part of the team I do not know the relative importance of the contributions made by these individuals. I also do not know how much Manning's ideas dominated both the initial outline and the final version of the document. However, some people close to the process have told me that Manning imposed his views on the final draft of the document, much to the dismay of Harper, who had put so much effort into making the fiscal platform sound economically and acceptable politically.

Caucus meetings offered me few opportunities for contributions to debates over fiscal and economic issues and matters of basic ideology. It seems to me, in retrospect, that the caucus agenda always was dominated by procedural and political issues. The important policies were formulated by Manning and his inner circle. In preceding chapters I have described in some detail my limited involvement in these deliberations.

However, on a few occasions I was able to influence the public position taken by Reform on important current fiscal issues brought up in caucus. Some of my ideas were voted down, some were accepted. Whatever the outcome of such caucus debates, I was pleased on such occasions to receive compliments from my colleagues on the extent to which I had helped them gain clarity of thought on difficult issues.

After my retirement one of my former colleagues noted that in the new caucus my name comes up occasionally as when someone is alleged to have said, "I wish Herb was here to explain this issue to us."

Indelibly etched into my mind will forever be the tension and excitement brought on by my speech on native policies and the ensuing media uproar. I am still embarrassed, because I handled the subject and the media like the amateur I was. I remain disappointed about the lack of support by

Manning, who distanced himself from me and forced me to apologize publicly for what I had said. But the experience also is a source of some satisfaction because I helped break the existing barriers of political correctness which surrounded the topic of government policies on natives. For years before my speech MPs had been afraid to raise questions which needed to be discussed for fear of being branded racist. Since then, genuine debate of native policies in Parliament has been more frequent and open.

In conversations with academics and people from the business community I have learned that the respect they had for Reform's economic platform had been enhanced by my presence in caucus and what they believed was my influence with Preston Manning. I cannot be certain how widespread this sentiment was, but almost certainly my reputation as a conservative economist developed during my career before politics did not damage the party's reputation with influential business interests. While I am glad that I could make this contribution to Reform's public image, I find it ironic that in fact I had so little involvement in policy formulation, as discussed above.

Some positive personal relationships

Work on the Finance Committee provided me with many pleasant memories. I learned much from expert witnesses, including those representing special interest groups. I had fun interacting with them. There was much cameraderie among the members of the committee from all three parties. The Liberals on the Committee took with humour and grace when I used my professional knowledge to discredit positions they had taken during some meetings.

I also have good memories of the few interactions I have had with Paul Martin. He paid close attention to what I said in speeches I made in the House, and always took seriously the questions I asked of him during the official question period, almost always answering them with a maximum of substance and a minimum of rhetoric. This treatment was in contrast with that afforded Monte Solberg, Deputy Finance Critic and the Chief Finance Critic after my announcement that I would not seek reelection. The trip to the IMF/World Bank meetings in Madrid in 1995 made possible through Martin's invitation and the private dinner I had with him and his closest advisers were one of the most interesting experiences as an MP.

Whenever people are united in a common cause and suffer together, be it political or real wars, special and valued ties develop among the participants. Caucus meetings, the battles with the media and the skirmishes in question period and debates on the floor of the House made for such bonding with other MPs. I am sure that, as with war veterans, eventually with the passage of time, my memories will increasingly be dominated by the happy times spent doing battle side by side with friends in arms. The heated disagreements and battles lost will be forgotten.

Unfortunately, circumstance of my life and that of my former caucus colleagues do not permit continuation of these bonds in practice. I have regular contact only with Ted White, the MP from North Vancouver, the riding adjacent to my former riding of Capilano Howe Sound. Contacts with Lynda Mackay, my former assistant in Ottawa and Andrew Kosnaski, the economist working in Reform Research, were frequent at first but are diminishing through time.

Reasons for leaving politics

In a sense, all the preceding narrative and analyses provide an answer to the question I have often been asked: "Why did you decide not to seek re-election?" Here is a brief summary. Basically, I have decided that my comparative advantage lies in teaching and research, not the work demanded of a politician. Milton Friedman expressed this reason in a letter he wrote to me in 1998: "Congratulations on not seeking re-election. I have no doubt whatsoever that you will be far more influential from the outside than would have been on the inside."

There were other, secondary, but obvious personal reasons for quitting politics. My health suffered under the stress of frequent trips across the continent, irregular and unhealthy meals, lack of exercise, emotional ups and downs and the constant stress of living in the limelight of the powerful media. It did not help that I was in my early sixties and suffered from bouts of irregular heartbeats which were aggravated by travel and tensions. I was lonely without family and friends during those long, cold evenings in Ottawa.

Money considerations also played a role. Pressures stemming from caucus solidarity had forced me into surrendering my rights to a pension in 1995. At that time, under pressure from Reform and other interest groups, the Liberals had introduced a modified pension plan for MPs, which was somewhat less generous than the original one but still too generous for Reform. We were then given the following ultimatum by the Liberals: Sign on to the new plan and implicitly support it or resign and give up your benefits for ever, thus putting your personal interests where your vote is. If I had not been forced into giving up the pension benefits, re-election in 1997 would have made me eligible to receive them upon retirement four years later at age 68. These benefits would have had a present value of several hundred thousand dollars. Suffice it to say that the absence of the possibility of getting such a return to seeking re-election played an important role in my decision.

Future teaching and research

One of the other important elements in my decision not to seek re-election was the existence of ready opportunities for interesting, well-paid employment where I could use both my professional background as an economist and the important perspectives on political economy I had gained during my political career. Since the election in June 1997 I have been employed half time by the Fraser Institute and half time in my old position as a Professor of Economics at Simon Fraser University. In the latter capacity I taught two courses in each fall semester in 1997 and 1998.

The return to teaching was a bit of a disappointment. Other professors had taken over the courses in International Finance for final year undergraduates and for post-graduate students that I had been teaching for 30 years before I stood for election. So I was assigned a course for second-year students. The course was designed to give an overview of Canadian fiscal and monetary policy in recent times. It was intended to show to students majoring in other fields the role economic policy played in their lives. It was also aimed at attracting students to economics as a major. The Department of Economics has been successful in achieving these goals of offering such courses to second year students. Ratings by students are good and the number of majors in economics has remained high while having declined in many other universities.

However, for me, teaching this second year course was somewhat of a come-down from teaching the higher level courses in the past. The percentage of students without any interest in the subject was very high. It was obvious to me throughout the course that these students were there to get attendance and examination credits on their way to getting a BA. They cared little about the substance of what I was teaching. It did not help that many of these students had very little background on recent Canadian economic history and politics. There was the normal but relatively small number of students who showed great interest in the readings and lectures in this course in Canadian monetary and fiscal policy. Their participation in class and search for understanding encouraged me and seemed to make worthwhile all the preparation, lecturing and examinations.

I was also given the assignment to teach a course on original economic research to a small group of fourth-year economics majors. The students were enthusiastic and produced some very fine papers. They provided me with much satisfaction. Two of the papers have resulted in publications. In February 1999 I will turn 65 years old and will be forced to retire from my university position under British Columbia law. This law is clearly in violation of the Canadian Charter of Rights and Freedoms since it discriminates in employment against a group of people on the basis of their age. The legislation had been challenged during the 1980s on these grounds. However, the challenge was rejected by the Supreme Court on the basis that such discrimination was 'in the public interest' and therefore permissible under the 'notwithstanding' clause of the charter.

Academic colleagues from the U.S. cannot believe that the Canadian Supreme Court reached such a verdict. They think that the life and professional experience makes many academics very effective teachers beyond the age of 65. It is therefore against and not in the public interest to force such individuals into retirement at that stage in their lives. Such policies reduce the overall productivity of the Canadian labour force and contribute to the country's economic malaise so evident in the late 1990s.

The Fraser Institute

Fortunately for me, the Fraser Institute has no age restrictions on employment. After my retirement from teaching I will work half time at the Institute to do research and assist younger people with their work.

Since 1997 I have already done some work at the Institute. In September of that year I attended a conference in Berlin organized by the Fraser Institute and the Friedrich Naumann Stiftung. It had in attendance researchers from 15 conservative institutes around the world reporting on their work on the Fraser Institute project on *Economic Freedom of the World*. I presented a brief paper on efforts to measure freedom in labour markets. As a result I was invited to publish an article on the subject in the German newspaper *Handelsblatt*. I also helped organize, present a paper and edit the proceedings of a conference in Ottawa on the subject 'What to do with the Fiscal Surplus.' In October I attended a conference in Dallas and presented a paper on the relationship between economic freedom and social indicators. In this paper I showed that greater economic freedom brings countries not just higher income per capita and greater economic growth but also better life expectancy, literacy rates and other measures of social well-being.

I was also able to show that income redistribution policies of governments are successful in creating a greater equality of income after taxes and transfers but that these effects are accompanied by substantial reductions in economic freedom, per capita income and other measures of well being. The paper has been refereed and will appear in a special issue of the professional journal *CATO Journal,* published in Washington by the Cato Institute.

By coincidence, in early 1998, John Dobson approached the Fraser Institute with the offer to endow a research chair through the Dobson Foundation he heads. Its occupant would engage in research on fiscal and taxation policies in Canada. I was happy to be chosen as the first occupant of this chair, and expect to work half-time for five years.

I plan to organize five annual conferences on taxation policies. The Canadian taxation system has many shortcomings which cause inefficiencies and reduce economic growth. I hope that the planned in-depth studies and their repeated public exposure will eventually pave the way for beneficial changes in policies.

Many other research projects tempt me. There is the study of the 'brain drain,' which is stimulated by the large and growing gap between personal

Chapter 15

income tax and capital gains tax rates between Canada and the U.S. I am also most eager to work on a major study about the way in which moral hazard has put into jeopardy social insurance programs in Canada and all industrial countries. I have already discussed the concept of moral hazard in an earlier chapter explained the positive relationships between the generosity of unemployment insurance benefits and the rate of unemployment. Here is a brief summary of the concept of moral hazard which refers to changes in the behaviour of individuals which accompanies the availability of insurance benefits.

These changes in behaviour are responsible for the fact that houses insured against burglary are broken into more often than houses which are not, and why people insured against unemployment and illness are more often afflicted by these hazards than people who are not. The problem is that while private insurance contracts stipulate effective measures to reduce risk, public social insurance programs do not.

For example, home owners who install burglary prevention systems enjoy lower insurance premiums, those who take good care of their health and relationships with employers are not rewarded with lower health or unemployment insurance premiums. A careful analysis of these differences between private and public insurance systems may be expected to result in important recommendations for policy changes that would improve the efficiency and equity of the public systems. One line of analysis is likely to lead to recommendations for the full or partial privatization of some social insurance programs.

I also look forward to working with the young researchers at the Fraser Institute on a wide range of projects of interest to them. My extensive experience in economic research will come in handy. From experience I know that working with such young, brilliant, energetic and promising people is a great source of pleasure and satisfaction. It will also help with the distribution of valuable ideas on how economic policies in Canada can be improved.

General Douglas MacArthur said that old soldiers never die, they just fade away. In the same vein it may be said that academic economists never retire, they just keep on writing. Milton Friedman turned 86 in 1998. He is still active and writing. I will try to emulate him.

Index of Names

A

Ablonczy, Diane 10, 139, 144, 211, 232, 235, 239
Alderman, Philip 121
Altschul, Frank 17
Anderson, David 262, 263
Anderson, Rick 168, 221, 222, 223
Arndt, Heinz 60
Arap Moi, Daniel 92
Arrow, Ken 37, 38
Axworthy, Lloyd 232, 258-260, 272

B

Baer, Donald 40
Balassa, Bela 44
Baran, Paul 37
Barlow, Maude 249
Barnard, Christian 97
Beck, John 156
Becker, Gary 170
Bertrand, Helene 85
Black, Conrad 213
Blaikie, Bill 258
Blaug, Mark 74, 110
Blume, Marshall 53
Boessenkool, Ken 6, 186, 219, 226, 249
Boland, Larry 75
Bonnici, Josef 89
Boyle, Pat 87
Breton, Albert 40
Brittain, Sam 92
Bromfield, Louis 16
Brown, Jan 16, 167, 180-183, 232-237
Brown, Robert 226
Buchanan, James 88
Buchanan, John 269
Bula, Frances 131
Byfield, Ted 199

C

Campbell, Barry 251
Campbell, Kim 9, 280
Cant, Eric 116, 117
Cardinal, Mike 165
Carpenter, Tony
Chant, John 131
Chao, Johnny 275
Charest, Jean 117, 147, 204
Chatters, David 9, 167, 173, 174, 201
Cherry, Don 162
Chretien, Jean 9, 117, 147-148, 162-163, 190, 205, 206, 209, 212, 256-258, 262, 272
Clark, Joe 280
Coase, Ronald 240
Cohen, Marjorie 132
Collins, Doug 113-115, 156
Collins, Mary 129, 135
Connally, John 26
Corden, Max 91
Courchene, Tom 88
Crow, John 10, 248
Cummins, John 265

D

Darwin, Charles 191
Day, Stockwell 285
de Gaulle, Charles 45
DeWald, William 49
Despres, Emile 37
Diefenbaker, John 9
Dobbin, Murray 155
Dobson, John 291
Dodge, David 141, 247
Dornbusch, Rudi 50
Douglas, Roger 281
D'Souza, Dinesh 215
Dyke, David 121
Dutton, Alan 128

E

Eaton, Curtis 76
Ebel, Rudi 18, 34
Eggleton, Art 9
Ehrlich, Paul 28
Elly, Reid 169
Epp, Ken 151
Erickson, Arthur 68

Index of Names

F

Fellner, William 25, 26
Finney, Ben 57
Fisher, Doug 150
Fisher, Irving 23
Flanagan, Tom 6, 154, 201-203
Fleming, John 92
Fogel, Bob 40
Forbes, Jim 225
Fortin, Pierre 57
Frankel, Jacob 50, 254
Friedman, Milton 25-27, 32, 39, 40-42, 49, 50, 59, 65, 104, 119, 248, 289, 292
Friend, Irwin 53
Frith, Darrell 121
Frum, David 198
Fryers, Cliff 123, 221
Furk, Margo 116, 117, 120

G

Getty, Don 210
Gibbons, Sam 268
Gibson, Gordon 283
Giersch, Herbert 39, 80
Gorbachev, Mikhail 106
Grafstein, Gerry 269
Gray, Herb 142
Grassley, Chuck 269
Green, Steve 149
Greene, Nancy 121, 124, 252
Greene, Stephen 145, 146
Greenspon, Ed 86, 141, 162, 235, 247, 255, 259
Grey, Deborah 138, 141, 168, 211, 265, 266
Grey, Lew 142
Griliches, Zvi 40
Grubel, Eric 37, 57, 58, 67, 81-83, 85, 86, 93, 95, 96
Grubel, Heidi 49, 57, 58, 67, 81, 83-85, 93, 95, 96
Grubel, Toni 20-22, 28, 34, 36, 37, 49, 57, 59, 67, 81, 82, 84, 85, 96
Gurley, Jack 37
Guttentag, Jack 53
Gwartney, Jim 103
Gzowski, Peter 133

H

Hall, Robert 225, 226
Hanger, Art 6, 167, 176-179, 182, 196
Harris, Mike 223
Harris, Richard 76
Hasan, Parvez 29
Harberger, Arnold 40-42, 49, 50
Harper, Stephen 123, 163, 184, 201, 206, 207, 212, 214, 219, 241, 264, 265, 285, 287
Hayek, Friedrich 88
Hayes, Sharon 199
Helleiner, Gerry 254
Hermanson, Elwin 142, 143, 210, 211
Hirsch, Fred 45
Honnecker, Ernst 106
Hoselitz, Bert 40
Howe, Gordie 252

J

Jewett, Pauline 113
Johnson, D. Gale 41
Johnson, Harry 34, 39, 41-45, 48, 50
Johnson, Harry (Rep.) 268
Johnson, Lyndon 26, 28, 29, 64, 65, 100

K

Kafka, Alexandre, 254
Kantor, Brian 97
Kaus, Renate 15
Kennedy, J. F. 26, 29, 60
Kenyatta, Jomo 92
Keran, Michael 62
Kidde, Walter 15
King, Mackenzie 252
Klaus, Vaclas 262, 263
Kosnaski, Andrew 289
Kruschev, Nikita 40
Kurihara, Kenneth 20

L

Laidler, David 249
Lange, Oscar 29

Index of Names

Lautens, Trevor 134, 155
Lawson, Richard 103
Leiserson, Mark 38
Leoncavallo 21
Lepine, Marc 175
Lewis, David 57
Lewis, Greg 40
Levi, Michael 34
Lipsey, Richard 75, 76, 88
Little, Ian 92
Littler, Karl 255, 256
Lloyd, Peter 58, 59
Loong, Lee Hsien 99
Lotka, Prof. 74
Loubier, Yvan 244
Lucas, Robert 27

M

MacArthur, Douglas 292
MacDougall, Brice 115, 116, 121, 122
Mack, Connie 268
MacKay, Lynda 136, 284
Maheux, Line 150
Maki, Dennis 56, 73
Mandela, Nelson 98
Manley, John 260
Manning, Preston 112, 114-120, 122, 123, 128, 129, 133, 138, 139, 142-147, 154-164, 168, 169, 181, 183, 184, 217, 219-226, 232-235, 238, 240-242, 246-252, 255, 257-263, 265, 270, 271, 277, 280, 283-288
Manning, Ernest 210
Martin, John 92
Martin, Paul 86, 141, 146, 148, 150, 232, 234-236, 241, 244, 247-248, 252-258, 260, 261, 266, 272, 273, 276, 288
Masera, Rainer 32
Masse, Marcel 261
Massey, Jeff 68
Mauser, Gary 176
McAdam, Ron 121
McClelland, Ian 234
McDonald, Donald 74
McLoughlin, Audrey 117
McMahon, Fred 260

McMartin, Pete 133
McTigue, Maurice 227
Meadows, A. 20
Meeker, Howie 252
Mercredi, Ovide 165, 166
Metzler, Lloyd 40
Miller, Merton 40
Mirrlees, Jim 92
Montias, Michael 29
Morgan, Walter 15
Moscovitch, Jason 182
Mulroney, Brian 9, 111, 113, 148, 191, 216, 226, 244, 278, 280
Mundell, Robert 40, 49
Murray, Lowell 227
Murzankowski, Senator 267
Mussa, Michael 50, 254

N

Nathan, Cedric 96
Naumetz, Tim 266
Neary, Peter 92
Newman, Graeme 179
Newman, John 140
Nicholson, Peter 146
Nixon, Richard 26, 61, 63-65
Nunziata, John 140

O

Okun, Arthur 24-26, 29, 64, 65
Olson, Bud 269
O'Neil, Peter 168, 173, 221
Oppenheimer, Peter 91
Owens, Owen 84
Oxtholm, Bent 121, 122

P

Pantazopoulos, Dimitri 123, 219, 287
Parent, Gib 10, 252
Pappon, Rainer 18
Pappon, Eberhard 18
Peitsch, Deana 121
Penson, Charlie 212, 266
Peterson, David 243
Peterson, Jim 243
Phelps, Edmund 27
Phillips, Bill 58

Index of Names

Pinochet, Augustine 98
Poddar, Satya 226
Polak, Jacques 79
Porter, Michael 44
Powell, Ray 24

R

Rabushka, Alvin 225, 226
Radler, David 213
Ramsay, Jack 167, 176, 177, 182
Ranis, Gustav 34
Reagan, Ronald 49, 55, 105, 106, 111, 215, 216, 223, 281, 286
Reese, Albert 40
Regan, Donald 55
Reid, Scott 6, 233
Reise, Heino 104
Reisman, Simon 73
Revell, Ian 126
Reynolds, John 136
Ricardo, David 43
Richard, 'Rocket' 25
Ringma, Bob 6, 144, 167-170, 173, 174, 196, 201, 211
Robinson, Svend 253
Robson, William 249
Rock, Allan 148, 175, 176, 262

S

Samarras, Lucas 21
Samuelson, Paul 25
Sandhu, Kernial 99
Sax, Shelley 56, 73
Scammell, William 69
Schneider, Jürgen 14
Schmitt, Wilson 60
Schwindt, Richard 70
Schulze, Charles 100
Schultz, Theodore
Schwartz, Rainer 105
Scott, Maurice 92
Scott, Mike 267
Scott, Tony 40, 46
Shaw, Edward 37
Shultz, George 40
Sidneysmith, Sam 72
Silye, Jim 141, 144, 146, 167, 180-182, 190, 210, 212, 213, 224, 226, 227-229

Sjaastad, Larry 40
Smith, Adam 25
Smith, Anthony Wilson
Smith, Michael 252
Solow, Robert 25
Sohmen, Egon 32
Sojonkey, Audrey 129, 135
Solberg, Monte 150,151, 223, 241, 252, 266, 277, 288
Sorensen, Ted 26
Sowell, Tom 171
Speaker, Ray 6, 143, 144, 146,147, 161, 168, 184, 200, 201, 204, 207-212, 214, 219, 222, 241, 253
Spindler, Zane 82
Stigler, George 40
Stoll, Hans 53
Strahl, Chuck 144
Strand, Ken 69
Stupich, Dave 71
Stursberg, Peter 117

T

Tarshis, Lorie 36
Telser, Lester 40
Thatcher, Margaret 87, 88, 111, 119, 281
Thiessen, Gordon 247
Thompson, Neil 114, 115, 117, 121
Thompson, Myron 167, 179, 180, 182
Tobin, James 23, 26, 29, 32, 34, 39, 104
Tobin, Brian 261
Trudeau, Pierre 9, 73, 88, 114, 185, 205, 212, 257, 269, 283
Triffin, Robert 31, 32, 34
Tsipsis, Costa 21

U

Uzawa, Hirofumi 40

V

Vanagas, Steve 113
Vander Zalm, Bill 112
Van Esch, John 71

Index of Names

Van Notten, Michael 89
Vickers, Doug 53, 54
Volker, Paul 60, 62, 64, 248
Von Hayek, Friedrich 23
Von Mieses, Ludvig 23

Walker, Michael 87, 88, 90, 91, 132
Walters, Sir Alan 88
Wallich, Henry 25
Wearing, Peter 112, 116, 121-124, 132
White, Randy 6, 139, 145, 146, 167, 179, 180, 182, 211
White, Ted 125-127, 141, 188, 190-192, 203, 281, 289
Willis, George 61
Wilson, Michael 148
Wilson-Smith, Anthony 235
Wood, Ron 149, 161

Y

Yamani, Sheik 79
Yew, Lee Kuan 99
Young, Doug 258, 272

ORDER FORM
(please detach)

For additional copies of the book *A Professor in Parliament,* please complete the form below and either

Mail to: Herbert Grubel
           Apt. 1202, 125 West Second St.,
           North Vancouver, B.C. V7M 1C5

Or fax to: (604) 980-6508

YOUR MAILING ADDRESS:

Name _____

Street Address _____

City _____ Postal Code _____

Number of copies required _____

Please enclose a check for $19.95 for each book and $5.00 for postage and handling for each book (20 percent discount for orders of 5 books or more). Allow 3 weeks for delivery.